OneStream Finance Rules and Calculations Handbook

Jon Golembiewski

Published in 2022 by OneStream Press.

Copyright (c) 2022 Jon Golembiewski. All rights reserved.

Portions of this book are Copyright (c) 2022 OneStream Software LLC, and courtesy of OneStream Software LLC. All rights reserved.

OneStream and the OneStream logo are trademarks of OneStream Software LLC, www.OneStream.com, and used with permission.

ISBN: 978-1-8382528-5-4

All Rights Reserved. No part of this publication may be reproduced, stored in a retrieval system, or transmitted in any form or by any means, electronic, mechanical, photocopying, recording or otherwise, without the prior permission of the publisher.

This book is sold subject to the condition that it shall not, by way of trade or otherwise, be lent, re-sold, hired out or otherwise circulated without the publisher's prior consent in any form of binding or cover other than that it which it is published and without a similar condition including this condition being imposed on the subsequent purchaser.

OneStream Press has endeavored to provide trademark information about all the companies and products mentioned in this book by the appropriate use of capitals. However, OneStream Press cannot guarantee the accuracy of this information. OneStream Press is an imprint of Play Technologies (England) Limited. 6 Woodside, Churnet View Road, Oakamoor, ST10 3AE, United Kingdom.

www.OneStreamPress.com

Disclaimer

While the advice and information in this book is believed to be true and accurate at the date of publication, OneStream Press, the author, and OneStream Software LLC do not guarantee the accuracy, adequacy, or completeness of any information, and are not responsible for any errors or omissions or the results obtained from the use of such information.

OneStream Press, the author, and OneStream Software LLC make no warranty, express or implied, with respect to the material contained herein, and hereby disclaim any liability to any party for any loss, damage, or disruption caused by errors or omissions, whether such errors or omissions result from negligence, accident, or any other cause.

About the Author

Jon Golembiewski is a Distinguished Architect on the OneStream Services Team. Jon joined OneStream in 2013 as one of the first members of the Services Team. Jon's experience stretches across both Consolidation and Planning projects. He has worked on projects in over 20 countries, including OneStream's first customers in South Africa, Australia, Finland, and Norway. Jon has also helped build and deliver training for both customers and consultants. He has lived in Amsterdam and currently resides in Pittsburgh, Pennsylvania.

Acknowledgments

First and foremost, I'd like to thank the founders of OneStream – Tom Shea, Bob Powers, Craig Colby, John Von Allmen, Todd Allen, Terry Shea, Eric Davidson and Matt Baranowski – for not only creating a brilliant product but fostering an infectious company culture too. They are not only insanely smart but genuinely good people that I am proud to call both colleagues and friends.

I'd also like to thank Peter Fugere for hiring me and both him, Steve Mebius, and Jerri McConnell for being my early and present mentors.

This book was far from a one-man show, and I'd like to thank the numerous colleagues that helped me with this book. Eric Osmanski and Tommy Sandi provided technical editing as well as direct content contribution. Matt DeCarlo for providing the very well-detailed and thought-out Consolidation Rule examples in Chapter 8. Additional editing and help by Chul Smith, Nick Bollinger, Ludo De Paz, Matt Ha, and Sam Richards. Finally, Amanda Goralewski and James Lumsden-Cook for their editing and logistical efforts.

Technical Reviewers

Eric Osmanski is a CPA who joined the OneStream Software Services organization in 2014 to deliver revolutionary corporate performance management (CPM) solutions. He is currently a Distinguished Architect focusing on the design, development, and maintenance of OneStream applications for OneStream's largest and most complex customers.

Tommy Sandi joined OneStream within the Pre-sales organization and focused on the creation of proof of concepts for the largest prospects and customers requiring unique solutions in the enterprise performance measurement area. He then moved to an engineering role where he became a Distinguished Architect working with the platform, MarketPlace development, and customers to constantly improve the OneStream platform.

Code Zip Download

There is a substantial archive of code material that accompanies this book, available as a free download. Download the file from: **www.OneStreamPress.com/FRC**

Note: Any Files provided for Exercises in this OneStream Press Book are for the use of Customers and Partners in an On-Premise environment and are not supported by the OneStream Support Team.

Errata

Despite best efforts, mistakes can sometimes creep into books. If you spot a mistake, please feel free to email us at **errata@OneStreamPress.com** (with the book title in the subject line).

The errata page for this book is hosted at **www.OneStreamPress.com/OneStreamFRC**

Table of Contents

Introduction   1
- Why I Wrote this Book   1
- Who are you?   1
  - The OneStream N00B   1
  - The OneStream Veteran   1
  - The <Insert Competing CPM Software Here> Veteran   2
  - Everyone Else   2
- Prerequisites   2
- Drowning in a Sea of Options   2
- Scope of the Book   2
- Code References   2
- The Reference Application   3

Chapter 1: Finance Engine Basics   5
- One Product, Many Engines   5
  - Stage Engine   5
  - Data Quality Engine   6
  - Data Management Engine   6
  - Presentation Engine   6
  - Workflow Engine   6
  - BI Blend Engine   6
- Engine Interaction via Business Rules   6
  - Business Rule Library   6
  - Business Rule Editor   7
  - Code and Script   8
    - VB.NET Basics   8
      - Data Types   8
      - Collection Classes   8
      - Classes & Methods   8
      - Other Relevant Concepts   9
  - The OneStream API Library   9
  - BRAPI   9
  - In-Solution Documentation   9
  - IntelliSense   10
- The Cube Stores, The Finance Engine Processes   10
  - Dimensions   10
  - Data Unit   11
- Functions of the Finance Engine   11
  - Consolidation Algorithm   11
  - Data Storage and In-Memory Aggregation   11
  - Finance Business Rules and Member Formulas   12
    - Finance Business Rules   12
      - Location   12
      - Finance Function Types   13
      - Advantages   13
    - Member Formulas   14
      - Location   14
      - Calculation Drill Down   15
      - Advantages   16
    - Which is Better – Business Rule or Member Formula?   16
    - Referencing Business Rules in Other Business Rules or Member Formulas   17
  - Cube Properties   18
    - Consolidation Algorithm Type   19

Standard	19
Stored Share	19
Org-By-Period Elimination	19
Stored Share and Org-By-Period Elimination	19
Custom	19
Translation Algorithm Type	19
Standard	20
Standard Using Business Rules for FX Rates	20
Custom	20
NoData Calculate Settings	20
When and How Do Calculations Run?	**21**
Data Unit Calculation Sequence (DUCS)	21
Consolidation Dimension	21
Assigning Business Rules to the Cube	22
Member Formulas	23
Triggering the DUCS	23
Data Management	24
Create the Step	24
Calculation Type	24
Define the Data Unit	25
From a Cube View	26
Dashboard Button	27
Workflow Process Step	28
Data Unit, Data Unit, Data Unit	29
Dependent Data Units	29
Parallel Processing	29
All or Nothing	30
Custom Calculate Function	30
Triggering a Custom Calculate Business Rule	30
Durable Data	32
Data Clearing	32
Other Differences	32
C#Aggregated	33
Dynamic Calculations	34
Clear as Mud	34
What Finance Function Type Should I Use?	34
DUCS vs. Custom Calculate	34
Conclusion	**35**

Chapter 2: Cube Data   37

Cube Building Blocks	**37**
Data Cells	37
Data Entering the Cube	39
The View Dimension	40
Data Cell Status	40
Real Data	41
NoData & Zeros	42
Derived Data	42
Derived Data Example	42
Storage Types	43
The Data Unit	43
The Data Buffer	44
Analogy To Excel	44
Perhaps a Better Analogy	44
Visualize the Data Buffer	45
A Data Buffer is an Object	45

Logging the Data Buffer	46
Anatomy of a Data Buffer	47
Common Members	48
Data Buffer Cell POV	48
Cell Amount	48
Cell Status	48
Storage Type	48
Filter and Remove Members from Data Buffers	48
Removing NoData & Zeros from Data Buffers	49
Conclusion	**49**

Chapter 3: api.Data.Calculate — 51

A Quick Revisit	**51**
With Great Power Comes Great Responsibility	**51**
Syntax	**51**
Simple Example	**52**
Breakdown	53
Data Buffer Math	53
Current Data Unit Being Processed	55
Data Unit Dimensions in the Destination Script	55
Data Unit Dimensions in the Source Scripts	56
Unbalanced Buffers	56
Data Explosion	57
Using #All	57
Unbalanced Functions	58
Syntax	58
Example	58
Even More Unbalanced	59
Potential Issues	59
Double Unbalanced	59
Divide and Subtract Unbalanced	59
Using Constants	**60**
An Interesting Use Case	60
Formula Variables	**61**
Syntax	61
Example	61
Converting Data Buffers with Differing Extensibility	**62**
Limiting Scope	**63**
Limit Data Unit Scope	63
Specific Data Unit Members	64
Translated Currency Only	64
Specific Scenario Types	64
Why Api.Pov.Account Won't Work	64
Dimension Filters	65
The Member Filter Builder	65
Applying the Member Filter	66
Base Members Only	68
No Duplicates	68
Know Your Hierarchies and Use Them to Your Advantage	69
Collapsing Detail	69
Origin Dimension	69
O#Import vs. O#Forms	69
Always Collapse When Possible	70
Remove NoData/Zeros	**71**
Durable Data	**73**
Clear Calculated Data	75

Custom Calculate	75
Api.Pov Functions	75
Linking to a Dashboard	76
Combo Box	77
Button	77
Data Management Step	78
Execution	78
Advanced Filtering with Eval	**79**
Putting It To Use	79
EventArgs	80
Eval Use Case	80
Breakdown of OnEvalDataBuffer	81
Returning to the Api.Data.Calculate Function	82
Eval2 Function	**82**
Use Case	82
The Code	83
Breakdown	84
The Result	84
Conclusion	**85**

Chapter 4: The Data Buffer Cell Loop — 87

The Recipe	**87**
Ingredients	87
Directions	87
Example	88
ResultDataBuffer	88
DestinationInfo	88
GetDataBufferUsingFormula	89
For, Each Loop	89
Result Cell	89
GetDataCell	89
Use the Source Cell Member Names	90
Use the Source Cell IDs to Build a DataCellPk	90
DimConstants	90
Api.Members.GetMemberId	90
Convert the Source Cell DataBufferCellPk to a Member Script	91
Performance	91
Setting the ResultCellPk	91
Setting the Result Cell Amount	92
Adding the Result Cell to the Result Data Buffer	92
Finishing the Loop and Setting the Data Buffer	92
Other Considerations	93
Setting Cell Status	93
SetDimension Extension	93
When to Use the DBCL	94
Flexibility	94
Transforming Dimensions	94
Analyzing Cell Status or Cell Amounts	94
Performance	94
Example of Setting Multiple Result Cells	95
DBCL vs. Eval	95
Guidelines	98
Loop Definition	98
Out of the Loop	98
Write Once	98
Conclusion	**98**

Chapter 5: Reporting Calculations — 99

When They Run — 99
Dynamic Calculation Example — 99
Where They are Located — 99
  Member Formulas — 100
  Dynamic Calculations in Business Rules — 102
    Benefits/Drawbacks — 102
  Cube Views — 103
    Benefits/Drawbacks — 103
  Results — 104
How They Work — 104
  Cell POV By Cell POV — 104
    Retrieving POV Members — 105
    Return — 105
      Numerical Data — 106
        Api.Data.GetDataCell — 106
        Api.Data.GetDataCell with a Formula — 107
        Data Cell Properties — 107
        Time Functions and Substitution Variables — 108
      Textual Data — 108
        DataCellEx — 109
        Return Text Properties — 109
    Name Value Pairs — 112
Functions — 112
  Variance — 113
  VariancePercent — 113
  BetterWorse — 113
  BetterWorsePercent — 113
  But Wait, There's More — 113
Use of UD8 — 114
  UD8 Example — 115
  UD8#None — 116
Referencing Other Dynamic Calcs — 117
  Relational Blending — 117
    Stage Table — 118
    Dynamic Calculation Using GetStageBlendText Function — 119
      CacheLevel — 120
      CacheName — 120
      wfProfileName — 120
      FieldList — 120
      Criteria — 121
      FieldToReturn — 121
    Results — 121
    Other Variations — 123
General Guidelines and Tips — 123
  Aggregation — 123
  Alternate Hierarchies — 124
  Complement Stored Calculations — 124
  Test on Small Report — 124
Conclusion — 125

Chapter 6: Managing Calculations — 127

Start at the Beginning — 127
  Create a Calculation Matrix — 127
    Basic Information — 127
      Calculation Name and Category — 128

Calculation Type	128
Finance Function Type	128
Calculation Location	128
Execution	128
Formula	128
Dependencies	128
Scope Information	128
Testing	129
Calculation Matrix Benefits	129
Tracking	129
Designing	129
Building, Testing, and Approving	129
Transferring Knowledge	129
Calculation Testing	**129**
Testing Tips	130
Calculation Reports	**130**
Formula Statistics	131
Formula List	132
Calculation Maintenance	**132**
Comments	133
Header	133
Inline	133
Regions	134
Maintenance Tips	134
Time Functions	134
Utilizing Hierarchies	136
Text Properties	137
Custom SQL Tables	138
Use Case	139
Create the Table	139
Populate the Table	140
Referencing the Table in a Calculation	141
Rule Context	141
The Code	141
The Breakdown	141
Get the SQL Table	141
Filter the Table using the .Select Method	141
Loop through the Table Rows	142
Clear the Previously Calculated Data and Execute the Calculation	142
Performance Note	142
Conclusion	**142**

Chapter 7: Troubleshooting and Performance — 143

Troubleshooting	**143**
Task Activity	143
Logging	145
Writing to the Error Log	146
Log a String	146
Log a Decimal	147
Logging Lists	147
String.Join	147
For, Each	148
Log Data Buffer	149
Stopwatch	150
Rubber Duck Debugging	151
Calculation Performance Troubleshooting	152

Calculation Drill Down 152
   Calculate with Logging 152
     Viewing the Result 153
  Common Calculation Errors 157
   Calculation Not Producing Results 157
     Drill Down From the Cube View 158
     Log the Data Buffers 159
     Fixing the Issue 160
   Calculation Producing Inconsistent or No Results 161
   Compilation Error 161
   Invalid Formula Script 162
     Invalid Member Name 162
     Unclosed Parentheses 163
   Unbalanced Buffer 163
   Declaring New Result Cell Outside of Loop 164
   Duplicate Members in Filter 164
   Undefined Members 165
   Unresolved Members 166
   Invalid Destination Script 168
   Object Not Set to Instance of an Object 169
   Given Key Not Present in Dictionary 170

Calculation Performance 172
Overview 172
  A Note on Multi-threading 173
Hardware and Server Settings 173
  Server Structure 173
   Server Designation 173
  CPU Specs 174
  Multi-threading Settings 174
Cube Design 175
  Data Unit Size and Volume 175
   Utilize Extensibility 175
   Increase The Number of Entities 175
   Optimize Entity Hierarchies 176
   Don't Store Unnecessary Data in the Cube 176
Consolidation/Calculation Execution Efficiency 176
  Use C#Aggregation When Possible 176
  Don't Force Consolidate/Calculate If Unnecessary 177
Formula Efficiency 177
Things to Do 177
  Use Custom Calculate When Possible 177
  Align Entity Dimensions with Calculations 178
  Use Dynamic Calculations Instead of Stored Calculations (and vice versa) 178
  Use RemoveZeros on All Data Buffers 178
  Limit Data Unit Scope 179
  Limit Account-Level Dimension Scope in Data Buffers 179
  Use Global Variables 179
  Formula Variables 180
  Use DimConstants 181
Things to Avoid 182
  Unnecessary Calculations in the Cube 182
  Copying Data in the DUCS 182
  Inside vs. Outside Loops 182
   Using Api.Data.Calculate Inside a Loop 182
   Using Api.Data.SetCell or SetDataCell Inside the Loop 183
   Api.Data.ClearCalculatedData 185
   Lookup of Constants 185
  Using Api.Data.ClearCalculatedData in DUCS 187

Stacking Api.Data.Calculate Functions With Similar Logic	187
Using BRAPI Calls	187
Hardcoding Time Periods	188
Forgetting to Comment Out Logging	189
System Diagnostics Solution	**189**
Conclusion	**191**

Chapter 8: Common Rule Examples — 193

Balance Sheet and Flow Calculations	**193**
Balance Sheet Calculations	193
Current Year Net Income	193
Reduce Data Unit Scope	194
Collapsing Detail	194
Key Account Properties	194
Formula Pass	194
Is Consolidated	194
Allow Input	194
Results	194
Retained Earnings Beginning Balance	195
Reduce Data Unit Scope	195
Only Pull from the Prior Year Once	195
Collapsing Detail	195
Key Account Properties	195
Formula Pass	195
Is Consolidated	195
Allow Input	196
Flow Calculations	196
Dimension Member Setup	196
Calculations	198
Beginning Balance	198
BegBalCalcYTD	198
BegBalDynamic	198
Activity	200
ActivityCalc	200
FX	201
Formulas	201
FXOpen	201
FXMovement	202
FXOverrideBalance and FXHistoricalOverrideMovement	202
CTA – Cumulative Translation Adjustment	202
Formula	203
Calculation	203
CTA Proof	203
Consolidation Calculations	**204**
Equity Pickup (EPU)	204
Background and Business Case	204
Example	205
Cube Setup	205
Metadata Setup	205
Entities	205
Accounts	210
Data Type Dimension	211
Data Setup	212
Rule Abstract	212
The Code Breakdown - Section 1	212
Abstract	212

Section 2	213
Abstract	213
Section 3	214
Abstract	214
Results	215
Noncontrolling Interest (NCI)	215
Example	216
Metadata	216
Entities	216
Accounts	218
Data Description	220
Rule Abstract	221
Code Breakdown	221
Section 1	221
Abstract	221
Section 2	222
Abstract	222
Section 3	223
Abstract	224
Section 4	224
Abstract	224
Section 5	225
Abstract	225
Results	226
Variations	226
Seeding Rules	**227**
What Rule Type to Use?	227
IsDurable and ClearCalculatedData	227
Simple Copy Data Example	227
Forecast Seeding Example	228
Using the Scenario Name	228
Using No Input Periods	229
Convert Extended Members	230
Allocation Calculations	**231**
Using Unbalanced Functions	231
The Setup	231
The Calculation	232
Using a Data Buffer Cell Loop	233
Calculation Abstract	233
Calculation Script and Breakdown	234
Allocations Across Entities	235
Example	236
The Setup	236
Calculation Breakdown	237
SGA Allocation	237
Rent Allocation	239
Results	239
Budget and Forecast Calculations	**240**
Variance Analysis Calculations	**240**
Simple Variance	240
Detailed Variance Calculation	242
Dimension Member Setup	243
FX Rate Variance Calculation	243
Required Data	243
Calculation Abstract	245
Calculation Script and Breakdown	245
Price and Volume Variance Calculation	248
Required Data	248

    Association of Driver to Account 248
    Calculation Abstract 250
       Price Variance 250
       Volume Variance 250
    Calculation Script and Breakdown 250
  Mix Calculation 253
  Results 253
Conclusion **253**

Index   255

25% OFF VOUCHER

Certification

Validate your technical competence and gain industry recognition with OneStream Software.

In purchasing this book, you are eligible to claim
a **25% discount** on any
OneStream Certification Exam.

Email Certification@OneStreamSoftware.com with proof of purchase for this book to claim your voucher today!

Terms & Conditions:
One (1) certification exam voucher per book, and each voucher is limited to one candidate per exam. All vouchers per receipt must be claimed at one time; if a receipt is for the purchase of 10 books, all 10 vouchers must be claimed at the same time. Vouchers are valid for post-beta production exams only. This offer cannot be combined with any other offer.

Introduction

Why I Wrote this Book

I started my career in 2008, after graduating from Penn State, and working at a Fortune 500 coatings company in Pittsburgh as essentially a glorified intern. About six months into the job, the 2008 financial crisis happened and – like most other large companies – the company I worked for did a massive restructuring, dissolving my department in the process. Luckily for me, an implementation of a CPM product was underway, and they needed someone to sit in a dark room and reconcile data. After two-and-a-half years of working on back-to-back implementations, I realized I had a knack for software and enjoyed project work, so I took a job at a local consulting company. Fast forward a few years, and I am interviewing for OneStream in their first office (above a sporting goods store in Rochester, Michigan). One of the founders, John Von Allmen, plus Steve Mebius (who started the same day as I did), worked as consultants for the software implementation at the Pittsburgh coatings company, too.

When I joined OneStream, I was still green but eager to learn and got many opportunities to do so. Working on hundreds of projects (and counting) over my career, I was fortunate to be mentored and coached by the same people who created the software.

Since I started at OneStream in 2013, the company has quickly ascended to become the dominant CPM leader. I have seen numerous colleagues – who worked with other software products – see the light, and eventually come over to OneStream. The abrupt rise of OneStream has created a knowledge gap in the industry as experts in legacy products, as well as novices attracted to the OneStream shooting star, are catching up to learn OneStream. While Finance Rules and Calculations are one of the most powerful features of the OneStream platform, they also have the steepest learning curve.

I experienced that steep learning curve first-hand and mostly learned the hard way – by making mistakes and good ol' trial and error. I am writing this book for myself nine years ago when I started at OneStream. I desperately wish I had read this book then; it would have saved me a lot of pain and suffering. I hope that it accomplishes good things for you.

Who are you?

I believe the audience for this handbook will fall into a number of categories. My goal in writing this book is to provide something for everyone, whether you are brand new to OneStream or have been working for years.

The OneStream N00B

Over the years, the OneStream community has exploded from a few dozen evangelical early adopters to thousands of employees, partners, and customers across the globe. If you are one of the hundreds of people just getting into OneStream, this book is written, first and foremost, for you. This book starts with explanations of the foundational concepts before advancing to the more technical coding stuff. I will do my best to break through the complexity and technical jargon and provide clear explanations in plain English.

The OneStream Veteran

Having worked at OneStream since 2013, I am about as veteran as you can be, and I still learned *a lot* while writing this book. Both through testing various use cases, and discussions with colleagues about a feature or function I hadn't used before and was curious about.

While this book will start with the absolute basics, it will eventually build to tackle more complex topics and use case examples. It should also satisfy some curiosity around *why* certain things in

Introduction

OneStream work the way they do, or provide an alternate way of doing something you've always done one way.

The bottom line is that if *I* learned something from writing this book, I am hopeful that you will learn something from reading it, no matter how experienced you are.

The <Insert Competing CPM Software Here> Veteran

This book does not draw comparisons or similarities between how OneStream handles Calculations and how they are handled in other products (besides Excel). The good news is that if you understand Calculations and data structures in other products, you have a good head start and making the transition to OneStream will be easy with the help of this book.

Everyone Else

Maybe you fall somewhere between beginner and veteran, or have dabbled in writing Finance Rules but aren't fully comfortable writing them on your own. Or maybe you've tiptoed carefully through several projects without having to write a Business Rule and feel it's about time to learn. I hope this book helps you get over the hump, and you become a proficient rules writer.

Prerequisites

While this book focuses on the underlying concepts relating to the Finance Engine, Cube data, and Finance Rules, writing Calculations and Business Rules *is writing code*. This book will not teach you how to code but rather teach how to write OneStream Finance Rules and Calculations *using* code.

At the very minimum, a basic understanding of VB.NET or another object-oriented programming language should be attained to gain the most value out of this book. That being said, you do not need to be an expert or even a half-decent programmer to write OneStream Calculations. Your author proudly admits that he has had no formal coding training, and is mostly self-taught. I hope this serves as an inspiration to the non-programmers out there.

While there is a plethora of VB.NET and other programming courses available online, the link below is a recommended resource that will help you gain a basic understanding of the VB.NET Framework. https://msdn.microsoft.com/en-us/library/2x7h1hfk.aspx

Drowning in a Sea of Options

OneStream offers an enormous variety of choices when it comes to writing Calculations. From where and how they are written to how they can be executed. My goal is to help you make sense of those choices and provide some guide rails based on my experiences. You can certainly veer off the paved road (in some instances, it is necessary!), but staying on the path will get you to your destination the vast majority of the time. I say this as a disclaimer… the way I show things may not be the *only* way. If you've written Calculations that look vastly different than mine, it does not necessarily mean they are wrong.

Scope of the Book

As will be explained in the first chapter, this book is focused solely on the OneStream Finance Engine and how to write and execute Calculations and Finance Rules. OneStream has a lot of functionality, so writing Business Rules in other OneStream Engines will be saved as topics for other books.

Code References

Throughout this book, code snippets for rule examples will be shown and, in some cases, broken down line by line with detailed explanations. Screenshots of the code as it is presented in the

OneStream Business Rule Editor are used instead of showing the code as plain text. The benefit is that the screenshotted code is much more readable as various keywords, functions, and comments are color-coded and formatted *exactly* how they are presented within the product. The disadvantage is that the code cannot be copied and pasted from the book PDF version, and the code can sometimes be squeezed down to fit on the printed page. To account for this, a full application with all referenced code examples (and more) will be available to download at
www.OneStreamPress.com/FRC

In this application, all rules and scripts can be accessed and executed against real data, and results can be matched up against what is shown in the book.

Learning technical concepts, especially involving code, can be challenging when only *reading* about it. Real learning takes place while *doing* it. I encourage you to use the example application in parallel with reading the book. Try to change the code, break it, and get it working again. Don't be afraid to get your hands dirty!

The Reference Application

The accompanying reference application (noted above) will be for a fictional company, run by The Three Stooges (Moe, Larry, and Curly), called StoogeCorp. StoogeCorp has several companies under its umbrella, including ACME Exterminators, Gypsum Good Antiques, Gottrox Jewelry, and Cheatum Investments. These companies have interesting operations that make for some hopefully interesting use cases for Calculations.

The Three Stooges was (and still is) one of my favorite shows, and I was happy to include watching reruns as part of my book 'research.'

1
Finance Engine Basics

Unless you are brand new to OneStream, you probably know that the OneStream platform contains *a lot* of functionality. If you are new to OneStream, don't be intimidated. Even if you are an experienced OneStream veteran, there are areas of the product that you likely know better than others. Learning the entire scope of the product takes time and patience.

We can follow the various functionalities of OneStream from the perspective of the data that moves through it – at its different stages. Data starts raw, living in disparate source systems, until finally appearing on a polished Report on the desk of the CFO. Along the way, the data can be parsed, transformed, validated, and loaded to a Cube. As data moves through OneStream, it is processed by different Engines; just as a car engine processes gasoline to make a vehicle accelerate, OneStream processes data to help propel a company forward.

Of the various Engines within the platform, the **Finance Engine** is the primary Engine used to enrich data and add financial intelligence. Within this Engine, sophisticated calculations can be written to add company-specific financial intelligence. This book focuses solely on writing calculations within the Finance Engine.

Before you start tinkering with the engine of your car, though, you had better know some basics about it. How do you turn it on? What smaller components is it comprised of? Where are the pistons located? What kind of gas does it need?

The same is true for the OneStream Finance Engine. This chapter will introduce and break down the Finance Engine, which is where calculations take place.

One Product, Many Engines

The Finance Engine is one of many Engines within the OneStream platform, with each suited to help process data as it moves within the product. The Finance Engine is an in-memory Financial Analytic Engine, which aggregates, consolidates, and provides financial intelligence to data.

The Finance Engine works closely with the other Engines to create a unified User Experience. To introduce another metaphor, think of each Engine as a workstation within a factory that makes loaves of bread. Each station performs a specific task to bring raw data (flour, yeast, water) to a polished Sales Report (loaf of bread on the store shelf). Below is an overview of each of the various Engines in OneStream and how they *interact* with the Finance Engine.

Stage Engine

The Stage Engine performs the task of parsing and transforming external data into the Cube, where it is then processed by the Finance Engine. It ensures that data is mapped to valid data points defined by the Finance Engine.

The Stage Engine performs the role of the sourcing manager within the factory, ensuring the raw ingredients are prepped and refined before being used in the baking process.

Data Quality Engine

The Data Quality Engine is responsible for the validation and certification of data within the Finance Engine.

Think of the Data Quality Engine as the quality assurance manager, testing the product before it goes into the market.

Data Management Engine

The Data Management Engine interacts with other Engines by providing the ability to automate tasks within those Engines. For example, the **Clear Data** step – within Data Management – clears data within the Finance Engine while the **Export Report** step interacts with the Presentation Engine.

Think of the Data Management Engine as a robot that is used to automate certain assembly line activities within the factory.

Presentation Engine

The Presentation Engine provides data visualization functionality. Data processed within the Finance Engine can be viewed on a Report or exported to Excel using the Presentation Engine.

Think of the Presentation Engine as the distribution mechanism that brings the factory's finished products to the store shelves.

Workflow Engine

The Workflow Engine coordinates the activities of the other Engines via defined processes and responsibility hierarchies. It provides the ability to show the status and audit trail for specific tasks performed across the other Engines.

The Workflow Engine is the factory manager, coordinating all the activities of the assembly line and reporting the status to superiors.

BI Blend Engine

The BI Blend Engine supports the reporting of large volumes of transactional or highly changing data. While BI Blend is a separate Engine from the Finance Engine, it does leverage metadata hierarchies from the Finance Engine to add structure and commonality to the data.

Think of a BI Blend as a separate section of the factory, which uses similar ingredients to produce donuts instead of bread.

Engine Interaction via Business Rules

Each Engine described above can be interacted with to supplement standard functionality by executing custom scripts through Business Rules.

Business Rule Library

The Business Rule library categorizes Business Rules by the Engines they relate to.

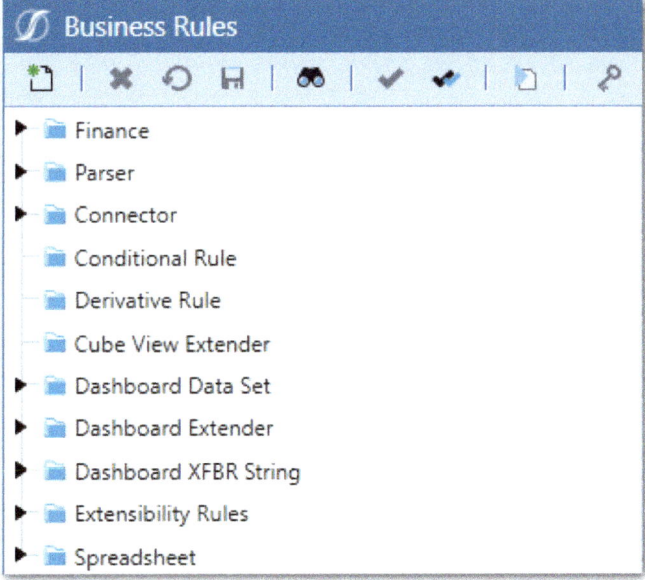

Figure 1.1

Business Rule Editor

Here are the components and key features of the Rule Editor:

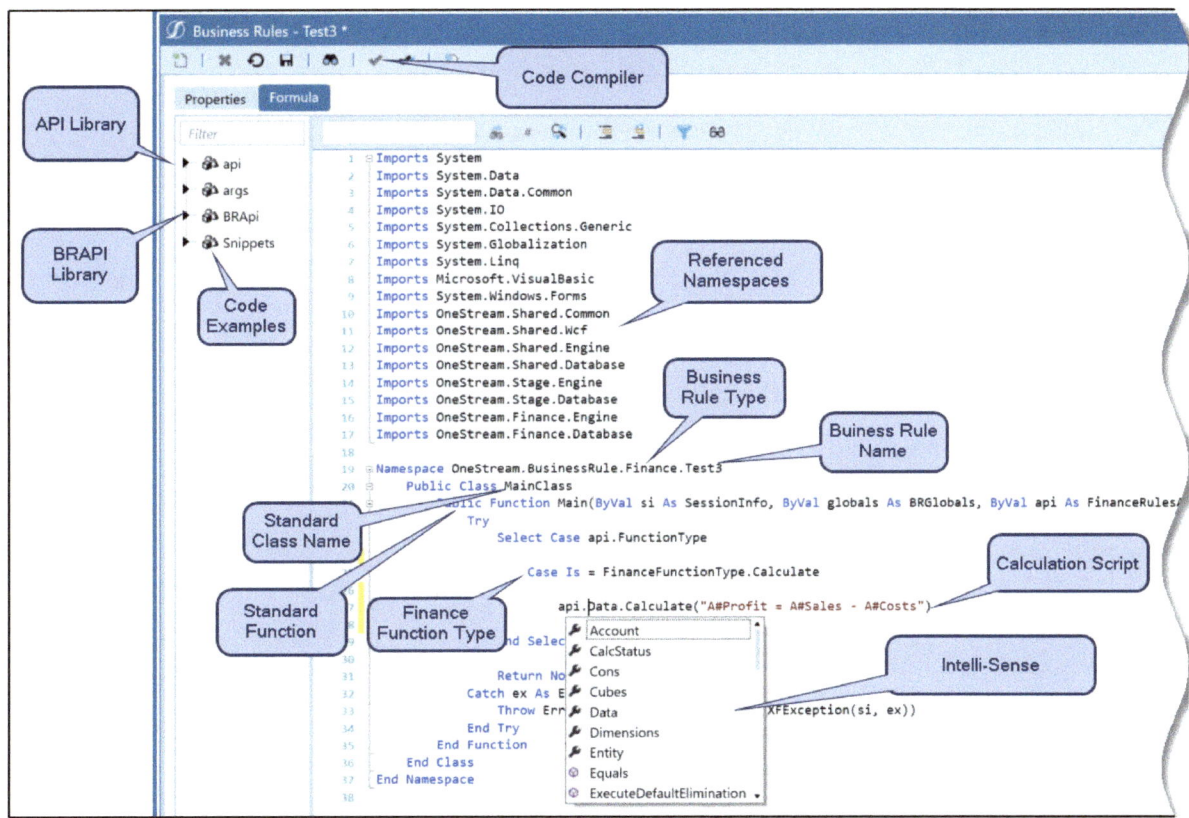

Figure 1.2

Chapter 1

Code and Script

The OneStream platform is based entirely on the Microsoft .NET Framework, as is the OneStream Business Rules Engine. Therefore, VB.NET is the logical choice for Business Rule syntax.

VB.NET is one of the most popular programming languages in use today. This language is prevalent amongst Business Users because the syntax is perceived to be more readable and Business User-friendly than other programming languages. VB.NET still shares many of the same syntax elements of older VB dialects, such as VB6, VBA, and VBScript. This means that Users who have written macros in Microsoft Excel or used VBScript to write Business Rules in first-generation CPM solutions should feel comfortable with the core syntax elements of VB.NET. The main learning challenge Business Users face when migrating to VB.NET is understanding the object-oriented nature of the language. In comparison to VBScript, VB.NET offers a more elegant coding paradigm.

As mentioned in this book's introduction, you don't need to be an expert-level coder to be proficient at writing Calculations. Does it help? Certainly, but it is *far more important* to grasp the OneStream-specific concepts around the data and understand the underlying business processes driving the Calculations. The coding part will come over time.

> **Note:** The C# programming language will be enabled for Business Rules in the future.

VB.NET Basics

This book will not teach you how to code VB.NET, but I will try to list common VB.NET concepts that will persist in many of your Calculations. There are a ton of online resources that can explain these concepts better than I can. This is far from a comprehensive list but a good starting point.

Data Types

- String (simple text string, e.g., "Hello")
- Integer (number without decimals, e.g., 123)
- Decimal (full 128-bit variable)
- Double (number with decimals, e.g., 123.45)
- Boolean (True or False)
- GUID (unique ID)
- Array

Collection Classes

- List(OfValueClass)
- Dictionary(Of KeyClass, ValueClass)

Classes & Methods

- Constructors
- Variables
- Properties
- Subs
- Functions
- Events

Other Relevant Concepts

- Namespace – provides a path to identify classes when their names are not unique within an assembly
- Imports – allow you to use someone's classes with their short names
- Public Variables – allow for the exposure of variables and functions to other classes (e.g., other Business Rules)
- If, Then, Else If, End If
- Select, Case
- For, For Each, Next

The OneStream API Library

Each Business Rule Type contains a plethora of API functions that allow you to interact with, and access, objects within that Engine. For example, using API functions, we can access Member names or descriptions from the Finance Engine, retrieve the Workflow status from the Workflow Engine, or parse Stage data from the Staging Engine. Getting familiar with the vast set of API functions will be a big part of Calculation writing.

API functions will be specific to the Type of Business Rule that you are working in. Since Cube Calculations are written in Finance Business Rules, we will primarily be using Finance-specific API Functions.

Throughout this book, you will be introduced to quite a few of these API functions, only scratching the surface of all that are available.

BRAPI

The BRAPI is common across all Business Rules and Engines. A BRAPI function runs outside of the other Engines and can orchestrate certain functions from within other Engines. In other words, a BRAPI function will allow you to execute functions outside of the Engine you are working in.

For example, a parser function can be executed from a Finance Business Rule. While not covered in detail in this book, learning the entire suite of API functions within other Engines can help your Calculation writing skills since these APIs can be accessed through the BRAPI library.

In-Solution Documentation

The **OneStream Business Rule Editor** includes context-sensitive help for API properties and Methods as well as snippets (code examples). In-solution documentation makes the process of writing a Business Rule more efficient because API documentation, objects, and samples are presented within the Business Rule Editor window. In addition, useful code snippets – accumulated by the OneStream engineering and consulting teams – are also presented in a context-sensitive manner within the Business Rule Editor.

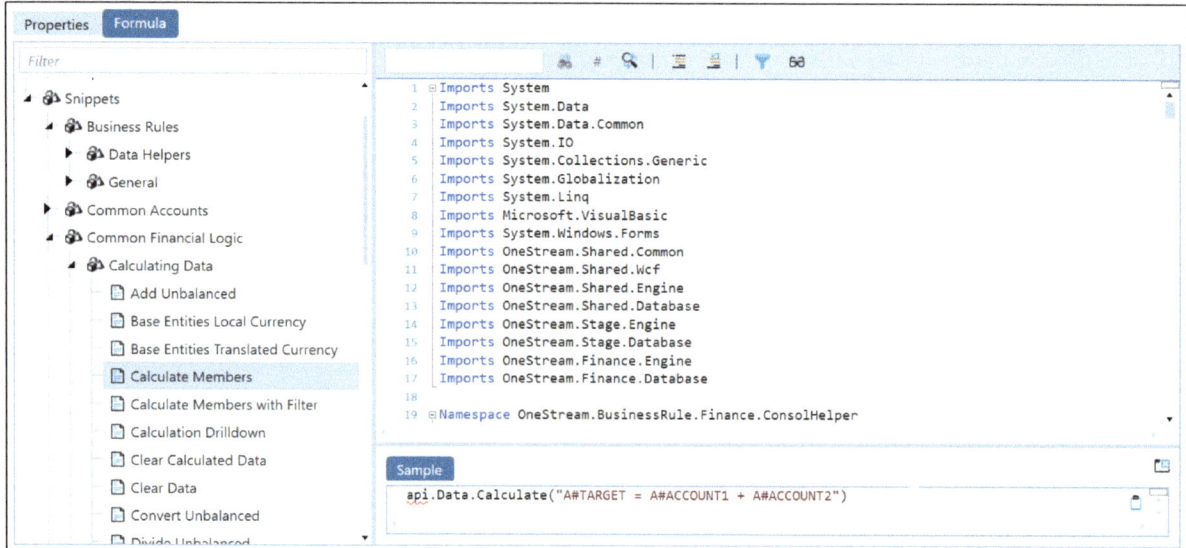

Figure 1.3

IntelliSense

IntelliSense is a code completion tool that is built into the OneStream Business Rule Editor. Start typing a function and IntelliSense will open available classes and functions right there on the screen, giving you the proper syntax and required parameters. It's like coding training wheels. If it isn't already, IntelliSense will soon become your best friend in rule writing.

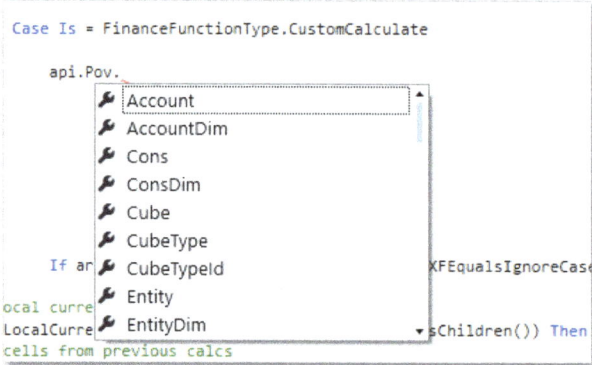

Figure 1.4

The Cube Stores, The Finance Engine Processes

Data that is processed by the Finance Engine resides in a multidimensional database called a Cube. Data processed by the Staging Engine is loaded into the Cube. Data can also be inputted directly into the Cube via the Workflow Engine through data entry Forms. Simply put, Cubes store the data, and the Finance Engine processes it.

Dimensions

Data is stored across the 18 Dimensions listed below. Some Dimensions are editable, and some are standard with a pre-defined list of Members.

Dimension Name	Editable
Time	N
Scenario	Y
Entity	Y
Parent	Y
Consolidation	N
View	N
Account	Y
Flow	Y
Origin	N
Intercompany	Y
UD1	Y
UD2	Y
UD3	Y
UD4	Y
UD5	Y
UD6	Y
UD7	Y
UD8	Y

Figure 1.5

Data Unit

The **Data Unit** acts as a grouping mechanism for data in the Cube and is defined as all data within a combination of Entity, Parent, Scenario, Consolidation, and Time Members. The Data Unit is the unit by which the Cube is partitioned and processed. In other words, Cube data is divided into Data Units, and the Finance Engine processes all the data within each Data Unit at once.

Understanding the Data Unit and how data is stored in the Cube is crucial to writing Calculations and is covered in more detail in the next chapter.

Functions of the Finance Engine

The Finance Engine describes the set of features and functionalities that process data within the Cube. Below is a brief description of the various functions the Finance Engine performs.

Consolidation Algorithm

The Consolidation algorithm encompasses several actions performed on Cube data:

- Data Storage and Aggregation
- Currency Translation via the Translation algorithm
- Calculation of `C#Share` by considering Entity Ownership %
- Intercompany elimination logic
- Company-specific Calculations via Business Rules and Member Formulas

The default Consolidation algorithm that performs the above functions can be modified in the Cube properties.

Data Storage and In-Memory Aggregation

Data storage occurs at the Base-level Members of the 18 Dimensions contained in the Cube. The Consolidation algorithm also writes and stores aggregated Base data to Parent Entity Members. Parent Members in non-Data Unit Dimensions are aggregated in-memory only.

Chapter 1

Finance Business Rules and Member Formulas

Sophisticated Calculation and business logic can be executed when the Finance Engine executes the Cube Consolidation or Calculation algorithms through **Finance Business Rules** or **Member Formulas**. This ability opens up infinite possibilities for how data can be manipulated and created. The majority of this book focuses on how to write Calculation Scripts via Business Rules and Member Formulas.

Calculations within the Finance Engine are written in the Business Rule or Member Formula Editor, right inside the OneStream software platform, from the desktop app or the browser-based web application.

In a practical sense, there is very little difference *where* you decide to write your Calculation logic. Both options have the same API functions available and can perform *mostly* the same things. There are, however, a few nuanced differences that I will describe below. Aside from these differences, everything else is essentially identical between them.

Finance Business Rules

Location

The **Business Rule Editor** can be accessed by going to **Business Rules** in the **Application** tab.

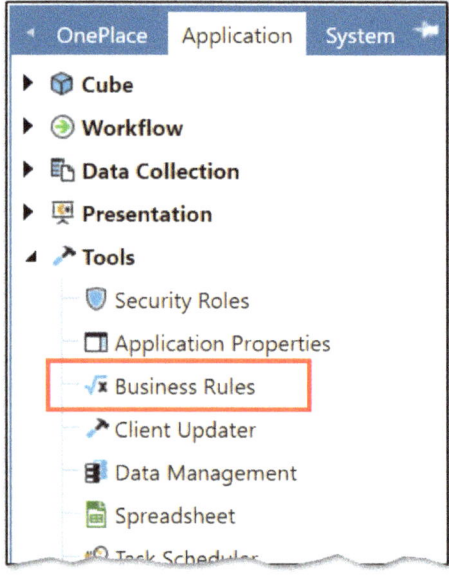

Figure 1.6

Finance Rules are grouped at the top, and each Rule created within is an independent object encapsulating VB.NET code.

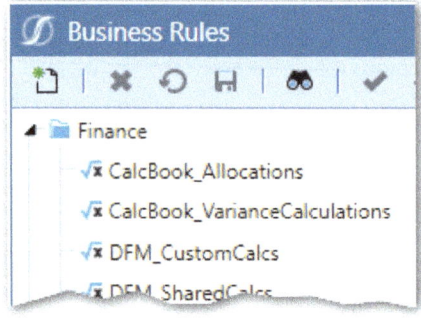

Figure 1.7

Each OneStream Business Rule has a pre-defined Namespace, a Public Class, and a Public Function that the OneStream platform Engines invoke when the Business Rule needs to be called.

```
Namespace OneStream.BusinessRule.Finance.CalcBook_Allocations
    Public Class MainClass
        Public Function Main(ByVal si As SessionInfo, ByVal globals As BRGlobals, ByVal api As FinanceRulesApi, ByVal args As FinanceRulesArgs) As Object
```

Figure 1.8

Finance Function Types

A unique attribute of Business Rules compared to Member Formulas is that Finance Function Types can be accessed to allow interactions with specific parts of the Calculation Engine.

Below are Finance Function Types relevant to Calculations:

```
Case Is = FinanceFunctionType.DataCell

Case Is = FinanceFunctionType.FxRate

Case Is = FinanceFunctionType.Calculate

Case Is = FinanceFunctionType.ConditionalInput

Case Is = FinanceFunctionType.CustomCalculate

Case Is = FinanceFunctionType.ConsolidateElimination

Case Is = FinanceFunctionType.ConsolidateShare

Case Is = FinanceFunctionType.DynamicCalcAccount

Case Is = FinanceFunctionType.Translate
```

Figure 1.9

Business Rules give the ability to execute any of the above Finance Function Types. This is a key difference from Member Formulas, especially when needing to run Calculations outside of the Data Units Calculation Sequence using the Custom Calculate Finance Function Type (more on that later).

Advantages

The biggest advantage of using Business Rules over Member Formulas is the ability to control behavior through Finance Function Types, which are not available in Member Formulas. For example, Custom Calculate functions – which are explained in detail later in this chapter – cannot be executed through Member Formulas.

Business Rules can also have some advantages when your Calculations have a high level of volume and complexity. For example, you may want to calculate multiple Accounts within the same script using some shared logic. While you technically could, it wouldn't make much sense to put that logic in a Member Formula since it doesn't apply to just one Member. You can also reuse variables and other objects through the duration of the Business Rule, which can save some redundancy if many Member Formulas are using the same variables.

With Business Rules, all your Calculations are in one place, so it can actually make management easier if Calculation volume is high.

Chapter 1

Member Formulas

Location

The **Member Formula Editor** can be accessed by going into any Scenario, Flow, Account, or UD Dimension Member's Formula property.

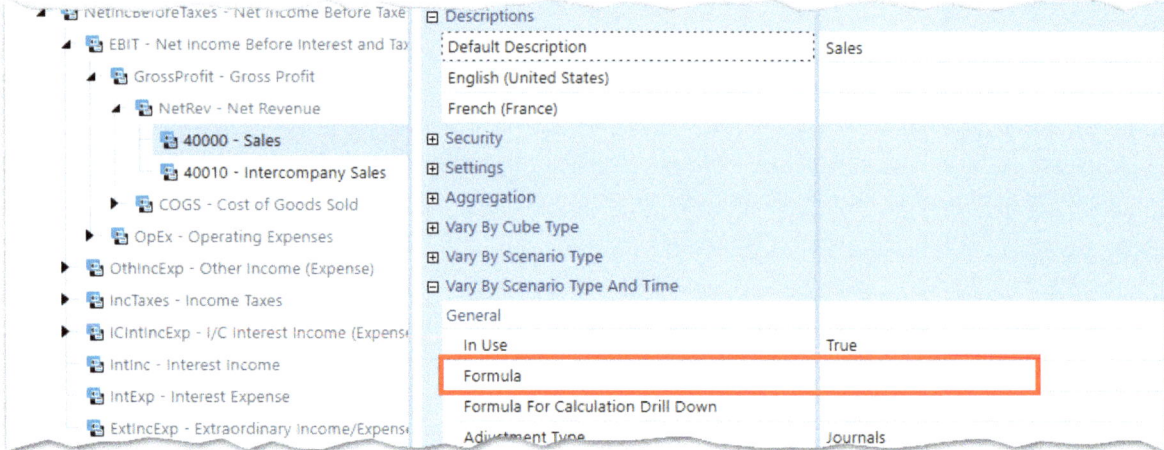

Figure 1.10

Menus are shown, which can allow Calculations to vary for specific Time periods and Scenario Types.

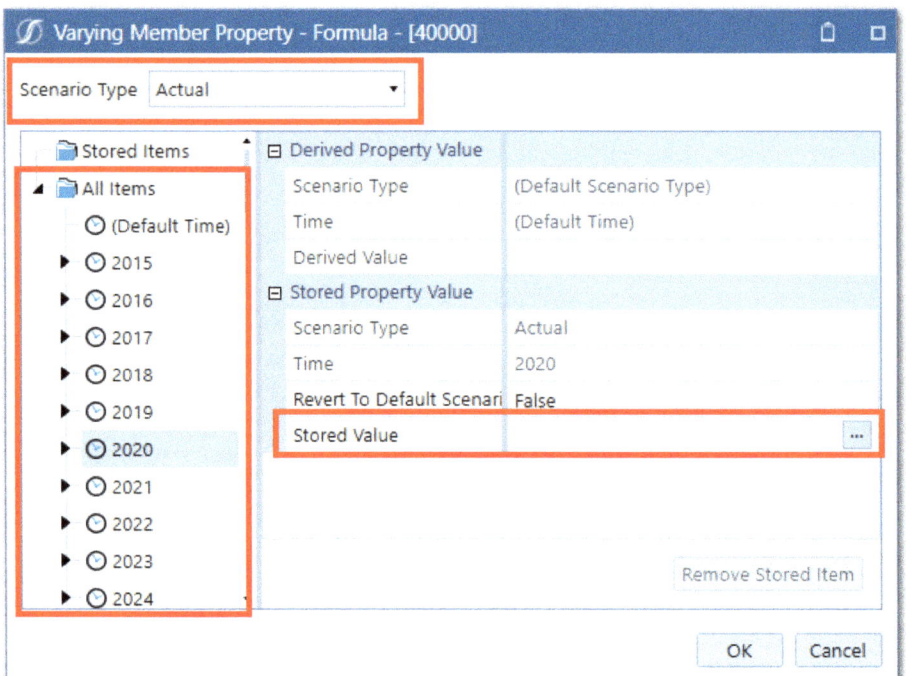

Figure 1.11

Clicking the Stored Value property opens the Formula Editor, which is similar in look, feel, and functionality to the Business Rule Editor.

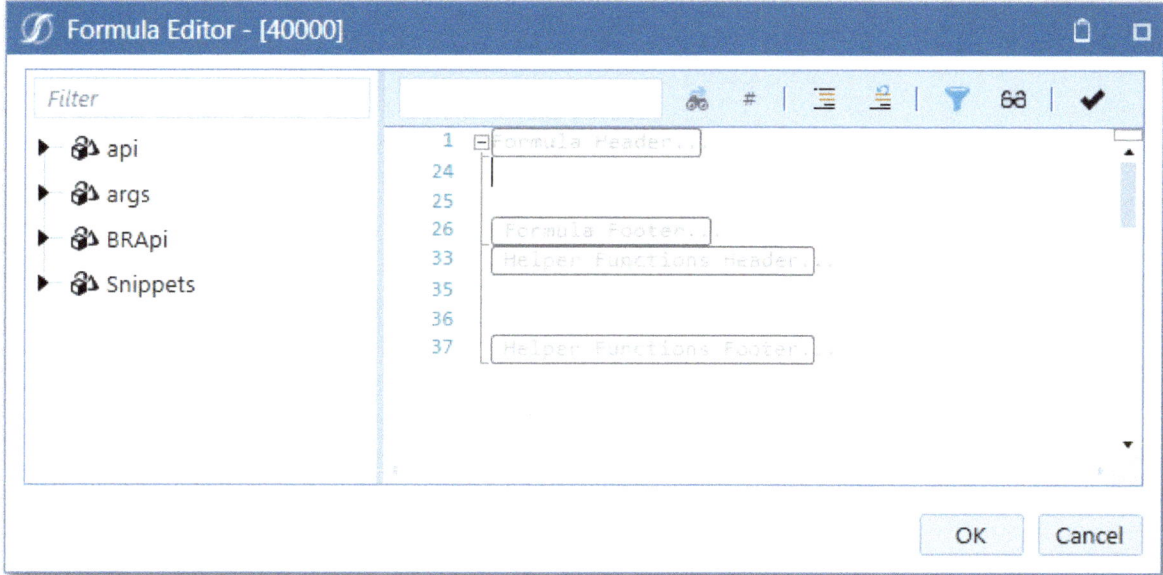

Figure 1.12

Assigning stored formulas to Members is for organizational purposes only. Formulas written to a particular Member are not restricted to writing data only for that Member. However, if a formula is attached to an unrelated Member, it can make the application difficult to maintain and understand. Therefore, decide to attach a formula that calculates multiple Members to the Scenario's Member Formula or a Business Rule instead.

Calculation Drill Down

When analyzing data from Cube Views or Quick Views, data can be drilled into, down to the base data, and even beyond to the Stage tables and source system. If a calculated Member is drilled down upon, **Calculation Drill Down** can be enabled so that the data can be drilled on further – to show the Calculation inputs. To enable this functionality, a drill down script is entered on the Member's Formula for Calculation Drill Down property.

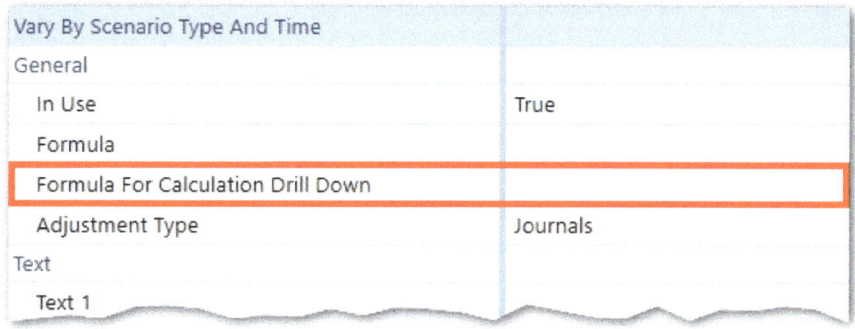

Figure 1.13

This formula will utilize specific drill down API functions and arguments.

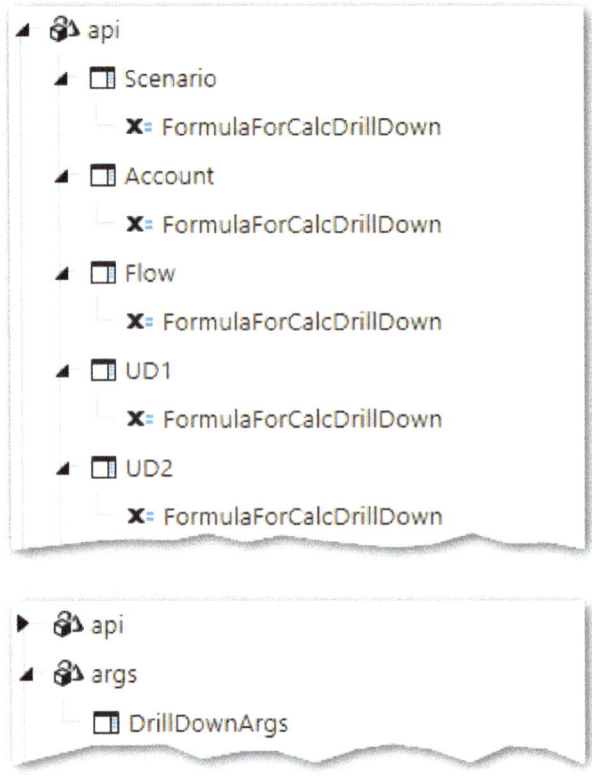

Figure 1.14

Advantages

The first benefit of Member Formulas is that they provide a natural organizational structure to your Calculation code that is maintenance-friendly. If you want to edit the Calculation Script for the Sales Account, you can quickly find it in the **Dimension Library**. There won't be a bunch of other scripts there, and it will generally be easier to read.

Member Formulas can vary by Scenario Type and/or Time without the need to write code. The Member Formula stores all these variations directly on the Member, via properties, through which the Administrator can carry out maintenance using drop-down menus. For example, you'll likely encounter a requirement for a Calculation to change as of a certain date, or to calculate things differently on an Actual Scenario than a Forecast Scenario. Again, the Member Formula accommodates this out-of-the-box without needing to write additional lines of code.

Another aspect of Member Formulas is the ability to assign a **Formula Pass**, which executes in order within the Data Unit Calculation Sequence (covered later in this chapter). Formulas running in the same pass multithread (run in parallel), so they do have a slight performance impact compared to Business Rules.

The drawbacks of Member Formulas lie in the fact that they are a bit less flexible and lack some functionality for certain types of rules. Member Formulas only give the ability to run Calculate and Dynamic Calc Finance Function Types. If you need to run a Custom Calculate function, you will need to use a Business Rule.

Lastly, with large Calculation volumes, it can become cumbersome to have to go Member by Member to find the Calculation, and it might be easier to manage all Calculations within one or a handful of Business Rules.

Which is Better – Business Rule or Member Formula?

Aside from the functionalities that Business Rules have, that Member Formulas do not, it comes down to which is easiest to maintain and administer when making the choice. The bottom line is that – in a given implementation – you will likely have a mix of both Business Rules and Member Formulas, and it is largely up to the Consultant or customer which Method is deployed.

Referencing Business Rules in Other Business Rules or Member Formulas

Business Rules can be called from other Business Rules, or from within Member Formulas. First, the shared Business Rule is created.

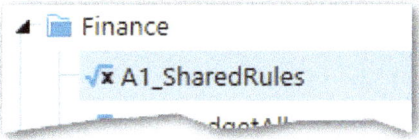

Figure 1.15

In the Properties tab of the Business Rule, make sure Contains Global Functions for Formulas is set to True.

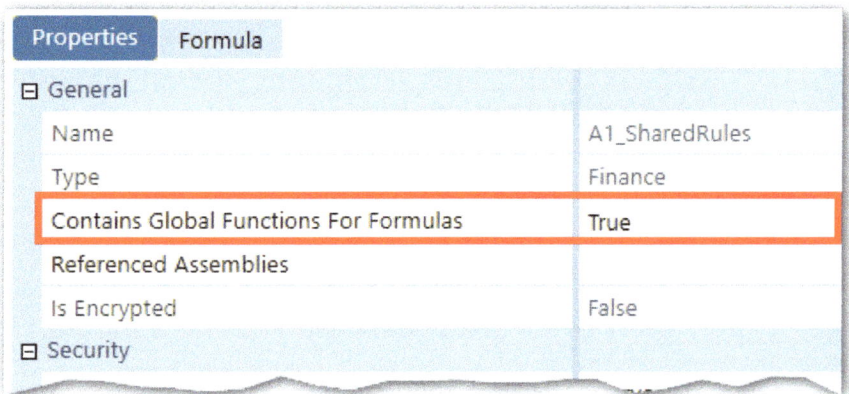

Figure 1.16

Inside this Rule, public functions are created and referenced by other Rules and Member Formulas. The function `Main` is included when creating the Rule, and other functions can be added if needed.

```vb
Namespace OneStream.BusinessRule.Finance.A1_SharedRules
    Public Class MainClass
        Public Function Main(ByVal si As SessionInfo, ByVal globals As BRGlobals, ByVal api As FinanceRulesApi, ByVal args As FinanceRulesArgs) As Object
            Try

                Return Nothing
            Catch ex As Exception
                Throw ErrorHandler.LogWrite(si, New XFException(si, ex))
            End Try
        End Function

        Public Function OtherFunction(ByVal si As SessionInfo, ByVal globals As BRGlobals, ByVal api As FinanceRulesApi, ByVal args As FinanceRulesArgs) As Object
            Try

                Return Nothing
            Catch ex As Exception
                Throw ErrorHandler.LogWrite(si, New XFException(si, ex))
            End Try
        End Function
    End Class
End Namespace
```

Figure 1.17

Next, call the Business Rule from a Member Formula using the below script:

```
Dim sharedFinanceBR As New
OneStream.BusinessRule.Finance.A1_SharedRules.MainClass
```

Each function within the Rule can then be called. Make sure all required parameters are passed in.

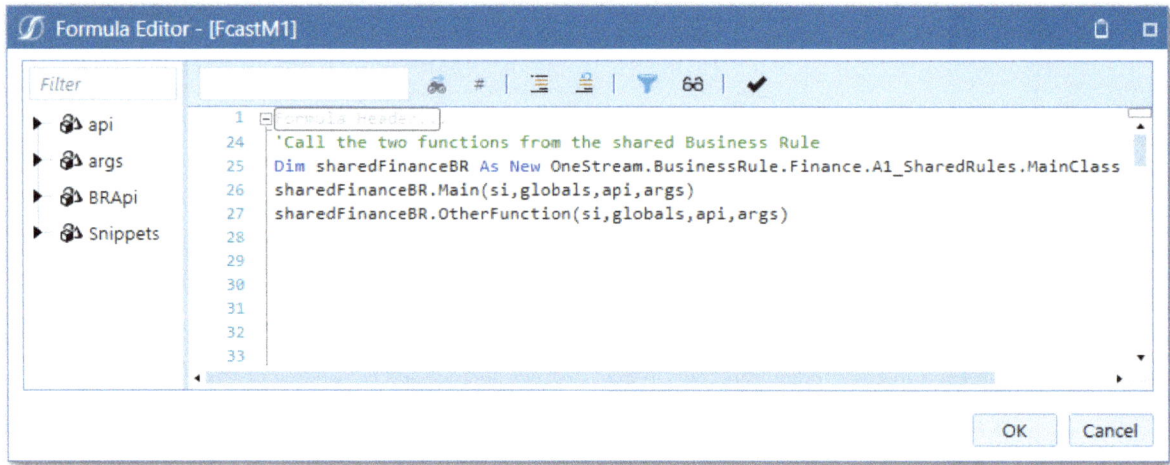

Figure 1.18

Figure 1.18 shows the shared Business Rule called from a Scenario Formula.

Using this technique can help streamline your Business Rules and Member Formulas as common logic or script does not need to be repeated in multiple rules.

Cube Properties

The below Cube properties can change the standard Consolidation algorithm

Calculation	
Consolidation Algorithm Type	Standard (Calc-On-The-Fly Share and Hierarchy Elimination)
Translation Algorithm Type	Standard
Calculate None Cons Member If No Data	False
Calculate Local Currency If No Data	True
Calculate Translated Currencies If No Data	False
Calculate OwnerPreAdj If No Data	False
Calculate Share Cons Member If No Data	False
Calculate Elimination Cons Member If No Data	False
Calculate OwnerPostAdj If No Data	False

Figure 1.19

Consolidation Algorithm Type

The Consolidation Algorithm Type has the below options:

- Standard (Calc-On-The-Fly Share and Hierarchy Elimination)
- Stored Share
- Org-By-Period Elimination
- Stored Share and Org-By-Period Elimination
- Custom

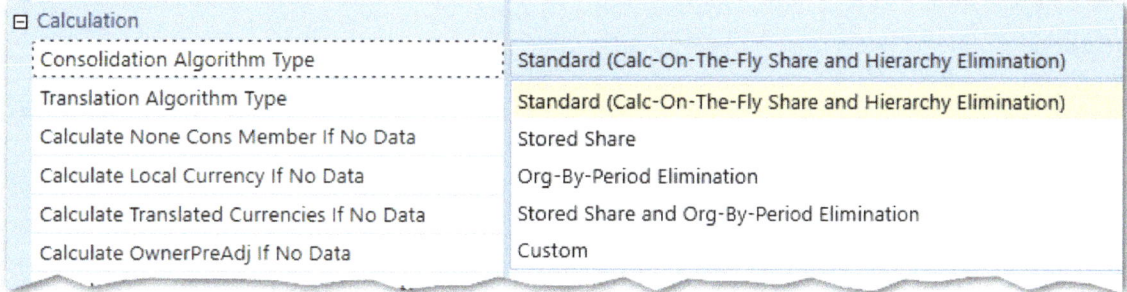

Figure 1.20

Standard
This is the default Consolidation algorithm. Amounts for the **Share Consolidation Member** are calculated dynamically and amounts for the **Elimination Consolidation Member** are calculated using built-in algorithms. Only in rare circumstances should Standard not be used.

Stored Share
This is similar to Standard, but values for the Share Member are stored instead of being calculated dynamically.

Org-By-Period Elimination
This differs from the standard Consolidation algorithm in that – when calculating the Elimination – this option considers the position of the IC Member in the Entity hierarchy and checks the percent Consolidation for every relationship down the hierarchy. If a percent Consolidation is zero, the IC Member is determined *not* to be a descendent of the Entity, and no elimination is calculated.

Stored Share and Org-By-Period Elimination
This option stores the Share Member and uses the Org-By-Period Elimination logic described above.

Custom
The Consolidation will utilize custom Business Rules to calculate amounts for the Share and Elimination Consolidation Members using the Finance Function Types of Consolidate Share and Consolidate Elimination.

Translation Algorithm Type

The Translation Algorithm Type has the following options:

- Standard
- Standard Using Business Rules for FX Rates
- Custom

Chapter 1

Calculation	
Consolidation Algorithm Type	Standard (Calc-On-The-Fly Share and Hierarchy Elimination)
Translation Algorithm Type	Standard
Calculate None Cons Member If No Data	Standard
Calculate Local Currency If No Data	Standard Using Business Rules For FX Rates
Calculate Translated Currencies If No Data	Custom
Calculate OwnerPreAdj If No Data	False

Figure 1.21

Standard
This setting runs the default Translation algorithm. Amounts calculated for a foreign currency Consolidation Member will be generated using the FX Rates determined by the Cube or Scenario settings.

Standard Using Business Rules for FX Rates
This setting will run the default Translation algorithm, described above, but also allow the ability to run specific different FX Rates, beyond what is assigned to the Cube or Scenario. For example, if the required FX Rates differ for certain Accounts, this setting would be chosen, and a Business Rule would hold the logic to determine which Accounts get different rates.

Custom
This setting assumes Translation will be run entirely through Business Rules assigned to the Cube that use the `FinanceFunctionType`.

NoData Calculate Settings

Calculation	
Consolidation Algorithm Type	Standard (Calc-On-The-Fly Share and Hierarchy Elimination)
Translation Algorithm Type	Standard
Calculate None Cons Member If No Data	False
Calculate Local Currency If No Data	True
Calculate Translated Currencies If No Data	False
Calculate OwnerPreAdj If No Data	False
Calculate Share Cons Member If No Data	False
Calculate Elimination Cons Member If No Data	False
Calculate OwnerPostAdj If No Data	False

Figure 1.22

These settings control whether the Finance Engine will execute Calculations against cells within the specified Consolidation Member, even if there is no data stored in the entire Data Unit. This can provide a performance benefit and False should be the default setting for all Members except for Local.

The use case for setting to True is when using a Business Rule or Member Formula to copy data from another Time period or Scenario. If not set to True, Data Units that are empty in the Target Data Unit will not run, even if there is data in the Source Data Unit and, thus, will not copy the data. Note that in most situations where data is copied from other Time periods or Scenarios, only copying `C#Local` data is suitable as the Consolidation algorithm will translate and consolidate the local data to the other Consolidation Members.

When and How Do Calculations Run?

How is the Finance Engine started so that our scripts inside Business Rules and Member Formulas execute? Going back to the car analogy, we need to know how to start the car and push the gas pedal. This section covers the mechanisms in which the Finance Engine can be initiated.

There are two underlying processes that are triggered to execute the Calculation Scripts stored in Business Rules and Member Formulas – the **Data Unit Calculation Sequence (DUCS)** and **Custom Calculate**.

Data Unit Calculation Sequence (DUCS)

The Data Unit Calculation Sequence (abbreviated to DUCS) is a series of steps that occurs each time a Calculation or Consolidation is run on the Cube.

Below are the steps involved in the DUCS:

- Clear previously calculated data (based on cell Storage Type – will not clear Durable Data). Note: OneStream will only perform this action if the calculated Scenario has its Clear Calculated Data During Calc setting set to True
- Run Scenario Member Formula
- Perform reverse Translations by calculating Flow Members from other alternate currency input Flow Members
- Execute Business Rules 1 and 2 (as assigned to Cube)
- Execute Formula Passes 1 through 4 (Account formulas, then Flow formulas, then UD1 formulas, UD2, … UD8)
- Execute Business Rules 3 and 4 (as assigned to Cube)
- Execute Formula Passes 5 through 8 (Account formulas, then Flow formulas, then UD1 formulas, UD2, … UD8)
- Execute Business Rules 5 and 6 (as assigned to Cube)
- Execute Formula Passes 9 through 12 (Account formulas, then Flow formulas, then UD1 formulas, UD2, … UD8)
- Execute Business Rules 7 and 8 (as assigned to Cube)
- Execute Formula Passes 13 through 16 (Account formulas, then Flow formulas, then UD1 formulas, UD2, … UD8)

Consolidation Dimension

The Consolidation Dimension is part of the Data Unit which means that the DUCS will run for each Member. There is a slight nuance I should point out, which is that some `FinanceFunctionTypes` mentioned earlier will only run at certain Consolidation Members. The below table shows which Finance Function Types run when each Consolidation Member is processed during a Consolidation.

Chapter 1

Consolidation Member	Relevant Finance Function Type
Local	Calculate
Translated*	Translate
OwerPreAdj	Calculate
Share*	ConsolidateShare
Elimination*	ConsolidateElimination
OwnerPostAdj	Calculate

*FinanceFunctionType.Calculate also executes at these members

Figure 1.23

Assigning Business Rules to the Cube

Finance Business Rules need to be assigned to the Cube for them to execute within the DUCS. In Cube Properties, there are up to 8 Finance Business Rules that can be assigned to the Cube.

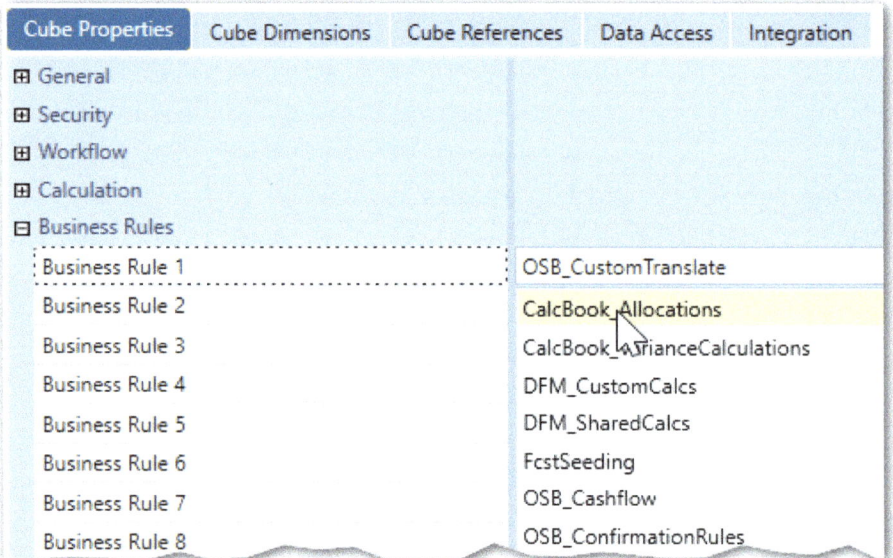

Figure 1.24

Note that some Business Rules may only run at certain Consolidation Members based on the `FinanceFunctionTypes` used.

Member Formulas

A Member Formula assigned to any Account, Flow, or UD Member with the Formula Pass Property set to FormulaPass1-16 will be included in the DUCS.

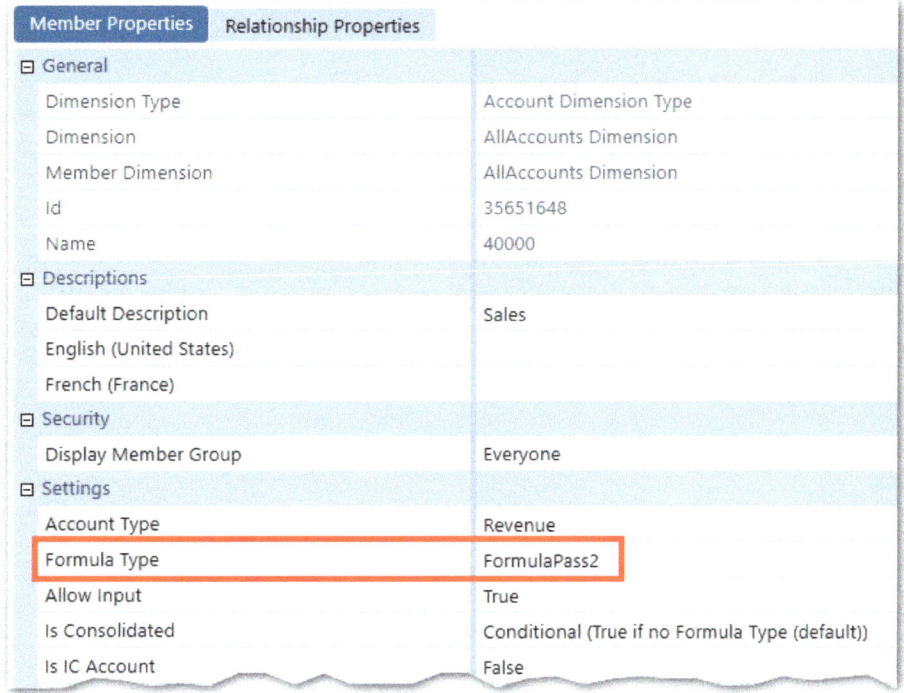

Figure 1.25

When storing Calculations on Member Formulas, it is important to pay attention to the Is Consolidated Property. The default setting of Conditional (True if no Formula Type (default)) means that data for this Account (calculated or otherwise) will not be consolidated. If you want data to be consolidated (as would be in most cases), this setting should be changed to True.

Triggering the DUCS

The DUCS is triggered by executing either a Consolidation or Calculation on one or more Data Units in a Cube. So, what's the difference between a Consolidation and Calculation?

A Calculation simply executes the DUCS for the selected Data Unit, while a Consolidation executes the DUCS and does several additional actions. A Consolidation will:

- Aggregate and store data at Parent Members in the Entity hierarchy
- Execute Currency Translations
- Execute Intercompany Eliminations
- Execute the DUCS

As with many things in OneStream, you are provided with a menu of options for where, when, and how you want your Calculations to execute. Below are all the places where Users can execute Consolidations and Calculations.

- Data Management
- Cube Views
- Dashboard Button
- Workflow Process Step

Chapter 1

Data Management

Let's start with the most common and logical place to execute Calculations. Data Management (DM) can be used to, amongst other things, calculate, clear, copy, and export data. DM is structured into steps that are assigned to **sequences**. Sequences are then executed either directly from the DM module, or attached to other OneStream objects like Dashboards.

Create the Step

The Calculate and Custom Calculate Step Types can be used to execute a Calculation.

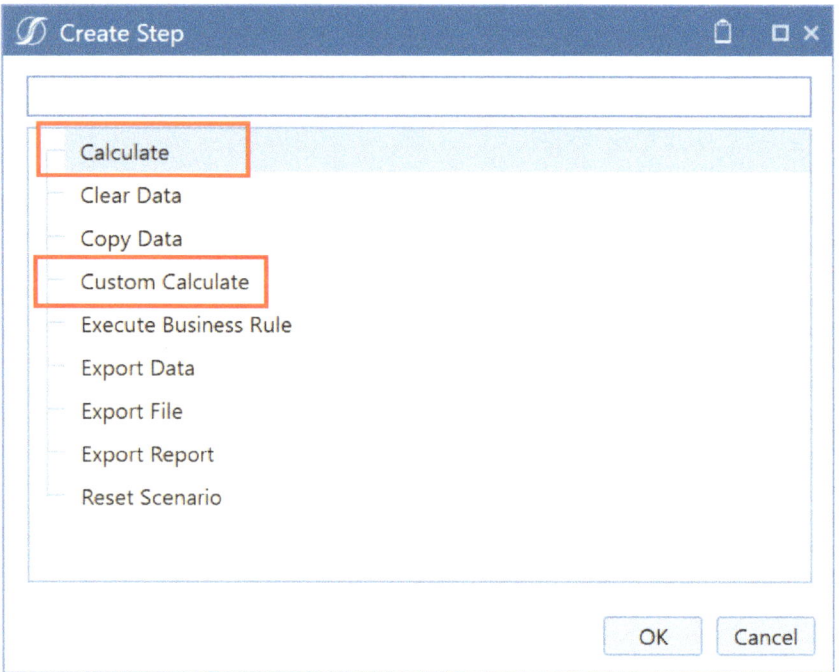

Figure 1.26

Calculation Type

Selecting the Calculate Step will require you to further specify the Calculation Type.

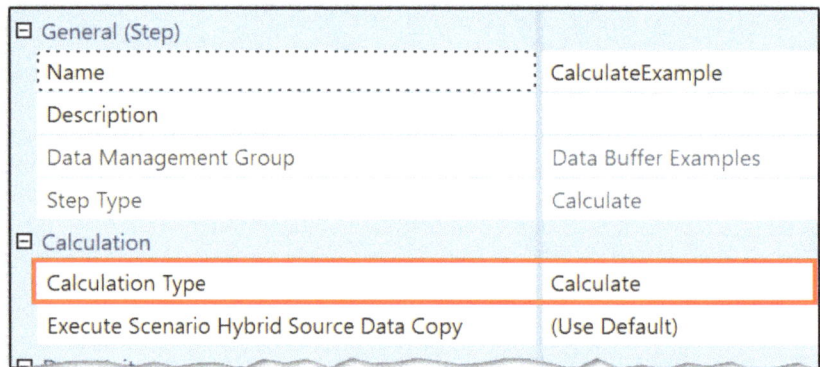

Figure 1.27

You can choose between Calculate, Translate, or Consolidate, which all contain With Logging and/or Force variations.

Finance Engine Basics

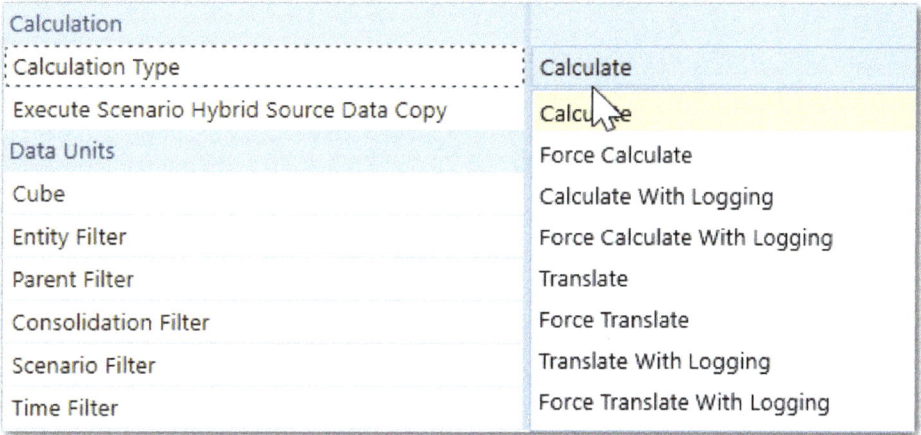

Figure 1.28

Define the Data Unit

Properties and required inputs will differ per the Step Type, but both Calculate DM steps require specification of the Data Unit Dimensions.

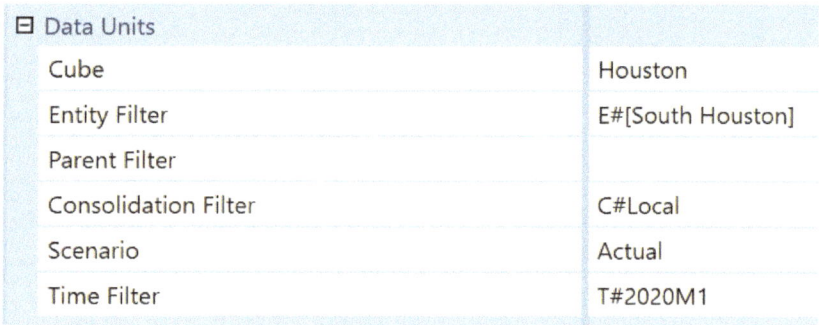

Figure 1.29

Note: The automation and scheduling of Data Management sequences can be configured through Windows PowerShell scripts running on the Application Server.

Chapter 1

From a Cube View

Users can execute Calculations and Consolidations directly from a Cube View by enabling those actions in the Cube View properties.

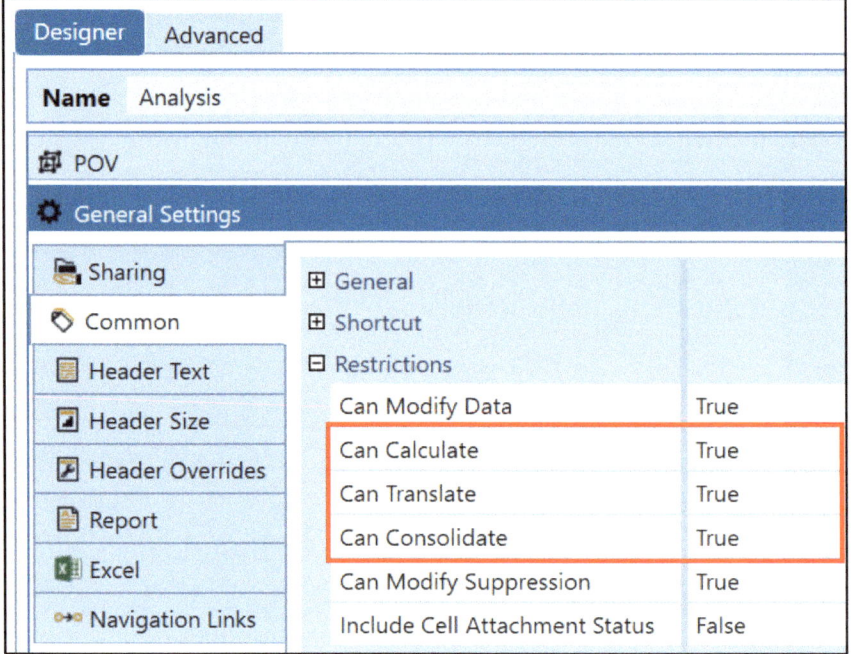

Figure 1.30

Setting these properties to True will activate those options in both the Data Explorer Header and in the right-click menu on each data cell.

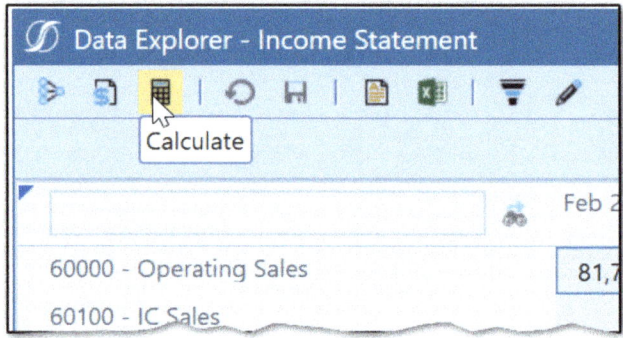

Figure 1.31

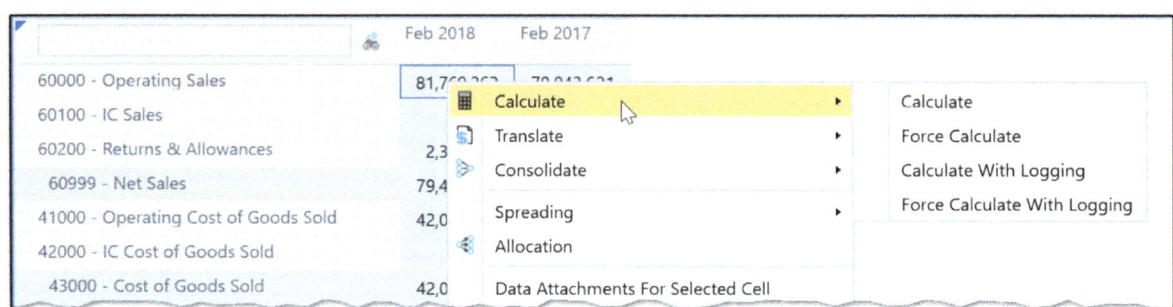

Figure 1.32

26

While not explicitly defined when clicking Calculate, the Data Unit(s) upon which the Calculation will run will be inherited from the POV of the clicked cell.

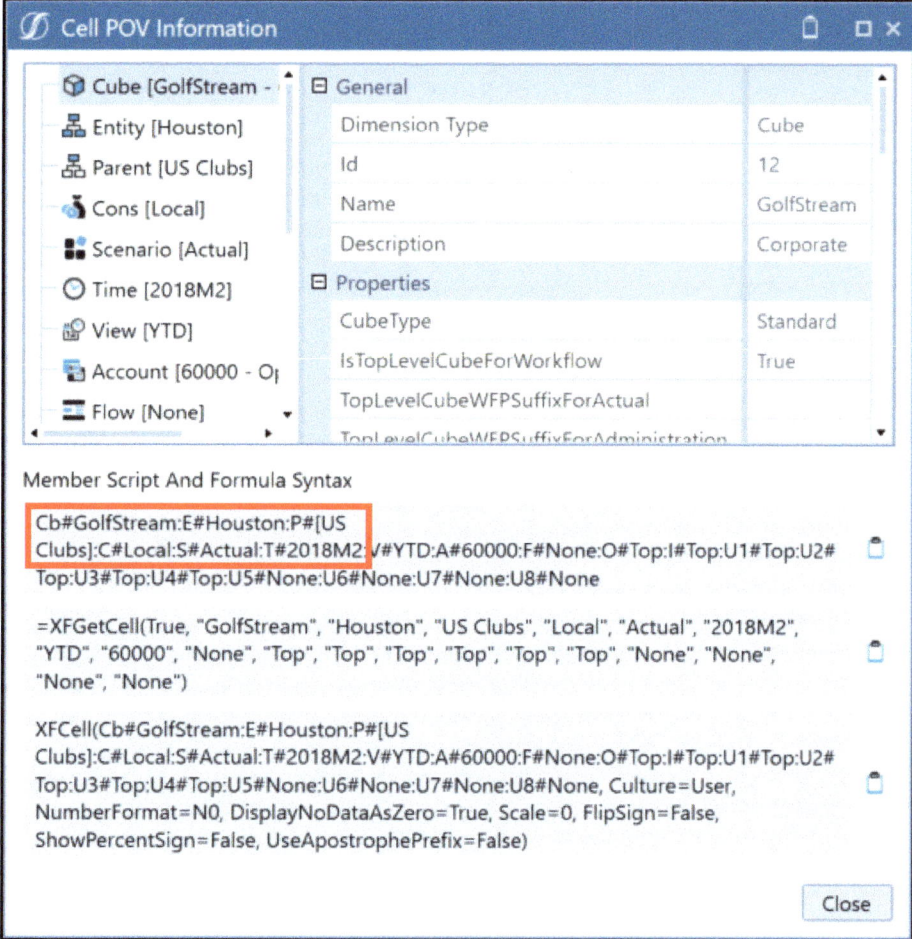

Figure 1.33

> **Note:** Custom Calculate Functions cannot be called from a Cube View.

Dashboard Button

Dashboards are collections of various Components in a nice, User-friendly layout. One of those Components is a button that, when clicked, can trigger an action to take place.

In the Action section of the button properties, the Server Task section allows you to either execute a DM Sequence (which would presumably contain a Calculate Step) or execute a Calculation directly.

Chapter 1

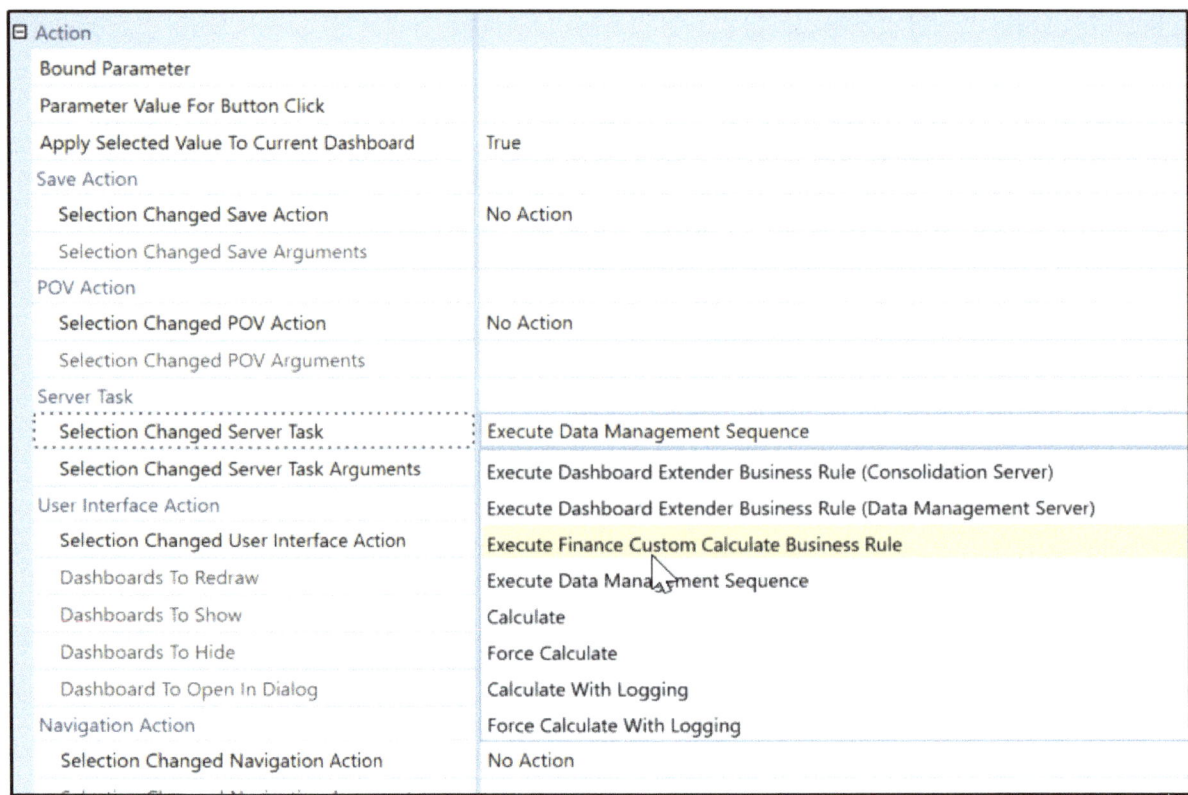

Figure 1.34

Arguments for the selected task will also need to be defined, which will control the Data Unit(s) that the task runs for.

Workflow Process Step

Built into OneStream's Workflow is the ability to execute Calculations through **Process** or **Pre-Process** steps. This is controlled through the **Workflow Name**, where various options are available depending on the requirements of that Workflow.

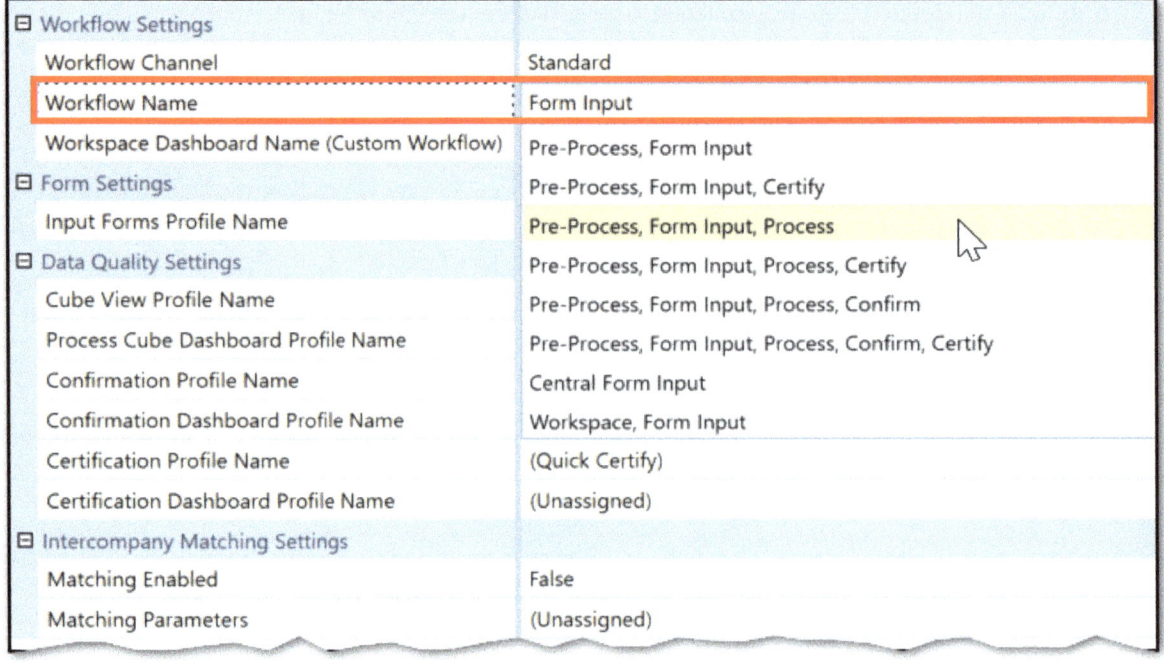

Figure 1.35

When selecting a Workflow Name that contains Process and/or Pre-Process, the Calculation Definitions tab will control the parameters in which the Calculation runs.

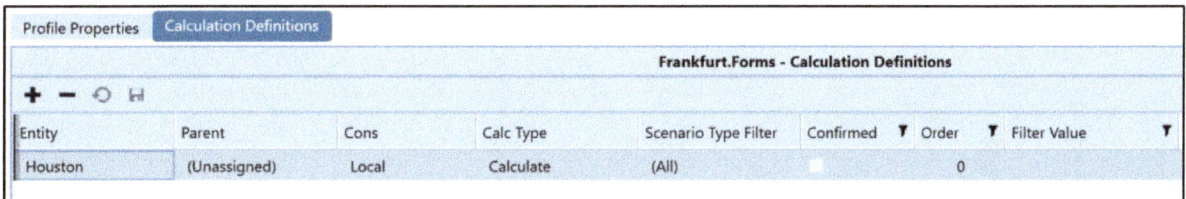

Figure 1.36

> **Note:** Custom Calculate Functions can be called from the Workflow Process Step via Data Management only.

Data Unit, Data Unit, Data Unit

It's important to call out that the Data Unit is defined *every time* a Consolidation or Calculation is triggered. If you think about it, this should make sense – the Data Unit Calculation Sequence needs a Data Unit to run for, and OneStream can't guess which one.

Dependent Data Units

Some Data Units have dependencies on other Data Units and, in some cases, should be consolidated or calculated first. An example of this is within the Time Dimension. June's data can be dependent on January-May. Entity and Consolidation Dimensions also have dependencies through **hierarchy relationships** (i.e., Children should Consolidate/Calculate before their Parents).

OneStream uses a concept called **Calculation Status** to determine whether data has changed since the last Calculation or Consolidation and, therefore, if dependent Data Units need to be processed. After the DUCS runs on a Data Unit, the Calculation Status of that Data Unit is changed to OK (No Calculation Needed, Data Has Not Changed). As soon as data changes in the Data Unit – either through a Form input, data load, or Journal – the Calculation Status will change to CN (Calculation Needed, Data Has Changed).

A **Force Consolidation** or **Force Calculation** can be used instead, which processes *all* dependent Data Units and ignores Calculation Status, while a normal Consolidate/Calculate will first check Calculation Status and will not run the DUCS if the Calculation Status for the Data Unit is OK.

There is a lot more detail and nuance around Calculation Status, which can be explored further in the *OneStream Design and Reference Guide*.

Parallel Processing

With the dependent Data Unit concept, it is likely that multiple Data Units will process when a Consolidation or Calculation is triggered. When the Finance Engine processes multiple Data Units, it processes **Sibling Data Units** in parallel (i.e., at the same time) to save time. Also referred to as **multi-threading**, this concept is primarily observed through the Entity Dimension. If consolidating the top Member of the Entity hierarchy, groups of sibling Entity Members will be processed simultaneously using multiple threads.

> **Note:** Because parallel processing results in sibling Entities being processed at the same time, the order in which two sibling Entities process can vary for each Consolidation. Special Entity properties are available, which can enable sibling Entities to process in order, using **sibling passes**. This use case is usually for **Equity Pickup Calculations**. An example is included in the last chapter of this book. 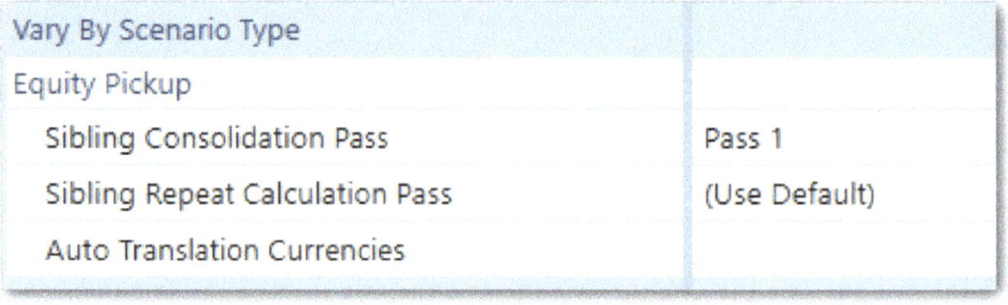
>
> | Vary By Scenario Type | |
> |---|---|
> | Equity Pickup | |
> | Sibling Consolidation Pass | Pass 1 |
> | Sibling Repeat Calculation Pass | (Use Default) |
> | Auto Translation Currencies | |
>
> Figure 1.37

All or Nothing

The DUCS is all or nothing. This is to say, all the steps run each time, no matter what. For example, you cannot choose to only execute Formula Pass 1 and bypass the other steps. This ensures that the entire Data Unit is always completely processed before data is then consolidated to its Parent Data Unit. Also, many Calculations have dependencies on other Calculations, so this ensures the Calculation order is never compromised. It also preserves data integrity by ensuring data is always cleared properly and completely before recalculating.

Custom Calculate Function

You may be thinking, "Isn't the DUCS a bit like overkill for certain situations? Do I really need to run every Calculation, even if I only want to calculate a handful of Accounts?" Indeed, if you were thinking something along those lines, you wouldn't be the first. That's where the Custom Calculate Function comes into play.

In house remodeling, the DUCS would be akin to a full demolition and rebuild. In contrast, the Custom Calculate Function would allow you to remodel the kitchen only.

Quite simply, Custom Calculate Functions only execute Calculation Scripts within that function. This allows the Calculation writer to be much more surgical with their Calculations and narrow the scope to specific elements of the financial process. There are, however, a couple of additional things that must be considered.

Triggering a Custom Calculate Business Rule

A Custom Calculate Function can only be triggered via a Data Management step or sequence. Simply create a step and select the Custom Calculate Step Type.

Finance Engine Basics

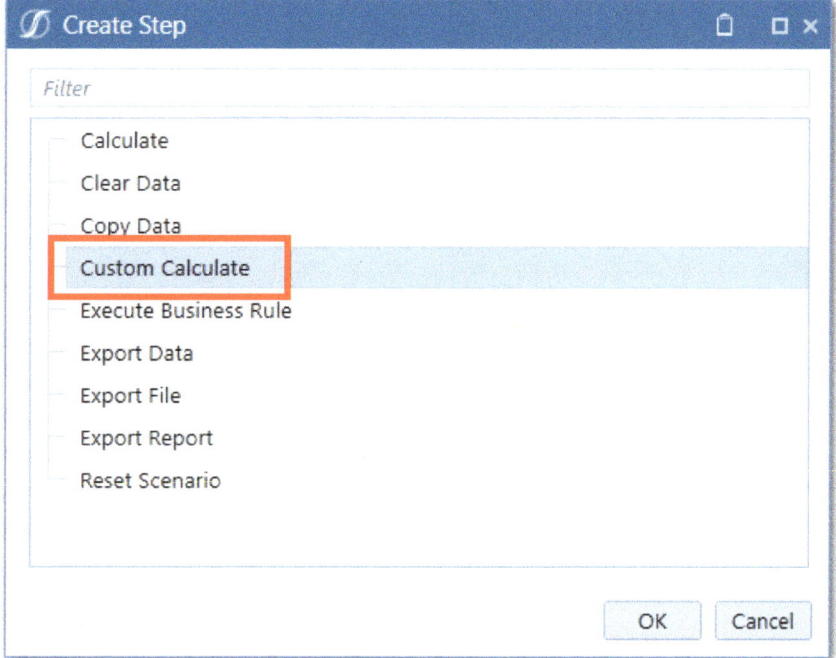

Figure 1.38

The Data Unit(s) will also need to be defined. A key difference with how Data Units are defined for Custom Calculate rules is that Calculation Status is not considered, so only Data Units explicitly defined will run. However, filters can be used for Entity, Consolidation, and Time which allow for multiple Members of those Dimensions to be included if needed.

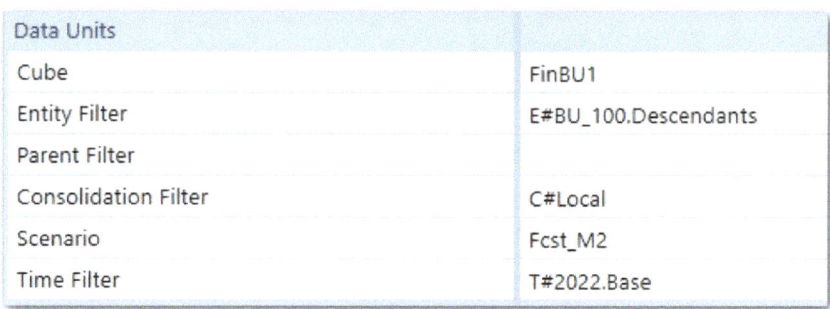

Figure 1.39

Figure 1.39, above, will run the Custom Calculate function for all Descendants of Entity BU_100 and all months in 2022. This will function like a Force Calculate because all Entity and Time Members within 2022 will be processed, regardless of Calculation Status.

The Business Rule and Function Name must be defined for Custom Calculate Steps. Parameter definition is optional but can be used to pass custom parameters or substitution variables in the Business Rule.

Figure 1.40

Chapter 1

Dimension POV Members can also be defined and referenced in the accompanied Business Rule:

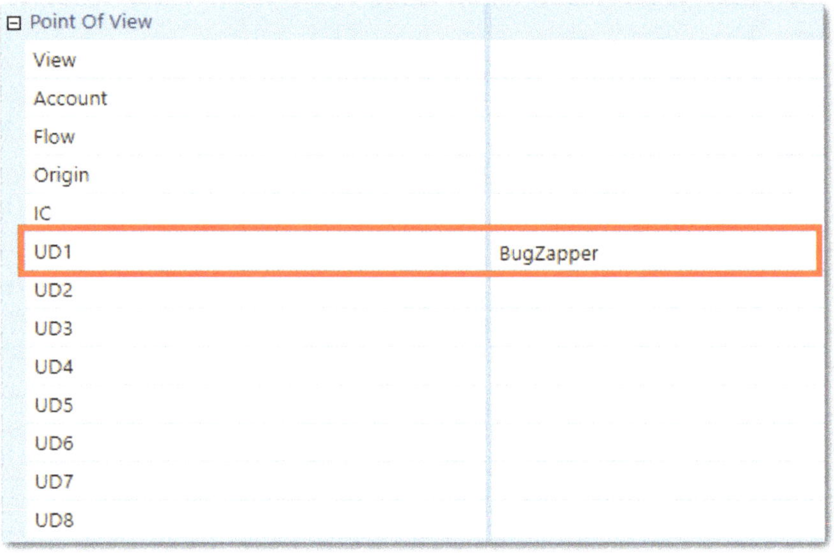

Figure 1.41

Durable Data

Let's say you've calculated data using Custom Calculate and subsequently run a Consolidation that executes the DUCS. What's the first step in the DUCS? I'll save you from needing to flip back a few pages – it's Clear Previously Calculated Data. Oh no! What will become of your Custom Calculated data? The answer will depend on whether you've flagged the data as `IsDurable` or not.

OneStream does not treat all calculated data the same. `DurableCalculatedData` is a data storage Type that is used to prevent calculated data from being cleared during the Clear Data step of the DUCS. The data that results from a Calculation can be set as `isDurable = True` which will protect it from being cleared during the DUCS. The data storage-type concept is expounded in the next chapter.

Data Clearing

Since you won't have the benefit of OneStream automatically clearing all previously calculated data for you (as during the DUCS), A **Clear Data Script** should be added at the top of every Custom Calculate rule so that all previously calculated data is cleared before recalculating. If you fail to include this, you could end up with data integrity issues such as 'old data' being left behind in the Cube, which could become very difficult to find and remedy. The `api.Data.ClearCalculatedData` function can be used.

```
api.Data.ClearCalculatedData(False,False,False,True,
   "A#AccountsToFilter.Base")
```

Other Differences

Custom Calculate Functions have a few other key properties which can make them much more flexible, User-friendly, and performant than Business Rules and Member Formulas that run inside the DUCS. Chapter 3 will explain those properties and how to use them in more detail.

C#Aggregated

The **Aggregated** Member of the Consolidation Dimension, when selected, allows for faster Aggregation and storage of data within the Entity Dimension by removing a lot of the functions of a Consolidation.

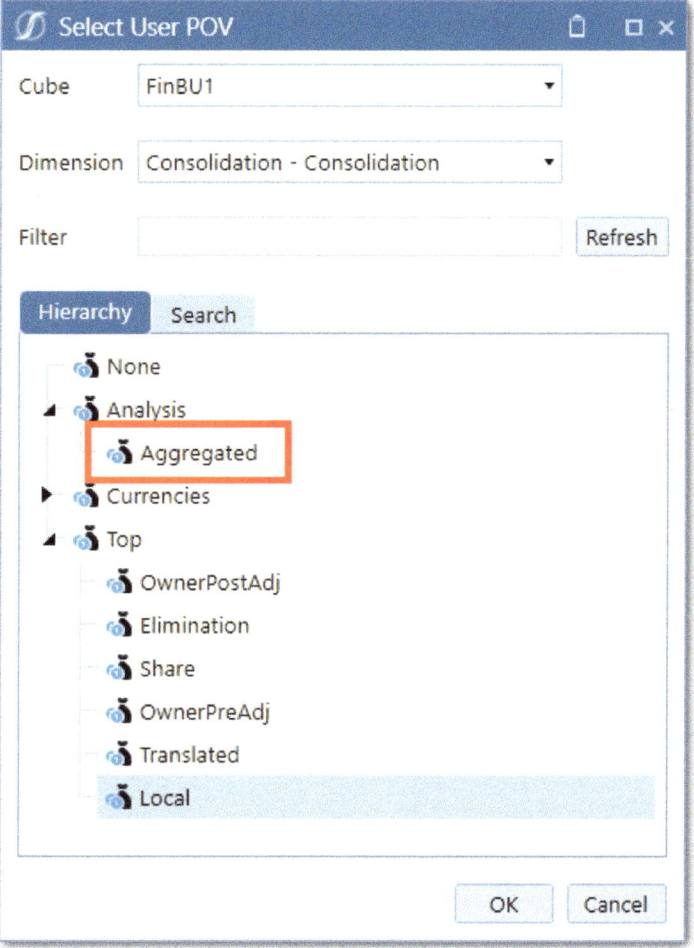

Figure 1.42

Aggregation can be triggered from the same mechanisms that trigger Consolidate or Calculate, described above. Simply define `C#Aggregated` as the Consolidation Member when defining the Data Unit.

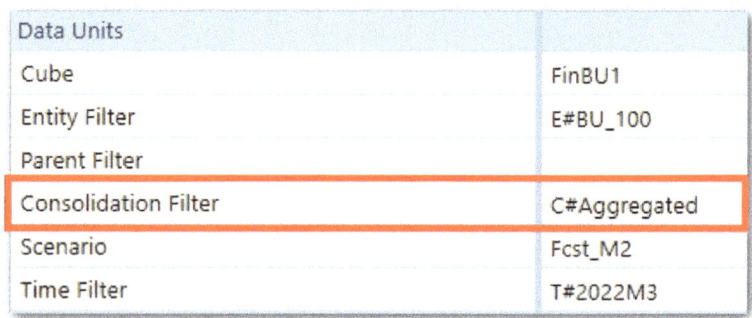

Figure 1.43

Chapter 1

When running a Calculation or Consolidation on `C#Aggregated`, a modified version of the Standard Consolidation algorithm is executed. The key differences when using `C#Aggregated` are:

- The DUCS is only executed at Base Entities
- No Intercompany elimination logic is performed
- No Share or Ownership Calculations are performed
- Data is stored at `C#Aggregated` at Parent Entities
- Only Direct Method Translation is performed

Dynamic Calculations

Calculations can also be written which do not execute during the DUCS or via Custom Calculate. These Calculations are called Dynamic (or Reporting) Calculations and only run when queried in a Report such as a Cube View or Excel Quick View. Dynamic Calculations differ fundamentally in terms of how they are written and behave compared to stored Calculations. A dedicated chapter – later in the book – will cover these in detail.

Clear as Mud

It may seem as though there is a lot to think about when trying to do something you'd expect to be simple, like executing a Calculation. I will do my best to simplify some questions that may be swirling through your head.

What Finance Function Type Should I Use?

Finance Function Types work hand in hand with the Consolidation Member being processed during the DUCS. Most Calculations and Business Rules will be restricted to run only at the Local Consolidation Member using `FinanceFunctionType.Calculate` or `FinanceFunctionType.CustomCalculate`. This allows data to calculate at Local and then get translated using the standard Translation.

Running Calculations at the other Consolidation Members – using other Finance Function Types – are reserved for specific requirements and more scarcely used.

DUCS vs. Custom Calculate

In many cases, most of what occurs during the Consolidation algorithm is only relevant for a Cube or Scenario with data that is heavily driven by financial and accounting rules. Executing Custom Calculate Rules and aggregating data using `C#Aggregated` is a simple way to execute Calculations and will be adequate for most solutions. Of course, if you have Elimination, Translation, or complex ownership structure requirements, then the full array of options described above will have to be considered.

The key benefit of the DUCS is that it removes a lot of the guesswork. Minimal thought needs to be given to clearing previously calculated data, dependent Data Units, and whether a Calculation was forgotten.

I try to avoid making blanket statements, but I'll make an exception in this case – Consolidation solutions should primarily run Calculations in the DUCS, and Planning solutions should primarily use Custom Calculations (outside the DUCS) with Entity Aggregation using `C#Aggregated`.

The reason for this lies in the underlying business processes that support each of those functions. Consolidation Calculations usually have a lot of dependencies – Trial Balance Calculations drive Flow Calculations, which in turn drive Cash Flow Calculations. Also, as their name implies, Consolidation Calculations are meant to be *consolidated*, so it is important that all Calculations run before data is moved up to a Parent Member. Data integrity is paramount, so full 'clear and replace' functionality is a necessity. In addition, the number of times data needs to be recalculated after an initial Consolidation is somewhat limited compared to more iterative Planning Calculations.

As just mentioned, things are much more iterative on the Planning side. Numbers are constantly massaged and changed. In addition, multiple Users often work within the same Data Unit. Having Users constantly running Calculations on the same Data Units would wreak havoc on the server, which would be constantly running each step in the DUCS – overlapping with another User's DUCS execution. This is where the Custom Calculate function saves the day.

Of course, blanket statements are often wrong. There could certainly be situations where Custom Calculates are used in Consolidations and DUCS Calculations are used in Planning. In fact, you're likely to have a mix of both.

I'll simply leave you with the knowledge of knowing the differences between each, and let you form your best judgment based on the specific requirements of your project.

Conclusion

This chapter has sought to give you context around the various Engines within OneStream and how they interact with the Finance Engine. You should also understand the core functions of the Finance Engine and how we can intervene within it to write powerful business logic and Calculations. Having a solid grasp of what the Engine is doing behind the scenes is important when writing Business Rules because you want your rules to work *with* the Finance Engine and not against it.

The next chapter will expound more on the Cube and break down the data within. Onwards!

2
Cube Data

As mentioned in the previous chapter, the Finance Engine processes data that resides in Cubes, which are powerful, multidimensional databases and the foundation of Consolidations and Financial Planning in OneStream.

In addition to the standard algorithms described in the previous chapter, the Finance Engine allows use-case specific financial intelligence and Calculations to be performed on Cube Data via Business Rules. When writing Calculations, you can perform complex arithmetic on large, multidimensional data sets with as little as one simple line of script.

But with great power comes great responsibility.

Writing effective and efficient Calculations relies on understanding the OneStream data architecture. The rest of this chapter will cover how OneStream stores and processes data in the Cube and how to properly use this data in Calculations.

Cube Building Blocks

We can identify three building blocks that comprise the structure of data within a Cube and how they relate to Calculations. These three building blocks are:

- Data Cells
- Data Buffers
- Data Units

Data Cells

Data cells represent a singular data point within the Cube. Each data cell has various properties associated with it. Just like everyone reading this book has a home, so does each data cell in the Cube. You live at a specific street number, on a street, in a city, in a state, in a country. That information is enough to pin you to a specific place. Outside of your family or roommates, no one else lives there. If someone is looking for you, they find you there. Cube data is the same. Each data point in a Cube resides at the unique intersection of 18 Dimensions called a **Member Script** or **Data Cell Primary Key** (Primary Key). The Primary Key is the address of the data.

Chapter 2

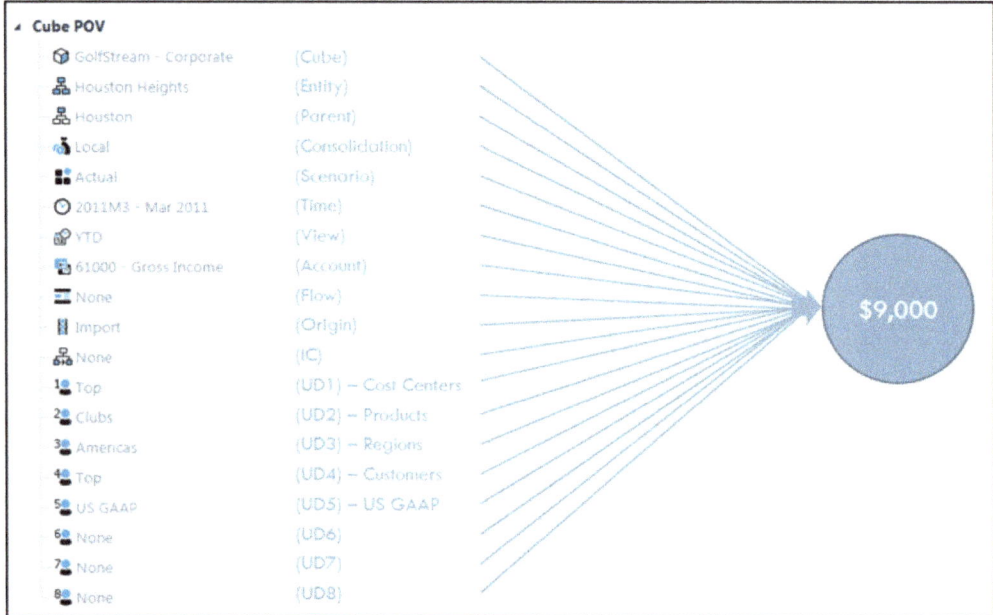

Figure 2.1

Dimension Name	Editable
Time	N
Scenario	Y
Entity	Y
Parent	Y
Consolidation	Y
View	N
Account	Y
Flow	Y
Origin	N
Intercompany	Y
UD1	Y
UD2	Y
UD3	Y
UD4	Y
UD5	Y
UD6	Y
UD7	Y
UD8	Y

Figure 2.2

Above are the 18 Dimensions which describe a data cell. Some of these Dimensions are fixed and contain default Members which cannot be modified.

The following is a Member Script which represents the intersection of all 18 Dimensions plus Cube. This is the address of the data.

```
Cb#ACME:E#ACME:P#StoogeCorp:C#Local:S#Budget:T#2023M1:V#Periodic:A#Pri
ce:F#EndBalLoad:O#Import:I#None:U1#BugZapper:U2#None:U3#None:U4#None:U
5#None:U6#None:U7#None:U8#None
```

Data Entering the Cube

When data enters the Cube – either via a data import, Form entry, or Journal posting – it is normally stored at a **Base Level** Member of each of the 18 Dimensions (as shown above). I qualify that previous statement with 'normally' because – in some rare instances – data can be entered on Parent Entity Members, but we'll ignore that for now.

Numeric Cube data is stored by year in one of 105 fully normalized fact tables from `DataRecord1996` to `DataRecord2100`. Each record contains the coordinates and numeric amounts for all stored data; this includes Dimension Member information, Cell Amount, and Cell Status. Each record in the data tables contains the data cells for all the periods of the specific year represented by the data table. These data tables are exposed to Administrator-level Users by going to Database in the System tab.

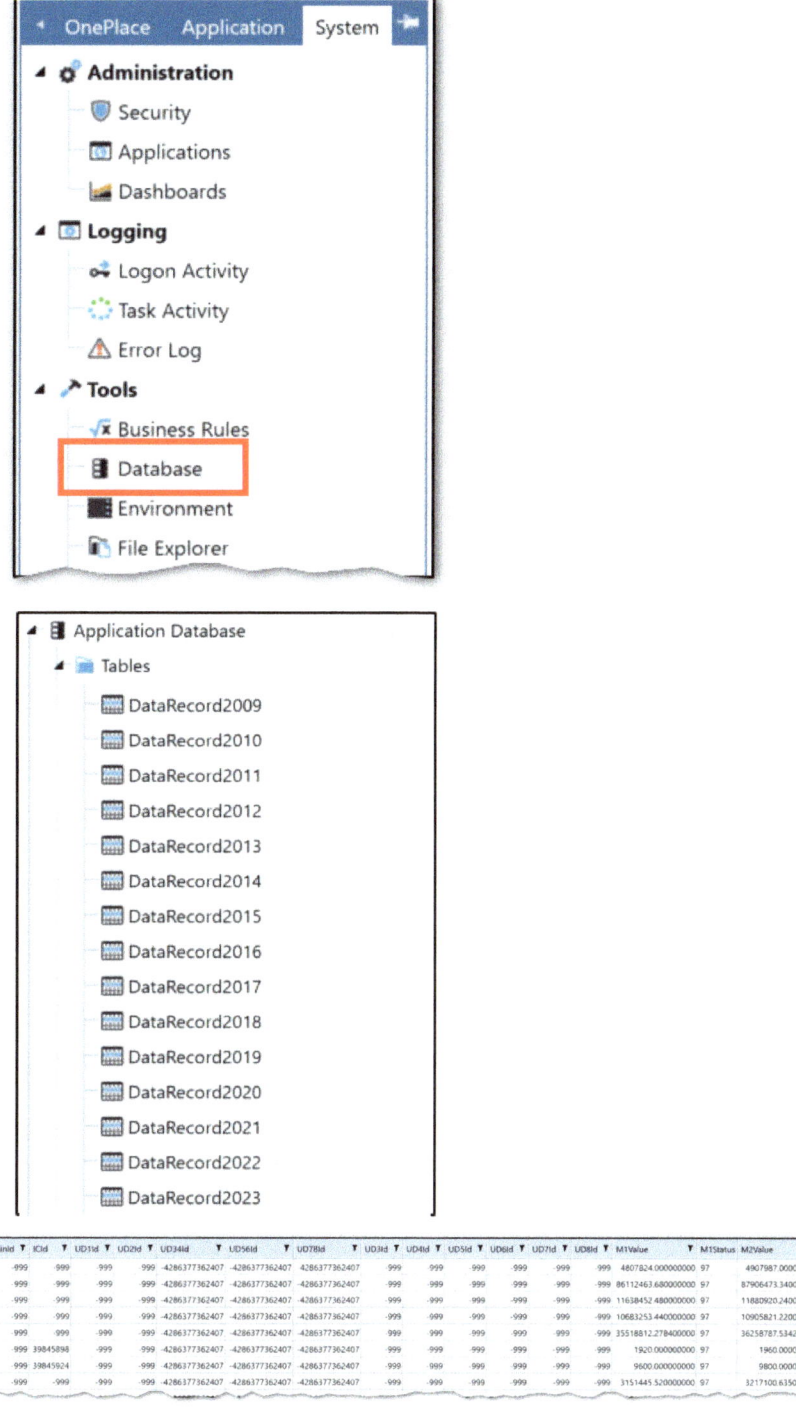

Figure 2.3

Chapter 2

The View Dimension

The View Dimension is one of the 18 Dimensions mentioned above. It is a 'fixed' Dimension, meaning that it contains a standard or fixed list of Members and no additional Members can be added or deleted.

The View Dimension works slightly differently from the other Dimensions in that all but one of the Members store numeric data. The other elements are either dynamically calculated or used to store text. Data is always stored at the `YTD` Member within the underlying database for numeric values, while it is stored in the corresponding annotation element for text data.

Numeric data can be entered on either `YTD` or `Periodic` but, again, is always stored at `YTD`. If entering data at `Periodic`, OneStream does dynamic math to determine the value that is stored.

> **Note:** Non-numeric (textual) data can be stored in the Cube using the `Annotation`, `Assumptions`, `AuditComment`, `Footnote`, or `VarianceExplanation` Members.
>
>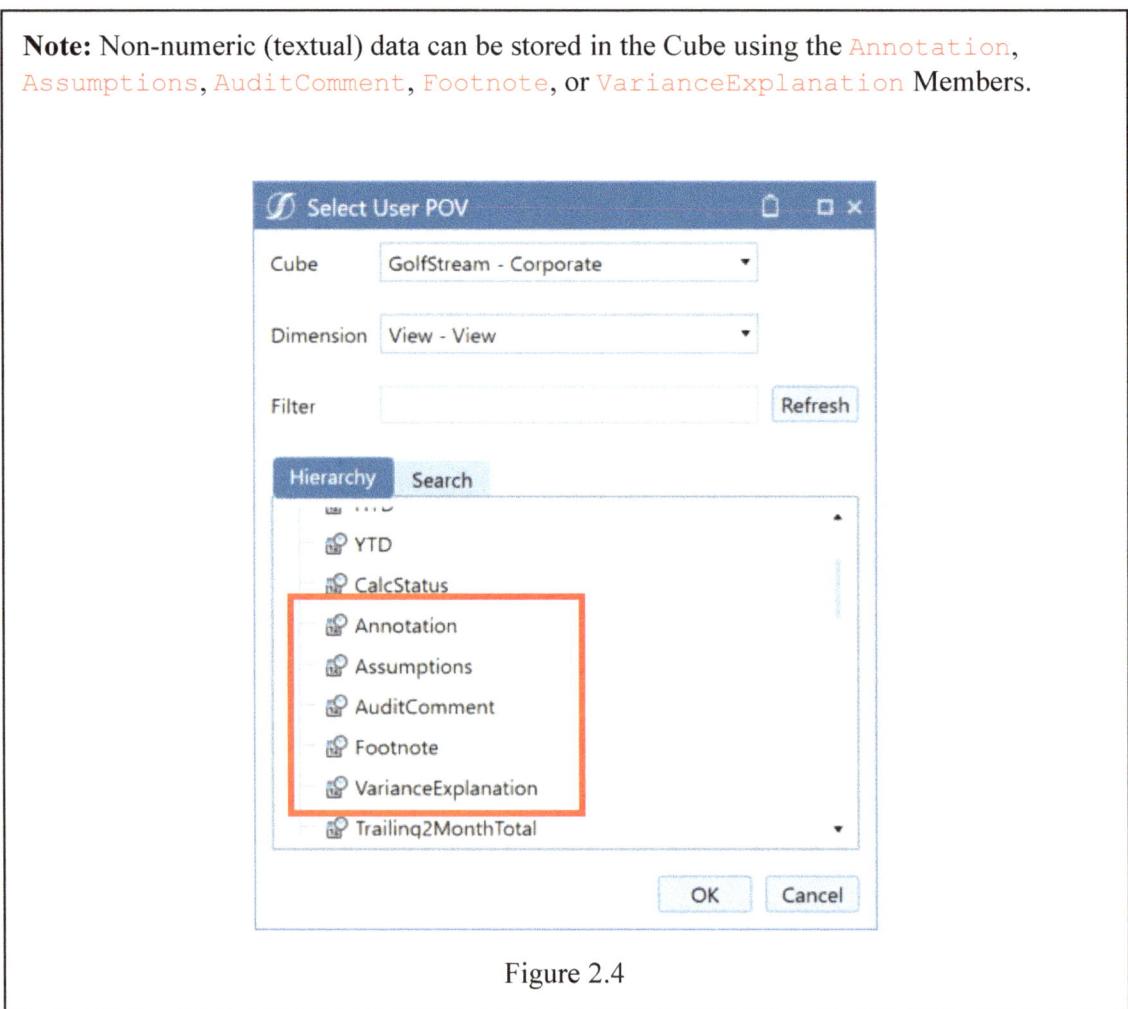
>
> Figure 2.4

Data Cell Status

Data Cell Status gives us some more information about the data cell.

Cell Status can be viewed directly from a Cube View and is comprised of the following statuses: Real Data, NoData & Zeros, Derived Data.

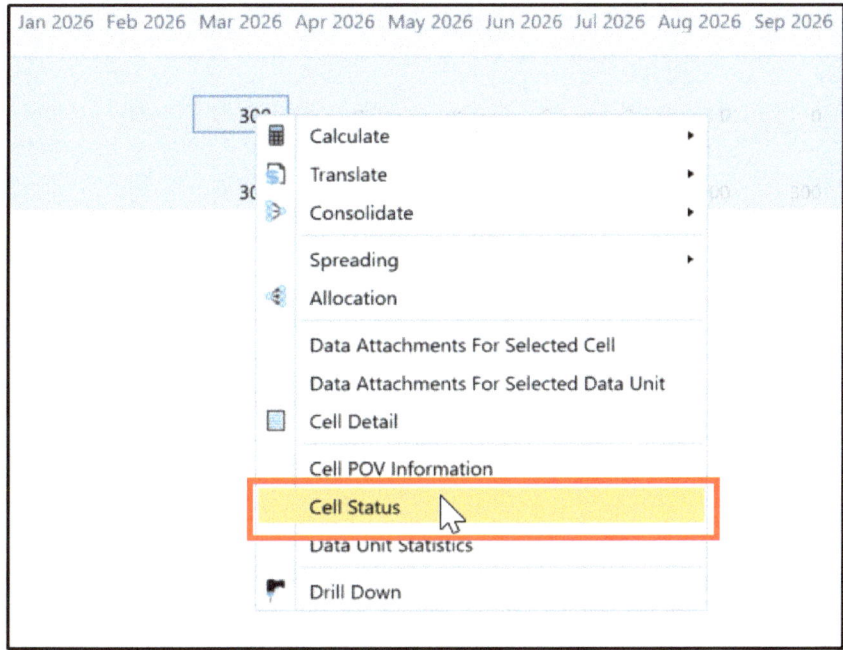

Figure 2.5

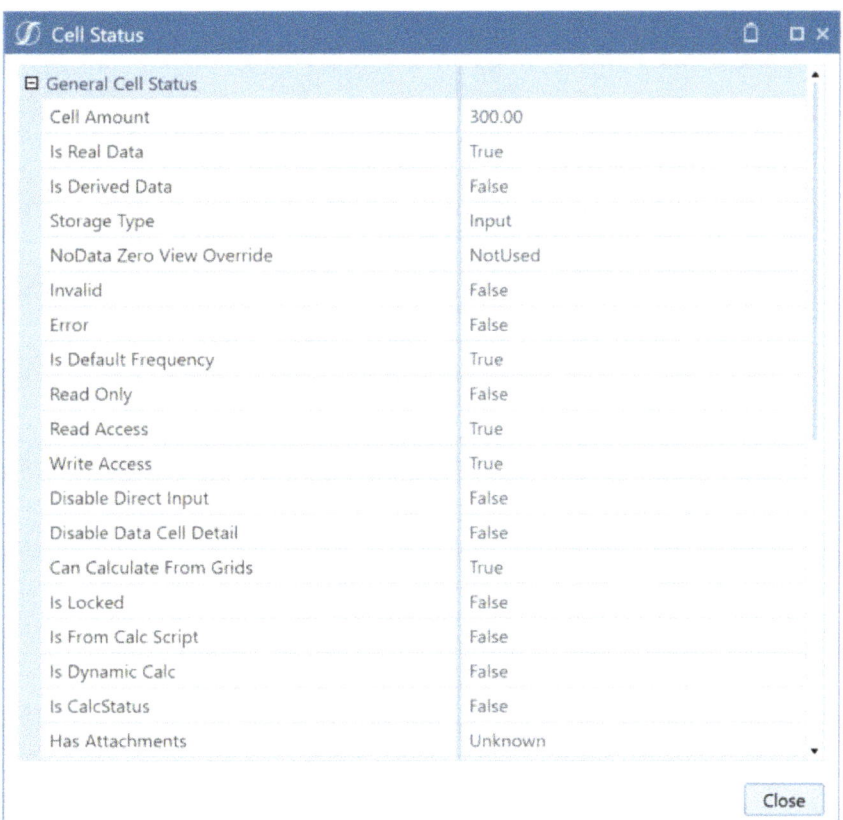

Figure 2.6

Real Data

Real Data is exactly what it sounds like. There's a record for it; it exists, so it's real. It refers to data that was physically written to the Cube by Form input, file import, or Journal entry. Calculated and Consolidated data is also Real Data. Real Data takes database space.

Chapter 2

NoData & Zeros

Cells that do not have any data stored are considered NoData. This would include blank cells. This is typically displayed as 0 on Reports even though a 0 is not actually stored. In some instances, there could be a stored zero in a data cell. If a zero is stored in the database, it is considered Real Data. OneStream takes great care not to store zeros to avoid wasting database space, but some situations warrant it. For example, when zeroing out a YTD balance in Periodic Scenario.

Derived Data

Derived Data can be a bit confusing because it's never considered *Real Data*, but it is considered *Stored Data*, and (in some instances) there is even a record in the `DataRecord` table for it!

To make sense of this, we need to take the View Dimension into account. As mentioned previously, data is always stored at the `YTD` View Member but, as you probably know, YTD Data is not always the way data comes into the Cube. Month-to-date can be entered and, in the background, OneStream determines what value needs to be stored at the YTD Member. The Default View, No Data Zero View For Adjustments/NonAdjustments, and Retain Next Period Data Using Default View properties on the Scenario Member will determine how data in subsequent periods is treated.

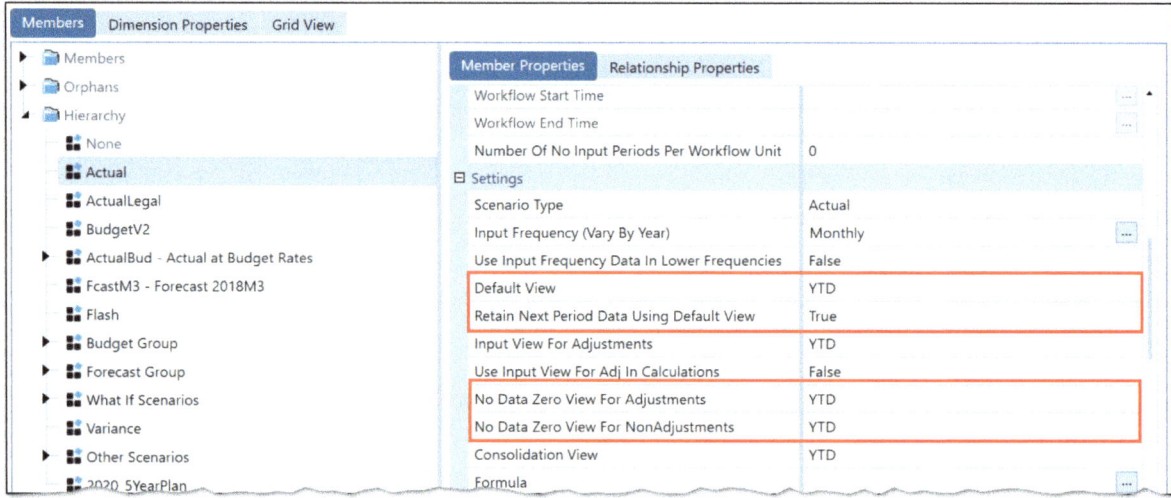

Figure 2.7

Derived Data Example
Let's look at four examples of data being entered into a Cube View for Scenarios with different Default View Settings.

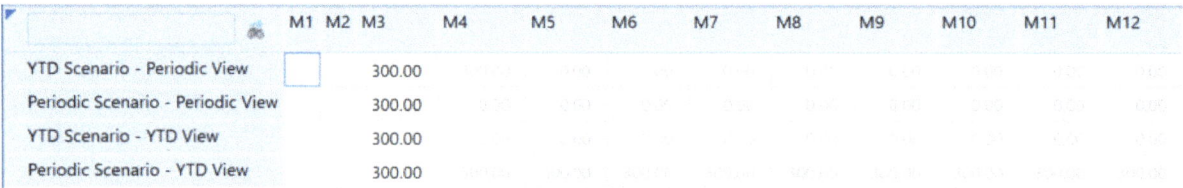

Figure 2.8

The value of 300 was entered into M3 in each of the four cells. Each of those cells will show a Cell Status of `IsRealData = True` and that number will be stored in `V#YTD`. What happens in the subsequent periods is where things get interesting.

Periods M4-M12 will show **Derived** values to get the data back in synch with the Scenario's Default View and NoData Zero View Properties. This data is shown as grayed out in Cube Views by default.

The Cell Status will show as `Is Derived Data` = `True` with a Storage Type of `StoredButNoActivity`.

Figure 2.9

The above example is meant to illustrate how Data Cell Status is affected by various Scenario settings. Consult the *OneStream Design & Reference Guide* for more information on these settings.

Storage Types

All data – either Real or Derived – will have a Storage Type. Below are the Storage Types that exist in OneStream.

- `Input`
- `Journal`
- `Calculation`
- `DurableCalculation`
- `Consolidation`
- `Translation`
- `StoredButNoActivity`

The Data Unit

The next building block of the Cube is the Data Unit which was briefly introduced in the last chapter. As a reminder, the Data Unit is defined as all the data cells within a unique combination of Cube, Scenario, Time, Consolidation, and Entity Dimensions.

To illustrate what purpose the Data Unit serves, let's go back to our address analogy. How many addresses are there in the US? In the world? Let's pretend we are interviewing at a company that loves to torture potential candidates with these weird questions. We might think about how many addresses are in a particular city or town and then extrapolate that number to arrive at the number of addresses in a state. Or maybe we could take the total population and divide it by an average number of people per address.

At the end of the day, the interviewer knows you won't guess correctly, but they want to see how you break the problem down into smaller parts and work up to an answer.

Now instead of addresses, let's take an example of a Cube and look at the number of potential intersections that exist.

Chapter 2

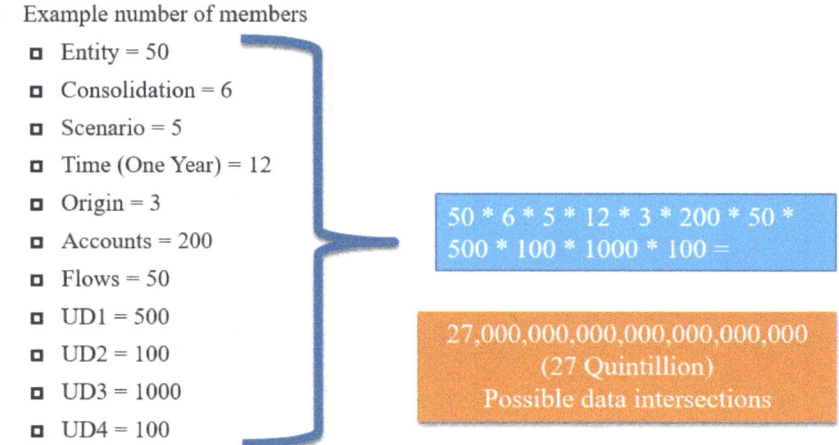

Figure 2.10

That's a lot of zeros (and yes, I had to Google what the name for that number was). Of course, the number of intersections where data is actually populated will be much lower, but the problem still persists. Just like our interview question riddle, we need a way to break the problem down into more manageable parts.

This same concept is why the Data Unit exists in OneStream. Quite simply, the Data Units breaks down the *Data* in the Cube into smaller *Units*. A Data Unit, therefore, is essentially a page of data used to break down the whole data set into chunks that can be read or processed at the same time by the server, and which can easily fit into server memory.

The Data Buffer

A **Data Buffer** is the term used to refer to a collection of data cells within a Data Unit. A Data Buffer *could* be all the data in a Data Unit but is likely a smaller subset. A Data Buffer can also be referred to as a chunk, block, or slice of data. Whichever word you prefer, the concept remains the same.

When we calculate data in the Cube, we will almost always work with Data Buffers. It's what makes the OneStream Calculation Engine so powerful. We can work with large data sets at one time and perform complex arithmetic on them. When defining Data Buffers for calculations, limiting the scope and size of Data Buffers will not only help calculations be more accurate but also help them perform well. We will explore this concept in great detail later in this chapter.

Analogy To Excel

Almost everyone has used Excel to perform calculations on data within a spreadsheet. Writing calculations in Excel is relatively straightforward – you take cell A1 and multiply it by cell B1, and the result is stored in C1… easy peasy. While you can get pretty fancy with `IF` statements and `Vlookups`, at the end of the day, the calculations boil down to arithmetic on individual cells.

Applying this same concept to OneStream Calculations quickly falls on its face. The OneStream Cube has simply too many data intersections to calculate cell by cell. Either you – the Calculation writer – or the server would start overheating from being overworked. Working with Data Buffers allows the Calculation writer and the server to do more (data) with less (code).

Perhaps a Better Analogy

Let's stay within our Excel spreadsheet world. Pretend we have two data sets for Price and Volume, each consisting of 15 cells. Now, instead of multiplying cell by cell (15 individual calculations), we could multiply two groups of 15 cells (arrays) in one calculation resulting in a new array of 15 calculated cells.

```
Array1 * Array2 = Array3
```

	Prices					Volumes					Sales		
	Product 1	Product 2	Product 3			Product 1	Product 2	Product 3			Product 1	Product 2	Product 3
United States	15	3	100		United States	1000	2500	50		United States	15000	7500	5000
Germany	10	5	150		Germany	500	2000	60		Germany	5000	10000	9000
Australia	20	8	125	X	Australia	500	2100	100	=	Australia	10000	16800	12500
Canada	5	10	80		Canada	100	2200	40		Canada	500	22000	3200
China	100	20	50		China	5000	1800	20		China	500000	36000	1000

Figure 2.11

Now we're much closer to what Data Buffers allow us to do. But instead of having two Dimensions to describe our data – Countries in rows and Products in columns – we have 18 Dimensions. THAT'S the power of the Data Buffer. Executing the same Calculation logic for a large volume of datapoints is, in fact, much more efficient than executing an independent Calculation for each of them, especially if the logic is the same across all the data points.

Visualize the Data Buffer

Since a Data Buffer is a subset of cells within a Data Unit, it can be visualized by querying the database for a specific Data Unit.

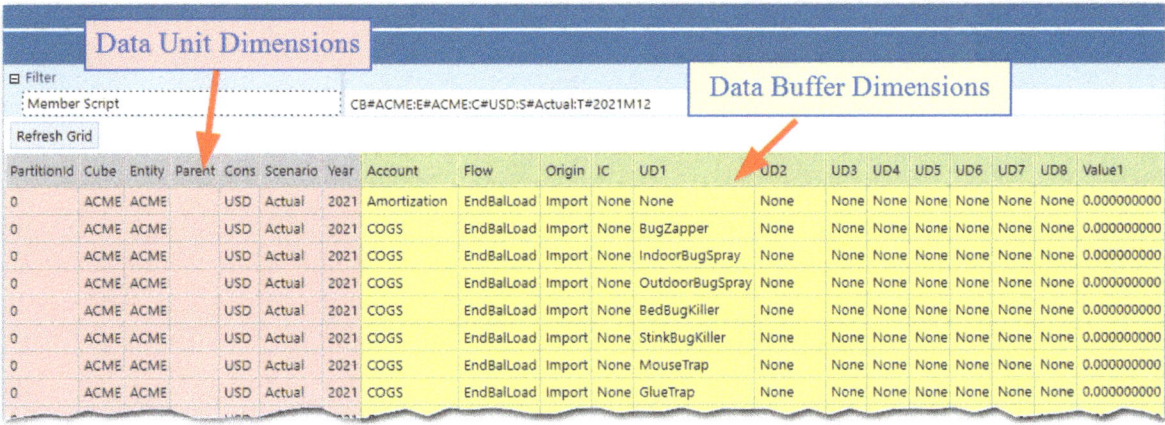

Figure 2.12

The above query shows rows for every data cell in the Data Unit specified in the Member Script field. These rows comprise a Data Buffer.

A Data Buffer is an Object

Just like a string or integer, a Data Buffer is an object in VB.NET with its own set of properties and methods. Data Buffers can be a declared variable, using one of several API functions.

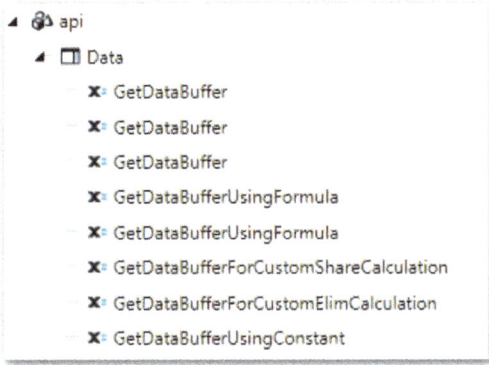

Figure 2.13

45

Chapter 2

The `api.Data.GetDataBuffer` function requires a `ScriptMethodType`, `DataBufferScript`, and `DestinationInfo`. The `ScriptMethodType` is an enumerable and the `DestinationInfo` can be declared as an object. The `DataBufferScript` is a Member Script string, (e.g., `A#Sales`).

```
Dim destinationInfo As ExpressionDestinationInfo = api.Data.GetExpressionDestinationInfo("")
api.Data.GetDataBuffer(DataApiScriptMethodType.Calculate,"A#Sales",destinationInfo)
```

The `api.Data.GetDataBufferUsingFormula` only requires the `DataBufferScript` string object.

While each of these functions are slightly different in the parameters they require, the end result is the same – a Data Buffer is brought into existence.

```
api.data.GetDataBufferUsingFormula("A#Sales")
```

For most of the examples in this book, I will use `GetDataBufferUsingFormula`.

Logging the Data Buffer

Once we have our Data Buffer object declared, we can do several things with it. IntelliSense shows us the available extension Methods associated with the object.

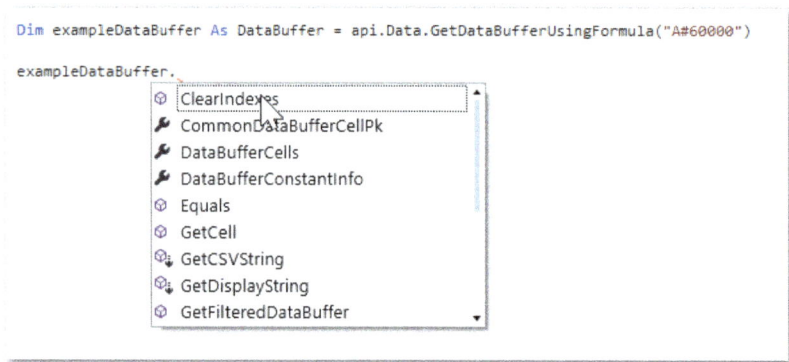

Figure 2.14

The `LogDataBuffer` Method requires some additional parameters for API, description, and an integer for the maximum number of cells to output.

```
(Extension) Sub DataBufferExtensions.LogDataBuffer(api As FinanceRulesApi, description As String, maxNumCellsInOutput As Integer)
```

Figure 2.15

The completed script now looks like this:

```
Dim exampleDataBuffer As DataBuffer = api.Data.GetDataBufferUsingFormula("A#Sales")
exampleDataBuffer.LogDataBuffer(api,"Example Data Buffer", 100)
```

After executing the script via a Data Management Step, the Data Buffer is logged in the Error Log.

Cube Data

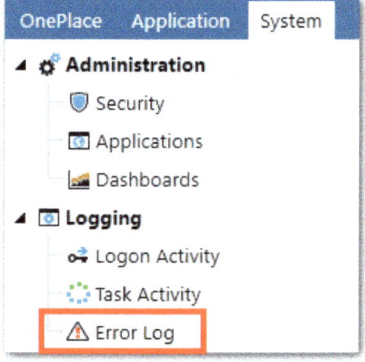

Figure 2.16

The logged Data Buffer is shown in the Error Log.

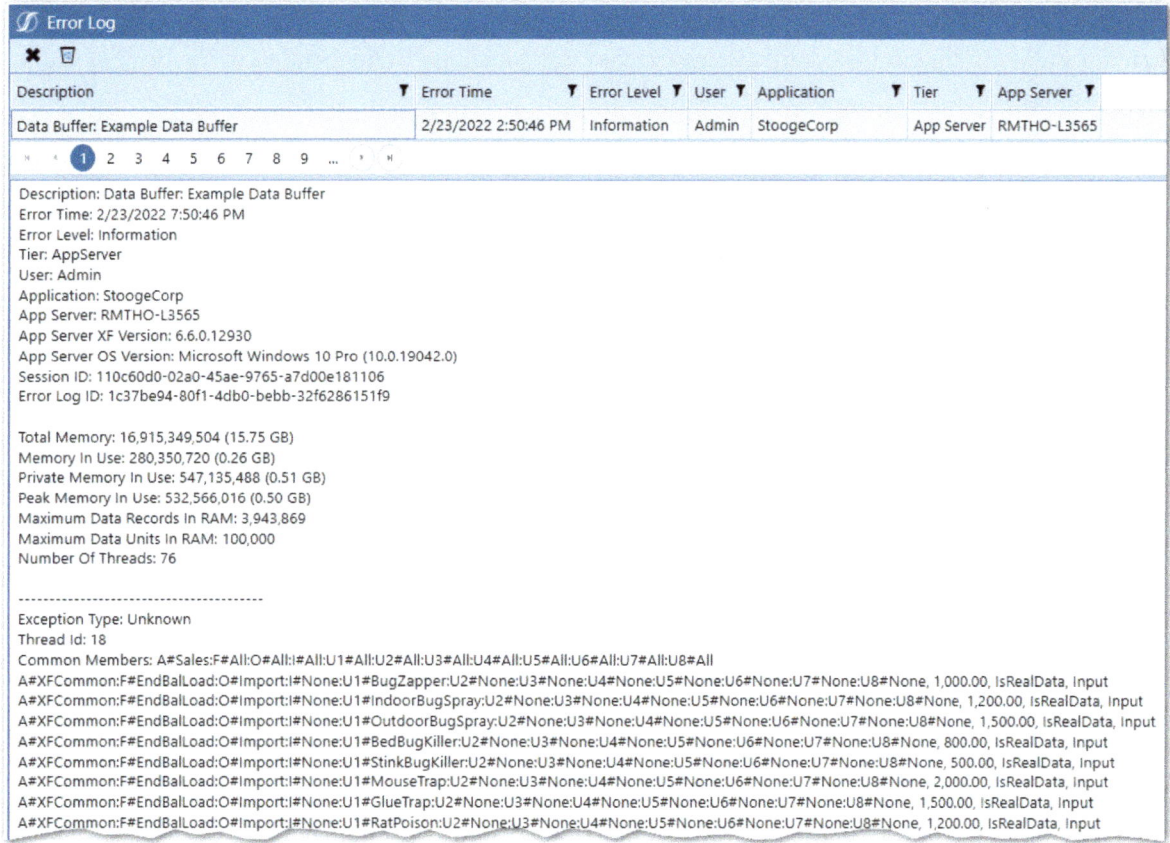

Figure 2.17

Anatomy of a Data Buffer

Data Buffers contain a lot of information about both the Data Buffer itself, and the data cells within it. Key components are highlighted below.

Chapter 2

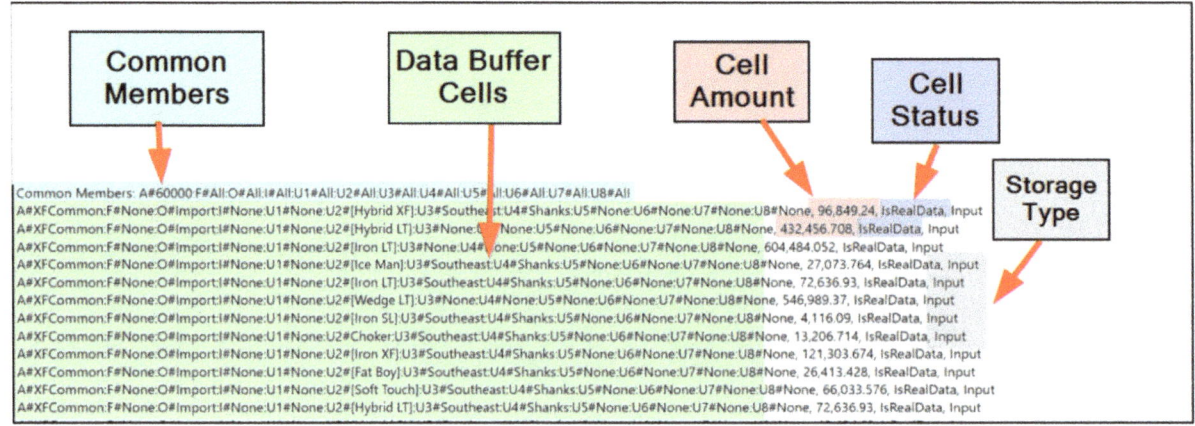

Figure 2.18

Common Members

The Common Members header refers to all the non-Data Unit or what is sometimes called **Account-Level** Dimensions. The Common Members represent Dimension Members that are shared for all rows in the Data Buffer. Each of the Account-Level Dimensions will either refer to a specific Member or #All.

#All means that the Data Buffer will include every intersection that has data for that Dimension. These will be the Members defined in the Member Script.

The reason for Common Members will be much clearer later, when we start using calculations, but for now, let's just say that only Data Buffers with the same Common Members can be used in the same Calculation.

Data Buffer Cell POV

Data Buffer Cells all have a Member Script or Primary Key, which is the intersection of all 18 OneStream Dimensions. This Member Script will be shown for all cells in the Data Buffer. You may be wondering why the Data Unit Dimensions aren't listed here. Well, technically, they *are* known because Data Buffers always execute on a Data Unit which is defined when executing the Calculation. Because of this, all Data Buffer Cells within the same Data Buffer will have the same Data Unit Dimension Members based on the current Data Unit being processed by the DUCS.

Cell Amount

The numeric data in the cell. This is truncated to two decimal places but is stored in the database tables to 9 decimals.

Cell Status

Refers to whether data is Real, Derived, or NoData.

Storage Type

When data is written to the Cube by either Form entry, data import, Calculation, or Consolidation, OneStream keeps track.

Filter and Remove Members from Data Buffers

Data cells within a Data Buffer can be filtered out based on their dimensional information. The FilterMembers and RemoveMembers functions offer capabilities that allow changing a Data Buffer to only include data cells for Dimension Members that are specified in the function parameters.

You can have as many parameters as you want to specify Member Filters and can even use different Member Filters for multiple Dimension Types. The resulting filtered Data Buffer will only contain numbers that match the Members in your filters. `RemoveMembers` has the same syntax, but it has the opposite effect. It takes away the data cells for the Members you specified, instead of keeping them.

```
api.Data.GetDataBufferUsingFormula("FilterMembers(A#Sales, U1#Insects.Base)")
api.Data.GetDataBufferUsingFormula("RemoveMembers(A#Sales, U1#Insects.Base)")
```

Removing NoData & Zeros from Data Buffers

NoData or Zero cells can also be filtered out of Data Buffers using the `RemoveNoData` and `RemoveZeros` functions.

- `RemoveNoData` – Removes all data cells with Cell Status of `NoData`.

- `RemoveZeros` – Removes all data cells with a Cell Amount of 0 or with a Cell Status of `NoData`.

Simply wrap `RemoveZeros`, or `RemoveNoData` with parentheses around any Data Buffer.

```
api.Data.GetDataBufferUsingFormula("FilterMembers(RemoveZeros(A#Sales), U1#Insects.Base)")
```

It makes sense that we would want to exclude Zeros and NoData cells from our Data Buffers as they provide no analytic value, and they only take up room in the database which degrades performance. These functions should be used by default, any time a Data Buffer is declared.

> **Note:** `FilterMembers`, `RemoveMembers`, `RemoveZeros`, and `RemoveNoData` can only be used with `api.Data.GetDataBufferUsingFormula` and not with `api.Data.GetDataBuffer`.

Conclusion

Understanding how data is stored and organized in the Cube is vital to writing efficient and effective Calculations and Business Rules. In this chapter, the three building blocks of the Cube have been identified and explained.

- Data cells are a singular data point at the intersection of all 18 Dimensions.
- The Data Unit breaks the Cube down into smaller parts based on the unique combination of Cube, Scenario, Time, Consolidation, and Entity.
- The Data Buffer is a subset of data cells within the Data Unit.

The Finance Engine processes data in the Cube by Data Units. When writing Calculations, we are always working with a subset of the data within the current Data Unit being processed, called a Data Buffer. A Calculation writer should always be thinking in terms of Data Buffers. The next chapter will explain how to write Calculations by performing math on Data Buffers.

3

api.Data.Calculate

If you've been skimming through the book thus far, now is the time to pay attention. In the first two chapters, the foundation of knowledge to understand how to write Calculations was laid. Now, we will apply much of that knowledge using the **api.Data.Calculate** function. For purposes of conciseness, I will also refer to it as the 'ADC' function going forward.

In OneStream's ocean-deep library of API functions, there isn't one that gets much more use than the ADC function. Its pervasive use is no doubt due to its power and flexibility, which allows it to be employed to solve a wide variety of Calculation requirements.

In this chapter, I will breakdown the ADC function and explain how it can handle the lion's share of your Calculation requirements.

A Quick Revisit

In Chapter 2, we defined a Data Buffer as a collection of data cells in a Data Unit. Aside from the Cell Amount and Dimension information, a Data Buffer contains other information about a data cell such as Cell Status and Storage Type. The ADC function allows you to perform arithmetic on Data Buffers. Simply put, the ADC function multiplies groups of data cells together, allowing you (potentially) to create thousands of calculated data cells with just one line of script.

With Great Power Comes Great Responsibility

Calculations can have a significant impact on Cube processing times and reporting performance. Creating additional data cells from Calculations increases Data Unit size which means servers need to use more memory and processing time to retrieve them. To that point, it is important to only calculate data that is necessary, and which provides analytic value. We know that while a Data Buffer *could* be all data cells in a Data Unit, most Calculations do not need to work with that much data. Most Calculations will work with Data Buffers that are smaller subsets of the Data Unit.

Techniques on how to increase Calculation efficiency and reduce Calculation scope will be introduced in this chapter and expounded on in Chapter 7.

Syntax

The ADC function will accept several arguments with the formula string being the only one that is required.

Syntax:
Public Sub Calculate(ByVal formula As String, Optional ByVal accountFilter As String, Optional ByVal flowFilter As String, Optional ByVal originFilter As String, Optional ByVal icFilter As String, Optional ByVal ud1Filter As String, Optional ByVal ud2Filter As String, Optional ByVal ud3Filter As String, Optional ByVal ud4Filter As String, Optional ByVal ud5Filter As String, Optional ByVal ud6Filter As String, Optional ByVal ud7Filter As String, Optional ByVal ud8Filter As String, Optional ByVal onEvalDataBuffer As EvalDataBufferDelegate, Optional ByVal userState As Object, Optional ByVal isDurableCalculatedData As Boolean)

```
api.Data.Calculate("FormulaString")
```

Chapter 3

The formula string is like any math formula you've written in elementary school e.g., 1 + 2 = 3 except we replace each numerical operand with the coordinates of a Data Buffer represented by a Member Script.

```
api.Data.Calculate("A#AccountA = A#AccountB + A#AccountC")
```

> **Note**: Syntax mistakes or typos within the formula string will pass compile checks successfully and will not reveal themselves until Calculation execution time. This is because the syntax used within `api.Data.Calculate` is interpreted at runtime to support dynamic objects (such as `T#PovYear` Time filter) by the Calculation Engine and not compiled by the .NET compiler on save.

The other arguments that can be passed into the ADC function are listed below with a brief definition and will be further explored later in this chapter:

- `<dimension>Filter` – a Member Script string which will limit the scope of the formula execution.
- `onEvalDataBuffer` – a customized function that runs on the Data Buffer enclosed in the `Eval()` syntax; used for particular use cases that will be later described.
- `userState` – a User State Object.
- `isDurableCalculate` – True/False which changes the `StorageType` from `Calculation` to `DurableCalculation`.

Simple Example

To illustrate how the ADC function works, let's dive into an example and I'll explain what is happening along the way.

As the Director of FP&A, Curly wants to create a simple driver-based Calculation to forecast Sales. Driver data for Volume and Price Accounts have been loaded to the Cube.

Curly creates a simple `api.Data.Calculate` which multiplies Price and Volume.

```
api.Data.Calculate("A#Sales = A#Price * A#Volume")
```

`A#Price`, and `A#Volume` represent Data Buffers containing multiple records of data cells; for example, they might have Product or Cost Center details. `A#Sales` represents the empty destination Data Buffer that will be filled with the cells of the formula Result Data Buffer.

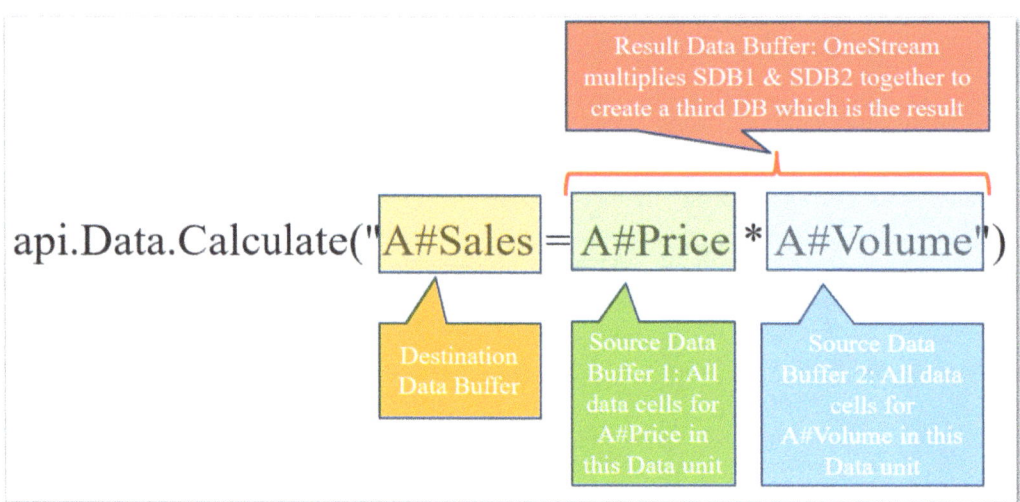

Figure 3.1

As shown above, the Calculation formula is contained within a string with each operand in our equation being a **Member Filter**. OneStream converts each Member Filter to a Data Buffer and multiplies the Price and Volume Data Buffers together, writing the result to a new Data Buffer defined by `A#Sales`.

> **Note**: The Formula String is *not* case sensitive – `a#price` will work the same as `A#Price`.

Breakdown

The simplicity of the `api.Data.Calculate` function has a downside, in that it can obscure what OneStream is really doing. So, what's really happening under the hood?

- The `A#Price` Data Buffer – from the current Data Unit being processed – is retrieved from storage in the Cube.
- The `A#Volume` Data Buffer – from the current Data Unit being processed – is retrieved from storage in the Cube.
- Data Buffer Math multiplies the two Data Buffer together and creates a new Data Buffer (multiplication of many numbers).
- An empty Data Buffer is created for `A#Sales`.
- The result cells are added to the `A#Sales` Data Buffer and saved to the Cube.

Data Buffer Math

Looking over the above series of steps, it's clear we've conveniently glazed over a pretty big concept – **Data Buffer math**. This is where the all the magic happens so let's dive into how it works.

Data Buffer math starts with the Data Buffers and ultimately results in math of individual cells – but how does it get there? OneStream analyzes each Data Buffer cell in the formula, 'matches them up' based on common Dimension Members, then performs the math on the individual cells. The result of the math creates a new Data Buffer which is added to a new Result Data Buffer. Let's continue the Sales Calculation example to see how it works.

First let's visualize the `A#Price` and `A#Volume` Data Buffers. We can do this by using the `api.Data.GetDataBufferUsingFilter` function along with `LogDataBuffer`.

```
Dim priceDataBuffer As DataBuffer = api.Data.GetDataBufferUsingFormula("A#Price")
Dim volumeDataBuffer As DataBuffer = api.Data.GetDataBufferUsingFormula("A#Volume")
priceDataBuffer.LogDataBuffer(api,"Price Data Buffer", 100)
volumeDataBuffer.LogDataBuffer(api,"Volume Data Buffer", 100)
```

If we execute this script (by either triggering the DUCS or a Custom Calculation), we can see both Data Buffers in the Error Log.

Chapter 3

Price Data Buffer:

```
Common Members: A#Price:F#All:O#All:I#All:U1#All:U2#All:U3#All:U4#All:U5#All:U6#All:U7#All:U8#All
A#XFCommon:F#EndBalLoad:O#Import:I#None:U1#BugZapper:U2#None:U3#None:U4#None:U5#None:U6#None:U7#None:U8#None, 15.00, IsRealData, Input
A#XFCommon:F#EndBalLoad:O#Import:I#None:U1#IndoorBugSpray:U2#None:U3#None:U4#None:U5#None:U6#None:U7#None:U8#None, 8.00, IsRealData, Input
A#XFCommon:F#EndBalLoad:O#Import:I#None:U1#OutdoorBugSpray:U2#None:U3#None:U4#None:U5#None:U6#None:U7#None:U8#None, 10.00, IsRealData, Input
A#XFCommon:F#EndBalLoad:O#Import:I#None:U1#BedBugKiller:U2#None:U3#None:U4#None:U5#None:U6#None:U7#None:U8#None, 12.00, IsRealData, Input
A#XFCommon:F#EndBalLoad:O#Import:I#None:U1#StinkBugKiller:U2#None:U3#None:U4#None:U5#None:U6#None:U7#None:U8#None, 13.00, IsRealData, Input
A#XFCommon:F#EndBalLoad:O#Import:I#None:U1#MouseTrap:U2#None:U3#None:U4#None:U5#None:U6#None:U7#None:U8#None, 4.50, IsRealData, Input
A#XFCommon:F#EndBalLoad:O#Import:I#None:U1#GlueTrap:U2#None:U3#None:U4#None:U5#None:U6#None:U7#None:U8#None, 6.50, IsRealData, Input
A#XFCommon:F#EndBalLoad:O#Import:I#None:U1#RatPoison:U2#None:U3#None:U4#None:U5#None:U6#None:U7#None:U8#None, 9.00, IsRealData, Input
A#XFCommon:F#EndBalLoad:O#Import:I#None:U1#Termicide:U2#None:U3#None:U4#None:U5#None:U6#None:U7#None:U8#None, 12.50, IsRealData, Input
A#XFCommon:F#EndBalLoad:O#Import:I#None:U1#PestControl:U2#None:U3#None:U4#None:U5#None:U6#None:U7#None:U8#None, 150.00, IsRealData, Input
A#XFCommon:F#EndBalLoad:O#Import:I#None:U1#TermiteTreatment:U2#None:U3#None:U4#None:U5#None:U6#None:U7#None:U8#None, 250.00, IsRealData, Input
A#XFCommon:F#EndBalLoad:O#Import:I#None:U1#Commercial:U2#None:U3#None:U4#None:U5#None:U6#None:U7#None:U8#None, 400.00, IsRealData, Input
A#XFCommon:F#EndBalLoad:O#Import:I#None:U1#BugBeaters:U2#None:U3#None:U4#None:U5#None:U6#None:U7#None:U8#None, 800.00, IsRealData, Input
```

Figure 3.2

Volume Data Buffer:

```
Common Members: A#Volume:F#All:O#All:I#All:U1#All:U2#All:U3#All:U4#All:U5#All:U6#All:U7#All:U8#All
A#XFCommon:F#EndBalLoad:O#Import:I#None:U1#IndoorBugSpray:U2#None:U3#None:U4#None:U5#None:U6#None:U7#None:U8#None, 175.00, IsRealData, Input
A#XFCommon:F#EndBalLoad:O#Import:I#None:U1#OutdoorBugSpray:U2#None:U3#None:U4#None:U5#None:U6#None:U7#None:U8#None, 175.00, IsRealData, Input
A#XFCommon:F#EndBalLoad:O#Import:I#None:U1#BedBugKiller:U2#None:U3#None:U4#None:U5#None:U6#None:U7#None:U8#None, 75.00, IsRealData, Input
A#XFCommon:F#EndBalLoad:O#Import:I#None:U1#StinkBugKiller:U2#None:U3#None:U4#None:U5#None:U6#None:U7#None:U8#None, 45.00, IsRealData, Input
A#XFCommon:F#EndBalLoad:O#Import:I#None:U1#MouseTrap:U2#None:U3#None:U4#None:U5#None:U6#None:U7#None:U8#None, 500.00, IsRealData, Input
A#XFCommon:F#EndBalLoad:O#Import:I#None:U1#GlueTrap:U2#None:U3#None:U4#None:U5#None:U6#None:U7#None:U8#None, 250.00, IsRealData, Input
A#XFCommon:F#EndBalLoad:O#Import:I#None:U1#RatPoison:U2#None:U3#None:U4#None:U5#None:U6#None:U7#None:U8#None, 140.00, IsRealData, Input
A#XFCommon:F#EndBalLoad:O#Import:I#None:U1#Termicide:U2#None:U3#None:U4#None:U5#None:U6#None:U7#None:U8#None, 60.00, IsRealData, Input
A#XFCommon:F#EndBalLoad:O#Import:I#None:U1#PestControl:U2#None:U3#None:U4#None:U5#None:U6#None:U7#None:U8#None, 20.00, IsRealData, Input
A#XFCommon:F#EndBalLoad:O#Import:I#None:U1#TermiteTreatment:U2#None:U3#None:U4#None:U5#None:U6#None:U7#None:U8#None, 10.00, IsRealData, Input
A#XFCommon:F#EndBalLoad:O#Import:I#None:U1#Commercial:U2#None:U3#None:U4#None:U5#None:U6#None:U7#None:U8#None, 5.00, IsRealData, Input
A#XFCommon:F#EndBalLoad:O#Import:I#None:U1#BugBeaters:U2#None:U3#None:U4#None:U5#None:U6#None:U7#None:U8#None, 5.00, IsRealData, Input
A#XFCommon:F#EndBalLoad:O#Import:I#None:U1#SpeedyBugSpray:U2#None:U3#None:U4#None:U5#None:U6#None:U7#None:U8#None, 8.00, IsRealData, Input
A#XFCommon:F#EndBalLoad:O#Import:I#None:U1#SpeedyTermiteSpray:U2#None:U3#None:U4#None:U5#None:U6#None:U7#None:U8#None, 8.00, IsRealData, Input
A#XFCommon:F#EndBalLoad:O#Import:I#None:U1#BugZapper:U2#None:U3#None:U4#None:U5#None:U6#None:U7#None:U8#None, 70.00, IsRealData, Input
```

Figure 3.3

We can see the individual data cells that make up each of our Data Buffers above. Note that – along with the dimensional information – we also see the Cell Amount, Cell Status, and Storage Type as discussed in detail in the previous chapter.

There are a few other things to take note of here. First, notice that A#Price and A#Volume are listed in the **Common Members** section and A#XFCommon is listed in the Member Script of the data cells. The reason for this is that Data Buffer math is only performed on cells with identical dimensional Member details.

Since we know from the previous chapter that the dimensional details of a data cell make up its Primary Key (PK), we know that one data cell PK in a Data Buffer can only correspond to a maximum of one data cell PK in another Data Buffer. OneStream will simply multiply the data cells from the Price Data Buffer with the data cells from the Volume Data Buffer *that have the same PK or dimensional details.* Since the Account is obviously different between the two Data Buffers, XFCommon takes its place.

Let's look at the resulting Data Buffer, logged after the ADC function runs.

```
Dim salesDataBuffer As DataBuffer = api.Data.GetDataBufferUsingFormula("A#Sales")
salesDataBuffer.LogDataBuffer(api,"Sales Data Buffer", 100)
```

```
Common Members: A#Sales:F#All:O#All:I#All:U1#All:U2#All:U3#All:U4#All:U5#All:U6#All:U7#All:U8#All
A#XFCommon:F#EndBalLoad:O#Import:I#None:U1#BugZapper:U2#None:U3#None:U4#None:U5#None:U6#None:U7#None:U8#None, 1,050.00, IsRealData, Calculation
A#XFCommon:F#EndBalLoad:O#Import:I#None:U1#IndoorBugSpray:U2#None:U3#None:U4#None:U5#None:U6#None:U7#None:U8#None, 1,400.00, IsRealData, Calculation
A#XFCommon:F#EndBalLoad:O#Import:I#None:U1#OutdoorBugSpray:U2#None:U3#None:U4#None:U5#None:U6#None:U7#None:U8#None, 1,750.00, IsRealData, Calculation
A#XFCommon:F#EndBalLoad:O#Import:I#None:U1#BedBugKiller:U2#None:U3#None:U4#None:U5#None:U6#None:U7#None:U8#None, 900.00, IsRealData, Calculation
A#XFCommon:F#EndBalLoad:O#Import:I#None:U1#StinkBugKiller:U2#None:U3#None:U4#None:U5#None:U6#None:U7#None:U8#None, 585.00, IsRealData, Calculation
A#XFCommon:F#EndBalLoad:O#Import:I#None:U1#MouseTrap:U2#None:U3#None:U4#None:U5#None:U6#None:U7#None:U8#None, 2,250.00, IsRealData, Calculation
A#XFCommon:F#EndBalLoad:O#Import:I#None:U1#GlueTrap:U2#None:U3#None:U4#None:U5#None:U6#None:U7#None:U8#None, 1,625.00, IsRealData, Calculation
A#XFCommon:F#EndBalLoad:O#Import:I#None:U1#RatPoison:U2#None:U3#None:U4#None:U5#None:U6#None:U7#None:U8#None, 1,260.00, IsRealData, Calculation
A#XFCommon:F#EndBalLoad:O#Import:I#None:U1#Termicide:U2#None:U3#None:U4#None:U5#None:U6#None:U7#None:U8#None, 750.00, IsRealData, Calculation
A#XFCommon:F#EndBalLoad:O#Import:I#None:U1#PestControl:U2#None:U3#None:U4#None:U5#None:U6#None:U7#None:U8#None, 3,000.00, IsRealData, Calculation
A#XFCommon:F#EndBalLoad:O#Import:I#None:U1#TermiteTreatment:U2#None:U3#None:U4#None:U5#None:U6#None:U7#None:U8#None, 2,500.00, IsRealData, Calculation
A#XFCommon:F#EndBalLoad:O#Import:I#None:U1#Commercial:U2#None:U3#None:U4#None:U5#None:U6#None:U7#None:U8#None, 2,000.00, IsRealData, Calculation
A#XFCommon:F#EndBalLoad:O#Import:I#None:U1#BugBeaters:U2#None:U3#None:U4#None:U5#None:U6#None:U7#None:U8#None, 4,000.00, IsRealData, Calculation
```

Figure 3.4

In this simplified example, all Dimensions but one – `U1` – Product – are at the `None` Member, so it is easy to see which ones have matching Dimension details.

`U1#BugZappers` results in 1,050 (70*15), `U1#IndoorBugSpray` results in 1,400 (175*8) and so on. The only Members that we see in one of the Source Data Buffers that we don't see in the result is `U1#SpeedyBugSpray` and `U1#SpeedyTermiteSpray`. Since there is no corresponding data cell for these Members in the `A#Price` Buffer, no Calculation is performed on these cells and no data cell is created in the Result Buffer.

Current Data Unit Being Processed

In the above breakdown, I was careful to specify that the Data Buffer was being retrieved from *the current Data Unit being processed.* As we already know, every data cell in the Cube is described by all 18 Dimension Types known as the **Data Cell Primary Key**. We can see that the Data Unit Dimensions – Cube, Entity, Scenario, Time, and Consolidation – are not shown in the Data Buffer at all. This is because those Dimensions are known by the Calculation Engine as it processes the DUCS. The Calculation Engine knows these Dimensions when they were defined on the execution of the Calculation (in our case a Data Management step).

Data Unit Dimensions in the Destination Script

Since the Data Unit being processed is known in the background by the Calculation Engine, the Data Unit Dimensions should never be included in the destination Member Script (the left side of the formula).

```
api.Data.Calculate("E#ACME:A#Sales = A#Price * A#Volume")
```

The above script shows incorrect use of a Data Unit Dimension in the destination Member Script, which results in an error upon execution.

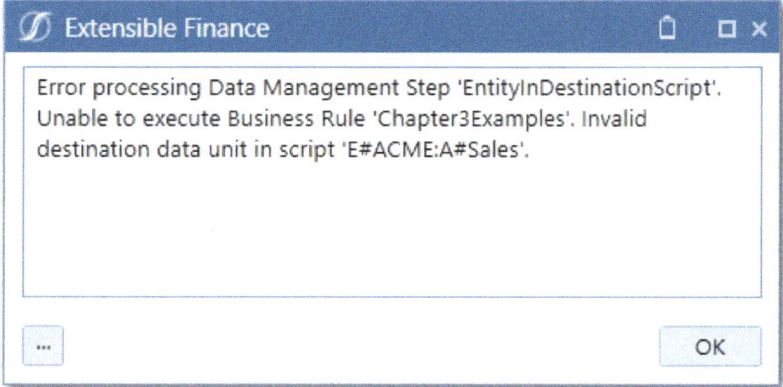

Figure 3.5

Chapter 3

ADC functions can never write to Data Units outside the one being processed. Instead, if needing to limit Calculations to specific Data Unit Dimensions, preceding `If` statements should be used. Their use is described in a later section in this chapter.

Data Unit Dimensions in the Source Scripts

Data Unit Dimensions *can* be used in Source Member Scripts (right side of the formula). Since Data Buffers do not include Data Unit Dimensions, Data Buffers from 'outside' Data Units will still match up with Data Buffers from the current Data Unit if cells within both Data Buffers have the same dimensionality.

```
api.Data.Calculate("A#Sales = A#Price * E#Global:C#Local:A#Volume")
```

The above example pulls the `A#Volume` Data Buffer from the Global Entity and multiplies it by the `A#Price` Data Buffer from the current Entity being processed.

> **Note:** When referencing Entity in a Source Member Script, `C#Local` should also be included. This is because if the Entity in the Data Unit currently being processed has a different currency assignment, then that currency will be used to retrieve the Data Buffer which will result in no data. Using `C#Local` will ensure that the data is pulled from the Entity's assigned currency where data is entered.

Unbalanced Buffers

We refer to Data Buffers with the same common Dimensions as **'Balanced' Data Buffers**. OneStream will only perform Data Buffer math on Balanced Data Buffers unless a special function is used (more on that later). The reason for this is the potential to cause **data explosion** which means that our Calculation might result in a lot of potentially unwanted data intersections. Let's look at an example.

Larry wants to calculate COGS for the Budget by multiplying the baseline Product manufacturing cost by an inflation rate. Manufacturing costs are entered for each Product while the inflation rate (think of the national CPI) is not specific to a Product so is entered at `U1#None`.

We might start by writing out the Calculation like this:

```
'This causes a data explosion error
api.Data.Calculate("A#COGS = A#ManufacturingCost * A#InflationRate:U1#None")
```

Larry, being the knucklehead that he is, assumed that each data record from the `A#ManufacturingCost` Data Buffer would multiply against the Inflation Rate entered in `U1#None`. This is not the case as the inclusion of the `U1` Member in the first operand makes this unbalanced. Let's look at what happens if we try to execute.

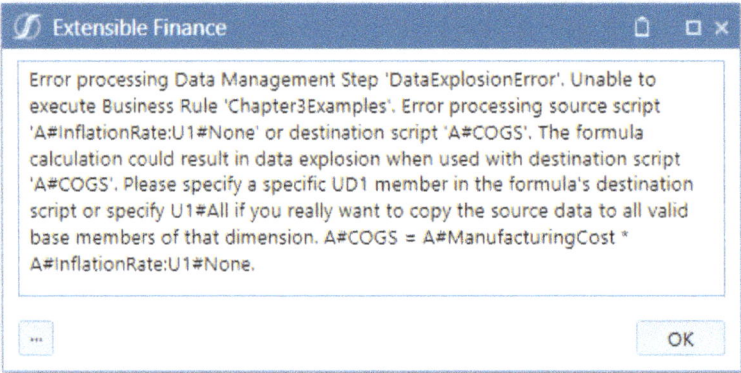

Figure 3.6

Whomp, Whomp! OneStream will immediately throw an error message at you when executing an unbalanced formula. Reading through the error message will give us a pretty good explanation of why this is explicitly prevented. Let's dig a little and log the `A#ManufacturingCost` and `A#InflationRate:U1#None` Data Buffers:

Inflation Rate Data Buffer:

```
Common Members: A#InflationRate:F#All:O#All:I#All:U1#None:U2#All:U3#All:U4#All:U5#All:U6#All:U7#All:U8#All
A#XFCommon:F#EndBalLoad:O#Import:I#None:U1#XFCommon:U2#None:U3#None:U4#None:U5#None:U6#None:U7#None:U8#None, 0.035, IsRealData, Input
```

Figure 3.7

Manufacturing Cost Data Buffer:

```
Common Members: A#ManufacturingCost:F#All:O#All:I#All:U1#All:U2#All:U3#All:U4#All:U5#All:U6#All:U7#All:U8#All
A#XFCommon:F#EndBalLoad:O#Import:I#None:U1#BugZapper:U2#None:U3#None:U4#None:U5#None:U6#None:U7#None:U8#None, 9.00, IsRealData, Input
A#XFCommon:F#EndBalLoad:O#Import:I#None:U1#IndoorBugSpray:U2#None:U3#None:U4#None:U5#None:U6#None:U7#None:U8#None, 2.75, IsRealData, Input
A#XFCommon:F#EndBalLoad:O#Import:I#None:U1#OutdoorBugSpray:U2#None:U3#None:U4#None:U5#None:U6#None:U7#None:U8#None, 2.25, IsRealData, Input
A#XFCommon:F#EndBalLoad:O#Import:I#None:U1#BedBugKiller:U2#None:U3#None:U4#None:U5#None:U6#None:U7#None:U8#None, 9.00, IsRealData, Input
A#XFCommon:F#EndBalLoad:O#Import:I#None:U1#StinkBugKiller:U2#None:U3#None:U4#None:U5#None:U6#None:U7#None:U8#None, 11.80, IsRealData, Input
A#XFCommon:F#EndBalLoad:O#Import:I#None:U1#MouseTrap:U2#None:U3#None:U4#None:U5#None:U6#None:U7#None:U8#None, 0.90, IsRealData, Input
A#XFCommon:F#EndBalLoad:O#Import:I#None:U1#GlueTrap:U2#None:U3#None:U4#None:U5#None:U6#None:U7#None:U8#None, 0.045, IsRealData, Input
A#XFCommon:F#EndBalLoad:O#Import:I#None:U1#RatPoison:U2#None:U3#None:U4#None:U5#None:U6#None:U7#None:U8#None, 0.10, IsRealData, Input
A#XFCommon:F#EndBalLoad:O#Import:I#None:U1#Termicide:U2#None:U3#None:U4#None:U5#None:U6#None:U7#None:U8#None, 4.50, IsRealData, Input
A#XFCommon:F#EndBalLoad:O#Import:I#None:U1#PestControl:U2#None:U3#None:U4#None:U5#None:U6#None:U7#None:U8#None, 50.00, IsRealData, Input
A#XFCommon:F#EndBalLoad:O#Import:I#None:U1#TermiteTreatment:U2#None:U3#None:U4#None:U5#None:U6#None:U7#None:U8#None, 75.00, IsRealData, Input
A#XFCommon:F#EndBalLoad:O#Import:I#None:U1#Commercial:U2#None:U3#None:U4#None:U5#None:U6#None:U7#None:U8#None, 70.00, IsRealData, Input
A#XFCommon:F#EndBalLoad:O#Import:I#None:U1#BugBeaters:U2#None:U3#None:U4#None:U5#None:U6#None:U7#None:U8#None, 120.00, IsRealData, Input
```

Figure 3.8

The `A#InflationRate` Data Buffer has `U1#XFCommon` in the dimensional details while the `A#ManufacturingCost` Data Buffer does not. Since the Data Buffers do not contain any cells with the same dimensional details, the Calculation doesn't result in any result cells.

Data Explosion

The error message we received suggests that our formula could cause data explosion. This sounds scary, and so it should! Data explosion can wreak havoc on a database by filling it with zeros or unwanted data.

The data explosion warning is triggered anytime a source script contains Dimensions not contained in the destination script.

```
api.Data.Calculate("A#COGS = A#ManufacturingCost:U1#BugZapper * A#InflationRate:U1#None")
```

The above script is a better example of a formula that could cause data explosion.

Since `U1` is included in both source scripts, Data Buffer math would execute and produce a resulting Data Buffer. However, it then needs to assign the combined Data Buffer to the destination script of `A#COGS`. Since `U1` was not included in the destination script, OneStream has nowhere to write this data. The system cannot use `U1#BugZapper` or `U1#None` because data cells were created by adding them together and it cannot arbitrarily choose one over the other. Because `#All` is the default setting for each unspecified Member, the formula will copy the Source Data Buffer to every Base-level `U1` Member. This could create a lot of data cells and is likely not wanted, so an error is thrown.

Using #All

I'll cut right to the chase and say that `#All` should very rarely be used in Member Scripts. At worst, you can cause data explosion, and at best there is a better way.

As the earlier error message suggests, `U1#All` can be added to the destination script to circumvent the error message and force data explosion. Below is an example to show what actually happens when `#All` is used on the destination script.

```
api.Data.Calculate("A#COGS:U1#All = A#ManufacturingCost:U1#BugZapper * A#InflationRate:U1#None")
```

```
Common Members: A#COGS:F#All:O#All:I#All:U1#All:U2#All:U3#All:U4#All:U5#All:U6#All:U7#All:U8#All
A#XFCommon:F#EndBalLoad:O#Import:I#None:U1#None:U2#None:U3#None:U4#None:U5#None:U6#None:U7#None:U8#None, 0.315, IsRealData, Calculation
A#XFCommon:F#EndBalLoad:O#Import:I#None:U1#BugZapper:U2#None:U3#None:U4#None:U5#None:U6#None:U7#None:U8#None, 0.315, IsRealData, Calculation
A#XFCommon:F#EndBalLoad:O#Import:I#None:U1#IndoorBugSpray:U2#None:U3#None:U4#None:U5#None:U6#None:U7#None:U8#None, 0.315, IsRealData, Calculation
A#XFCommon:F#EndBalLoad:O#Import:I#None:U1#OutdoorBugSpray:U2#None:U3#None:U4#None:U5#None:U6#None:U7#None:U8#None, 0.315, IsRealData, Calculation
A#XFCommon:F#EndBalLoad:O#Import:I#None:U1#BedBugKiller:U2#None:U3#None:U4#None:U5#None:U6#None:U7#None:U8#None, 0.315, IsRealData, Calculation
A#XFCommon:F#EndBalLoad:O#Import:I#None:U1#StinkBugKiller:U2#None:U3#None:U4#None:U5#None:U6#None:U7#None:U8#None, 0.315, IsRealData, Calculation
A#XFCommon:F#EndBalLoad:O#Import:I#None:U1#Termicide:U2#None:U3#None:U4#None:U5#None:U6#None:U7#None:U8#None, 0.315, IsRealData, Calculation
A#XFCommon:F#EndBalLoad:O#Import:I#None:U1#SpeedyBugSpray:U2#None:U3#None:U4#None:U5#None:U6#None:U7#None:U8#None, 0.315, IsRealData, Calculation
A#XFCommon:F#EndBalLoad:O#Import:I#None:U1#SpeedyTermiteSpray:U2#None:U3#None:U4#None:U5#None:U6#None:U7#None:U8#None, 0.315, IsRealData, Calculation
A#XFCommon:F#EndBalLoad:O#Import:I#None:U1#MouseTrap:U2#None:U3#None:U4#None:U5#None:U6#None:U7#None:U8#None, 0.315, IsRealData, Calculation
A#XFCommon:F#EndBalLoad:O#Import:I#None:U1#GlueTrap:U2#None:U3#None:U4#None:U5#None:U6#None:U7#None:U8#None, 0.315, IsRealData, Calculation
A#XFCommon:F#EndBalLoad:O#Import:I#None:U1#RatPoison:U2#None:U3#None:U4#None:U5#None:U6#None:U7#None:U8#None, 0.315, IsRealData, Calculation
A#XFCommon:F#EndBalLoad:O#Import:I#None:U1#PestControl:U2#None:U3#None:U4#None:U5#None:U6#None:U7#None:U8#None, 0.315, IsRealData, Calculation
A#XFCommon:F#EndBalLoad:O#Import:I#None:U1#TermiteTreatment:U2#None:U3#None:U4#None:U5#None:U6#None:U7#None:U8#None, 0.315, IsRealData, Calculation
A#XFCommon:F#EndBalLoad:O#Import:I#None:U1#Commercial:U2#None:U3#None:U4#None:U5#None:U6#None:U7#None:U8#None, 0.315, IsRealData, Calculation
A#XFCommon:F#EndBalLoad:O#Import:I#None:U1#BugBeaters:U2#None:U3#None:U4#None:U5#None:U6#None:U7#None:U8#None, 0.315, IsRealData, Calculation
```

Figure 3.9

The Calculation indeed resulted in data explosion as a number was saved in every Base Member of the `U1` Dimension. Because of the risk of creating many unwanted data cells, `#All` should never be used.

Unbalanced Functions

Going back to Larry's problem, we still need a way to apply the Inflation Rate which is not specific to a Product and saved on `U1#None` by the Manufacturing Cost which exists for each Product. In other words, Larry wants to multiply the same Inflation Rate by each cell in the `A#ManufacturingCost` Data Buffer.

To do exactly this, Larry can use **Unbalanced Math Functions** which are specifically designed to safely combine Data Buffers that don't balance. Below is a list of the available unbalanced functions:

- `MultiplyUnbalanced`
- `DivideUnbalanced`
- `AddUnbalanced`
- `SubtractUnbalanced`

Syntax

To use these functions, wrap the unbalanced function in parentheses, and separate each Data Buffer with a comma. A third argument will reference the unbalanced part of the script.

```
UnbalancedFunction(DataBuffer1, DataBuffer2, UnbalancedScript)
```

> **Note:** The Unbalanced Data Buffer (Data Buffer with more Dimensions defined) should always be the second argument.

Example

Let's correct Larry's earlier error by rewriting our COGS formula using the `MultiplyUnbalanced` function.

```
api.Data.Calculate("A#COGS = MultiplyUnbalanced(A#ManufacturingCost, A#InflationRate:U1#None, U1#None)")
```

Let's see what the resulting Data Buffer looks like after applying the unbalanced function.

```
Dim multiplyUnbalancedDataBuffer As DataBuffer
multiplyUnbalancedDataBuffer = api.Data.GetDataBufferUsingFormula("MultiplyUnbalanced(A#ManufacturingCost, A#InflationRate:U1#None, U1#None)")
multiplyUnbalancedDataBuffer.LogDataBuffer(api,"Multiply Unbalanced Data Buffer", 100)
```

```
Common Members: A#ManufacturingCost:F#All:O#All:I#All:U1#All:U2#All:U3#All:U4#All:U5#All:U6#All:U7#All:U8#All
A#XFCommon:F#EndBalLoad:O#Import:I#None:U1#BugZapper:U2#None:U3#None:U4#None:U5#None:U6#None:U7#None:U8#None, 0.315, IsRealData, Input
A#XFCommon:F#EndBalLoad:O#Import:I#None:U1#IndoorBugSpray:U2#None:U3#None:U4#None:U5#None:U6#None:U7#None:U8#None, 0.09625, IsRealData, Input
A#XFCommon:F#EndBalLoad:O#Import:I#None:U1#OutdoorBugSpray:U2#None:U3#None:U4#None:U5#None:U6#None:U7#None:U8#None, 0.07875, IsRealData, Input
A#XFCommon:F#EndBalLoad:O#Import:I#None:U1#BedBugKiller:U2#None:U3#None:U4#None:U5#None:U6#None:U7#None:U8#None, 0.315, IsRealData, Input
A#XFCommon:F#EndBalLoad:O#Import:I#None:U1#StinkBugKiller:U2#None:U3#None:U4#None:U5#None:U6#None:U7#None:U8#None, 0.413, IsRealData, Input
A#XFCommon:F#EndBalLoad:O#Import:I#None:U1#MouseTrap:U2#None:U3#None:U4#None:U5#None:U6#None:U7#None:U8#None, 0.0315, IsRealData, Input
A#XFCommon:F#EndBalLoad:O#Import:I#None:U1#GlueTrap:U2#None:U3#None:U4#None:U5#None:U6#None:U7#None:U8#None, 0.001575, IsRealData, Input
A#XFCommon:F#EndBalLoad:O#Import:I#None:U1#RatPoison:U2#None:U3#None:U4#None:U5#None:U6#None:U7#None:U8#None, 0.0035, IsRealData, Input
A#XFCommon:F#EndBalLoad:O#Import:I#None:U1#Termicide:U2#None:U3#None:U4#None:U5#None:U6#None:U7#None:U8#None, 0.1575, IsRealData, Input
A#XFCommon:F#EndBalLoad:O#Import:I#None:U1#PestControl:U2#None:U3#None:U4#None:U5#None:U6#None:U7#None:U8#None, 1.75, IsRealData, Input
A#XFCommon:F#EndBalLoad:O#Import:I#None:U1#TermiteTreatment:U2#None:U3#None:U4#None:U5#None:U6#None:U7#None:U8#None, 2.625, IsRealData, Input
A#XFCommon:F#EndBalLoad:O#Import:I#None:U1#Commercial:U2#None:U3#None:U4#None:U5#None:U6#None:U7#None:U8#None, 2.45, IsRealData, Input
A#XFCommon:F#EndBalLoad:O#Import:I#None:U1#BugBeaters:U2#None:U3#None:U4#None:U5#None:U6#None:U7#None:U8#None, 4.20, IsRealData, Input
```

Figure 3.10

The resulting Data Buffer has been successfully created and still balances with our destination Data Buffer. No data explosion has occurred. All is good!

Even More Unbalanced

When you're using unbalanced functions, you are not limited to your Data Buffers being unbalanced by just one Dimension. The unbalanced functions can handle multiple unbalanced Dimensions in the unbalanced Data Buffer by concatenating them in the third argument.

```
api.Data.Calculate("A#COGS = MultiplyUnbalanced(A#ManufacturingCost,
A#InflationRate: U1#None:U2#None:U3#None,
U1#None:U2#Accounting:U3#None")
```

Potential Issues

Double Unbalanced

If both Data Buffers in your expression are unbalanced by *different* Dimensions, then things get tricky.

```
api.Data.Calculate("A#COGS = A#ManufacturingCost:U2#Sales,
A#InflationRate:U1#None")
```

For this example, unbalanced functions will not work, and we will need to employ a different technique. Stay tuned as we cover this in the next chapter.

Divide and Subtract Unbalanced

When using the unbalanced functions, the order in which each operand appears in the function matters, as the second operand must always be the Member Script with the additional Dimensions. This presents a conflict with the subtract and divide functions as the order of operations *also* matters when dividing and subtracting.

```
DivideUnbalanced(NumeratorMemberScript, DenominatorMemberScript,
UnbalancedScript)
```

Given the above required syntax, only the denominator can have the unbalanced Dimensions attached to it. What do we do when the numerator contains the unbalanced Dimensions?

The answer is to use some basic third grade math and convert division into multiplication. We can divide the numerator by 1 and use `MultiplyUnbalanced` instead, since the order of multiplication does not matter.

```
MultiplyUnbalanced(DenominatorMemberScript, Divide(1,
NumeratorMemberScript), UnbalancedScript)
```

Chapter 3

For subtraction, we can still use `SubtractUnbalanced` while switching the intended order of the operands and simply multiplying by `-1`.

Intended expression: MemberScript1 – MemberScript2 with MemberScript1 being unbalanced:

Using `SubtractUnbalanced`:

```
SubtractUnbalanced(MemberScript2, MemberScript1, UnbalancedScript) * -1
```

Using Constants

Constants can be easily integrated into ADC functions and Data Buffer math still works as expected.

```
api.Data.Calculate("A#NewPrice = A#Price * 10")
```

To calculate the result, OneStream will simply take each data cell in the `A#Price` Data Buffer and multiply it by `10`, creating a new Result Data Buffer.

You cannot, however, set a destination Data Buffer equal to a constant.

```
api.Data.Calculate("A#NewPrice = 10")
```

The above would cause data explosion since OneStream might assume that you wanted to set every possible Base intersection of `A#NewPrice` to `10`. Executing this script will result in the data explosion error.

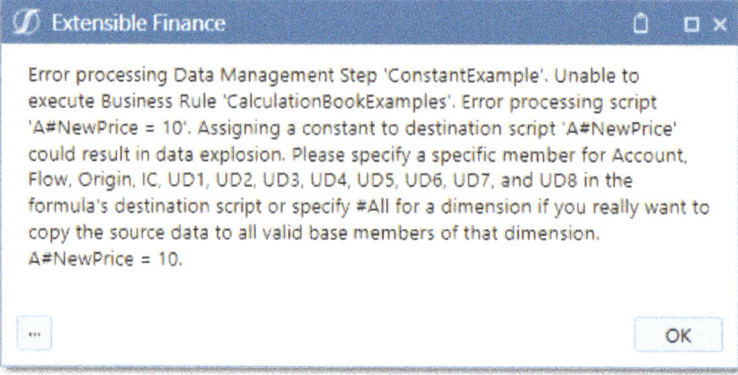

Figure 3.11

An Interesting Use Case

Let's look at a real-world Calculation example involving a constant and inspect what happens. In this example, we are using a **Growth Rate** to extrapolate a future cost.

```
api.Data.Calculate("A#Cost = T#POVPriorYearM12:A#Cost * (1 + A#GrowthRate)")
```

- The `A#Cost` Data Buffer from the Prior Year Month 12 is retrieved from storage in the Cube.
- A new Data Buffer is created in memory by adding the `A#GrowthRate` Data Buffer to `1`.
- Data Buffer Math multiplies the `A#Cost` Data Buffer by the new `A#GrowthRate` Data Buffer.

- The newly-created Data Buffer is saved to the Cube.

The above is hopefully not too surprising. But what happens if the `A#GrowthRate` Buffer is Zero or NoData?

Adding an empty Data Buffer by a constant, results in nothing which means that `T#POVPriorYearM12:A#Cost` gets multiplied by nothing which equals… you guessed it… nothing.

In other words, if no growth rate is entered, the Calculation produces no results. This may be desired behavior but most likely, you would want to treat an empty growth rate as a zero which would result in `A#Cost` being equal to `T#POVPriorYearM12:A#Cost` if no growth rate was entered.

To remedy this, simply rewrite the Calculation as follows:

```
api.Data.Calculate("A#Cost = T#POVPriorYearM12:A#Cost + (T#POVPriorYearM12:A#Cost * A#GrowthRate)")
```

Using addition will still result in a Result Data Buffer, even if the `A#GrowthRate` is empty, which is the desired result.

Formula Variables

We learned in the previous chapter that a Data Buffer can be assigned to a variable using the `api.Data.GetDataBuffer` and `api.Data.GetDataBufferUsingFormula` functions. Once created, this Data Buffer variable can be used inside an `api.Data.Calculate` function by using a **Formula Variable**. Formula Variables allow the Data Buffer object to be referenced in the formula string of the ADC function. This provides a lot of flexibility, and it can even improve performance because you can calculate a Data Buffer once and re-use the variable multiple times.

Syntax

Use the `api.Data.FormulaVariables.SetDataBufferVariable` function to name your Data Buffer. Pass in any name followed by the Data Buffer variable and then a `True` or `False` value. The final `True` or `False` value is for Use Indexes To Optimize Repeat Filtering. Use `True` if you intend to re-use the same Data Buffer using `FilterMembers` (performance improvement). Otherwise, use `False`. After you name the Data Buffer, use a `$` plus the name when referencing it in the script.

Example

We can rewrite our *Sales = Price * Volume* equation using Formula Variables as the Price and Volume Data Buffers instead of Member Scripts.

```
Dim priceDataBuffer As DataBuffer = api.Data.GetDataBufferUsingFormula("A#Price")
api.Data.FormulaVariables.SetDataBufferVariable("Price", priceDataBuffer, False)

Dim volumeDataBuffer As DataBuffer = api.Data.GetDataBufferUsingFormula("A#Volume")
api.Data.FormulaVariables.SetDataBufferVariable("Volume", volumeDataBuffer, False)

api.Data.Calculate("A#Sales = $Price * $Volume")
```

Chapter 3

Converting Data Buffers with Differing Extensibility

OneStream Extensible dimensionality allows different levels of dimensional detail by Entity, Scenario, or Cube. This means that Base Members in one Scenario may be Parents in another.

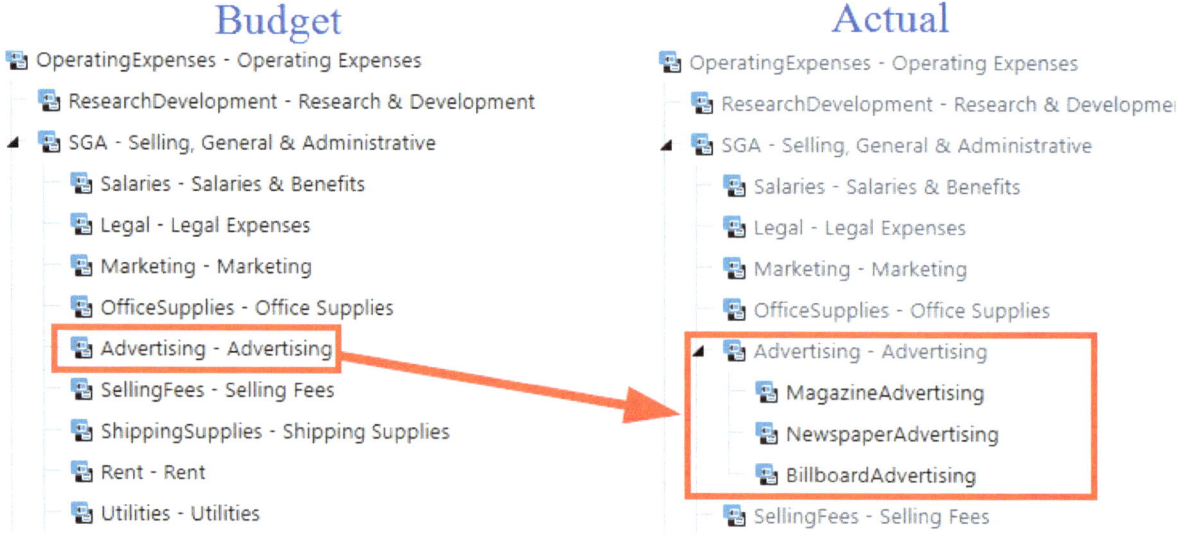

Figure 3.12

Figure 3.12 shows this concept within the Account Dimension across Actual and Budget Scenarios. Actual data is at a lower level of detail than the Budget data but a common Member – A#Advertising – is still shared.

The api.Data.ConvertDataBufferExtendedMembers function can be used to convert a Data Buffer to the dimensionality of another Cube or Scenario. The function automatically aggregates the data for extended Members in order to create data cells for Parent Members that are Base-level Members in the destination Dimensions. This is used when copying data from a Source Data Buffer created in another Cube or Scenario where one or more Dimensions have been extended.

The below script shows how to use this function to convert a Data Buffer from the Budget Scenario to the dimensionality of the Actual Scenario by collapsing the detail in the Budget to the common Member.

```
'Get the Actual Data Buffer and convert it
Dim actualDataBuffer As DataBuffer = api.Data.GetDataBufferUsingFormula("S#Actual:T#POVPriorYearM12")
actualDataBuffer.LogDataBuffer(api,"Actual Data Buffer",1000)
Dim convertedActualDataBuffer As DataBuffer
convertedActualDataBuffer = api.Data.ConvertDataBufferExtendedMembers(api.Pov.Cube.Name,"Actual",actualDataBuffer)
convertedActualDataBuffer.LogDataBuffer(api,"Converted Data Buffer",100)

'Store the converted actual data buffer in a data buffer variable
api.Data.FormulaVariables.SetDataBufferVariable("ConvertedActuals",convertedActualDataBuffer,True)

'Execute the ADC function with the Converted Data Buffer variable
api.Data.Calculate("S#" & api.Pov.Scenario.Name & " = $ConvertedActuals")
```

Once the Data Buffer is converted, it can be assigned to a variable using Formula Variables and used in ADC functions. We can see the detailed Accounts in the S#Actual Data Buffer:

```
A#Insurance:F#EndBalLoad:O#Import:I#None:U1#None:U2#Facilities:U3#None:U4#None:U5#None:U6#None:U7#None:U8#None, 36.00, IsRealData, Input
A#MagazineAdvertising:F#EndBalLoad:O#Import:I#None:U1#None:U2#Marketing:U3#None:U4#None:U5#None:U6#None:U7#None:U8#None, 144.00, IsRealData, Input
A#NewspaperAdvertising:F#EndBalLoad:O#Import:I#None:U1#None:U2#Marketing:U3#None:U4#None:U5#None:U6#None:U7#None:U8#None, 120.00, IsRealData, Input
A#BillboardAdvertising:F#EndBalLoad:O#Import:I#None:U1#None:U2#Marketing:U3#None:U4#None:U5#None:U6#None:U7#None:U8#None, 96.00, IsRealData, Input
A#Inventory:F#EndBalLoad:O#Import:I#None:U1#None:U2#None:U3#None:U4#None:U5#None:U6#None:U7#None:U8#None, 24,666.83, IsRealData, Input
```

Figure 3.13

After using the `ConvertExtendedMembers` function on the Data Buffer, we can see the three detailed Accounts collapsed to one:

```
A#Insurance:F#EndBalLoad:O#Import:I#None:U1#None:U2#Facilities:U3#None:U4#None:U5#None:U6#None:U7#None:U8#None, 36.00, IsRealData, Input
A#Advertising:F#EndBalLoad:O#Import:I#None:U1#None:U2#Marketing:U3#None:U4#None:U5#None:U6#None:U7#None:U8#None, 360.00, IsRealData, Input
```

Figure 3.14

The data now matches the dimensionality of the Budget Scenario and can be copied.

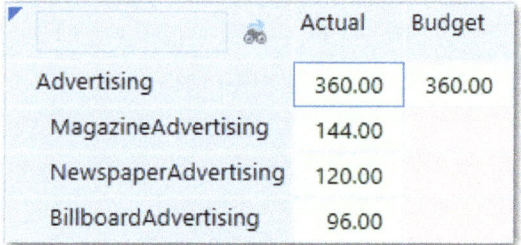

Figure 3.15

Limiting Scope

So far, we've used very limited data sets in our examples. Our Data Buffer examples have had only a handful of cells so we could reduce noise and visualize what was really happening. Data sets in the real world are much larger and messier. Anomalies in the data will cause inconsistencies and Calculation performance will often be at the forefront of your mind. Also, Calculation logic may need to vary for subsets of Dimensions. For example, Products in a certain group may calculate material costs differently than Products in another group. For these reasons, limiting the number of data cells created by your Calculations is important. Below are the ways in which we can limit the scope of Calculations:

- Limit Data Unit scope using `If` Statements
- Reducing Data Buffer size using Dimension Filters
- Collapsing detail within Data Buffers

Limit Data Unit Scope

Calculations within assigned Business Rules and Member Formulas will run for every Data Unit defined at runtime. However, we likely don't want *every* Calculation to run at *every* Data Unit. There are up to seven Calculation operations per Entity in the Consolidation process. It would be very rare to have a Calculation that needed to run at all of them.

We want our Calculations to work *with* the Finance Engine and not against it.

Conditional statements should be added to formulas to limit which Consolidation Calculation processes will run for a particular formula. This will let Calculations run only where needed and then get picked up and processed by the standard algorithms.

Chapter 3

The most common application of this concept is restricting Calculations to only run at `C#Local` and Base Entities.

```
If api.Cons.IsLocalCurrencyForEntity()And Not api.Entity.HasChildren() Then
    api.data.Calculate("A#Cost = A#Price * A#Volume")
End If
```

The idea here is that Calculations will run at `C#Local` only and then use default Translation to translate the calculated amount and consolidate the result to its Parent. This lets the default Translation and Consolidation/Aggregation components of the OneStream Calculation Engine algorithm do most of the legwork.

Below are some other API functions which will limit the Data Unit scope of the Calculation.

Specific Data Unit Members

We can exclude Calculations from running on certain Data Units by using various API functions. For example, if we wanted to limit a Calculation to only run on one Entity or Scenario, we could do something like this:

```
If api.Pov.Entity.Name.XFEqualsIgnoreCase("Pittsburgh") Then…
If api.Pov.Scenario.Name.XFEqualsIgnoreCase("Budget") Then…
```

The above script would result in all Data Units except the Entity of `Pittsburgh` and Scenario of `Budget`.

Translated Currency Only

```
If api.Cons.IsForeignCurrencyForEntity Then
```

Specific Scenario Types

```
If api.Scenario.GetScenarioType() = ScenarioType.Budget
```

Why Api.Pov.Account Won't Work

You may be thinking that you could use `api.Pov.Account`, `Flow`, or `UD` to limit the data cells created in an ADC. You certainly wouldn't be the first and it is, after all, a valid function. If you did try to use it, your script would compile and execute without error. And since we're able to use `api.Pov.Entity` in this way, it should work, right? Wrong.

`api.Pov.Entity`, `Scenario`, `Time`, or `Consolidation` works because those Dimensions are in the Data Unit which OneStream has full context of. Remember from Chapter 2 that we always define the Data Unit when executing Calculations. All other Dimensions are within the Data Buffer which the Calculation Engine has no context of until it is performing Data Buffer math dictated by the formula string in the ADC.

What we instead need to do is conditionally remove cells from our Data Buffers either before or after Data Buffer math is performed.

Dimension Filters

Functionality to filter cells from Data Buffers is built right into the ADC function. The ADC function will accept optional Dimension filter parameters in the form of a **Member Filter**.

```
Sub DataApi.Calculate(formula As String, Optional accountFilter As String, Optional flowFilter As String, Optional originFilter As String, Optional icFilter As String, Optional ud1Filter As String, Optional ud2Filter As String, Optional ud3Filter As String, Optional ud4Filter As String, Optional ud5Filter As String, Optional ud6Filter As String, Optional ud7Filter As String, Optional ud8Filter As String, Optional onEvalDataBuffer As EvalDataBufferDelegate, Optional userState As Object, Optional isDurableCalculatedData As Boolean)
```

Figure 3.16

A Member Filter returns a list of Members, and through various expansion functions, `Where` clauses, and other tricks, can be manipulated to return just about any combination of Dimension Members that you need. Here are some examples:

- `A#IncomeStatement.Base`
- `A#IncomeStatement.Base.Where(AccountType = Revenue)`
- `U1#Top.Base.Where(Name Contains Bug)`

Using Member Filters, you can restrict the data cells created in your ADC functions, based on the Member's position in the hierarchy or its properties.

The Member Filter Builder

The **Member Filter Builder** is a tool within OneStream that provides a Graphical User Interface for creating Member Filters.

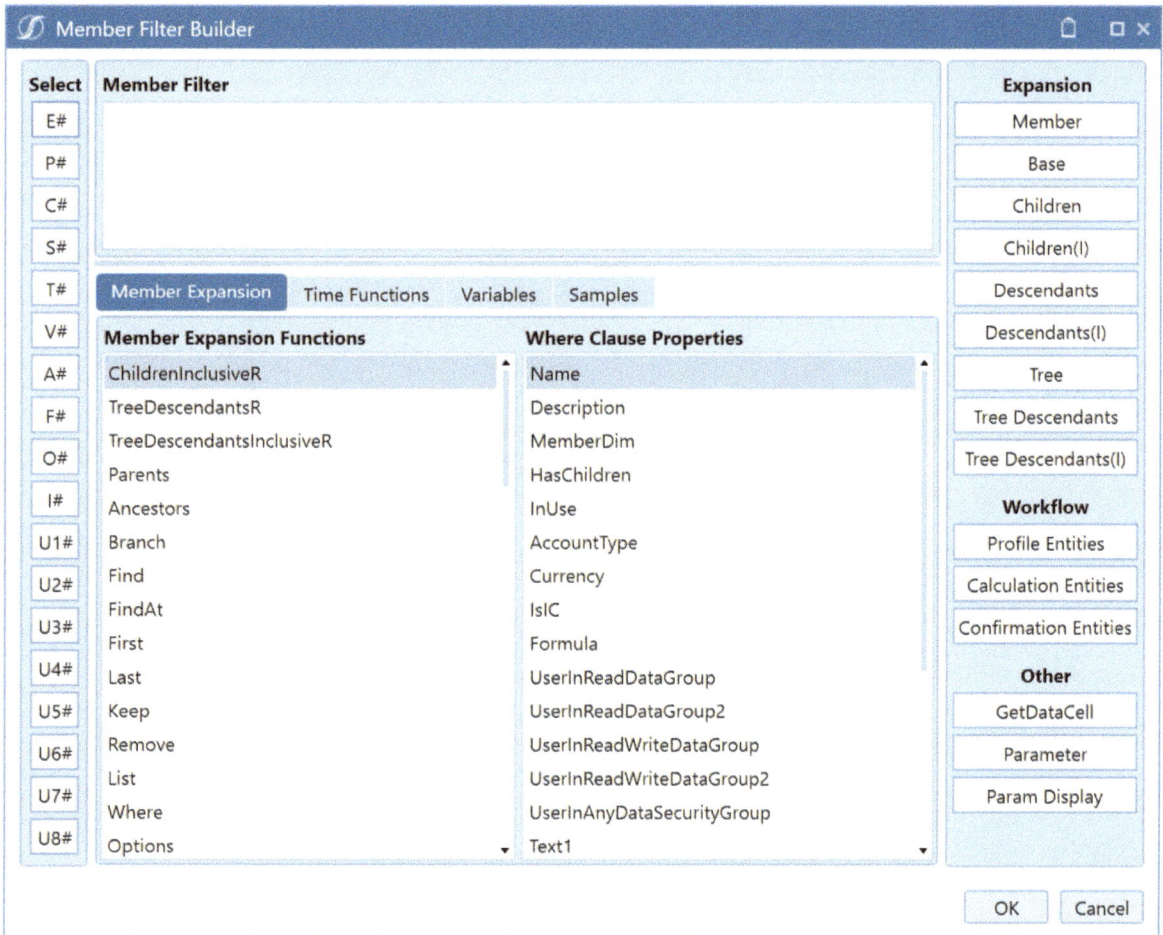

Figure 3.17

Chapter 3

The Member Filter Builder not only helps you use the correct syntax, but provides examples and sample scripts which will help you get to the exact list of Members you need. I strongly recommend getting familiar with the Member Filter Builder and learning its expansive functionality.

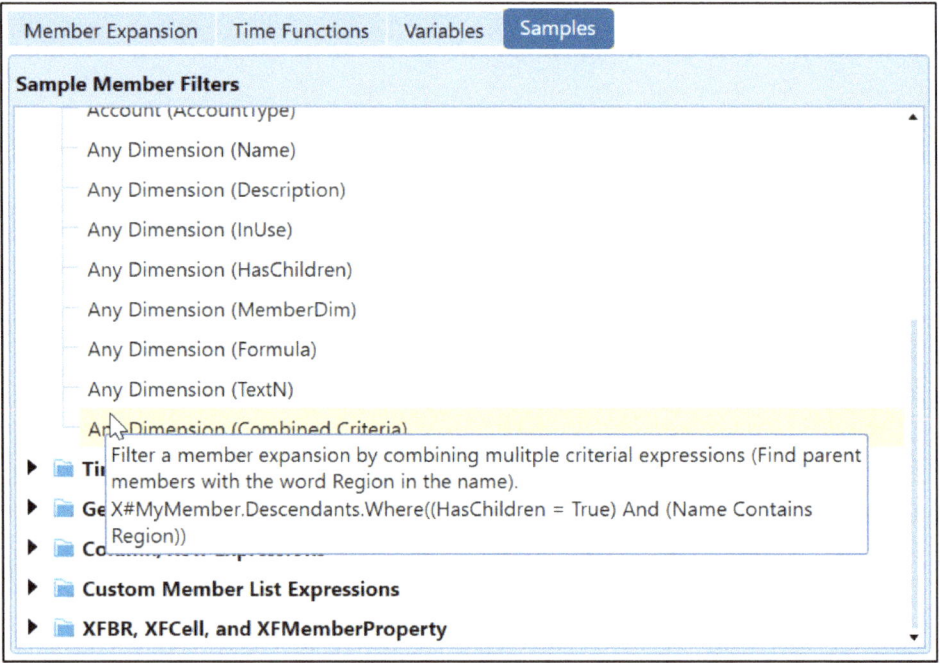

Figure 3.18

Applying the Member Filter

Let's take our previous Sales Calculation example and apply a Member Filter to it so that the result is only written on Base Members of `U1#Insects`.

```
api.Data.Calculate("A#Sales = A#Price * A#Volume",,,,,"U1#Insects.Base")
```

> **Note**: If you need filters for certain Dimension Types, simply leave the filters empty for Dimensions you don't need. Also, pay careful attention to the position of commas when applying Dimension filters. Use Intelli-Sense to ensure each Dimension is in the right argument position. For example, `UD1` needs to always be in the fifth position as shown above.

The Calculation now only saves Data Buffer cells with a `U1` Member that is a Base Member of the `Insects` Parent. The `U1` hierarchy is shown below for reference.

66

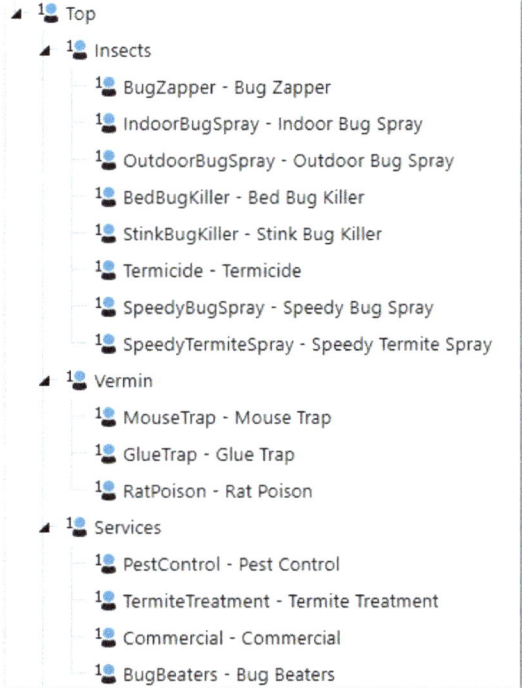

Figure 3.19

Let's look at what OneStream does under hood when executing the ADC with the filter applied.

- The `A#Price` Data Buffer is retrieved from storage.
- The `A#Volume` Data Buffer is retrieved from storage.
- Data Buffer math multiplies the two Data Buffers together and creates a new Data Buffer.
- The new Data Buffer is filtered to exclude any `U1` Members not contained in the Member Filter.
- The newly created and filtered Data Buffer is saved to the Cube.

The added step before saving the Data Buffer will remove data cells from the Data Buffer. Here is what the Calculation result looks like before and after applying the filter.

Before Filter:

Sales		
	BugZapper - Bug Zapper	13,150.00
	IndoorBugSpray - Indoor Bug Spray	15,780.00
	OutdoorBugSpray - Outdoor Bug Spray	19,725.00
	BedBugKiller - Bed Bug Killer	10,520.00
	StinkBugKiller - Stink Bug Killer	6,575.00
	Termicide	9,205.00
	SpeedyBugSpray - Speedy Bug Spray	
	SpeedyTermiteSpray - Speedy Termite Spray	
	MouseTrap - Mouse Trap	26,300.00
	GlueTrap - Glue Trap	19,725.00
	RatPoison - Rat Poison	15,780.00
	PestControl - Pest Control	28,930.00
	TermiteTreatment - Termite Treatment	23,012.50
	Commercial	10,914.50
	BugBeaters - Bug Beaters	18,410.00

Figure 3.20

After Filter:

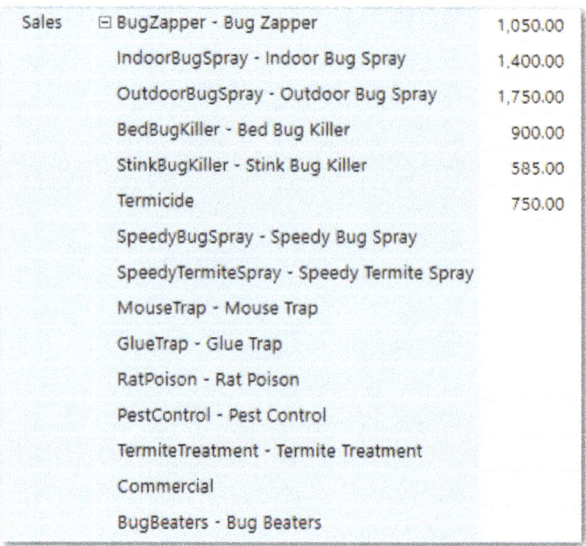

Figure 3.21

Only Base U1 Members that exist beneath Insects remain in the Result Data Buffer. We have reduced the scope of this Calculation from 13 data cells to six.

Base Members Only

Data Buffers will only contain data cells that are writable to the Cube. As explained previously, data can only be written to Base Members of a Cube (however, bear in mind that thanks to Extensibility, Base cells of a Cube can be Parent cells of another Cube or Scenario Type). To this point, your Member Filters used in ADC functions should also only contain Base Members. If they don't, the filter will still work, but will technically perform slower.

No Duplicates

It is possible to create a Member Filter that includes the same Member twice. Here is an example:

    U1#Insects.Base, U1#BugZapper

U1#BugZapper is also a Base Member within U1#Insects, so it is contained twice in the resulting Member List. If using this Member Filter elsewhere in OneStream, (e.g., a Cube View), OneStream will simply display the Member twice, clearly showing your error. Used in a formula, however, OneStream will throw an error.

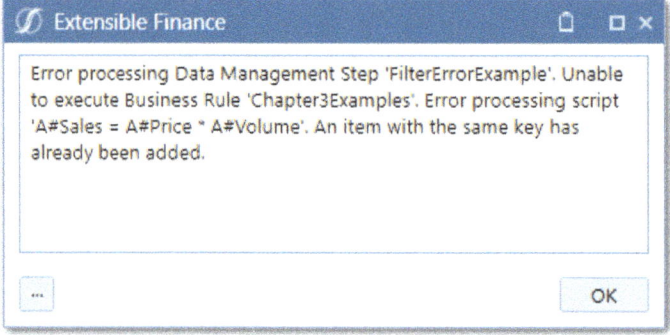

Figure 3.22

You could also theoretically have the same Member appear twice within a hierarchy, which is most likely unwanted as data could aggregate twice, throwing off the total. Using the `.Base` expansion on a Parent with a duplicate Member beneath it will also cause the same error, so keep this in mind when troubleshooting.

The reason for this error is because OneStream converts the Member List to a Dictionary (VB.NET class) and Dictionaries cannot contain duplicate keys.

Know Your Hierarchies and Use Them to Your Advantage

Creating effective Member Filters used in Calculations will require knowledge of the Dimension Member hierarchies. These hierarchies often support reporting or may have little to no structure at all, so they may not align well with your Calculation logic. In these cases, inserting Parents or creating hierarchies to support Calculations can be a useful technique.

There is minimal Calculation performance cost to adding Parent groupings within Account, Flow, and UD Dimensions. The only cost to consider is maintenance as new Members may need to be added to the groups over time, but this can be mitigated through the sharing of Parents between the main hierarchy and your alternate hierarchies used to support Calculations.

Collapsing Detail

The resultant Data Buffer (left side of the formula) inherits the dimensional detail of the Source Data Buffers after all Data Buffer math has been executed (right side of the equation). Leaving Dimensions off the Member Scripts is called leaving the Dimension 'open'.

```
api.Data.Calculate("A#Sales = A#Price * A#Volume")
```

In the above formula, Flow, Origin, Intercompany, and all UDs are 'open'. This means that the resulting Data Buffer will include all Members for those Dimensions where there is data (assuming we don't apply a filter). If detail for one of those Dimensions is not necessary, we can remove it by adding that Dimension to all Data Buffer operands in the formula.

```
'This collapses detail from Origin and Flow Top to O#Import and F#EndBalLoad
Api.Data.Calculate("A#Sales:O#Import:F#EndBalLoad = A#Price:O#Top:F#Top * A#Volume:O#Top:F#Top")
```

The formula has now been changed to include the Origin and Flow Dimensions. Remember, that we need to include `O#` in every Buffer so that our formula remains balanced. Now, all the detail in the Origin and Flow Dimensions will be collapsed to `Top` and written to `O#Import` and `F#EndBal`.

Since the destination Data Buffer can only contain writable Base Members, we need to pick one to write the data to. In this example, we picked `O#Import` and `F#EndBal`, but we could have also picked any other Base Member in those Dimensions.

Origin Dimension

Collapsing Origin Dimension detail is very common practice and should be used in almost all Calculations. Not doing so can produce unwanted results as data could exist at different Origin Members causing them not to match up when Data Buffer math is performed. Imagine if a Price was entered through a Form at `O#Forms`, and the related Volume imported through a file, at `O#Import`. Performing Data Buffer math on this data would not yield any result because the data exists at different Origin Members.

While the above example used `O#Import` as the destination Origin Member, `O#Forms` can be used as well. Both options have advantages and disadvantages.

O#Import vs. O#Forms

The Origin Dimension has a special feature built in which allows a User to type directly into the `BeforeAdj` Member.

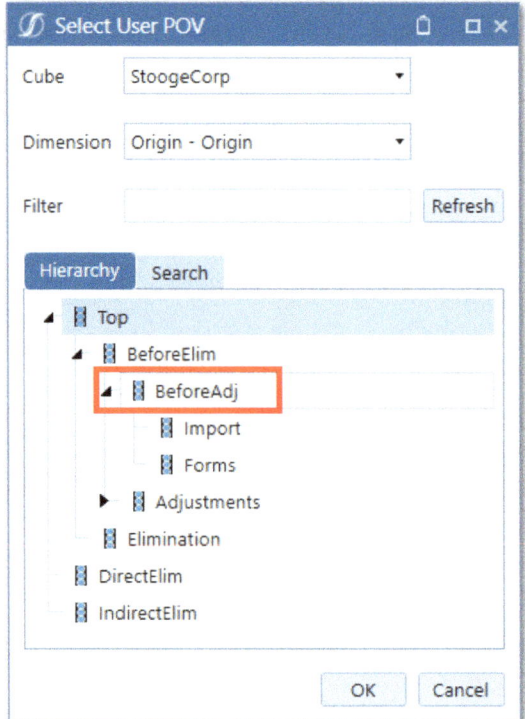

Figure 3.23

If an amount exists on the `Import` Member, then the difference between that amount and the typed in amount on `BeforeAdj` is written to the `Forms` Member. This allows Users to easily make adjustments to calculated data, preserving an audit trail of what was calculated versus adjusted. If Calculations are written to `Forms`, then this does not work as cleanly. When a User types a number at `BeforeAdj`, the entire calculated amount would be overwritten, destroying the audit trail of the originally calculated number.

Other issues can exist when calculated data is written to the same intersection as imported data. A situation may arise where data is imported to `Import` before a Calculation runs which writes to `Import` at the same intersection. The calculated number would override what was imported. Conversely, imported data would clear out calculated data written to `Import`. Both of these situations are unwanted because data integrity is lost. Writing Calculations to `Forms` instead may solve the issue and be the best approach in some cases. However, it is generally not recommended to have both imported and calculated data write to the same intersection. Use a UD or Flow Member to make a separation between the data, which will prevent any chance of data integrity issues.

Always Collapse When Possible

While collapsing detail to `Forms` or `Import` is commonly used for the Origin Dimension, it can also apply to any other Dimension. When writing Calculations, it is important to consider each Dimension and inquire whether detail is needed for analytical or other purposes. If not, there is no reason to create unnecessary data records that can impair performance and bloat database size.

Origin, Flow, and Intercompany Dimensions are always almost collapsed. A useful technique is to save source and destination defaults to strings so that they can be reused across multiple Calculations.

```
'Save source and destination dimensions to variables to reuse
Dim sourceDims As String = "O#Top:I#Top:F#Top"
Dim destinationDims As String = "O#Import:I#None:F#EndBalLoad"

'Substitute the variables on the source and destination Member Scripts
Api.Data.Calculate("A#Sales:" & destinationDims & " = A#Price:" & sourceDims & " * A#Volume:" & sourceDims & "")
```

This can save time, improve consistency, and make Calculations more readable.

Remove NoData/Zeros

To prevent Calculations from creating Zeros or NoData cells, the `RemoveNoData` and `RemoveZeros` functions introduced in the previous chapter should be used within ADC functions.

- `RemoveNoData` – Removes cells with a `CellAmount` of `NoData`.
- `RemoveZeros` – Removes cells with a `CellAmount` of `NoData` and cells with a stored Zero.

Simply wrap `RemoveZeros` or `RemoveNoData` around the source script and all Zeros and NoData cells will be removed from the Data Buffer.

```
api.Data.Calculate("A#Sales = RemoveZeros(A#Price * A#Volume)")
```

You may be wondering why Calculations would create NoData or Zero cells. Let's look at an example.

		Jan 2021	Feb 2021
Price	⊟ BugZapper - Bug Zapper	10.00	20.00
	IndoorBugSpray - Indoor Bug Spray	5.00	
	OutdoorBugSpray - Outdoor Bug Spray	6.00	0.00
	BedBugKiller - Bed Bug Killer	12.00	
Volume	⊟ BugZapper - Bug Zapper	5.00	10.00
	IndoorBugSpray - Indoor Bug Spray	8.00	
	OutdoorBugSpray - Outdoor Bug Spray	7.00	
	BedBugKiller - Bed Bug Killer	4.00	

Figure 3.24

Figure 3.24 shows Price and Volume data in a YTD Scenario. Amounts were entered in January for several Products; in February, data was only entered for one Product. The Products with no data entered will appear as DerivedData with a Storage Type of StoredButNoActivity.

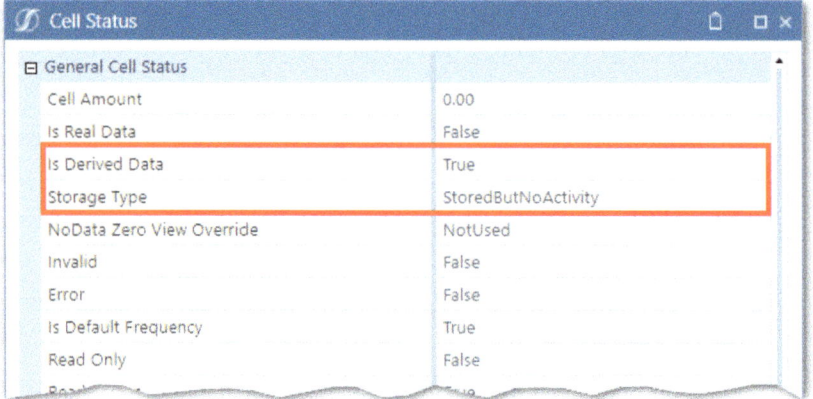

Figure 3.25

```
Dim priceDataBuffer As DataBuffer = api.Data.GetDataBufferUsingFormula("A#Price")
Dim volumeDataBuffer As DataBuffer = api.Data.GetDataBufferUsingFormula("A#Volume")
priceDataBuffer.LogDataBuffer(api,"Price Data Buffer", 100)
volumeDataBuffer.LogDataBuffer(api,"Volume Data Buffer", 100)
```

The above script logs the Price and Volume Data Buffers. Let's look at each Data Buffer:

Price Data Buffer:

Figure 3.26

Volume Data Buffer:

Figure 3.27

We can see the Stored, Derived, Zero Amount data cells in the Price and Volume Data Buffers.

Next, an ADC function will calculate the cost by performing Data Buffer math on the Price and Volume Data Buffers. We can simulate the result of the ADC function using a formula within the `GetDataBufferUsingFormula` function.

```
Dim salesDataBuffer As DataBuffer = api.Data.GetDataBufferUsingFormula("A#Price * A#Volume")
salesDataBuffer.LogDataBuffer(api,"Sales Data Buffer", 100)
```

api.Data.Calculate

Sales Result Data Buffer:

```
Common Members: F#All:O#All:I#All:U1#All:U2#All:U3#All:U4#All:U5#All:U6#All:U7#All:U8#All
A#XFCommon:F#EndBalLoad:O#Forms:I#None:U1#BugZapper:U2#None:U3#None:U4#None:U5#None:U6#None:U7#None:U8#None, 200.00, IsRealData, Input
A#XFCommon:F#EndBalLoad:O#Forms:I#None:U1#IndoorBugSpray:U2#None:U3#None:U4#None:U5#None:U6#None:U7#None:U8#None, 0.00, isDerivedData, Input
A#XFCommon:F#EndBalLoad:O#Forms:I#None:U1#OutdoorBugSpray:U2#None:U3#None:U4#None:U5#None:U6#None:U7#None:U8#None, 0.00, IsRealData, StoredButNoActivity
A#XFCommon:F#EndBalLoad:O#Forms:I#None:U1#BedBugKiller:U2#None:U3#None:U4#None:U5#None:U6#None:U7#None:U8#None, 0.00, IsDerivedData, StoredButNoActivity
```

Figure 3.28

The Cost Data Buffer shows six cells of which four have a status of `IsRealData`. This is interesting because even though the Cell Amount is zero, the data is saved to the Cube. To prevent these types of cells from being written to the Cube, we can use the `RemoveZeros` function when performing Data Buffer math.

```
Dim salesDataBufferRemoveZeros As DataBuffer = api.Data.GetDataBufferUsingFormula("RemoveZeros(A#Price * A#Volume)")
salesDataBufferRemoveZeros.LogDataBuffer(api,"Sales Data Buffer Remove Zeros", 100)
```

Figure 3.29

Logging the Result Data Buffer after using the `RemoveZeros` function shows the number of cells resulting from the Calculation have been reduced to one.

```
Common Members: F#All:O#All:I#All:U1#All:U2#All:U3#All:U4#All:U5#All:U6#All:U7#All:U8#All
A#XFCommon:F#EndBalLoad:O#Forms:I#None:U1#BugZapper:U2#None:U3#None:U4#None:U5#None:U6#None:U7#None:U8#None, 200.00, IsRealData, Input
```

Figure 3.30

The `RemoveZeros` function eliminated unnecessary data cells from our Result Data Buffer and should be used as a default for all ADC and `GetDataBuffer` functions.

Durable Data

Another way we can manipulate our Data Buffer cells before writing them to the Cube is to change the data Storage Type. By default, calculated data is stored with the Storage Type of `Calculation`.

We can see the Storage Type assigned to the data cells of our resulting Data Buffer, `A#Sales`.

```
Common Members: A#Sales:F#All:O#All:I#All:U1#All:U2#All:U3#All:U4#All:U5#All:U6#All:U7#All:U8#All
A#XFCommon:F#EndBalLoad:O#Import:I#None:U1#BugZapper:U2#None:U3#None:U4#None:U5#None:U6#None:U7#None:U8#None, 1,050.00, IsRealData, Calculation
A#XFCommon:F#EndBalLoad:O#Import:I#None:U1#IndoorBugSpray:U2#None:U3#None:U4#None:U5#None:U6#None:U7#None:U8#None, 1,400.00, IsRealData, Calculation
A#XFCommon:F#EndBalLoad:O#Import:I#None:U1#OutdoorBugSpray:U2#None:U3#None:U4#None:U5#None:U6#None:U7#None:U8#None, 1,750.00, IsRealData, Calculation
A#XFCommon:F#EndBalLoad:O#Import:I#None:U1#BedBugKiller:U2#None:U3#None:U4#None:U5#None:U6#None:U7#None:U8#None, 900.00, IsRealData, Calculation
A#XFCommon:F#EndBalLoad:O#Import:I#None:U1#StinkBugKiller:U2#None:U3#None:U4#None:U5#None:U6#None:U7#None:U8#None, 585.00, IsRealData, Calculation
A#XFCommon:F#EndBalLoad:O#Import:I#None:U1#MouseTrap:U2#None:U3#None:U4#None:U5#None:U6#None:U7#None:U8#None, 2,250.00, IsRealData, Calculation
A#XFCommon:F#EndBalLoad:O#Import:I#None:U1#GlueTrap:U2#None:U3#None:U4#None:U5#None:U6#None:U7#None:U8#None, 1,625.00, IsRealData, Calculation
A#XFCommon:F#EndBalLoad:O#Import:I#None:U1#RatPoison:U2#None:U3#None:U4#None:U5#None:U6#None:U7#None:U8#None, 1,260.00, IsRealData, Calculation
A#XFCommon:F#EndBalLoad:O#Import:I#None:U1#Termicide:U2#None:U3#None:U4#None:U5#None:U6#None:U7#None:U8#None, 750.00, IsRealData, Calculation
A#XFCommon:F#EndBalLoad:O#Import:I#None:U1#PestControl:U2#None:U3#None:U4#None:U5#None:U6#None:U7#None:U8#None, 3,000.00, IsRealData, Calculation
A#XFCommon:F#EndBalLoad:O#Import:I#None:U1#TermiteTreatment:U2#None:U3#None:U4#None:U5#None:U6#None:U7#None:U8#None, 2,500.00, IsRealData, Calculation
A#XFCommon:F#EndBalLoad:O#Import:I#None:U1#Commercial:U2#None:U3#None:U4#None:U5#None:U6#None:U7#None:U8#None, 2,000.00, IsRealData, Calculation
A#XFCommon:F#EndBalLoad:O#Import:I#None:U1#BugBeaters:U2#None:U3#None:U4#None:U5#None:U6#None:U7#None:U8#None, 4,000.00, IsRealData, Calculation
```

Figure 3.31

Viewing the Cell Status in a Cube View also shows the Storage Type of Calculation.

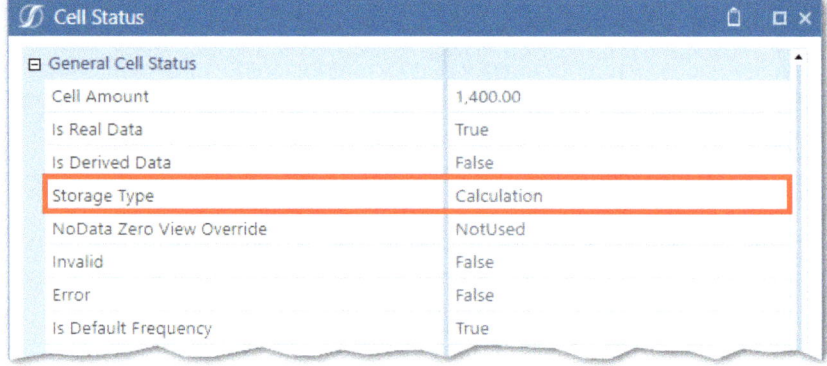

Figure 3.32

Data with this Storage Type will be cleared in the Clear Previously Calculated Data step of the DUCS. The assumption is that the Calculation Script will run again and re-calculate the data. We can prevent the clearing of this data from happening by changing the Storage Type to Durable Calculation. Data with this Storage Type will not be cleared by the DUCS.

The ADC function will accept an optional Boolean argument for `isDurableData`.

```
▲ 3 of 3 ▼   Sub DataApi.Calculate(formula As String, isDurableCalculatedData As Boolean)
```

Figure 3.33

This is set to `False` by default. Setting it to `True` will change the Storage Type of the resultant Data Buffer. This is illustrated by modifying our example:

```
api.Data.Calculate("A#Sales = A#Price * A#Volume",True)
```

The logged `A#Sales` Data Buffer (post-Calculation execution):

Figure 3.34

The new Storage Type:

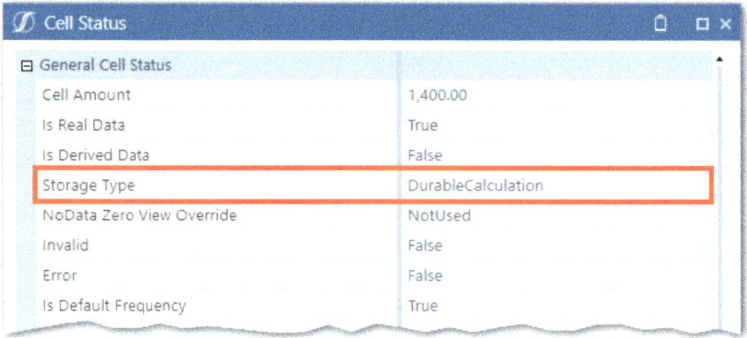

Figure 3.35

Clear Calculated Data

When using durable calculated data, it's important to include a clear data script to preserve data integrity as running Calculations multiple times could leave behind data from previous Calculations. This can be done with the **api.Data.ClearCalculatedData** function. This function accepts arguments for the types of data you want to clear as well as Dimension filters similar to the ADC function. You can specify if you want to clear translated, consolidated, and/or durable data.

```
Syntax:
Public Sub ClearCalculatedData(ByVal clearCalculatedData As Boolean, ByVal clearTranslatedData As Boolean, ByVal clearConsolidatedData As Boolean, ByVal clearDurableCalculatedData As Boolean, Optional ByVal accountFilter As String, Optional ByVal flowFilter As String, Optional ByVal originFilter As String, Optional ByVal icFilter As String, Optional ByVal ud1Filter As String, Optional ByVal ud2Filter As String, Optional ByVal ud3Filter As String, Optional ByVal ud4Filter As String, Optional ByVal ud5Filter As String, Optional ByVal ud6Filter As String, Optional ByVal ud7Filter As String, Optional ByVal ud8Filter As String)
```

Figure 3.36

It is good practice to mirror the destination Member Script and any Dimension filters from your ADC function in your `ClearCalculatedData` function.

```
api.Data.ClearCalculatedData(True,True,True,True,"A#Sales",,,"U1#Insects.Base")

api.Data.Calculate("A#Sales = A#Price * A#Volume",,,,,"U1#Insects.Base")
```

Figure 3.37

In doing this, we can be confident we are always clearing the data generated by the previous ADC function before calculating new data.

Custom Calculate

The `ClearCalculatedData` function and `isDurableData = True` is almost always used in conjunction with Calculations that are executed in a **Custom Calculate**. This is because data is not automatically cleared as it is in the DUCS. Conversely, writing the data as `Durable` ensures that the DUCS does not clear the Custom Calculate data. The Custom Calculate function also enables a few other features, which DUCS Calculations do not have.

Api.Pov Functions

Earlier, we demonstrated using POV functions for Data Unit Dimensions to help limit the scope of Calculations. We also mentioned that `api.Pov.Account` would not work in the same way because Account is in the Data Buffer and Data Buffers are filtered differently.

In Custom Calculate functions, Account-level POV Dimensions can be set within the Data Management step properties and referenced in the Calculation Script.

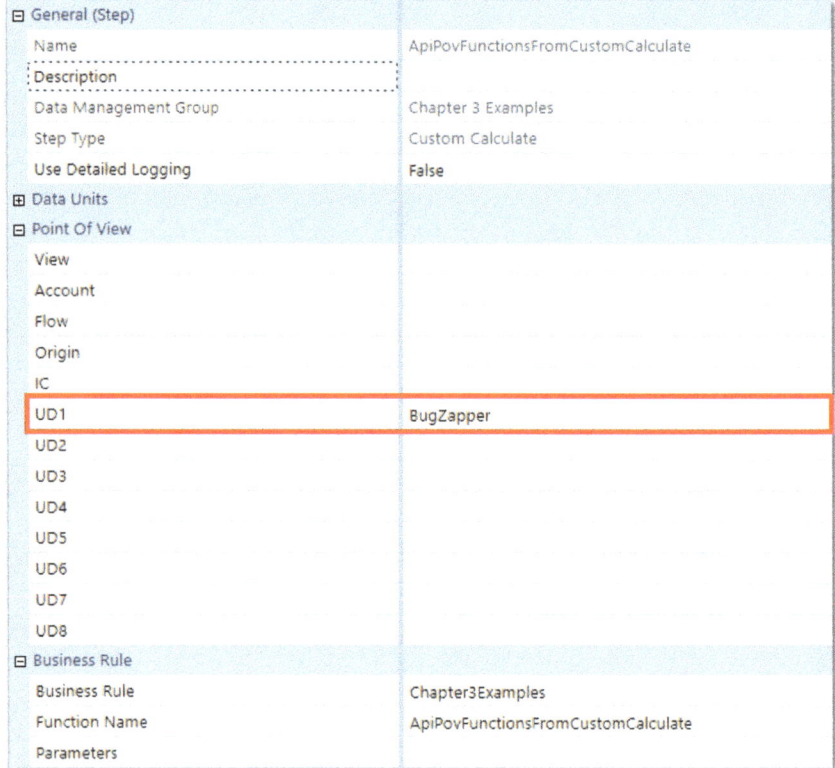

Figure 3.38

The POV from the Data Management step is set to a variable which is referenced in both the Clear Data and ADC functions.

```
'Get the product from Custom Calculate properties
Dim povUD1 As String = api.Pov.UD1.Name
'Clear data for the Sales Account and UD1 from POV
api.Data.ClearCalculatedData(True,True,True,True,"A#Sales",,,"U1#" & povUD1 & "")
'Calculate sales for the POV UD1 only
api.Data.Calculate("A#Sales:U1#" & povUD1 & " = A#Price:U1#" & povUD1 & " * A#Volume:U1#" & povUD1 & "",True)
```

Let's take this example a step further and make the POV User-driven by linking the Calculation to a Dashboard.

Linking to a Dashboard

First, a simple Dashboard is setup, which a User can interact with.

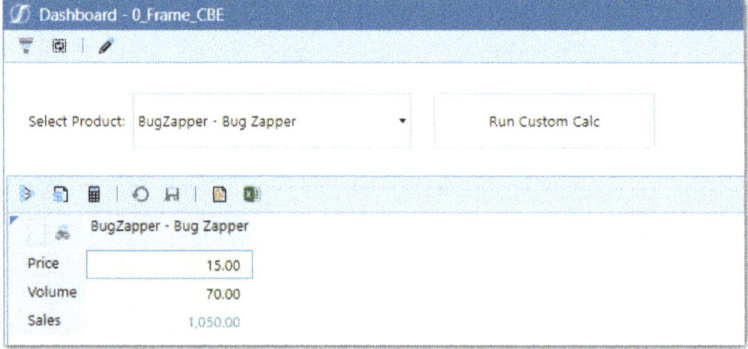

Figure 3.39

A User can select a Product (UD1) from a combo box, which will change the Product displayed in the Cube View. A button will execute the Custom Calculate function.

Combo Box

The combo box references a **Member List Parameter** which is defined as U1#Insects.Base.

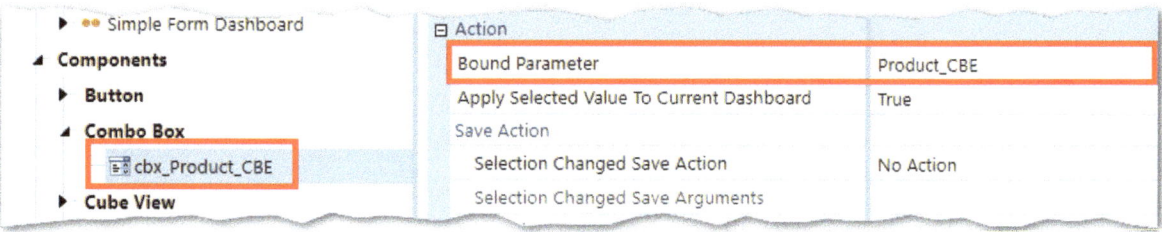

Figure 3.40

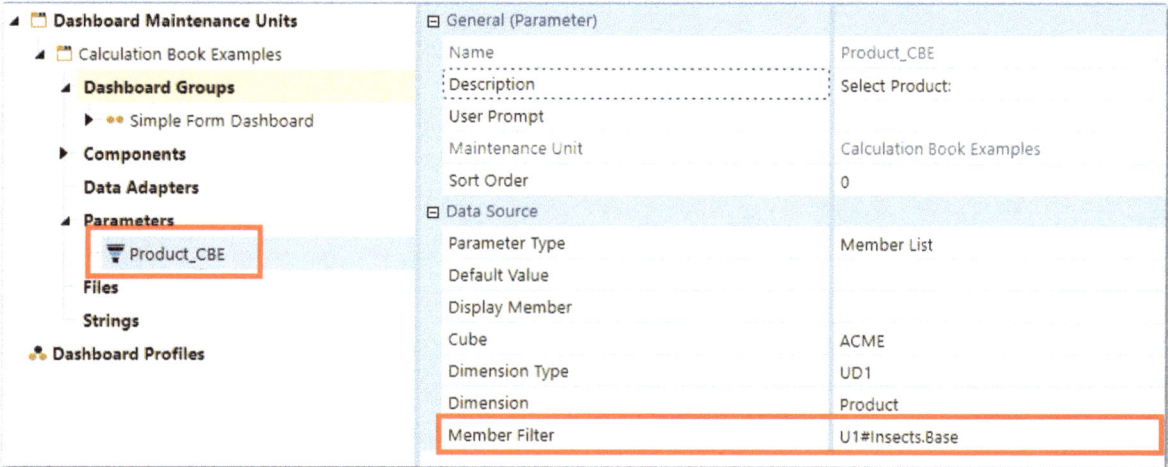

Figure 3.41

Button

The Dashboard button calls the Data Management Sequence and the parameter is referenced in the Name Value pairs.

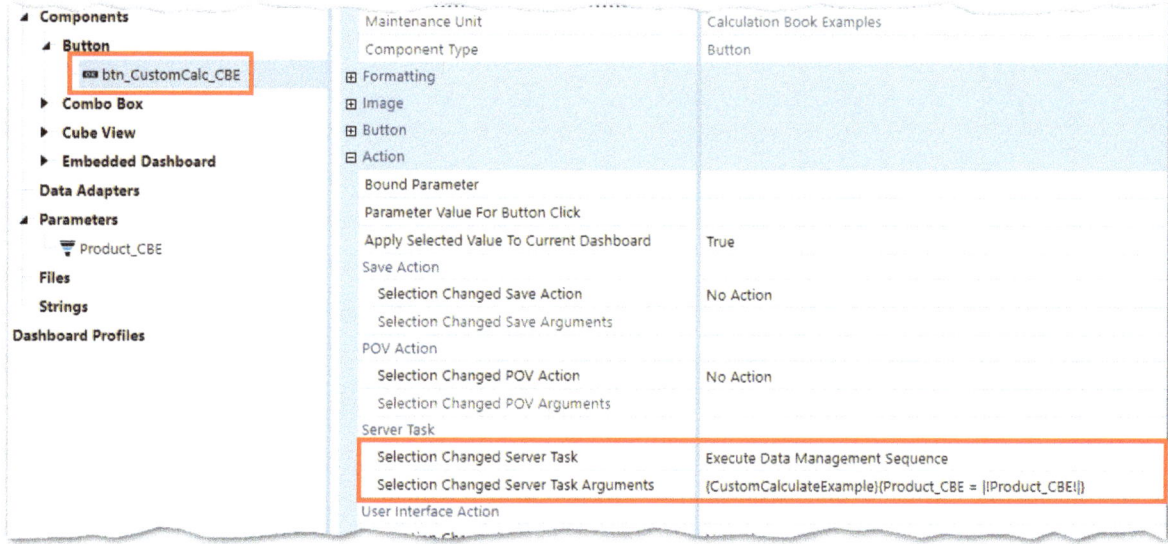

Figure 3.42

Chapter 3

Data Management Step

The Data Management Step will now have the parameter reference in the UD1 POV field.

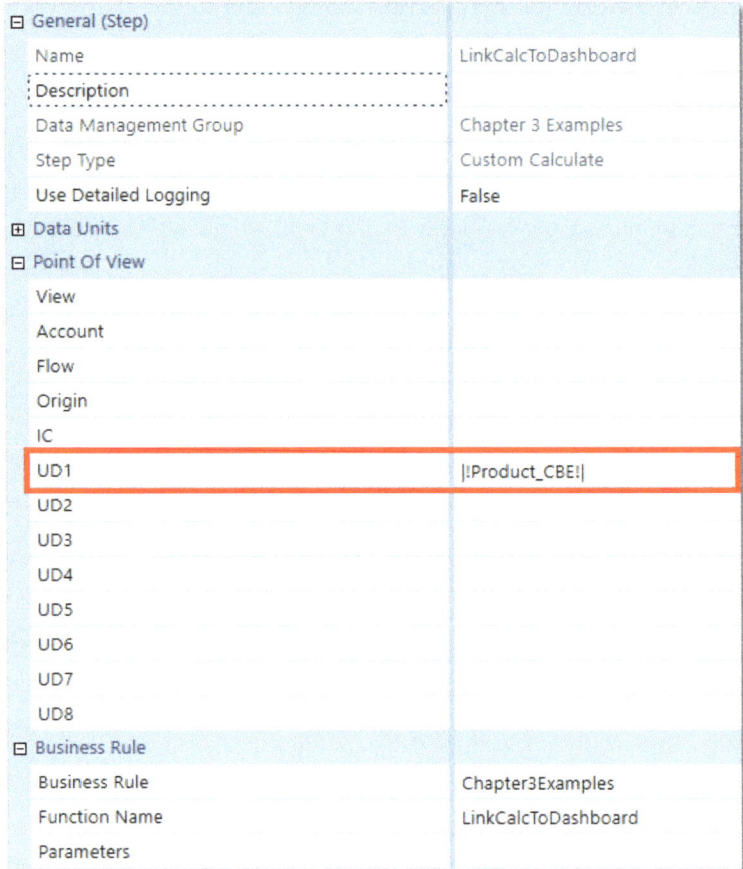

Figure 3.43

Execution

Now, when the button is clicked, the Product selection from the combo box will be transferred into the script. The Calculation scope is now User-driven, reduced in scope to only one selected Product.

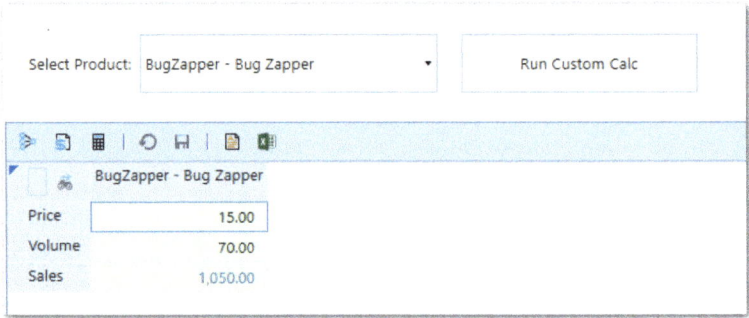

Figure 3.44

Advanced Filtering with Eval

The examples described above have conveyed the various options we have to filter Data Buffers used in Calculations to reduce scope. But what happens when we have filtering requirements that the above options don't address? What if we need to filter data cells by Cell Amount, or run complex logic on the Dimension Members of the data cells within our Data Buffers?

OneStream accommodates these requirements using a function called **Eval**. When implementing ADC functions, Eval provides the ability to evaluate (that's where the Eval moniker comes from) the individual data cells in any Data Buffer. The Eval function can even be used to filter one operand in the formula instead of filtering the entire result.

Putting It To Use

To put this to use, simply precede any Member Script in an ADC with an `Eval` wrapped in parentheses.

```
api.Data.Calculate("A#Sales = Eval(A#Price) * A#Volume")
```

or:

```
api.Data.Calculate("A#Sales = Eval(A#Price * A#Volume)")
```

Next, we must call a subfunction which we will add to our Calculation Script. The subfunction is referenced as another optional argument in the ADC function.

```
Sub DataApi.Calculate(formula As String, onEvalDataBuffer As EvalDataBufferDelegate, Optional userState As Object)
```

Figure 3.45

The syntax for the `EvalDataBufferDelegate` is `AddressOf SubFunctionName`. The standard subfunction name is usually `OnEvalDataBuffer` but this could be changed to any name you like.

```
api.Data.Calculate("A#Sales = Eval(A#Price) * A#Volume",AddressOf OnEvalDataBuffer)
```

The subfunction is then called below.

```
Private Sub OnEvalDataBuffer(ByVal api As FinanceRulesApi, ByVal evalName As String, ByVal eventArgs As EvalDataBufferEventArgs)
    'Make sure the Result Data Buffer is empty
    eventArgs.DataBufferResult.DataBufferCells.Clear
    'Check to make sure the Data Buffer isn't empty before continuing
    If Not eventArgs.DataBuffer1 Is Nothing Then
        'Loop through the cells of the Data Buffer
        For Each cell As DataBufferCell In eventArgs.DataBuffer1.DataBufferCells.Values
            'Check the cell amount and if greater than 100 add it to the result Data Buffer
            If (Not cell.CellAmount > 100) Then
                eventArgs.DataBufferResult.SetCell(api.si,cell)
            End If
```

Figure 3.46

The `Api`, `evalName`, and `eventArgs` arguments are required to be supplied for this function to work. The logic within the sub function will do the following:

- Loop through the data cells of the Eval Data Buffer (from the ADC function).
- Perform some logic on each data cell.

Chapter 3

- Add the data cell to the Result Data Buffer object retrieved from `eventArgs`.

EventArgs

`Eventargs` is supplied to the sub function and contains various information that is passed between the ADC function and the `Eval` subfunction. It is used to access various objects related to the Data Buffer that our `Eval` function is wrapped around. We can retrieve the Data Buffer itself as well as the `DestinationInfo` and the `ResultDataBuffer`.

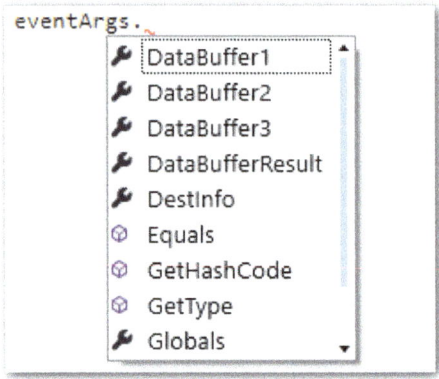

Figure 3.47

Eval Use Case

Let's go through an example to better illustrate the above. Let's say we want to remove all data cells from our `A#Price` Data Buffer with a Cell Amount greater than 500. This is a somewhat arbitrary example but it's nice and straightforward for illustration purposes. This would not be possible using any of the other filtering Methods described so far, so we have a good use case for the `Eval`.

First, let's look at our Price Data Buffer before the `Eval` is applied:

```
Common Members: A#Price:F#All:O#All:I#All:U1#All:U2#All:U3#All:U4#All:U5#All:U6#All:U7#All:U8#All
A#XFCommon:F#EndBalLoad:O#Import:I#None:U1#BugZapper:U2#None:U3#None:U4#None:U5#None:U6#None:U7#None:U8#None, 15.00, IsRealData, Input
A#XFCommon:F#EndBalLoad:O#Import:I#None:U1#IndoorBugSpray:U2#None:U3#None:U4#None:U5#None:U6#None:U7#None:U8#None, 8.00, IsRealData, Input
A#XFCommon:F#EndBalLoad:O#Import:I#None:U1#OutdoorBugSpray:U2#None:U3#None:U4#None:U5#None:U6#None:U7#None:U8#None, 10.00, IsRealData, Input
A#XFCommon:F#EndBalLoad:O#Import:I#None:U1#BedBugKiller:U2#None:U3#None:U4#None:U5#None:U6#None:U7#None:U8#None, 12.00, IsRealData, Input
A#XFCommon:F#EndBalLoad:O#Import:I#None:U1#StinkBugKiller:U2#None:U3#None:U4#None:U5#None:U6#None:U7#None:U8#None, 13.00, IsRealData, Input
A#XFCommon:F#EndBalLoad:O#Import:I#None:U1#MouseTrap:U2#None:U3#None:U4#None:U5#None:U6#None:U7#None:U8#None, 4.50, IsRealData, Input
A#XFCommon:F#EndBalLoad:O#Import:I#None:U1#GlueTrap:U2#None:U3#None:U4#None:U5#None:U6#None:U7#None:U8#None, 6.50, IsRealData, Input
A#XFCommon:F#EndBalLoad:O#Import:I#None:U1#RatPoison:U2#None:U3#None:U4#None:U5#None:U6#None:U7#None:U8#None, 9.00, IsRealData, Input
A#XFCommon:F#EndBalLoad:O#Import:I#None:U1#Termicide:U2#None:U3#None:U4#None:U5#None:U6#None:U7#None:U8#None, 12.50, IsRealData, Input
A#XFCommon:F#EndBalLoad:O#Import:I#None:U1#PestControl:U2#None:U3#None:U4#None:U5#None:U6#None:U7#None:U8#None, 150.00, IsRealData, Input
A#XFCommon:F#EndBalLoad:O#Import:I#None:U1#TermiteTreatment:U2#None:U3#None:U4#None:U5#None:U6#None:U7#None:U8#None, 250.00, IsRealData, Input
A#XFCommon:F#EndBalLoad:O#Import:I#None:U1#Commercial:U2#None:U3#None:U4#None:U5#None:U6#None:U7#None:U8#None, 400.00, IsRealData, Input
A#XFCommon:F#EndBalLoad:O#Import:I#None:U1#BugBeaters:U2#None:U3#None:U4#None:U5#None:U6#None:U7#None:U8#None, 800.00, IsRealData, Input
```

Figure 3.48

The highlighted data cell within the Data Buffer is the only one that meets the criteria of being > 500. This is the data cell we want to remove using the `Eval`.

First, we must modify the ADC function by wrapping the `Eval` keyword around our `A#Price` operand and add the `EvalDataBufferDelegate` argument.

```
api.Data.Calculate("A#Cost = Eval(A#Price) * A#Volume", AddressOf OnEvalDataBuffer)
```

Finally, we add our subfunction.

```vbnet
360 Private Sub OnEvalDataBuffer(ByVal api As FinanceRulesApi, ByVal evalName As String, ByVal eventArgs As EvalDataBufferEventArgs)
361     'Make sure the Result Data Buffer is empty
362     eventArgs.DataBufferResult.DataBufferCells.Clear
363     'Check to make sure the Data Buffer isn't empty before continuing
364     If Not eventArgs.DataBuffer1 Is Nothing Then
365         'Loop through the cells of the Data Buffer
366         For Each cell As DataBufferCell In eventArgs.DataBuffer1.DataBufferCells.Values
367             'Check the cell amount and if greater than 500 add it to the result Data Buffer
368             If (Not cell.CellAmount > 500) Then
369                 eventArgs.DataBufferResult.SetCell(api.si,cell)
370             End If
371         Next
372     End If
373 End Sub
```

When the ADC function runs, the `Eval` function will run on the Price Data Buffer and the logic within our subfunction will filter out any cells with `Amounts` greater than 500. Data Buffer math will then be performed on the modified `A#Price` Data Buffer and the `A#Volume` Data Buffer. The steps performed by the Calculation Engine are:

- The `A#Price` Data Buffer is retrieved from storage.
- The `Eval` function filters the `A#Price` Data Buffer.
- The `A#Volume` Data Buffer is retrieved from storage.
- Data Buffer math multiplies the modified Price Data Buffer and Volume Data Buffer together and creates a new Result Data Buffer.
- The Sales Account from the destination script is added to the new Result Data Buffer.
- The Result Data Buffer is saved to the Cube.

Breakdown of OnEvalDataBuffer

The script that runs in the `OnEvalDataBuffer` function may look intimidating to unseasoned coders. In reality, what the code is actually doing is quite simple. Let's break down the code, line by line.

Lines 360-364

```vbnet
360 Private Sub OnEvalDataBuffer(ByVal api As FinanceRulesApi, ByVal evalName As String, ByVal eventArgs As EvalDataBufferEventArgs)
361     'Make sure the Result Data Buffer is empty
362     eventArgs.DataBufferResult.DataBufferCells.Clear
363     'Check to make sure the Data Buffer isn't empty before continuing
364     If Not eventArgs.DataBuffer1 Is Nothing Then
```

The subfunction is called and the Result Data Buffer is cleared to ensure we start with an empty set; the Result Data Buffer will be filled with new cells. The Price Data Buffer is checked to ensure it is not empty before continuing.

Lines 365-373

```vbnet
365     'Loop through the cells of the Data Buffer
366     For Each cell As DataBufferCell In eventArgs.DataBuffer1.DataBufferCells.Values
367         'Check the cell amount and if greater than 500 add it to the result Data Buffer
368         If (Not cell.CellAmount > 500) Then
369             eventArgs.DataBufferResult.SetCell(api.si,cell)
370         End If
371     Next
372 End If
373 End Sub
```

Chapter 3

The cells of the Price Data Buffer are looped through, using a `For Each` loop. Each iteration of the loop will be one of the data cells in the `A#Price` Data Buffer. For each iteration of the loop, we now have access to data cell information such as Dimension Members (contained in the `DataBufferCellPk`), Storage Type, Cell Status, and Cell Amount.

Each data cell is then checked to see if its amount is greater than 500. If it is not, it is added to the Result Data Buffer which is returned to the ADC function.

Returning to the Api.Data.Calculate Function

The manipulated Price Data Buffer is then returned to the ADC function where Data Buffer math will multiply it by the Volume Data Buffer with the result writing to the Cost Account.

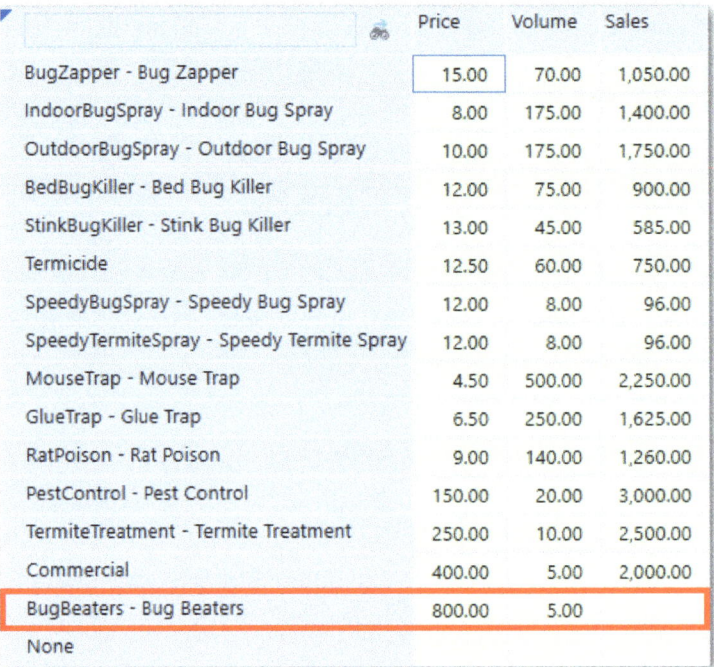

Figure 3.49

We can see that BugBeaters, with a Price greater than 500, was excluded from the Calculation result.

Eval2 Function

As shown above, the `Eval` function allows you to analyze the individual cells within one Data Buffer. The `Eval2` function can be used to analyze two Data Buffers and even compare cells between them. `Eval2` is the same as `Eval` except two Member Scripts are specified and separated by a comma. Using the `Eval2`, both Data Buffers can be analyzed in the subfunction.

Use Case

For the Budget Scenario, Sales are calculated across Products. Advertising Expense, meanwhile, is based on a fixed percentage of Sales of 10% for existing Products and 20% for new Products. Curly is hoping to automate this process, so he has more time to wisecrack with Moe and Larry.

To accomplish this, new Sales could be determined by comparing the Actual Sales to Budget Sales and determining which Products had Sales in the Budget but nothing in Actuals.

The `Eval2` function can be used to retrieve the Sales Data Buffer for the last period of Actuals and the current Budget and compare the cells within the two Data Buffers. If a cell exists in the Budget

Scenario, but not in the Actual Scenario, we can safely assume that it is a new Product and can apply the Advertising Expense percentage accordingly.

The Cube View, below, shows the Sales by Product for Month 12 of Actuals and M1 of the Budget Scenario. Our Calculation will populate the last column for Advertising costs.

	Actual Sales	Budget Sales	Advertising
BugZapper - Bug Zapper	13,150.00	1,050.00	
IndoorBugSpray - Indoor Bug Spray	15,780.00	1,400.00	
OutdoorBugSpray - Outdoor Bug Spray	19,725.00	1,750.00	
BedBugKiller - Bed Bug Killer	10,520.00	900.00	
StinkBugKiller - Stink Bug Killer	6,575.00	585.00	
Termicide	9,205.00	750.00	
SpeedyBugSpray - Speedy Bug Spray		96.00	
SpeedyTermiteSpray - Speedy Termite Spray		96.00	
MouseTrap - Mouse Trap	26,300.00	2,250.00	
GlueTrap - Glue Trap	19,725.00	1,625.00	
RatPoison - Rat Poison	15,780.00	1,260.00	
PestControl - Pest Control	28,930.00	3,000.00	
TermiteTreatment - Termite Treatment	23,012.50	2,500.00	
Commercial	10,914.50	2,000.00	
BugBeaters - Bug Beaters	18,410.00	4,000.00	

Figure 3.50

The Code

An `api.Data.Calculate` is used with the `Eval2` function and the two Data Buffers which we want to compare.

```
'Compare Actual and Budget Data Buffers using Eval2 and apply a percentage based on sales
api.Data.Calculate("A#52030 = Eval2(S#Budget, T#POVPriorYearM12:S#Actual:V#YTD)", AddressOf OnEvalDataBuffer2)
```

The `OnEvalDataBuffer2` subfunction is called from the ADC and shown below.

```
558 Private Sub OnEvalDataBuffer2(ByVal api As FinanceRulesApi, ByVal evalName As String, ByVal eventArgs As EvalDataBufferEventArgs)
559     'Start with an empty result buffer
560     eventArgs.DataBufferResult.DataBufferCells.Clear()
561     'Check to make sure both Data Buffers aren't empty first
562     If Not eventArgs.DataBuffer1 Is Nothing And Not eventArgs.DataBuffer2 Is Nothing Then
563         'For each cell in DataBuffer1, try to find a number for the same intersection In DataBuffer2.
564         For Each cell1 As DataBufferCell In eventArgs.DataBuffer1.DataBufferCells.Values
565             If (Not cell1.CellStatus.IsNoData) Then
566                 'Check if the sales data is in the Actual Data Buffer
567                 Dim cell2 As DataBufferCell = eventArgs.DataBuffer2.GetCell(api.SI,cell1.DataBufferCellPk)
568                 If cell2 Is Nothing Then 'This is a new product
569                     Dim resultCell As New DataBufferCell(cell1)
570                     resultCell.CellAmount = cell1.CellAmount * .2
571                     eventArgs.DataBufferResult.SetCell(api.SI,resultCell, False)
572                 Else 'The cell exists in the Actual Data Buffer so this product is not new
573                     Dim resultCell As New DataBufferCell(cell1)
574                     resultCell.CellAmount = cell1.CellAmount * .1
575                     eventArgs.DataBufferResult.SetCell(api.SI, resultCell,False)
576                 End If
577             End If
578         Next
579     End If
580 End Sub
```

Chapter 3

Breakdown

Lines 558-562

```
558  Private Sub OnEvalDataBuffer2(ByVal api As FinanceRulesApi, ByVal evalName As String, ByVal eventArgs As EvalDataBufferEventArgs)
559     'Start with an empty result buffer
560     eventArgs.DataBufferResult.DataBufferCells.Clear()
561     'Check to make sure both Data Buffers aren't empty first
562     If Not eventArgs.DataBuffer1 Is Nothing And Not eventArgs.DataBuffer2 Is Nothing Then
```

The `EventArgs` function is part of the `Eval` functionality and is used to access the Data Buffer objects we will be working with.

The `OnEvalDataBuffer2` sub-function is called and the Result Data Buffer is called from `EventArgs` and cleared to ensure we start with an empty set. The Result Data Buffer will be filled with new cells. Next, both Data Buffers are checked to ensure they are not empty. If they are empty the Calculation will not continue and processing time will be saved.

Lines 563-567

```
563     'For each cell in DataBuffer1, try to find a number for the same intersection In DataBuffer2.
564         For Each cell1 As DataBufferCell In eventArgs.DataBuffer1.DataBufferCells.Values
565             If (Not cell1.CellStatus.IsNoData) Then
566                 'Check if the sales data is in the Actual Data Buffer
567                 Dim cell2 As DataBufferCell = eventArgs.DataBuffer2.GetCell(api.SI,cell1.DataBufferCellPk)
```

The first Data Buffer (`S#Budget`) specified after `Eval2` in the ADC function is accessed through `EventArgs` as `DataBuffer1`. The cells of this Data Buffer will be looped through. Each cell in the loop will be check against the `S#Actual` Data Buffer using the `GetCell` function. If the cell exists, it will be stored in the `cell2` variable.

Lines 568-576

```
568                 If cell2 Is Nothing Then 'This is a new product
569                     Dim resultCell As New DataBufferCell(cell1)
570                     resultCell.CellAmount = cell1.CellAmount * .2
571                     eventArgs.DataBufferResult.SetCell(api.SI,resultCell, False)
572                 Else 'The cell exists in the Actual Data Buffer so this product is not new
573                     Dim resultCell As New DataBufferCell(cell1)
574                     resultCell.CellAmount = cell1.CellAmount * .1
575                     eventArgs.DataBufferResult.SetCell(api.SI, resultCell,False)
576                 End If
```

The `cell2` variable is then checked to see if it exists. If it doesn't, we know that this is a new Product and we can calculate our result cell (`A#Advertising`) as the Budget Sales (`cell1`) multiplied by .2. The Result Cell Amount is set and then it is added to the `DataBufferResult` object.

The Result

After the `OnEvalDataBuffer2` subfunction runs, the `DataBufferResult` is written to the destination script of `A#Advertising`.

Figure 3.51

We can see that our logic was correctly applied. We have now automated our advertising cost Budget Calculation.

Conclusion

As described in the examples above, OneStream's Data Buffer math is extremely powerful in that it can be used to process hundreds or thousands of numbers with just one simple equation. Without Data Buffer math, or an equivalent scripting capability, a large multidimensional financial application would not be feasible because every intersection would need to be considered separately.

In addition to facilitating powerful Data Buffer math, the `api.Data.Calculate` function has built-in capabilities that allow you to manipulate the resulting data cells. This affords the Calculation writer with flexibility and precision when attempting to serve the complex financial processes employed by today's corporations.

4
The Data Buffer Cell Loop

In your Calculation-writing travels, there will be cases where ultimate flexibility is necessary, whether it's for tackling complex logic or improving Calculation performance. For all its power, the `api.Data.Calculate` function can prove inadequate in some situations. Another technique, the **Data Buffer Cell Loop** (abbreviated to DBCL), will prove to be a valuable tool to have on your belt.

What it lacks in simplicity, the DBCL makes up for in flexibility. It is similar in concept to the `Eval` function explained in the previous chapter; however, the DBCL abandons the `api.Data.Calculate` (ADC) function altogether. We can think of this Method as the long-hand, manual way of doing what the ADC function does behind the scenes.

The Recipe

I always hate how – when I look for a recipe online – I must first scroll through a long, drawn-out story of how the author stayed in a small, Spanish village and discovered a love for paella. I'll spare you the personal anecdote and cut right to the chase.

Ingredients

The DBCL technique requires a mix of coding concepts and API functions. Here is what we need at a minimum:

- New `DataBuffer` object
- `DestinationInfo` object
- `api.Data.GetDataBuffer` or `api.Data.GetDataBufferUsingFilter` function
- `For each`, `Next` loop, or `For` loop
- `api.Data.GetDataCell` function (three variations are explained)
- Data Buffer Cell objects
- `api.Data.SetDataBuffer` function

Directions

1. First, create new Data Buffer and `DestinationInfo` objects and set them aside for later.
2. Next, create a Data Buffer and loop through each cell.
3. While inside the loop, create a Result Data Buffer Cell and change its properties with the desired logic.
4. Add the Result Data Buffer Cell to the new Data Buffer created in step 1.
5. Exit the loop and write the new Data Buffer to the Cube.
6. Execute a Calculation and enjoy your freshly-calculated data with a garnish of lemon and parsley.

Chapter 4

Example

Like any good cooking show, we have the finished dish ready to pull out of the oven.

```vb
'Create a result data buffer and destination info to add the cells to later
Dim resultDataBuffer As DataBuffer = New DataBuffer()
Dim destinationInfo As ExpressionDestinationInfo = api.Data.GetExpressionDestinationInfo("")

'Declare starting data buffer to loop through
Dim priceDataBuffer As DataBuffer = api.Data.GetDataBufferUsingFormula("RemoveZeros(A#Price:O#Top:I#Top)")

'Retrieve the Sales Account Id before the loop so we don't retrieve it for each iteration
Dim salesId As Integer = api.Members.GetMemberId(dimtypeid.Account, "Sales")

'Loop through the cells of the data buffer
For Each sourceCell As DataBufferCell In priceDataBuffer.DataBufferCells.Values
    'Retrieve the volume data cell using source cell names
    Dim volumeDataCell As DataCell
    volumeDataCell = api.Data.GetDataCell("F#EndBalLoad:I#Top:O#Top:A#Volume:" & _
                                "U1#" & sourceCell.DataBufferCellPk.GetUD1Name(api) & ":" & _
                                "U2#" & sourceCell.DataBufferCellPk.GetUD2Name(api) & ":" & _
                                "U3#" & sourceCell.DataBufferCellPk.GetUD3Name(api) & ":" & _
                                "U4#" & sourceCell.DataBufferCellPk.GetUD4Name(api) & ":" & _
                                "U5#" & sourceCell.DataBufferCellPk.GetUD5Name(api) & ":" & _
                                "U6#" & sourceCell.DataBufferCellPk.GetUD6Name(api) & ":" & _
                                "U7#" & sourceCell.DataBufferCellPk.GetUD7Name(api) & ":" & _
                                "U8#" & sourceCell.DataBufferCellPk.GetUD8Name(api) & "")

    'Create a new result cell to eventually add to the result data buffer
    'The cell properties of the source cell will be inherited
    Dim resultCell As New DataBufferCell(sourceCell)

    'Set the result cell to the destination account
    resultcell.DataBufferCellPk.OriginId = DimConstants.Import
    resultCell.DataBufferCellPk.ICId = DimConstants.None
    resultCell.DataBufferCellPk.AccountId = salesId

    'Do the logic to calculate the result amount
    resultCell.CellAmount = sourceCell.CellAmount * volumeDataCell.CellAmount

    'Set the target members for the XFCommon members
    resultcell.DataBufferCellPk.OriginId = DimConstants.Import
    resultCell.DataBufferCellPk.ICId = DimConstants.None
    resultDataBuffer.SetCell(si,resultCell)
Next

'Save the Data Buffer using the Result Data Buffer and Destination Info
api.Data.SetDataBuffer(resultDataBuffer,destinationInfo)
```

The above example replicates the result of the earlier `api.Data.Calculate("A#Sales = A#Price * A#Volume")` example. Think of the DBCL as the long-hand version of the ADC function. While using this Method is unnecessarily complex for this use case, it helps to illustrate the key components. Let's break it down.

ResultDataBuffer

We've already learned that a Data Buffer is just a Dictionary of data cells, like a spreadsheet. The Result Data Buffer is an empty Dictionary (spreadsheet) to which we will add data cells later in the process.

DestinationInfo

The Destination Info object is a required parameter in the `SetDataBuffer` function, which is used – at the end – to write the data to the Cube. This object will specify Dimension Members via a string, to which the Result Data Buffer will be written to. This part is the equivalent of the left side of the formula in an ADC function.

Our example passes in an empty string for the Member Filter, as we will define all destination Dimensions in the result cell. Later in this chapter, I will explain how to use `DestinationInfo` instead of setting the Dimensions for each result cell.

The Data Buffer Cell Loop

GetDataBufferUsingFormula

To state the obvious, the Data Buffer Cell Loop requires a Data Buffer to loop through. This can be done using one of two API functions.

1. `api.Data.GetDataBuffer`
2. `api.Data.GetDataBufferUsingFormula`

Your author prefers to use the `api.Data.GetDataBufferUsingFormula` as it allows formulas (Data Buffer math) and the use of functions like `FilterMember` and `RemoveZeros`.

Think of this part as the right side of the formula in the ADC function. Typically, one of the Member Script operands is used to define the loop. For this example, we could have theoretically looped through the `A#Volume` Data Buffer instead of the `A#Price`, or looped through the result of `A#Price * A#Volume`, and achieved the same result.

For, Each Loop

The Data Buffer from the previous step is a Dictionary of data cells. A `For, Each` loop allows looping through each data cell in the Dictionary. The idea is that we will execute some logic on the source data cell properties and/or use the Source Data Cell Amount in a Calculation.

Result Cell

As the loop iterates through the source cells, result cells will be added to the Result Data Buffer. Before that can happen, the result cell must first be brought into existence. When brought into existence, that result cell will be completely devoid of any properties such as Dimension Members, Cell Amount, and Cell Status. Each of those properties must be defined before we try to write the cell to the Cube, or an error will be thrown. Instead of defining each property individually, it can sometimes be useful to have the result cell inherit the properties of the source cell.

```
Dim resultCell As New DataBufferCell(sourceCell)
```

At this point, the result cell and source cell are identical copies, with the idea being the result cell properties will be modified without impacting the source cell. This often makes sense because the Result Data Buffer usually shares most of its Dimension properties with the Source Data Buffers. In the `api.Data.Calculate("A#Cost = A#Price * A#Volume")` example, the Dimension properties are identical between all three with the exception of Account.

> **Note**: The result cell needs to be declared inside the loop as `New` so that the same cell is not reused for each loop iteration.

GetDataCell

Performing Calculations will require numbers from other data cells. To get numbers from other data cells, the `api.Data.GetDataCell` function is deployed. This function requires a Member Script or a DataCellPk, both of which define all Account-level Dimensions. The Data Unit is inherited from the POV and can be overwritten if there is a need to retrieve data outside the current Data Unit being processed by adding those Dimensions to the Member Script or `DataCellPk`. Again, we can use some information from the source cell to help us define those Dimensions. There are a couple of options for how we can retrieve the data cell:

1. Use the source cell Member names.
2. Use the source cell IDs to build a `DataCellPk`.
3. Convert the source cell `DataBufferCellPk` to a Member Script.

Chapter 4

Use the Source Cell Member Names

In this Method, a full Member Script string will be passed into the `GetDataCell` function.

```vb
'Retrieve the volume data cell using source cell names
Dim volumeDataCell As DataCell
volumeDataCell = api.Data.GetDataCell("F#EndBalLoad:I#Top:O#Top:A#Volume:" & _
                                "U1#" & sourceCell.DataBufferCellPk.GetUD1Name(api) & ":" & _
                                "U2#" & sourceCell.DataBufferCellPk.GetUD2Name(api) & ":" & _
                                "U3#" & sourceCell.DataBufferCellPk.GetUD3Name(api) & ":" & _
                                "U4#" & sourceCell.DataBufferCellPk.GetUD4Name(api) & ":" & _
                                "U5#" & sourceCell.DataBufferCellPk.GetUD5Name(api) & ":" & _
                                "U6#" & sourceCell.DataBufferCellPk.GetUD6Name(api) & ":" & _
                                "U7#" & sourceCell.DataBufferCellPk.GetUD7Name(api) & ":" & _
                                "U8#" & sourceCell.DataBufferCellPk.GetUD8Name(api) & "")
```

> **Note**: Line breaks are used via the `& _` syntax to increase readability.

All Account-level Dimensions are defined, and source cell information is retrieved using the `GetDimensionName` function. Note that for the Origin and IC Dimensions, we cannot use the Member names from the source cell because they have been defined in the Member Script within the `GetDataBuffer` function and would be defined as `XFCommon`. Instead, we define those as hardcoded values.

Use the Source Cell IDs to Build a DataCellPk

In this Method, a new `DataCellPk` object will be created, manipulated, and then passed into the `api.Data.GetDataCellFunction`.

```vb
'Retrieve the volume data cell using a Data Cell Pk Object
'Information from the Source Cell will be used to define the Data Cell
Dim volumeDataCellPk As DataCellPk = New DataCellPk
volumeDataCellPk.ICId = DimConstants.Top
volumeDataCellPk.OriginId = DimConstants.Top
volumeDataCellPk.AccountId = volumeId
volumeDataCellPk.UD1Id = sourceCell.DataBufferCellPk.UD1Id
volumeDataCellPk.UD2Id = sourceCell.DataBufferCellPk.UD2Id
volumeDataCellPk.UD3Id = sourceCell.DataBufferCellPk.UD3Id
volumeDataCellPk.UD4Id = sourceCell.DataBufferCellPk.UD4Id
volumeDataCellPk.UD5Id = sourceCell.DataBufferCellPk.UD5Id
volumeDataCellPk.UD6Id = sourceCell.DataBufferCellPk.UD6Id
volumeDataCellPk.UD7Id = sourceCell.DataBufferCellPk.UD7Id
volumeDataCellPk.UD8Id = sourceCell.DataBufferCellPk.UD8Id

Dim VolumeDataCell As DataCell = api.Data.GetDataCell(volumeDataCellPk)
```

Each Dimension ID for the new `DataCellPk` must be defined. The Origin and IC Dimensions will be defined using **DimConstants** and the Account Member set to the Volume Account Member ID, which was retrieved before starting the loop to save having to retrieve the same value for each loop iteration. The Source Cell Member IDs are used for the UD Dimensions to stay consistent with the source cell.

DimConstants
The `DimConstants` class can be called to retrieve IDs for default or system Dimension Members. For example, the Origin contains a fixed list of Members that cannot be edited. The `DimConstants` class serves as a way to easily retrieve those IDs since they will exist in every Cube.

Api.Members.GetMemberId
Member IDs for User-created Members within any Dimension can be retrieved using the `api.Members.GetMemberID` function. The `DimTypeID` and Member name must be passed into the function.

Convert the Source Cell DataBufferCellPk to a Member Script

Yet another way to retrieve a data cell is to build a Member Script using a `MemberScriptBuilder` object. The Source Cell Dimension information can be directly converted to a Member Script using the `ApplyDataBufferCellPkToMemberScriptBuilder` function.

As each source cell is looped through, the `DataBufferCellPk` is known so that object can be used to create our Member Script, which can then be passed into the `GetDataCell` function.

```
Dim mbrScriptBuilder As MemberScriptBuilder = api.Data.CreateMemberScriptBuilder("")
api.Data.ApplyDataBufferCellPkToMemberScriptBuilder(mbrScriptBuilder, sourceCell.DataBufferCellPk)
mbrscriptbuilder.Account = "Volume"
mbrscriptbuilder.Origin = "Top"
mbrscriptbuilder.IC = "Top"
Dim mbrScriptBuilderString As String = mbrscriptbuilder.GetMemberScript

Dim VolumeDataCell As DataCell = api.Data.GetDataCell(mbrScriptBuilderString)
```

A new `MemberScriptBuilder` object is created, and then the `ApplyDataBufferCellPkToMemberScriptBuilder` function is used to transfer the data cell information from the source cell to the `MemberScriptBuilder`. At this point, the `MemberScriptBuilder` and the source data cell are identical. Then the `MemberScriptBuilder`'s Members are manipulated to get the desired result.

Performance

Each of the three Methods described to retrieve a data cell produces the same result. There are, however, some slight performance differences. Using the MemberIDs to define a `DataCellPk` will perform the best due to the source cell IDs already being in memory. The `MemberSciptBuilder` should perform second-best and using `SourceCell` names to define the Member Script should perform the worst as the names need to be retrieved and then converted into MemberIDs.

Ultimately, performance results may vary based on the use case. For example, source cell names may be used for other logic – and already declared – which would require no further processing time to use them in a `GetDataCell`.

It's always good to have options.

Setting the ResultCellPk

Back to our example, we now need to manipulate the Dimension details of the result cell. If the result cell was initially set with the source cell information, much of the work has already been done. The result cell can be manipulated by setting the Dimension Member IDs using the `api.Members.GetMemberID` function.

```
'Set the target members for the XFCommon members
resultcell.DataBufferCellPk.OriginId = DimConstants.Import
resultCell.DataBufferCellPk.ICId = DimConstants.None
resultcell.DataBufferCellPk.AccountId = salesId
```

This can also be done via the `DestinationInfo` object, which will set all of the result cells in the Result Data Buffer at once.

```
Dim destinationInfo As ExpressionDestinationInfo = api.Data.GetExpressionDestinationInfo("A#Sales:O#Import:I#None")
```

Both Methods outlined above for setting result cell Dimension Members will have the same result. Setting the result cells within the loop should be used when needing to perform logic to determine the result cell destination. For example:

```
If sourceCell.CellAmount > 100 Then
    resultCell.DataBufferCellPk.AccountId = salesId
Else
    resultCell.DataBufferCellPk.AccountId = anotherAccountId
End If
```

All else being equal, using `DestinationInfo` performs better because it is applied to the *entire* Data Buffer, converting all the cells within it at once. Again, it's good to have options.

> **Note:** `DestinationInfo` will overwrite setting the Dimensions of the individual cells if both are used for the same Dimension.

Setting the Result Cell Amount

Now, it's time to do the math. The result cell's Amount will be set using the source cell (Price) multiplied by the Volume data cell.

```
'Perform the logic to calculate the result amount
resultcell.CellAmount = sourceCell.CellAmount * volumeDataCell.CellAmount
```

Adding the Result Cell to the Result Data Buffer

The result data cell is then added to the Result Data Buffer using the `SetCell` function.

```
'Add the new cell to the Result Data Buffer
resultdatabuffer.SetCell(si,resultcell)
```

`AccumulateIfCellAlreadyExists` is an optional True/False argument that can be passed into the function. This option defaults to False, which means that if you have cells with identical destination Dimensions (CellPks), the last one added will overwrite. This should be set to True if there is a potential for identical data intersections (Data Buffer Cell Pks) to be added to the Result Data Buffer. Otherwise, the last cell added will overwrite.

```
Sub DataBuffer.SetCell(si As SessionInfo, dataCell As DataCell, accumulateIfCellAlreadyExists As Boolean)
```

Figure 4.1

Finishing the Loop and Setting the Data Buffer

After all the source data cells have been looped over, the Result Data Buffer will be filled with cells. Those cells are committed to the Cube via the `SetDataBuffer` function. The `DestinationInfo` object is passed in, as well as optional arguments for Dimension filters which is similar to how we use filters in the ADC function.

```
Sub DataApi.SetDataBuffer(dataBuffer As DataBuffer, expressionDestinationInfo As ExpressionDestinationInfo, Optional accountFilter As String, Optional flowFilter As String, Optional originFilter As String, Optional icFilter As String, Optional ud1Filter As String, Optional ud2Filter As String, Optional ud3Filter As String, Optional ud4Filter As String, Optional ud5Filter As String, Optional ud6Filter As String, Optional ud7Filter As String, Optional ud8Filter As String, Optional isDurableCalculatedData As Boolean)
```

Figure 4.2

Other Considerations

The example used above was fairly simple and straightforward so that the main components of the DBCL could be illustrated. There are a few additional variations that can be used that may prove useful in some situations.

Setting Cell Status

The Cell Status for the Result Data Buffer Cell can be set using the `CreateDataCellStatus` function.

```
Function DataCellStatus.CreateDataCellStatus(isNoData As Boolean, isInvalid As Boolean) As DataCellStatus
```

Figure 4.3

The `CreateDataCellStatus` function accepts two arguments, both Booleans, for `IsNoData` and `IsInvalid` data. If you need to save data to the Cube, use `False` for both.

```
resultcell.CellStatus = DataCellStatus.CreateDataCellStatus(False,False)
```

This function should be used if looping over a Data Buffer that contains `NoData` cells (and they haven't been purposely removed with the `RemoveZeros` function). It can also be used if the result cell does not inherit the source cell information since a new result cell is created with a Cell Status of `NoData` by default.

This function is also useful when trying to remove or clear data that was either imported or entered through a Form. This data can be looped over, and the cells set to `NoData = True`, which – when written back to the Cube – will effectively clear it.

Below is an example of using a DBCL to clear data in `O#Forms`.

```
'Create a result data buffer and destination info
Dim resultDataBuffer As DataBuffer = New DataBuffer()
Dim destinationInfo As ExpressionDestinationInfo = api.Data.GetExpressionDestinationInfo("A#Sales:O#Forms")

'Declare starting data buffer to loop through
Dim formsDataBuffer As DataBuffer = api.Data.GetDataBufferUsingFormula("RemoveZeros(A#Sales:O#Forms)")

'Loop through the cells of the data buffer
For Each sourceCell As DataBufferCell In formsDataBuffer.DataBufferCells.Values
    'Create a new result cell to eventually add to the result data buffer
    'The cell properties of the source cell will be inherited
    Dim resultCell As New DataBufferCell(sourceCell)
    resultcell.CellStatus = DataCellStatus.CreateDataCellStatus(True,False)

    'Add the new cell to the Result Data Buffer
    resultdatabuffer.SetCell(si,resultCell)
Next
api.Data.SetDataBuffer(resultdatabuffer,destinationinfo)
End If
```

SetDimension Extension

In the above example, the Dimensions of the result cells were defined by setting their MemberIDs.

```
'Set the result cell to the destination account
resultcell.DataBufferCellPk.OriginId = DimConstants.Import
resultCell.DataBufferCellPk.ICId = DimConstants.None
resultCell.DataBufferCellPk.AccountId = salesId
```

Chapter 4

There is also a `SetDimension` extension that can be used to achieve the same result.

```
'Set the result cell to the destination account
resultCell.SetOrigin(api,"Import")
resultCell.SetIC(api,None)
resultCell.SetAccount(api,"Sales")
```

There is a slight performance benefit to using the MemberID Methods since OneStream needs to perform the extra step of converting names to IDs in the `Set` Method.

When to Use the DBCL

If the previous example produces the same result as the ADC function, what is the point of using it? The reason for using the DBCL approach comes down to flexibility and performance.

Flexibility

The DBCL affords the ability to filter, analyze, or otherwise manipulate each result cell before it is added to the Result Buffer. This opens up endless possibilities for applying logic that can't be applied using the ADC function. Two examples are:

- Transforming Dimensions
- Analyzing Cell Status or Cell Amounts

Transforming Dimensions

Result cells may need to be transformed to different Dimension Members using a **mapping table** or some other mechanism. This can be especially useful when data is pulled from other Cubes with unrelated Dimensions or non-Cube data from Staging, Register, or External Tables.

Analyzing Cell Status or Cell Amounts

The CellStatus or CellAmount of Data Buffer Cells can be analyzed and used within logic.

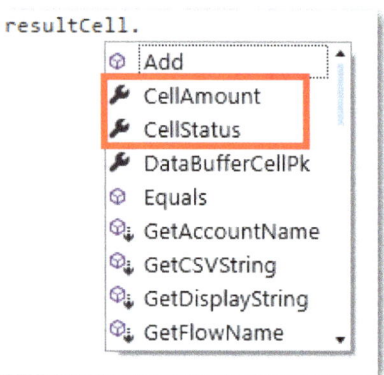

Figure 4.4

Performance

Using the DBCL approach – when the ADC function could have otherwise been used – will perform slightly worse. However, one DBCL could replace what would take multiple ADC functions, which would improve overall performance. This is because multiple result cells can be created inside the loop and added to the Result Data Buffer, which is then written once to the database where multiple ADC functions would write multiple times.

Example of Setting Multiple Result Cells

Curly wants to budget Returns as a function of Sales. Historically, Returns have been 1% of Sales. In a rare moment of intelligence, Curly decides that the logic for Returns can exist within the same Calculation as Sales. He adds the Returns Calculation logic to the existing DBCL for Sales.

```vb
api.Data.ClearCalculatedData(True,True,True,True,"A#Sales, A#Returns")

'Create a result data buffer and destination info to add the cells to later
Dim resultDataBuffer As DataBuffer = New DataBuffer()
Dim destinationInfo As ExpressionDestinationInfo = api.Data.GetExpressionDestinationInfo("O#Import:I#None")

'Declare starting data buffer to loop through
Dim priceDataBuffer As DataBuffer = api.Data.GetDataBufferUsingFormula("RemoveZeros(A#Price:O#Top:I#Top)")

'Retrieve the Sales Account Id before the loop so we don't retrieve it for each iteration
Dim salesId As Integer = api.Members.GetMemberId(dimtypeid.Account, "Sales")
Dim returnsId As Integer = api.Members.GetMemberId(dimtypeid.Account, "Returns")
'Loop through the cells of the data buffer
For Each sourceCell As DataBufferCell In priceDataBuffer.DataBufferCells.Values
    'Retrieve the volume data cell using a Member Script Builder
    'The Source Cell members will be set to the Member Script Builder
    Dim mbrScriptBuilder As MemberScriptBuilder = api.Data.CreateMemberScriptBuilder("")
    api.Data.ApplyDataBufferCellPkToMemberScriptBuilder(mbrScriptBuilder, sourceCell.DataBufferCellPk)
    mbrscriptbuilder.Account = "Volume"
    mbrscriptbuilder.Origin = "Top"
    mbrscriptbuilder.IC = "Top"
    Dim mbrScriptBuilderString As String = mbrscriptbuilder.GetMemberScript

    Dim VolumeDataCell As DataCell = api.Data.GetDataCell(mbrScriptBuilderString)

    'Create a new result cell to eventually add to the result data buffer
    'The cell properties of the source cell will be inherited
    Dim resultCellSales As New DataBufferCell(sourceCell)
    Dim resultCellReturns As New DataBufferCell(sourceCell)

    'Set the target members For the XFCommon members
    resultCellSales.DataBufferCellPk.AccountId = salesId
    resultCellReturns.DataBufferCellPk.AccountId = returnsId

    'Do the logic to calculate the result amount
    resultCellSales.CellAmount = sourceCell.CellAmount * volumeDataCell.CellAmount
    resultCellReturns.CellAmount = resultCellSales.CellAmount * .01

    'Add the new cell to the Result Data Buffer
    resultdatabuffer.SetCell(si,resultCellSales)
    resultdatabuffer.SetCell(si,resultCellReturns)
Next

'Save the Data Buffer using the Result Data Buffer and Destination Info
api.Data.SetDataBuffer(resultdatabuffer,destinationinfo)
```

Notice that two result cells are declared with different logic setting the Cell Amounts for each. Also, notice that `A#Returns` was added to the Account filter in the `ClearCalculateData` function at the top.

DBCL vs. Eval

The `Eval` function, used in conjunction with the ADC, can be used almost interchangeably with the DBCL. The choice of which to use mostly comes down to User preference, although there can be situations where a DBCL is clearly the better choice. Let's use the **Double Unbalanced** example mentioned in the previous chapter.

For this example, Curly needs to budget Shipping Expenses – across both Products and Cost Centers – by taking Volume multiplied by Shipping Cost Drivers.

Shipping Cost Drivers are entered across the various Shipping Cost Centers and Volumes are entered by Product.

Curly starts with a simple `api.Data.Calculate`, multiplying the `A#Volume` by `A#ShippingDrivers`.

```
api.Data.Calculate("A#ShippingExpense = A#Volume * A#ShippingDrivers")
```

This Calculation produces no results to Curly's dismay. Viewing the Drivers in a Cube View, it is clear that their dimensionality does not align.

		Volume	ShippingDrivers
BugZapper - Bug Zapper	None	70.00	
IndoorBugSpray - Indoor Bug Spray	None	175.00	
OutdoorBugSpray - Outdoor Bug Spray	None	175.00	
BedBugKiller - Bed Bug Killer	None	75.00	
StinkBugKiller - Stink Bug Killer	None	45.00	
Termicide	None	60.00	
SpeedyBugSpray - Speedy Bug Spray	None	8.00	
SpeedyTermiteSpray - Speedy Termite Spray	None	8.00	
MouseTrap - Mouse Trap	None	500.00	
GlueTrap - Glue Trap	None	250.00	
RatPoison - Rat Poison	None	140.00	
PestControl - Pest Control	None	20.00	
TermiteTreatment - Termite Treatment	None	10.00	
Commercial	None	5.00	
BugBeaters - Bug Beaters	None	5.00	
None	⊟ Packaging		0.01
	PackagingMaterials - Packaging Materials		0.01
	ShippingPrep - Shipping Preparation		0.02
	ShippingTransportation - Shipping Transportation		0.03

Figure 4.5

Next, Curly tries to align the Dimensions within the Calculation by adding UD1 and UD2 to the source and destination Member Scripts.

```
api.Data.Calculate("A#ShippingExpense:U1#None:U2#None =
A#Volume:U1#Top:U2#Top * A#ShippingDrivers:U1#Top:U2#Top")
```

The Calculation now produces results, but they aren't correct and lack detail for Product and Cost Center. Trying one more time, Curly rewrites the Calculation.

```
api.Data.Calculate("A#ShippingExpense = A#Volume:U2#None *
A#ShippingDrivers:U1#None")
```

Curly runs this Calculation and receives an **Unbalanced Data Buffer error** and is now thoroughly confused.

After doing the Curly shuffle for a few minutes to get his brain working, he decides to use a DBCL to solve the problem.

The Data Buffer Cell Loop

```vb
'Create a result data buffer and destination info to add the cells to later
Dim resultDataBuffer As DataBuffer = New DataBuffer()
Dim destinationInfo As ExpressionDestinationInfo = api.Data.GetExpressionDestinationInfo("O#Import:I#None")

'Declare the Volume data buffer with U2 fixed on None
Dim volumeDataBuffer As DataBuffer = api.Data.GetDataBufferUsingFormula("RemoveZeros(A#Volume:O#Top:I#Top:U2#None)")

'Retrieve the Sales Account Id before the loops so we don't retrieve it for each iteration
Dim shippingExpenseId As Integer = api.Members.GetMemberId(dimtypeid.Account, "ShippingExpense")

'Loop through the cells of the Volume data buffer
For Each sourceCellVolume As DataBufferCell In volumeDataBuffer.DataBufferCells.Values
    'Retrieve the volume amount to be used in the calculation later
    Dim volumeAmount As Decimal = sourceCellVolume.CellAmount
    'Declare the Shipping Drivers data buffer with U1 fixed on None
    Dim shippingDataBuffer As DataBuffer = api.Data.GetDataBufferUsingFormula("RemoveZeros(A#ShippingDrivers:O#Top:I#Top:U1#None)")

    For Each sourceCellShipping As DataBufferCell In shippingDataBuffer.DataBufferCells.Values

        Dim shippingAmount As Decimal = sourceCellShipping.CellAmount

        'Create a new result cell to eventually add to the result data buffer
        'The cell properties of the source cell will be inherited
        Dim resultCell As New DataBufferCell(sourceCellShipping)

        'Set the target members For the XFCommon members
        resultCell.DataBufferCellPk.AccountId = shippingExpenseId
        'Inherit the UD1 detail from the Volume Cell
        resultCell.DataBufferCellPk.UD1Id = sourceCellVolume.DataBufferCellPk.UD1Id
        'Inherit the UD2 detail from the Shipping Driver Cell
        resultCell.DataBufferCellPk.UD2Id = sourceCellShipping.DataBufferCellPk.UD2Id

        'Do the logic to calculate the result amount
        resultCell.CellAmount = volumeAmount * sourceCellShipping.CellAmount

        'Add the new cell to the Result Data Buffer
        resultdatabuffer.SetCell(si,resultCell)
    Next
Next

'Save the Data Buffer using the Result Data Buffer and Destination Info
api.Data.SetDataBuffer(resultdatabuffer,destinationinfo)
```

To get the Calculation to work, Curly first looped through the `A#Volume` Data Buffer and then created another loop through the `A#ShippingDrivers` Data Buffer nested within the first loop. Within the second loop, the result cell's `UD1` is inherited from the Volume cell and `UD2` is inherited from the `ShippingDrivers` cell.

The Shipping Expense Account is now populated with detail for both `UD1` and `UD2`.

		Volume	ShippingDrivers	ShippingExpense - Shipping Supplies
BugZapper - Bug Zapper	⊟ Packaging			0.84
	PackagingMaterials - Packaging Materials			0.70
	ShippingPrep - Shipping Preparation			1.54
	ShippingTransportation - Shipping Transportation			1.75
	None	70.00		
IndoorBugSpray - Indoor Bug Spray	⊟ Packaging			2.10
	PackagingMaterials - Packaging Materials			1.75
	ShippingPrep - Shipping Preparation			3.85
	ShippingTransportation - Shipping Transportation			4.38
	None	175.00		
OutdoorBugSpray - Outdoor Bug Spray	⊟ Packaging			2.10
	PackagingMaterials - Packaging Materials			1.75
	ShippingPrep - Shipping Preparation			3.85
	ShippingTransportation - Shipping Transportation			4.38
	None	175.00		
BedBugKiller - Bed Bug Killer	⊟ Packaging			0.90
	PackagingMaterials - Packaging Materials			0.75
	ShippingPrep - Shipping Preparation			1.65
	ShippingTransportation - Shipping Transportation			1.88

Figure 4.6

Accomplishing this with an `Eval` or `Eval2` is also possible but would be much more complex.

Chapter 4

Guidelines

The flexibility provided by the DBCL presents the opportunity for a lot of variation in the way it can be used. Regardless of the use case, the below guidelines should be adhered to.

Loop Definition

The term Data Buffer Cell Loop assumes that a Data Buffer is defining the loop. Looping over a Data Buffer makes sense in most cases because:

- Only cells containing data will be looped through.
- Dimensionality from the source cells can be transferred to the result cells.

This is not, however, necessary as any list could be looped through. For example, a list of Members could be retrieved using the `api.Members.GetMembersUsingFilter` function and then looped over. This should only be done in rare cases when data needs to be generated for each Member within the list. This Method is limited because only one Dimension Member can be supplied to the result cells. Rows of a custom table could also be looped through with fields from the rows being provided to the result cells.

Also, be careful when looping over Data Buffers that contain a high volume of cells. Use the `Count` function to log the total number of cells that are being looped over, and limit the scope using filters if possible.

```
'Declare the Volume data buffer
Dim volumeDataBuffer As DataBuffer = api.Data.GetDataBufferUsingFormula("RemoveZeros(A#Volume:O#Top:I#Top:U2#None)")
'Log the number of Data Buffer Cells
api.LogMessage(volumeDataBuffer.DataBufferCells.Count.XFToString)
```

Out of the Loop

It's important to be very judicial in regard to what is done *inside* the loop versus *outside* the loop. Anything done inside the loop will be repeated for every iteration of the loop, which can be hundreds or thousands of times. Things like Dimension Member IDs can be retrieved *before* the loop if they do not change for each iteration.

For example, if the Calculation required a Data Cell Amount for a global inflation rate, it is likely that this rate will remain the same for each iteration of the loop. Retrieving this data cell before starting the loop will ensure that processing time isn't wasted retrieving the same number over and over again.

Write Once

One of the most expensive actions when processing is writing to the database. To optimize performance, cells should be added to the Result Data Buffer in memory, and the `SetDataBuffer` function is called once, after the loop completes. Even though you may get the correct results, it is *never* a good idea to use an `api.Data.Calculate`, `api.Data.SetDataBuffer`, or `api.Data.SetDataCell` inside the loop.

Conclusion

The `api.Data.Calculate` function, introduced in the last chapter, is powerful but somewhat limited. When it proves inadequate for more complex Calculations, having the Data Buffer Cell Loop in your Calculation-writing arsenal will prove to be a powerful weapon. The DBCL allows logic to be applied at the individual cell level giving you ultimate flexibility and precision in Calculations. Multiple result cells can also be created inside the same loop, affording you the capability to combine Calculations using the same inputs, which can improve performance.

In this chapter, the basic concepts, and components of the DBCL were explained as well as several examples of how it can be applied for real-world solutions. Mastering this technique will allow you to tackle the most complex Calculation requirements. If our lovable stooge – Curly – can learn it, you can too!

5
Reporting Calculations

The lion's share of this book, thus far, has focused on Calculations that result in data being stored in the Cube. Writing data to any multidimensional database requires care and precision and is not very forgiving of mistakes. But not all Calculations need to result in stored Cube data. Sometimes referred to as **Dynamic Calcs**, reporting Calculations are generally simpler in how they are written and allow greater flexibility since data is not written back to the Cube.

Dynamic Calculations encompass all Calculations where the result is determined **in-memory** and displayed to the User via a Report, like a Cube View. Dynamic Calcs work fundamentally differently from the stored Calculations discussed so far. This chapter will cover the When, Where, and How of reporting Calculations.

When They Run

Unlike stored Calculations, dynamic Calculations do not need to be explicitly executed via the DUCS or a Data Management step. Rather, they will run anytime they are referenced, most commonly when opening a Report like a Cube View or Quick View. If a Report contains references to dynamic Calculations, then the formula logic will be processed in memory as OneStream renders the Report on the screen. Dynamic Members can also be referenced in stored Calculations via Business Rules and Member Formulas using the `api.Data.GetDataCell` function.

Aside from Cube View and Quick View Reports, dynamic Calcs will not execute in most other places in OneStream where data is processed. This includes:

- Data Exports via Data Management Export Data step
- Data Buffers
- Data Unit Method Queries

Dynamic Calculation Example

Let's start with a simple example of a dynamic Calculation that calculates the gross profit percentage of Sales.

```
'Calculate the Gross Profit Percentage of Sales
Return api.Data.GetDataCell("Divide(A#GrossProfit, A#Sales)")
```

How and where they are written – and the required syntax – is a bit different for stored Calculations than for dynamic Calculations. Let's dive in further, using the above example as a reference.

Where They are Located

Just like stored formulas, there are options for where dynamic Calculation Scripts can be stored.

Chapter 5

Member Formulas

Dynamic Calculation formulas can be stored in the Member Filter Property on Account, Flow, and UD Dimensions. To enable Dynamic Calculations on a Member, the Formula Type Member property should be set to DynamicCalc. For Account Members, both Account Type and Formula Type need to be set to DynamicCalc.

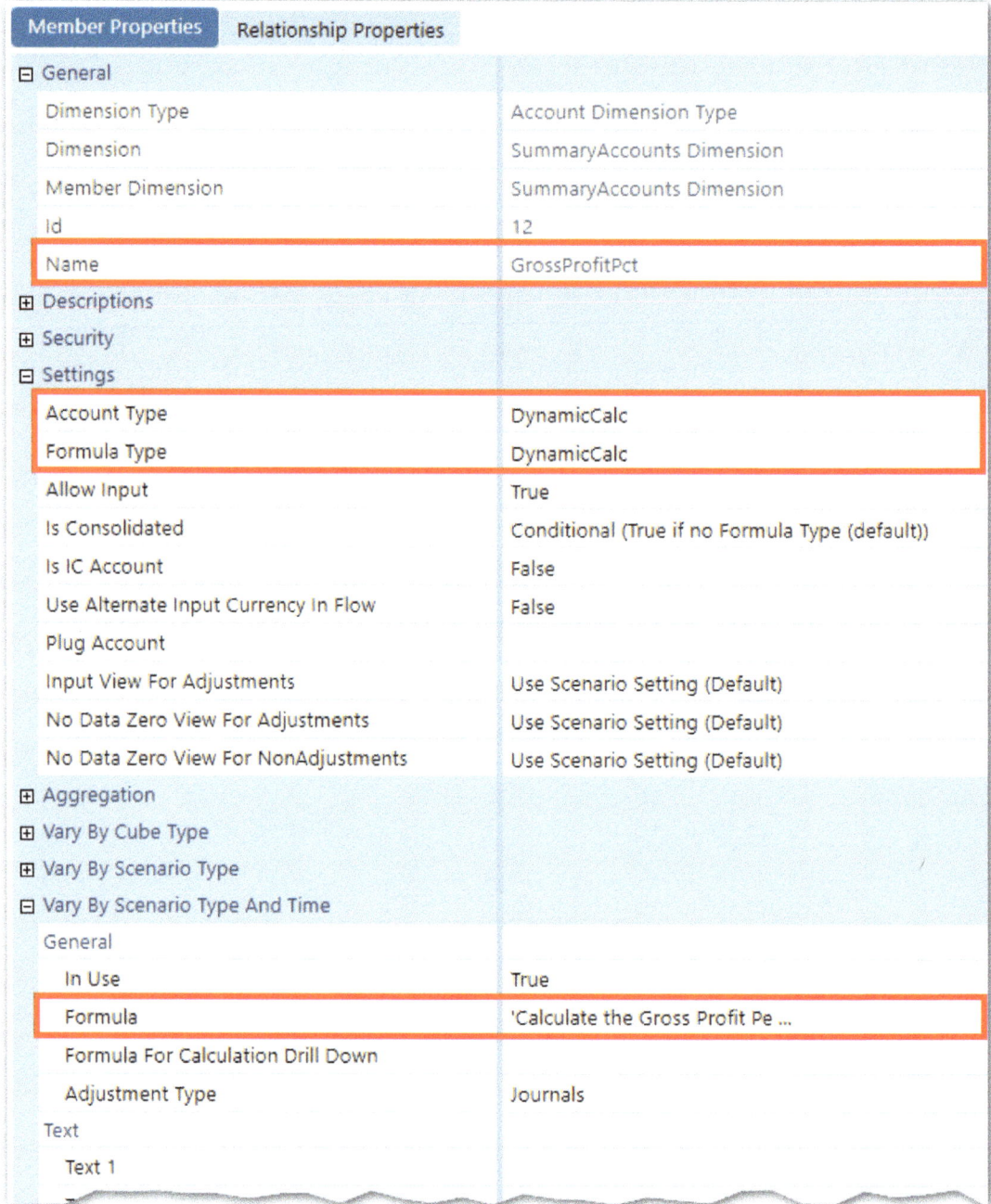

Figure 5.1

Just like for stored Calculations, the formula can vary by Time and Scenario Type.

Reporting Calculations

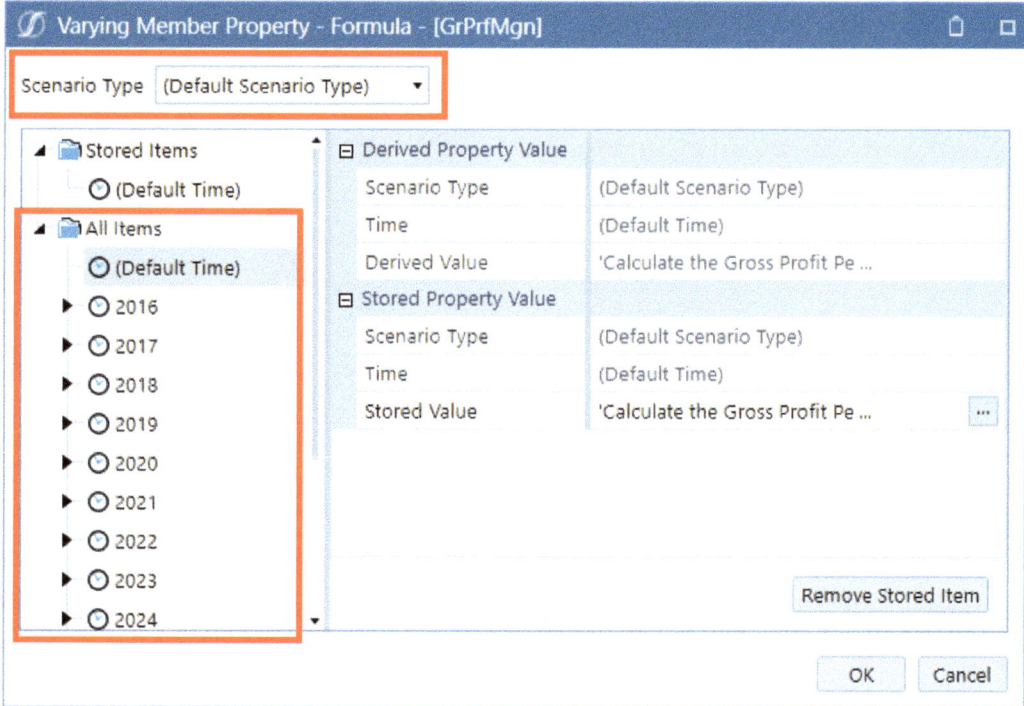

Figure 5.2

When storing the dynamic formula logic on a Member Formula, the formula will run anytime that Member is referenced, e.g., in a Cube View.

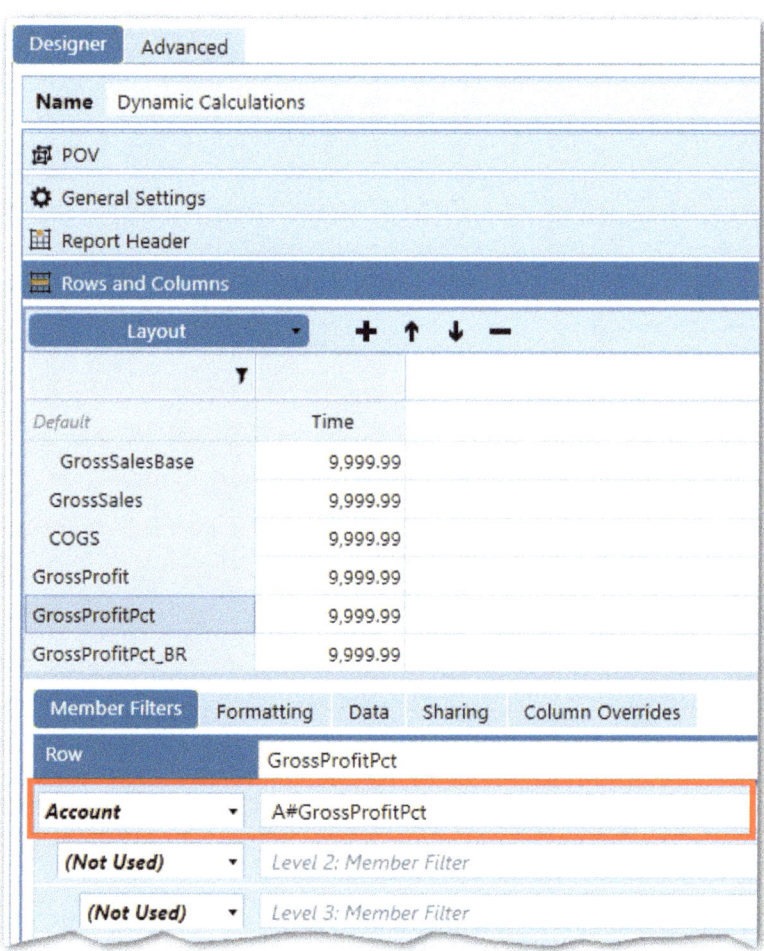

Figure 5.3

101

Chapter 5

Dynamic Calculations in Business Rules

Dynamic Calculations can be stored in Business Rules using the `FinanceFunctionType` of `DataCell`.

```
Case Is = FinanceFunctionType.DataCell
    If args.DataCellArgs.FunctionName.XFEqualsIgnoreCase("GrossProfitPct") Then

        Return api.Data.GetDataCell("Divide(A#GrossProfit,A#Sales)")

    End If
```

`DataCellArgs` are used to declare a `FunctionName` which is referenced when called. The Business Rule is then called from a Cube View using the below syntax:

```
GetDataCell(BR#[BRName=Chapter5Examples,
FunctionName=GrossProfitPct]):Name(Gross Profit % - BR)
```

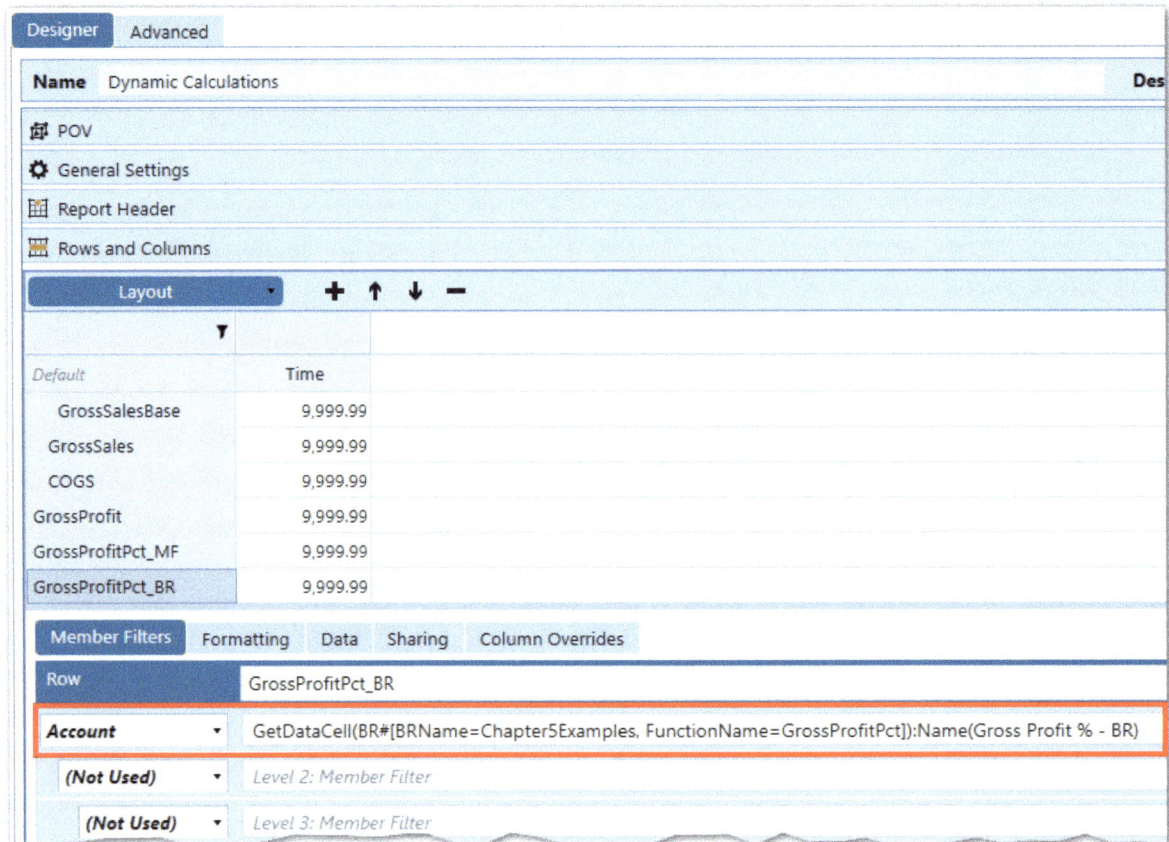

Figure 5.4

> **Note**: Square brackets `[ ]` must be put around the syntax that comes after `BR#`.

Benefits/Drawbacks

The main benefits of using Business Rules to store Dynamic Calculations is that they are not assigned to a specific Dimension and can leverage Name Value pairs (described later), which can make them more flexible.

The downside is that a data cell Business Rule cannot return textual data. Also, the syntax to call them is slightly more complex than if the same logic was stored in a Member Formula.

Cube Views

`GetDataCell` functions can also be used directly in Cube Views.

> `GetDataCell(Divide(A#GrossProfit, A#Sales)):Name(Gross Profit % - CV)`

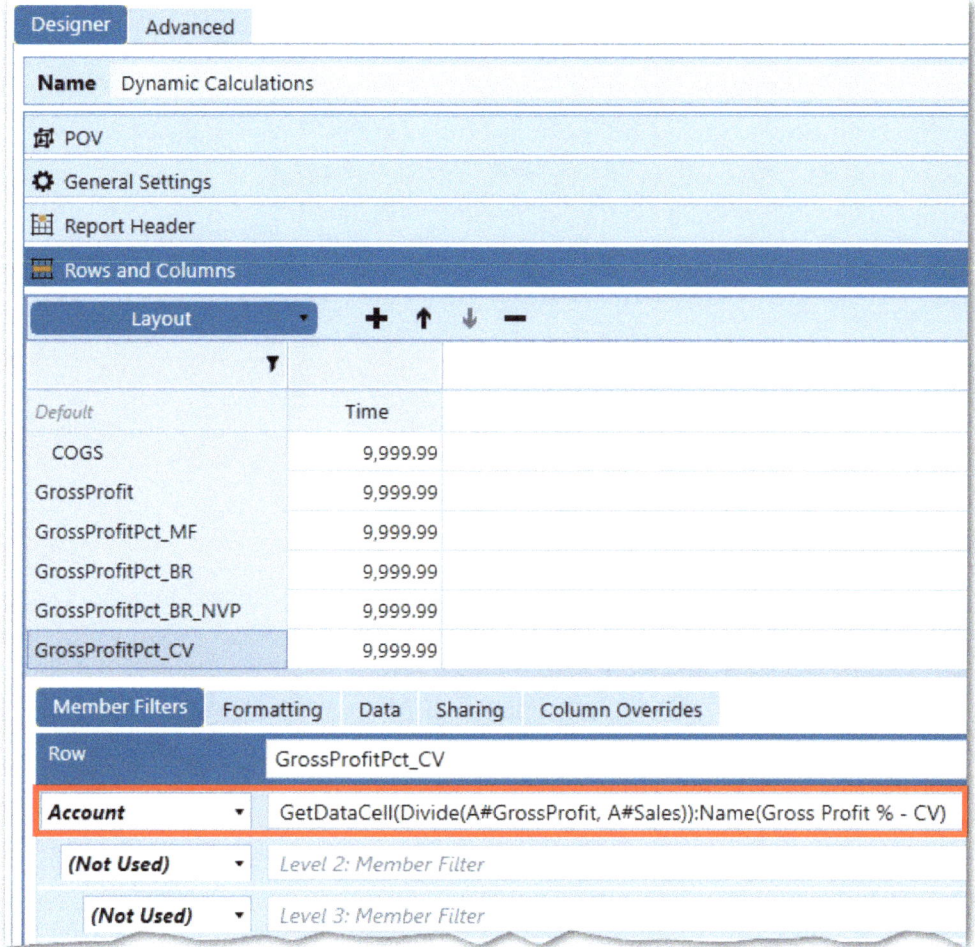

Figure 5.5

Benefits/Drawbacks

The advantage to using the `GetDataCell` function directly in a Cube View is that substitution variables and Column/Row math can be used.

Substitution Variable: `GetDataCell("S#Actual:T#[YearPrior1(|CVTime|)] – T#Actual")`

Column/Row math: `GetDataCell(CVC(SomeColumnName) – CVC(SomeOtherColumnName))`

> **Note**: Nested functions inside a `GetDataCell` should be wrapped in square brackets `[ ]`.

The downside of using `GetDataCell`(s) in Cube Views is that the logic cannot be referenced in other Cube Views, making this Method less maintenance-friendly. In addition, `GetDataCell` cannot be used in the Excel Add-in or Spreadsheet tool, so it is usually better to store the logic in a Member Formula or Business Rule so that it can be used universally.

Results

All the Methods described to calculate the gross profit percent of Sales yield the same results.

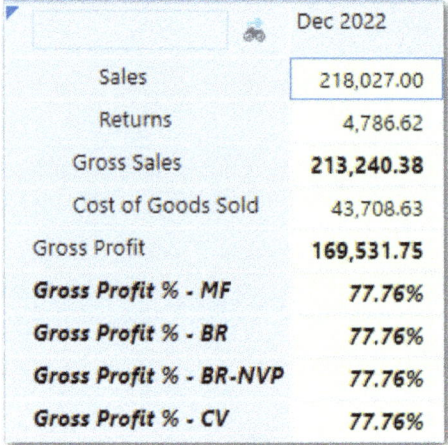

Figure 5.6

How They Work

In Chapter 2, we compared the OneStream Calculation Engine to Excel and said that Calculations do not work on a cell-by-cell basis (like they do in Excel) but rather in groups of cells called Data Buffers. While this is certainly true for stored Calculations, this does not apply to dynamic Calculations. Dynamic Calculations work on the individual data cell level, rather than at the Data Buffer level which more closely mirrors the way Excel works.

Cell POV By Cell POV

Let's look at dynamic Calculations in the context of the most common reporting mechanism in OneStream – the Cube View. Cube Views comprise of rows and columns which – *together* – form a data grid made up of data cells. As the data grid is processed, each cell is analyzed and processed. As it renders the data cells in the grid, each cell is either retrieved from storage or dynamically calculated in memory.

Figure 5.7

The above Cube View has 6 rows and 2 columns for a total of 12 data cells. Each one of these data cells has a full 18-Dimension POV that results in one data point or number. The POV is very important when writing and running dynamic Calcs since the Calculation will inherit the POV of each Cube View cell. This means the same dynamic Calculation can produce different results depending on the Cube View (or other reporting mechanism) in which it is referenced.

Reporting Calculations

Retrieving POV Members

Since each cell in a Cube View has a full 18-Dimension POV, the `api.Pov` Method can be used for any Dimension, not just the Data Unit Dimensions (which is the case for stored Calculations).

This is useful when needing to vary the Calculation logic for certain Members or can prevent the Calc from running on some cells (which can help Report performance).

The below example varies the Calculation logic based on the UD1 for each data cell.

```
'Get the UD1 from the POV of each Data Cell
Dim povUD1 As String = api.Pov.UD1.Name

If povUD1.XFEqualsIgnoreCase("BugZapper")
    'Return nothing for BugZapper product
    Return Nothing
Else
    'Return the Gross Profit %
    Return api.Data.GetDataCell("Divide(A#GrossProfit,A#Sales)")
End If
```

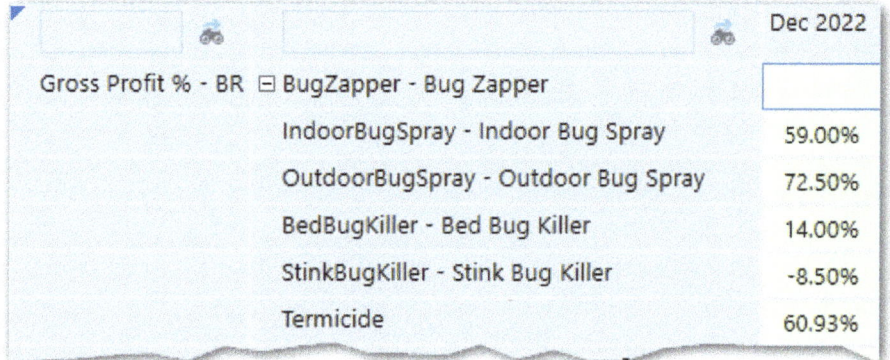

Figure 5.8

Note: For logic statements with many conditions, a `Case When` statement performs better than an `If` Statement.

Return

Dynamic Calcs require a `Return` statement followed by an object to be returned. The object that is returned can either be numerical or textual data, depending on the View Member of the data cell being processed.

View Members for displaying numerical data:

- `YTD`
- `Periodic`
- `QTD`
- `MTD`
- `HTD`

Chapter 5

View Members for displaying textual data:
- `Annotation`
- `Assumptions`
- `AuditComment`
- `Footnote`
- `VarianceExplanation`

Most dynamic Calculations return numerical data; however, having the ability to display textual data alongside numerical can be very useful. Let's explore how to display both numerical and textual data and later go through an example of displaying both in a technique called **Relational Blending**.

Numerical Data

The simplest example for displaying numerical data in a dynamic Calculation is returning a constant, (e.g., 123.4).

```
Return 123.4
```

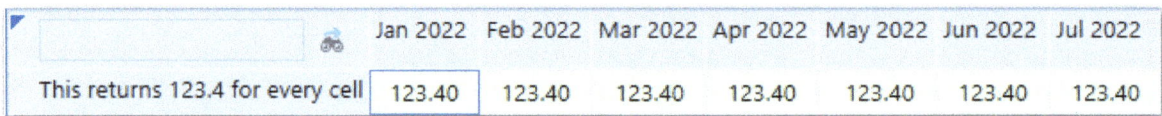

Figure 5.9

While this is easy and illustrates a simple example, it is not very useful. A better and more commonly used approach is to return a data cell using the `api.Data.GetDataCell` function.

Api.Data.GetDataCell
We've already seen the `GetDataCell` function used within a Data Buffer Cell Loop to retrieve a data cell's Cell Amount from the Cube. When used in Stored Formulas, a full Member Script of all Account-level Dimensions must be defined. When used in dynamic Calculations, a minimum of one Dimension can be defined with the rest of the Dimensions inherited from the Report settings.

```
Return api.Data.GetDataCell("A#Sales")
```

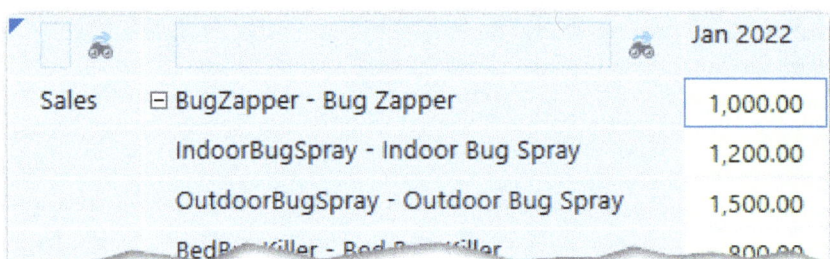

Figure 5.10

When referenced in a Cube View, the script returns multiple data cells, all with `A#Sales` in their Member Script. The other Dimensions are defined in the properties of the Cube View.

Reporting Calculations

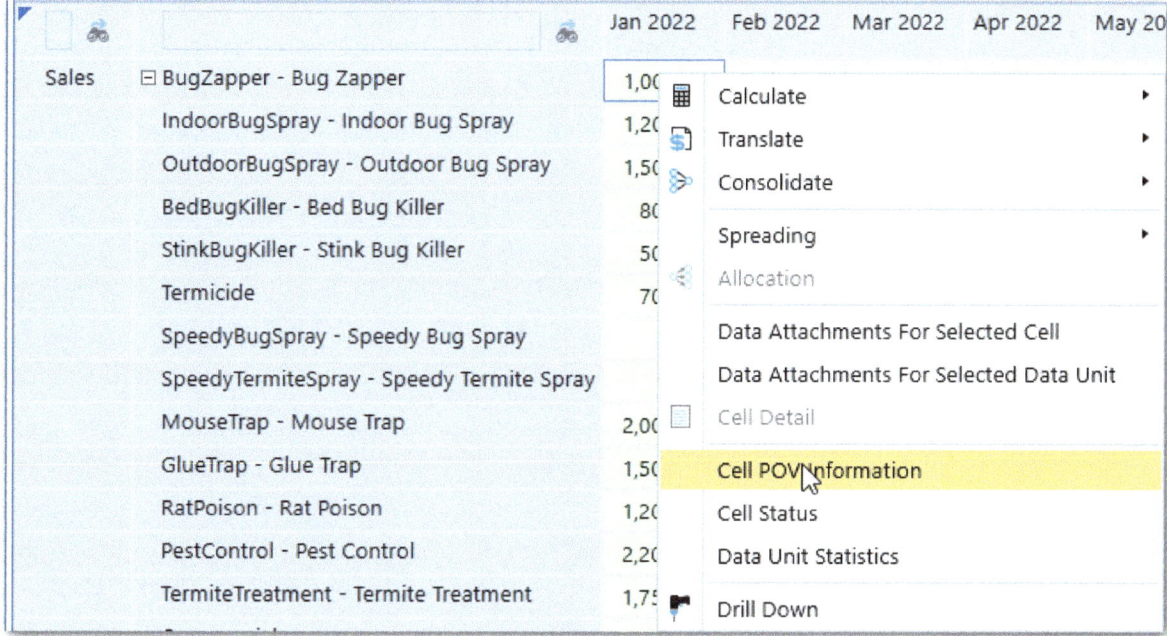

Figure 5.11

```
Cb#ACME:E#ACME:P#StoogeCorp:C#Local:S#Actual:T#2022M1:V#YTD:A#Sales:F#EndBalLoad:O
#Top:I#Top:U1#BugZapper:U2#Top:U3#None:U4#None:U5#None:U6#None:U7#None:U8#None
```

Figure 5.12

The above example is again trivial as there would be no need to write a dynamic Calculation to return `A#Sales`; however, it illustrates how other Dimension Members are applied to the dynamic Calculations script from the underlying Report.

Api.Data.GetDataCell with a Formula

`GetDataCell`'s use is often expanded to perform math operations on multiple data cells.

```
'Calculate the Gross Profit Percentage of Sales
Return api.Data.GetDataCell("Divide(A#GrossProfit, A#Sales)")
```

Just like the `api.Data.Calculate` function, each operand within the formula is defined by a **Member Script**. A key difference, however, is that the `GetDataCell` function does not perform Data Buffer math like the ADC function. Math is performed cell by cell with each Member Script resulting in a singular data point.

Data Cell Properties

The `GetDataCell` function returns a data cell object which has several properties associated with it.

- `CellAmount` – The Data Cell Amount as a decimal

- `CellAmountAsText` – The Data Cell Amount as a string

- `CellStatus` – The Cell Status as a `DataCellStatus` object (can be converted to a string)

- `DataCellPk` – The data cell Primary Key as a `DataCellPk` object

- `Get`/`Set` Dimension names – Functions that retrieve or set a Dimension name to the data cell

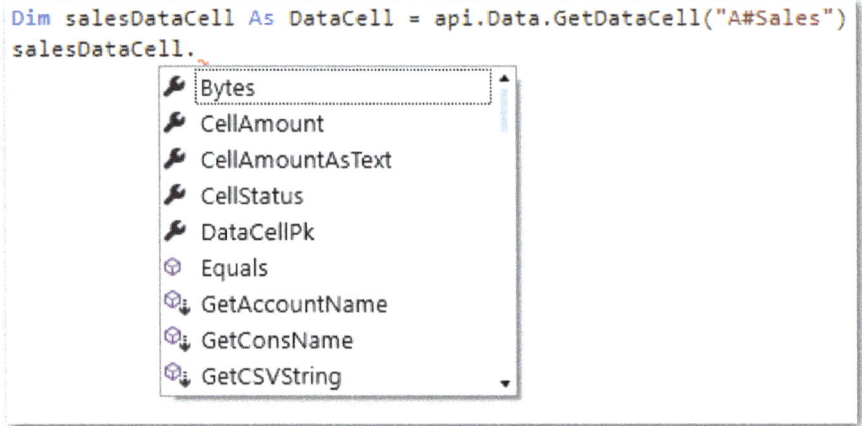

Figure 5.13

When using the `GetDataCell` object in dynamic Calculations, only the data cell object needs to be returned. An implicit conversion to a decimal will occur when rendering the data cell object on the Cube View. The `CellAmount` property can also be returned but will display zeros as actual 0s on the Report (instead of blank cells). For this reason, it is best to return the data cell object.

The `CellAmount` property is mostly used when utilizing the `GetDataCell` function in a stored Calculation, as we did in the Data Buffer Cell Loop example in the last chapter.

Time Functions and Substitution Variables

Time functions can be used within the Member Scripts used in formulas in `GetDataCell` functions.

```
Return api.Data.GetDataCell("A#Sales:T#POVPrior")
```

Textual Data

Textual data can also be displayed on a Report when using the Annotation-type View Members listed below:

- `Annotation`
- `Assumptions`
- `AuditComment`
- `Footnote`
- `VarianceExplanation`

The simplest example is returning a string.

```
Return "Hello"
```

Figure 5.14 shows the text string Hello returned only for Annotation-type View Members.

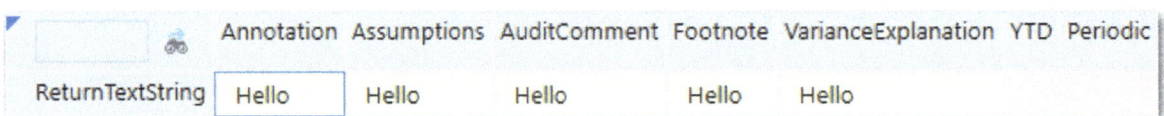

Figure 5.14

Reporting Calculations

DataCellEx

The `DataCellEx` object is like the `DataCell` object but has several properties which allow it to return some additional information about the data cell.

A `DataCellEx` object has the below properties associated with it:

- `AccountTypeID` – the Account Type ID of the data cell's Account Member.
- `CurrencyID` – the currency ID of the data cell's Entity Member.
- `DataCellAnnotation` – any text stored in the data cell's Annotation-type View Member.
- `DataCellDetail` – information regarding cell detail (if available) entered for this cell. This property has additional properties related to cell detail, such as line items and cell view type.

The following example checks the View Member of each data cell and returns either a text string or decimal constant, depending on whether the View Member is an Annotation-type.

```
Dim objViewMember As ViewMember = ViewMember.GetItem(api.Pov.View.MemberId)
    If objViewMember.IsAnnotationType Then
        Dim objDataCellEx As DataCellEx = New DataCellEx()
        objDataCellEx.DataCell.CellStatus = New DataCellStatus(True)
        objDataCellEx.DataCellAnnotation = "Hello"
        Return objDataCellEx
    Else
        Dim objDataCell As DataCell = New DataCell()
        objDataCell.CellStatus = New DataCellStatus(True)
        objDataCell.CellAmount = 123.4
        Return objDataCell
End If
```

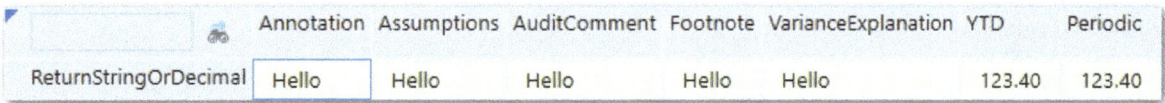

Figure 5.15

Return Text Properties

Another common application of using dynamic Calculations to return text is to display text properties associated with Dimension Members. Let's go through an example:

Moe, Larry, and Curly have decided to divide the management of all the Products sold by StoogeCorp amongst themselves. When looking at a Sales Report for all Products, they want to also see the name of the product manager in the first column next to the Product name. Larry decides that they will store the name of the product manager in the `Text1` property of the Product Member.

Chapter 5

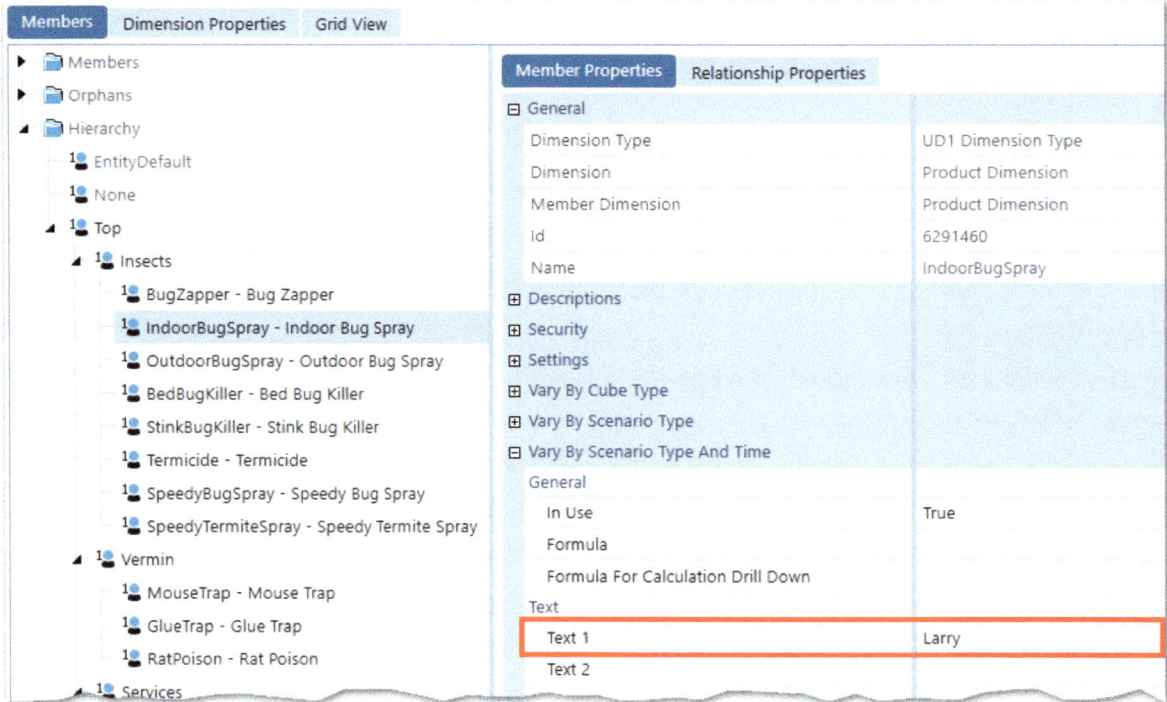

Figure 5.16

A UD8 dynamic Calculation Member is created with a formula to retrieve the `Text1` property of the Product in the POV.

```
Dim objViewMember As ViewMember = ViewMember.GetItem(api.Pov.View.MemberId)

If objViewMember.IsAnnotationType Then
    Dim productText1 As String = api.UD1.Text(api.Pov.UD1.MemberId, 1)
    Return productText1
Else
    Return Nothing
End If
```

The first column of the Sales Report references the UD8 Member with the Annotation View Member.

Reporting Calculations

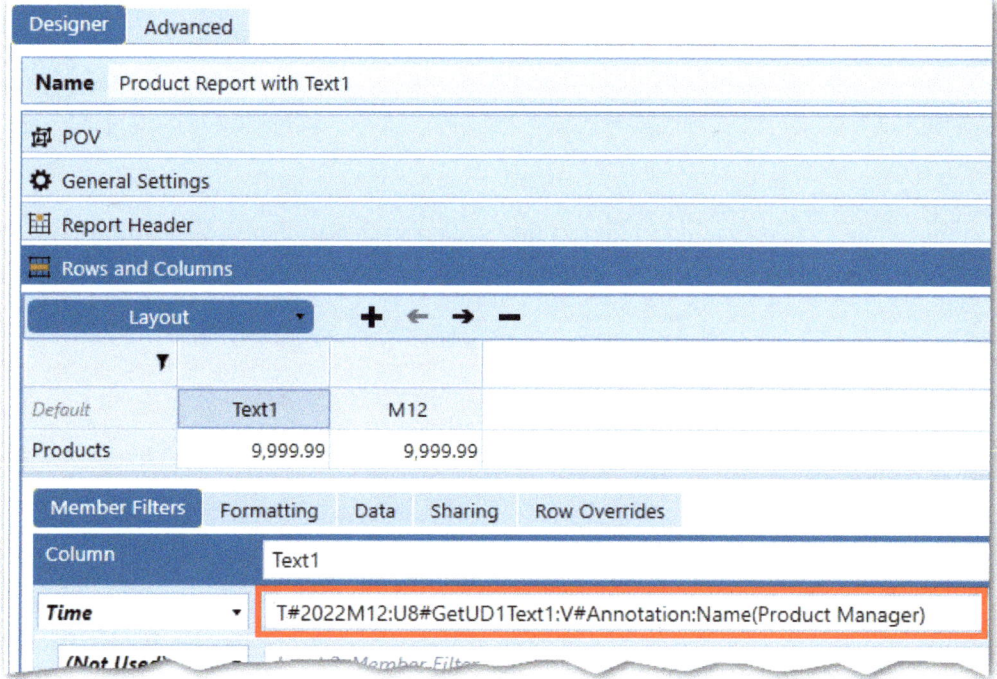

Figure 5.17

The first column shows the name – from the Product in the row's Text1 property – in the first column.

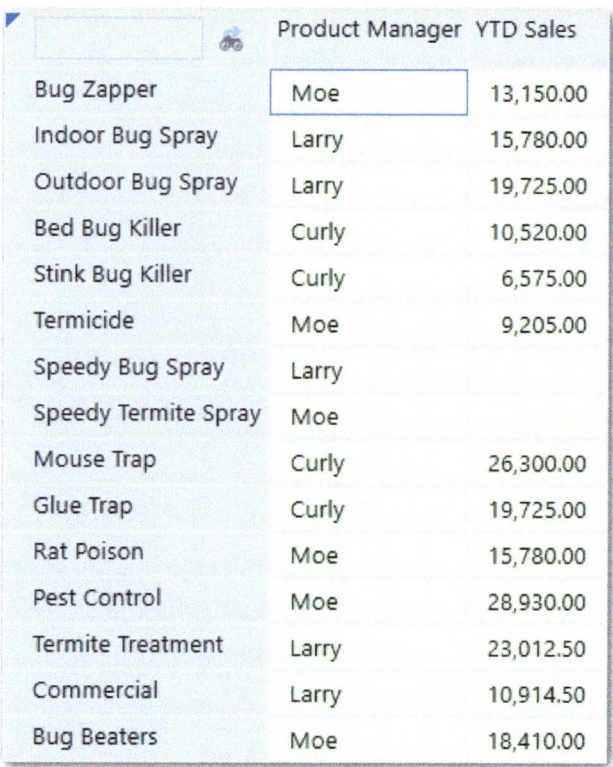

Figure 5.18

Chapter 5

Name Value Pairs

When calling a dynamic Calculation from a Business Rule, Name Value pairs can be used to pass values from the Cube View to the Business Rule. The advantage is that the logic of the Business Rule can change, based on the value passed into the rule, which makes the Business Rule more versatile.

Name Value pairs can be defined and brought into the Business Rule via `args.DataCellArgs.NameValuePairs`. After setting the Name Value pair equal to a string variable, the variable can be interpolated into the formula of the `GetDataCell` function.

```
Else If args.DataCellArgs.FunctionName.XFEqualsIgnoreCase("PctOfSales") Then

    Dim cvAccount As String = args.DataCellArgs.NameValuePairs.XFGetValue("Account")

    Return api.Data.GetDataCell("Divide(A#" & cvAccount & ",A#Sales)")

End If
```

The Name Value pair is then defined in the Cube View when calling the Business Rule and function name.

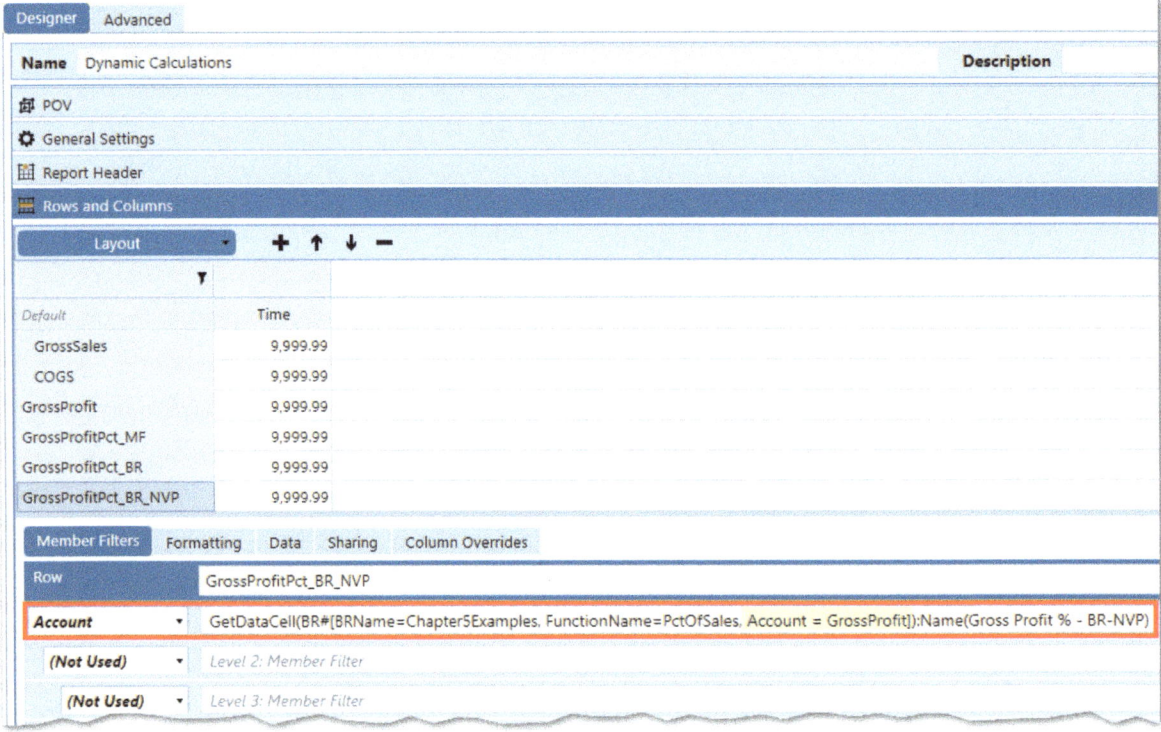

Figure 5.19

The `PctOfSales` function can now be reused with different values passed in via the Name Value pairs to make the function more versatile.

Functions

Our above example utilized the `Divide` function, and other math functions are available to use as well. These functions are designed to improve performance and save the Calculation writer time by shortening the formula and – in some cases – providing some built-in error handling. Specifically, the `Divide` function avoids errors caused when the denominator resolves to zero. Instead, zero values in the denominator are treated as NoData.

Variance

The `Variance` function shortens the syntax required to do simple variance percentage math with the same divide-by-zero protection as the `Divide` function.

Abstract: (A - B) / Abs B

Example:
```
GetDataCell(Variance(S#Actual,S#Budget)):Name(Variance)
```

VariancePercent

The `VariancePercent` is the same as `Variance` but multiplies the result by 100.

Abstract: (A - B) / Abs B * 100

Example:
```
GetDataCell(VariancePercent(S#Actual,S#Budget)):Name(Var %)
```

BetterWorse

Better/Worse (BW) functions calculate a variance, taking the Account Type property of the Account into consideration. Increases in Revenue/Asset Accounts over comparative periods or Scenarios will be displayed as a positive variance, while increases in Expense/Liability Accounts over comparative periods will be displayed as negative variances.

```
GetDataCell(BWDiff(S#Actual, S#BudgetV1)):Name("BetterWorse
Difference")
```

BetterWorsePercent

This function expands upon the Better/Worse function described above and calculates the variance as a percent.

```
GetDataCell(BWPercent(S#Actual, S#BudgetV1)):Name("BetterWorse
Difference %")
```

But Wait, There's More

A complete list of these functions is available in the OneStream Design and Reference Guide. There are also examples and samples in the **Member Filter Builder**.

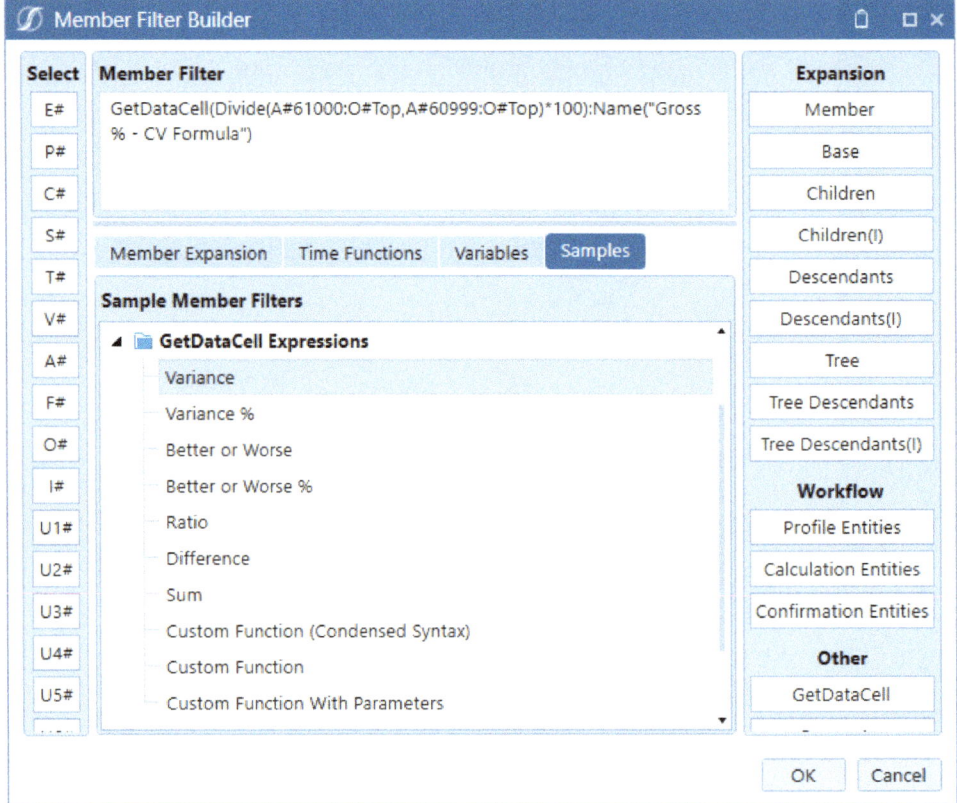

Figure 5.20

There are other more business-specific functions such as `api.functions.GetDSODataCell`. Days Sales Outstanding (DSO) is a common formula that is a required Calculation for many OneStream applications. Consequently, OneStream has provided a pre-built function to encapsulate the logic required for this function.

```
Return api.Functions.GetDSODataCell("AcctsRec", "Sales")
```

Use of UD8

A common technique is to store dynamic Calculations in the UD8 Dimension. The idea is that UD8 is the least-commonly used Dimension, so storing a dynamic Calculation there allows the Calculation to inherit the POV for all other Dimensions from the Report, giving it ultimate flexibility.

To use UD8 to store dynamic Calcs, simply create a Dimension (e.g., `ReportingCalculations`) and create Members there.

Figure 5.21

Since no *data* is being stored within the Members of this Dimension, it does not need to be assigned to the Cube. In fact, a different UD8 can be assigned to the Cube, and dynamic Calculations created within both will work.

UD8 Example

The most common UD8 dynamic Calculation is 'percentage of Net Sales'. The desired Report would look something like this:

	Dec 2022	% of Net Sales
Sales	218,027.00	102.24%
Returns	4,786.62	2.24%
Net Sales	**213,240.38**	**100.00%**
Cost of Goods Sold	43,708.63	20.50%
Research & Development	1,800.00	0.84%
Salaries & Benefits	3,660.00	1.72%
Legal Expenses	180.00	0.08%
Marketing	300.00	0.14%
Office Supplies	240.00	0.11%
MagazineAdvertising	144.00	0.07%
NewspaperAdvertising	120.00	0.06%
BillboardAdvertising	96.00	0.05%
Selling Fees	60.00	0.03%
Shipping Supplies	48.00	0.02%
Rent	84.00	0.04%
Utilities	72.00	0.03%
Insurance	36.00	0.02%
Other Expenses	1,200.00	0.56%
Operating Expenses	**8,040.00**	**3.77%**
Earnings before Interest, Taxes, Depreciation & Amortization	**161,491.75**	**75.73%**
Depreciation Expense	960.00	0.45%
Amortization Expense	240.00	0.11%
Earnings before Interest & Taxes	**162,691.75**	**76.30%**
Interest Expense	2,400.00	1.13%
Income Taxes	40,072.94	18.79%
Net Income	**120,218.81**	**56.38%**

Figure 5.22

The second column of the Report shows the first column's amount as a percentage of Net Sales. One way to accomplish this would be to create a percentage of Net Sales dynamic Calculation for each Account in the Report.

```
'Logic for A#COGS
Return api.Data.GetDataCell("Divide(A#COGS, A#NetSales)")
'Logic for A#Advertising
Return api.Data.GetDataCell("Divide(A#Advertising, A#NetSales")
```

While this approach would work, it would be terribly inefficient and not maintenance-friendly. Every new Account added to the Report would need a corresponding dynamic Calc written for it. Since each Account is using the exact same logic, there is a better way!

Storing the formula in a Member of another Dimension allows the Calculation to inherit the Account defined in the row of the Report, and eliminates the need to write a separate Calculation for each Account.

The logic could be stored in any Dimension but (as mentioned above) UD8 is often picked since it is the least used. This allows the Calculation to work with any Dimension in the row of the Report.

Chapter 5

There may be a need to see a similar Report with Product or Cost Center in the rows. By storing the formula in a UD8 Member, any Dimension (other than UD8) could be used.

The logic for the UD8 Calculation looks like this:

```
'Inherit the account from the Cube View Row
Dim povAccount As String = api.Pov.Account.Name
'Return the percentage of Net Sales
Return api.Data.GetDataCell("Divide(A#" & povAccount & ":U8#None, A#NetSales:U8#None)")
```

Declaring the POV Account and passing it into the formula is done to increase the readability of the formula but isn't necessary as it happens automatically. The below formula would also work:

```
'Return the percentage of Net Sales
Return api.Data.GetDataCell("Divide(U8#None, A#NetSales:U8#None)")
```

The UD8 Member is called in the Cube View column.

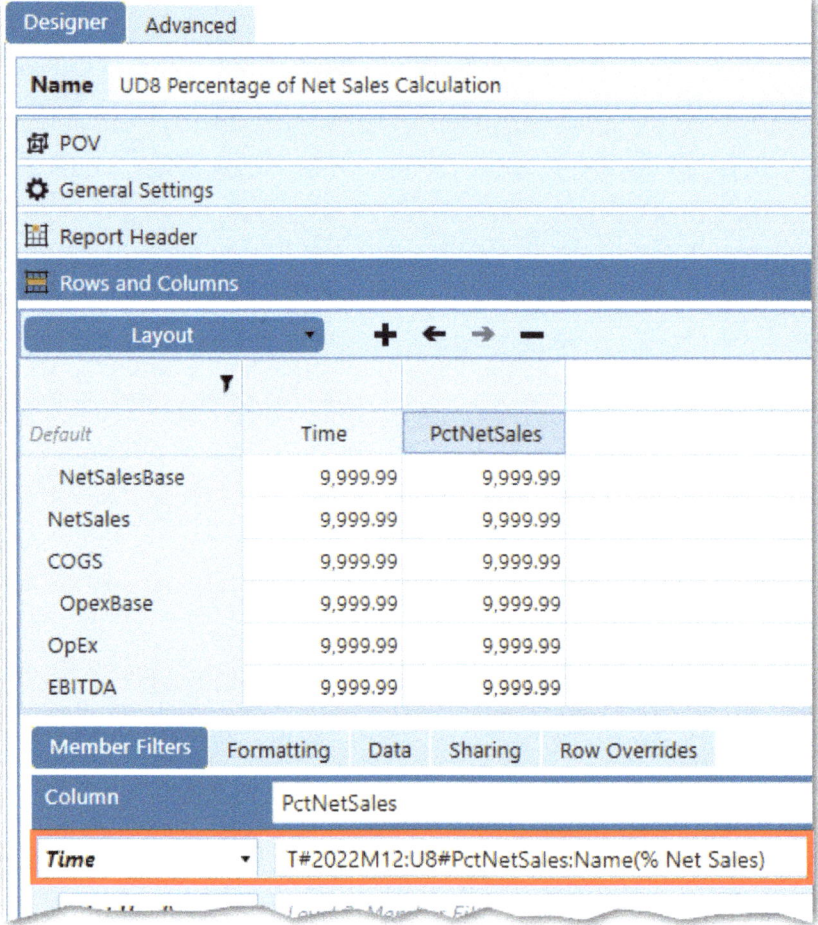

Figure 5.23

UD8#None

You may have noticed `UD8#None` in each of the Member Scripts. Without specifying the UD8 Member, the formula would try to inherit the `UD8#PctNetSales` Member from our Cube View column definition – creating a recursive reference. The error message below would occur.

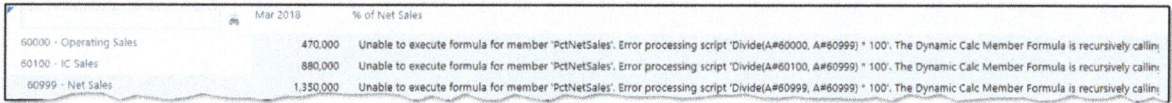

Figure 5.24

If a UD8 Dimension is assigned to the Cube, replace None with whatever the top Member of the hierarchy is named.

Referencing Other Dynamic Calcs

A dynamically calculated Member can be referenced in the formula of another dynamically calculated Member.

For example, let's say we create a dynamic Calculation Account to calculate Total Sales excluding Intercompany Sales.

Account: OpExExclRD

```
Return api.Data.GetDataCell("A#OperatingExpenses - A#ResearchDevelopment")
```

> **Note**: This type of Calculation could also be accomplished via an alternate Account hierarchy utilizing Aggregation weights to subtract A#ResearchDevelopment from A#OperatingExpenses.

This Account can now be used in the formula of another dynamic Calculation. Let's create another calculated Account that refers to the OpExExclRD Account.

Account: OpExExclRDandSalaries

```
Return api.Data.GetDataCell("A#OpExExclRD - A#Salaries")
```

Viewing both of these Accounts in a Cube View shows that one is able to reference the other. You will also notice that the percent of Net Sales UD8 dynamic Calc is also working on both Accounts.

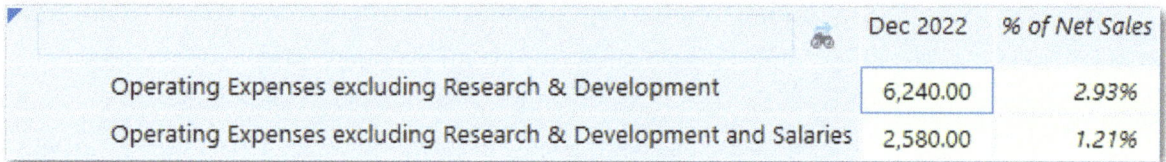

Figure 5.25

> **Note**: Since the UD8 dynamic Calculation is referenced in the column, it will run after the Account dynamic Calculations in the rows due to the order of operations in which Cube Views process.

Relational Blending

Relational Blending refers to blending data from a Cube with data outside of the Cube stored in relational tables. Dynamic Calculations can leverage Relational Blending API functions which can efficiently lookup values in relational tables using dimensional information from the Cube View, like Member names.

Chapter 5

There are three main Methods of Relational Blending:

- **Drill-Back Blending** (One-to-Many Relationship) – This Method of Relational Blending is used to provide access to detailed information that does not exist in the analytic model. This capability is delivered right out-of-the-box with its predefined drill back to Stage detail data. In addition, the Stage Integration Engine provides drill back and drill around capabilities against external data.

- **Application Blending** (One-to-Many Relationship) – This Method of Relational Blending leverages the OneStream MarketPlace Specialty Planning and Compliance applications. This collects information in a Transactional Register format and seamlessly maps/loads summarized data into an analytic model. These applications also provide predefined transactional-level Reports, as well as predefined drill back connectors, allowing drill down from a summarized analytic model to the detailed Register transaction data.

- **Model Blending** (One-to-One Relationship) – This Method of Relational Blending combines the power of the in-memory Analytic Engine with the flexibility of relational database storage. This functionality is provided as part of the Finance Engine API and can be integrated into dynamic Calculations to display relational data alongside data from the Cube.

Let's go back to our Sales Report, which shows the product manager alongside the Product. In our previous example, the information was stored and maintained in text properties within the UD1 Member properties. For this example, the product manager information is contained right in the source data file, which is imported through Stage before being summarized and loaded to the Cube. This type of information is typically not loaded into the Cube as it is constantly changing and maintaining Dimensions to support it would be cumbersome and inefficient. This information is better kept in Stage or Custom tables, where it can be accessed using the Relational Blending API functions.

Stage Table

The Stage table is out-of-the-box functionality; the only configuration required is to enable a Text Attribute field in the Cube Properties.

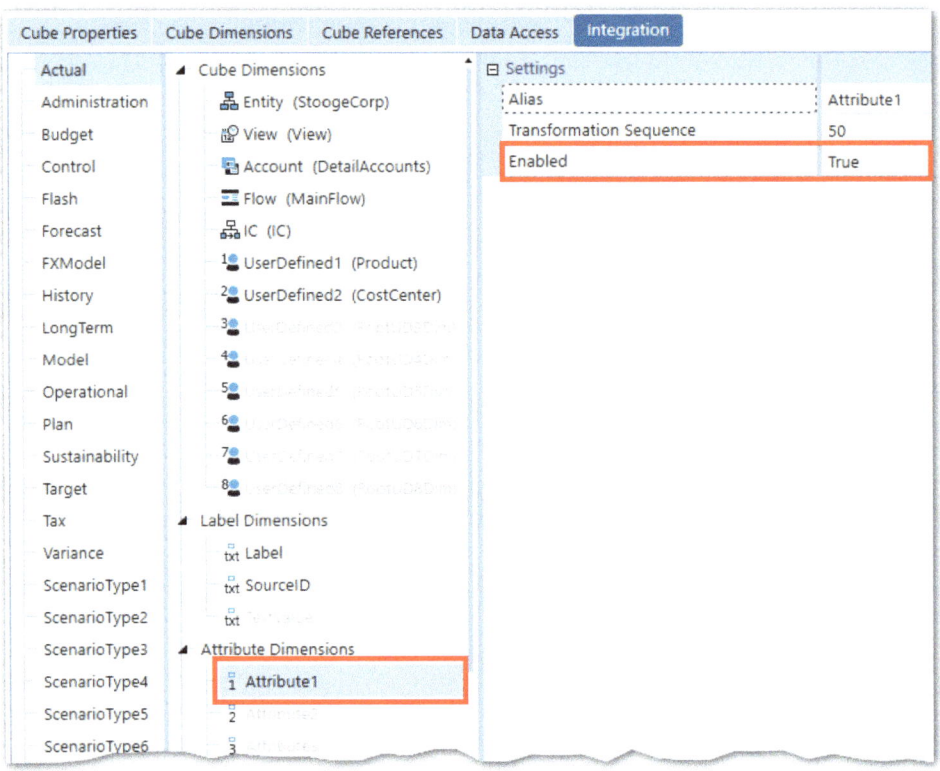

Figure 5.26

Reporting Calculations

Attribute1 is populated in Stage from the source file.

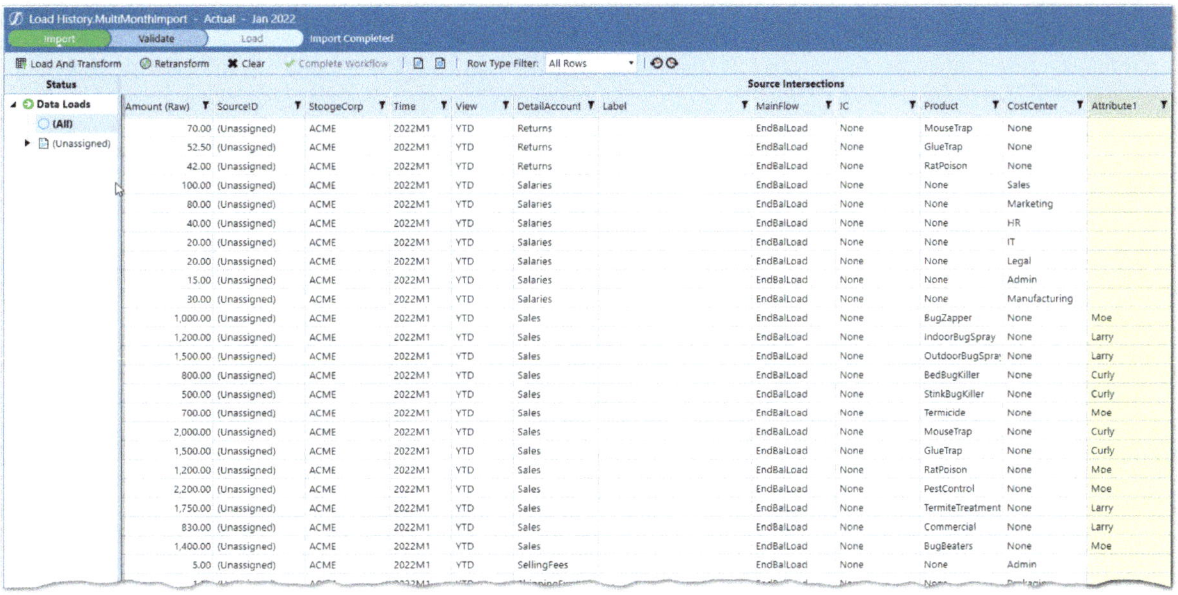

Amount (Raw)	SourceID	StoogeCorp	Time	View	DetailAccount	Label	MainFlow	IC	Product	CostCenter	Attribute1
70.00	(Unassigned)	ACME	2022M1	YTD	Returns		EndBalLoad	None	MouseTrap	None	
52.50	(Unassigned)	ACME	2022M1	YTD	Returns		EndBalLoad	None	GlueTrap	None	
42.00	(Unassigned)	ACME	2022M1	YTD	Returns		EndBalLoad	None	RatPoison	None	
100.00	(Unassigned)	ACME	2022M1	YTD	Salaries		EndBalLoad	None	None	Sales	
80.00	(Unassigned)	ACME	2022M1	YTD	Salaries		EndBalLoad	None	None	Marketing	
40.00	(Unassigned)	ACME	2022M1	YTD	Salaries		EndBalLoad	None	None	HR	
20.00	(Unassigned)	ACME	2022M1	YTD	Salaries		EndBalLoad	None	None	IT	
20.00	(Unassigned)	ACME	2022M1	YTD	Salaries		EndBalLoad	None	None	Legal	
15.00	(Unassigned)	ACME	2022M1	YTD	Salaries		EndBalLoad	None	None	Admin	
30.00	(Unassigned)	ACME	2022M1	YTD	Salaries		EndBalLoad	None	None	Manufacturing	
1,000.00	(Unassigned)	ACME	2022M1	YTD	Sales		EndBalLoad	None	BugZapper	None	Moe
1,200.00	(Unassigned)	ACME	2022M1	YTD	Sales		EndBalLoad	None	IndoorBugSpray	None	Larry
1,500.00	(Unassigned)	ACME	2022M1	YTD	Sales		EndBalLoad	None	OutdoorBugSpray	None	Larry
800.00	(Unassigned)	ACME	2022M1	YTD	Sales		EndBalLoad	None	BedBugKiller	None	Curly
500.00	(Unassigned)	ACME	2022M1	YTD	Sales		EndBalLoad	None	StinkBugKiller	None	Curly
700.00	(Unassigned)	ACME	2022M1	YTD	Sales		EndBalLoad	None	Termicide	None	Moe
2,000.00	(Unassigned)	ACME	2022M1	YTD	Sales		EndBalLoad	None	MouseTrap	None	Curly
1,500.00	(Unassigned)	ACME	2022M1	YTD	Sales		EndBalLoad	None	GlueTrap	None	Curly
1,200.00	(Unassigned)	ACME	2022M1	YTD	Sales		EndBalLoad	None	RatPoison	None	Moe
2,200.00	(Unassigned)	ACME	2022M1	YTD	Sales		EndBalLoad	None	PestControl	None	Moe
1,750.00	(Unassigned)	ACME	2022M1	YTD	Sales		EndBalLoad	None	TermiteTreatment	None	Larry
830.00	(Unassigned)	ACME	2022M1	YTD	Sales		EndBalLoad	None	Commercial	None	Larry
1,400.00	(Unassigned)	ACME	2022M1	YTD	Sales		EndBalLoad	None	BugBeaters	None	Moe
5.00	(Unassigned)	ACME	2022M1	YTD	SellingFees		EndBalLoad	None	None	Admin	

Figure 5.27

Dynamic Calculation Using GetStageBlendText Function

A Dynamic Calculation can now be written to look up the `Attribute` column of the Stage table based on the UD1 in the Report.

```
If Not api.Entity.HasChildren Then
    If objViewMember.IsAnnotationType Then
        Dim criteria As New Text.StringBuilder
        criteria.Append("AcT = '" & api.Pov.Account.Name & "' ")
        criteria.Append("And U1T = '" & api.Pov.UD1.Name & "' ")
        Return api.Functions.GetStageBlendTextUsingCurrentPOV(BlendCacheLevelTypes.WfProfileScenarioTime, " & _
        ""DU", "Load History.MultiMonthImport","AcT,U1T,A1", criteria.ToString, "A1",BlendTextOperationTypes.FirstValue)
    Else
        Return Nothing
    End If
Else
    Return Nothing
End If
```

The above script will query the Stage table based on some defined criteria and return the Attribute1 column. The `api.Functions.GetStageBlendTextUsingCurrentPOV` function is used to query the Stage table in an efficient manner using criteria from the Cube View in which the function is called from. Using this function will ensure optimal performance as the table will be queried once and then stored in cache. After the initial query, all cell references will read from cache.

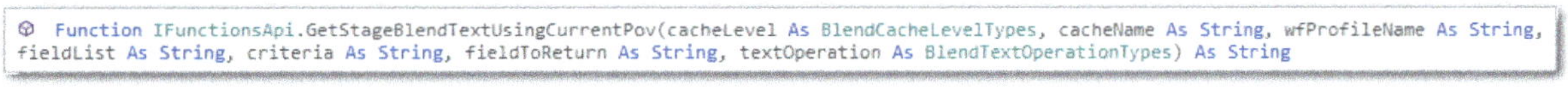

```
Function IFunctionsApi.GetStageBlendTextUsingCurrentPov(cacheLevel As BlendCacheLevelTypes, cacheName As String, wfProfileName As String, fieldList As String, criteria As String, fieldToReturn As String, textOperation As BlendTextOperationTypes) As String
```

Figure 5.28

This function is all about efficiency and performance. Querying tables from a Dynamic Calculation is a dangerous endeavor due to the potential high processing time required. Remember that a Dynamic Calculation will run for every cell in a Cube View, Quick View, or other Report. If you query a large relational table 120 times for a simple 10 row, 12 column Report, you are going to have a bad time. This function eliminates that risk and provides parameters to operate as efficiently as possible. This means querying the table as few times as possible, storing the query result in memory (caching it), and referring back to the stored (cached) table instead of re-querying the table each time.

Let's breakdown the function and the parameters which it requires.

CacheLevel

The `CacheLevel` is used to control the granularity of the cache. In other words, this controls how many times the table needs to be queried and the volume of records brought into cache. The `BlendCacheLevelTypes` enumerable can be used to view and set the options.

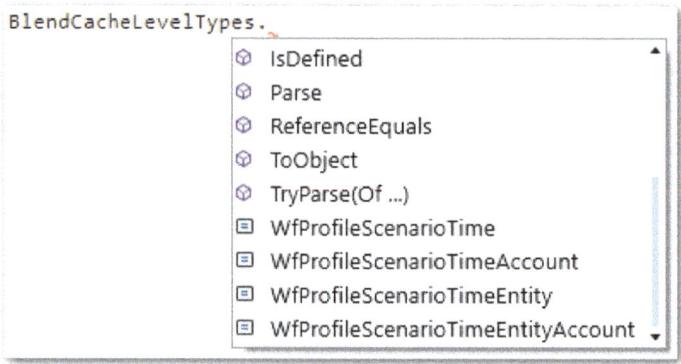

Figure 5.29

The option chosen here should align with the Cube View (or other reporting mechanism) in which it is used. If the Cube View only shows data for one Scenario, Time Period, Entity, and Account, then `WFProfileScenarioTimeEntityAccount BlendCacheLevel` should be used. The other options would also work but would be less efficient as more data is brought into cache than necessary; this will increase the time of the initial query as well as subsequent lookups of the cached data.

If multiple Accounts are shown in the Report, then `WFProfileScenarioTimeEntity` should be used. Conversely, using `WFProfileScenarioTimeEntity` when multiple Accounts are in the Cube View will mean that the table will be queried more times.

In summary, choose the cache level that will minimize the number of queries to the table and result in data that is only required for the scope of the Report.

CacheName

A short name used to identify the values placed in the cache (Full `CacheID` will be `CacheName` + `CacheLevel` values). This name can be any string and should be different for each reference of this function within a Member Formula or Business Rule.

wfProfileName

Name of the import Workflow Profile containing the values to be looked up. (Pass an empty string to look up the Workflow based on the POV Entity; use `*.YourWFSuffix` to get all Workflow Profiles with the specified suffix.)

FieldList

List of Stage table fields that will be used as criteria and/or returned. To view the column names of the Stage table, go to the Database page within the System tab and navigate to the various Stage tables.

Reporting Calculations

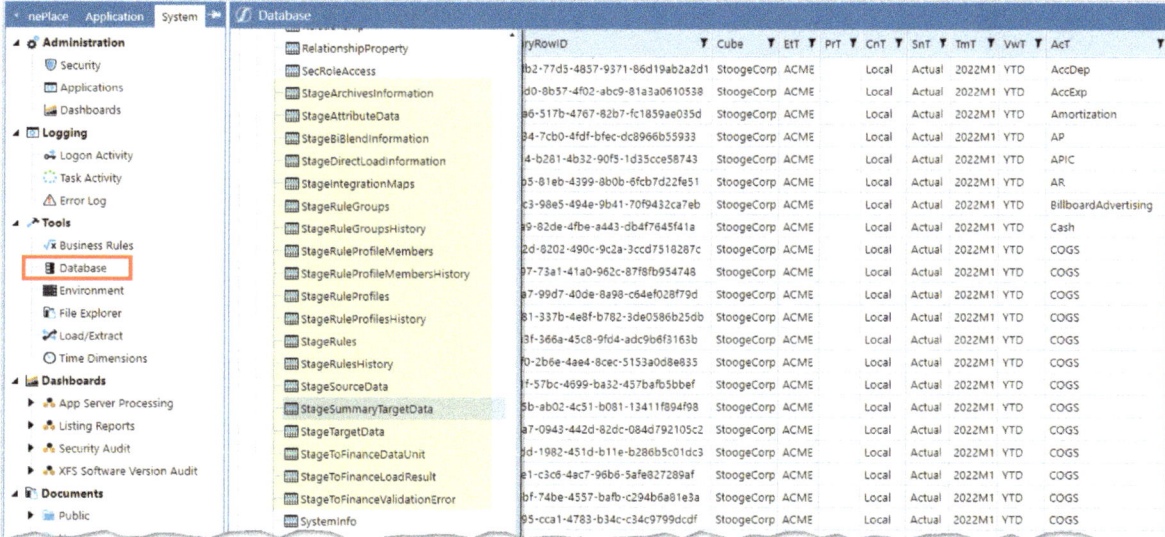

Figure 5.30

Criteria

`Criteria` statement used to select rows in the cached data table. A `StringBuilder` is used to build the criteria string. This will be like a SQL `Where` Clause with the 'Where' omitted. The `Where` clause used in the example will include the Product and Account from the Cube View.

```
Dim criteria As New Text.StringBuilder
criteria.Append("AcT = '" & api.Pov.Account.Name & "' ")
criteria.Append("And U1T = '" & api.Pov.UD1.Name & "' ")
```

FieldToReturn

Name of the Stage field to return. Our example will return the field from the `Attribute1` column, so `A1` is used. This can be seen in the `StageAttributeData` table.

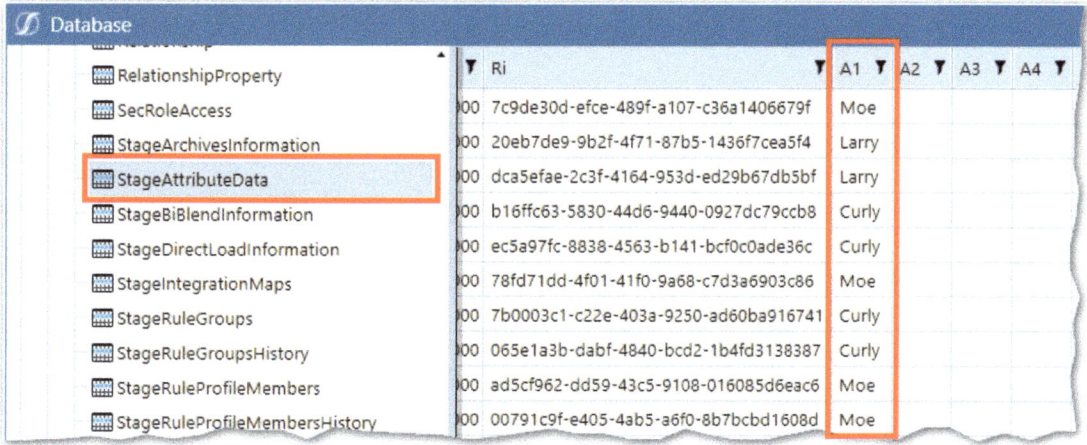

Figure 5.31

Results

The full script is stored in a UD8 Member and referenced in a Cube View with the `V#Annotation` Member.

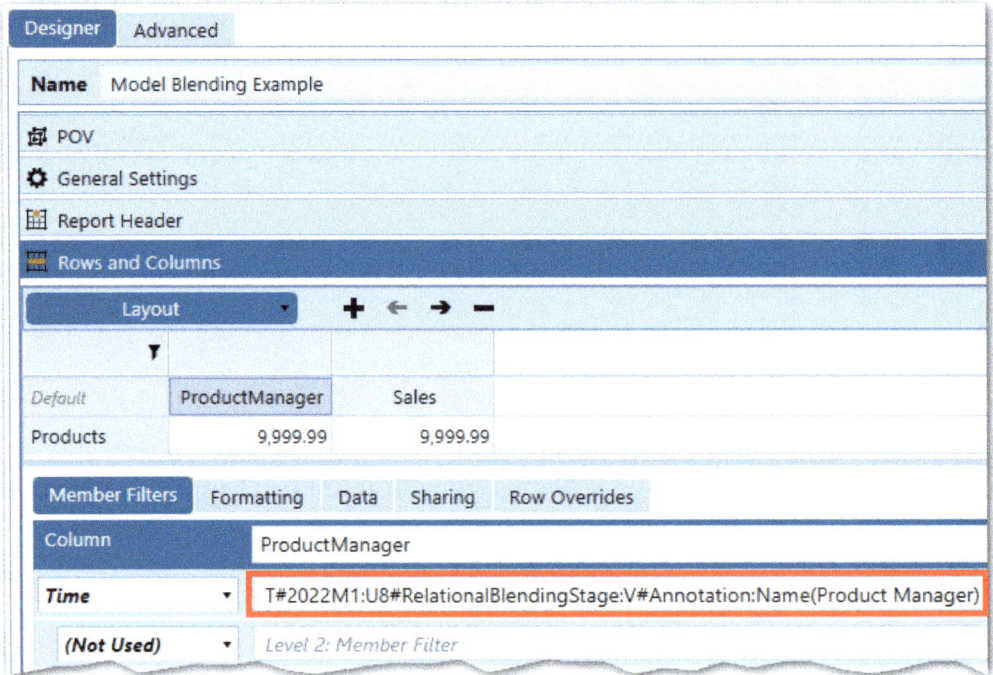

Figure 5.32

The results should mirror the earlier Product Report with the names now pulled from Stage instead of UD1 Member properties.

Figure 5.33

Reporting Calculations

Other Variations

Other `GetStageBlend` functions exist for different purposes. They all behave similarly to the example described above. Refer to the OneStream Design and Reference Guide for more information about them.

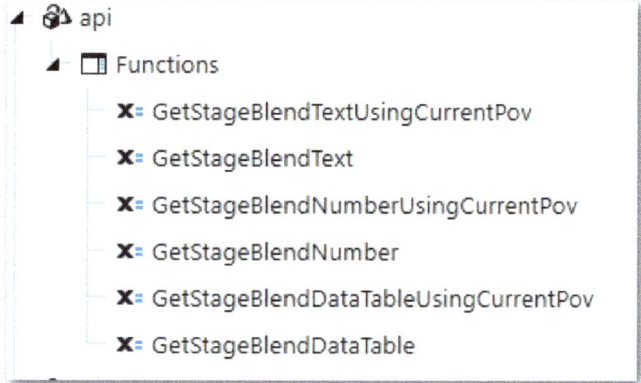

Figure 5.34

General Guidelines and Tips

Aggregation

Only stored data aggregates within Dimension hierarchies, so Dynamic Calculations will not naturally aggregate to Parent Members. For example, a Parent Account with two Dynamic Calculation Children will not display the aggregated total of both Calculations.

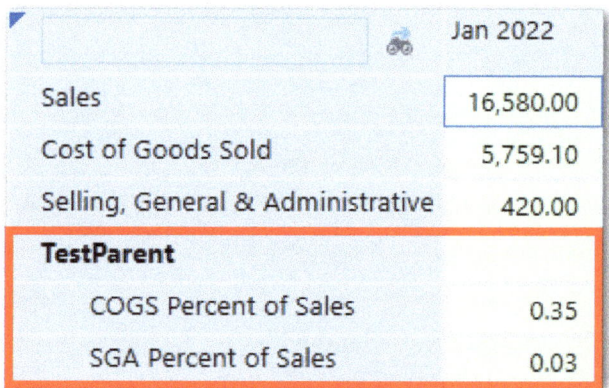

Figure 5.35

The above figure shows two dynamically calculated ratio Accounts rolling up to a Parent Account. The Parent Account does not aggregate the two ratios… which wouldn't make much sense anyway. Instead, a Dynamic Calculation can be written directly on the `TestParent` Account. The formula logic will add COGS and SGA together and divide the result by Sales to get a new ratio.

```
Return api.Data.GetDataCell("Divide((A#COGS + A#SGA), A#Sales)")
```

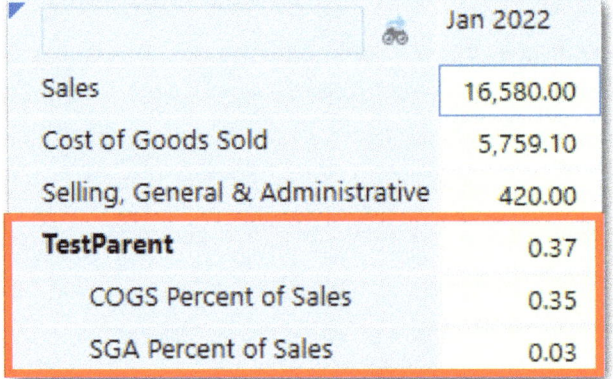

Figure 5.36

Alternate Hierarchies

For simple addition and subtraction, alternate hierarchies within Dimensions can also achieve the same result as a Dynamic Calculation and should be used when possible. The earlier example, where a Dynamic Calculation was used to calculate operating expenses excluding research & development, would have been better as an alternate hierarchy.

Figure 5.37

The above is achieved by creating a new Account with OperatingExpenses and ResearchDevelopment as Children. The Aggregation weight of ResearchDevelopment is set to -1 to subtract it from Operating Expense. This Method will perform better, be easier to maintain, and more transparent to End Users because it will be drillable.

Complement Stored Calculations

Dynamic Calculations can be written to mirror the logic of stored Calculations that will run as part of the DUCS or as Custom Calculate. They can be included on data entry Forms to give Users immediate feedback as to the result of inputs.

Test on Small Report

If you have a large Cube View or Report that returns hundreds of data cells, it is a good idea to test Dynamic Calculations on a smaller Report to increase speed and avoid server overload if the Calculations result in an error or error logging is enabled.

Conclusion

Not all calculated data needs to be stored in the Cube. For Calculations that are needed to support reporting, Dynamic Calcs are much more flexible and forgiving than stored Calculations. They can run within the dimensional context of the Report that they are called from, and run completely in memory. They also afford the ability to return text from Dimension properties or relational tables, which can enhance reporting. Use Dynamic Calculations whenever possible as they should be a part of every project's holistic Calculation build.

6

Managing Calculations

As we've learned by now, Calculations can exist in – and be executed from – many places within OneStream. Without a proper system for managing Calculations, things can get chaotic quickly.

It's also important to write Calculations in a maintenance-friendly manner, so this chapter will discuss guidelines for the efficient maintenance and management of Calculations from the beginning to the end of a project.

Start at the Beginning

Calculation management and documentation should start in the **Design and Requirements** phase of the project and continue to the end, where it is ultimately handed off to the application Administrator. Even though Design and Requirements meetings typically stray away from detailed discussion about Calculations, there will be indicators to look for that should trigger deeper dives for Calculations later in the project. For example, a customer may list things like "Automated Cash Flow," "Complex Ownership," and "Driver-Based Forecasting," which are likely candidates for the heavy use of Calculations. Keep a log of these items through Design and Requirements with the intent of extrapolating more detail later.

Create a Calculation Matrix

As more Calculation details are uncovered, it's a good idea to create an inventory of each Calculation along with some other pertinent information in a Calculation Matrix. The Calculation Matrix will also prove handy later in the project when it's time to test Calculation results with Users.

An initial Calculation Matrix can be quite simple, capturing only basic Calculation details such as Calculation name, Type, and location. As the Design and Build phases of a project move forward, the initial Calculation Matrix becomes a living document that grows and changes as the project progresses. Depending on the complexity of a client's implementation and required Calculations, the Calculation Matrix could evolve to capture more detail along the way, such as the Calculation scope and testing results.

Basic Information

Below is an example of the basic information that can be captured in a Calculation Matrix.

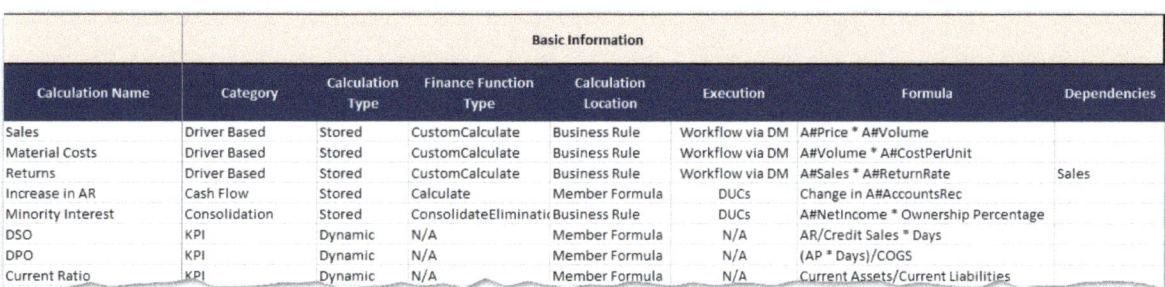

Figure 6.1

Chapter 6

Calculation Name and Category

The Calculation name and category will help organize and classify your Calculations. Categories can be based on the functional area they cover, the User audience, or the Scenario they are specific to.

Calculation Type

Calculation Type will distinguish between stored and dynamic; these Calculation Types are fundamentally different in how they are written and tested.

Finance Function Type

For stored Calculation Types, the **Finance Function Type** should be indicated as this will determine how and when the Calculations are executed.

> **Note:** Member Formulas automatically use the **Calculate Finance Function Type**, which is not explicitly defined like it is in Business Rules.

Calculation Location

Calculation location refers to where the Calculation syntax is physically written and maintained, either in a Business Rule or a Member Formula.

Execution

Refers to where the Calculation is executed from. This information isn't relevant for Dynamic Calcs because they will run any time they are called.

Formula

A simple, plain-English description of the logic. Don't worry about capturing every nuance or exception here.

Dependencies

Any other Calculations that this Calculation depends on. This will help to determine Formula Pass or the sequence within a Business Rule.

Scope Information

Calculation scope information will help performance and ensure Calculations don't conflict or cause unexpected results. Data Unit scope will result in preceding `IF` statements or an assignment to specific Scenario Types or Time periods in Member Formulas. Scope for Account-level Dimensions will help define what is included in the destination and source Member Scripts, as well as the filter (if needed).

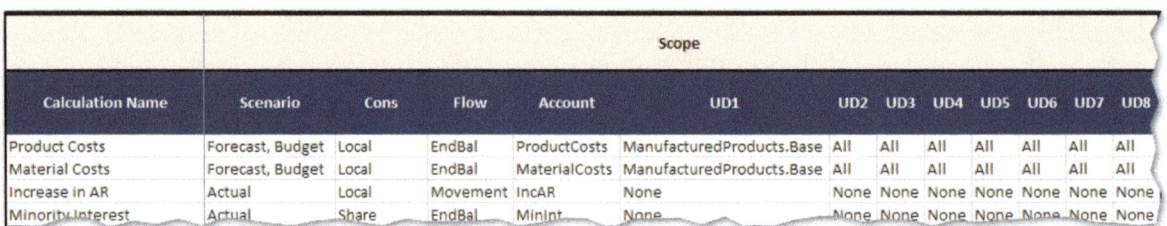

Figure 6.2

Testing

Once it's time for testing, the Calculation Matrix will be a great starting point for logging results. It is highly likely that, as you test, many of the fields in the matrix will change as production data gets used and previous assumptions are proven incorrect.

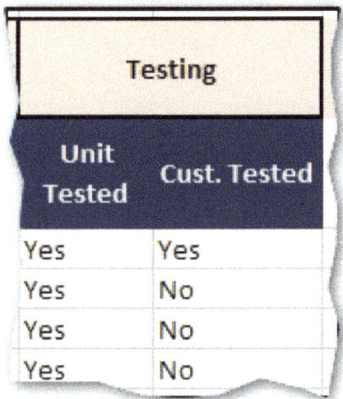

Figure 6.3

Calculation Matrix Benefits

Tracking

Keeping a centralized list of all Calculations:

- Reduces the risk of losing track of critical Calculations that *must* be built.
- Provides useful details for estimating the level of effort required to build Calculations.
- Creates a single source to quickly reference the status of the Calculation build.
- Streamlines the process for identifying missing Calculations by having a referenceable list of all defined Calculations in one location.

Designing

The design of Calculations often requires an iterative process. A Calculation Matrix can be used to review all proposed Calculation logic – with a client – prior to building Calculations. A client can review the proposed logic, make edits where necessary, and approve the Calculations before beginning the build.

Building, Testing, and Approving

A Calculation Matrix can be used to track the progress of building Calculations, and to document additional testing and approval milestones (e.g., unit-tested, customer-tested, Calculation complete).

Transferring Knowledge

A Calculation Matrix that is kept up-to-date serves as a valuable reference for System Administrators, enhancing their knowledge of all Calculations that have been built in OneStream.

Calculation Testing

The thorough testing of all Calculations is a critical success factor for OneStream implementations. It is important to complete detailed unit testing as well as client testing for each Calculation.

Chapter 6

Completing comprehensive and systematic testing helps to ensure that Calculation logic is functioning as intended.

Testing Tips

- If possible, try to replicate results against legacy systems or historical results.
- Create a Cube View that contains a `GetDataCell` formula that mirrors the logic of the Calculation (stored or dynamic) being tested. Use the Cube View to check the results after running the Calculation. Note that this may be difficult or impossible for complex Calculations.
- Create a Cube View that shows data for both the Calculation inputs and outputs. If using Dimension filters, include Members *outside* the filters to ensure the Calculation is correctly applying the filter.
- Use the functions available in the Excel Add-in to create a worksheet that mirrors the logic of the Calculation being tested. Use the Excel worksheet to check the results after running the Calculation.

Calculation Reports

OneStream includes a suite of standard **Application Reports** to assist in managing Calculations. If not already loaded into the application, Application Reports can be downloaded and installed from the OneStream MarketPlace.

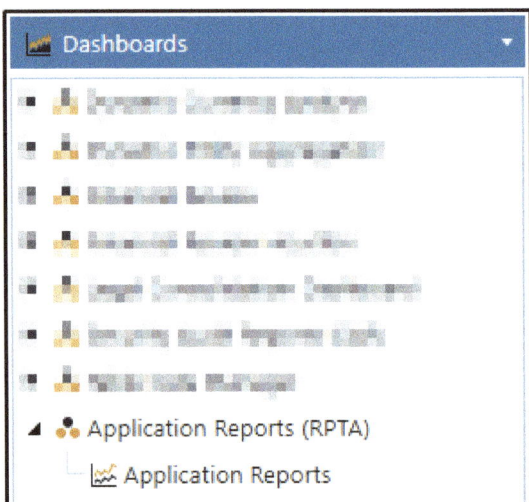

Figure 6.4

Application Reports contain several useful Reports but specific to Calculations are the Formula Statistics and Formula List Reports.

Managing Calculations

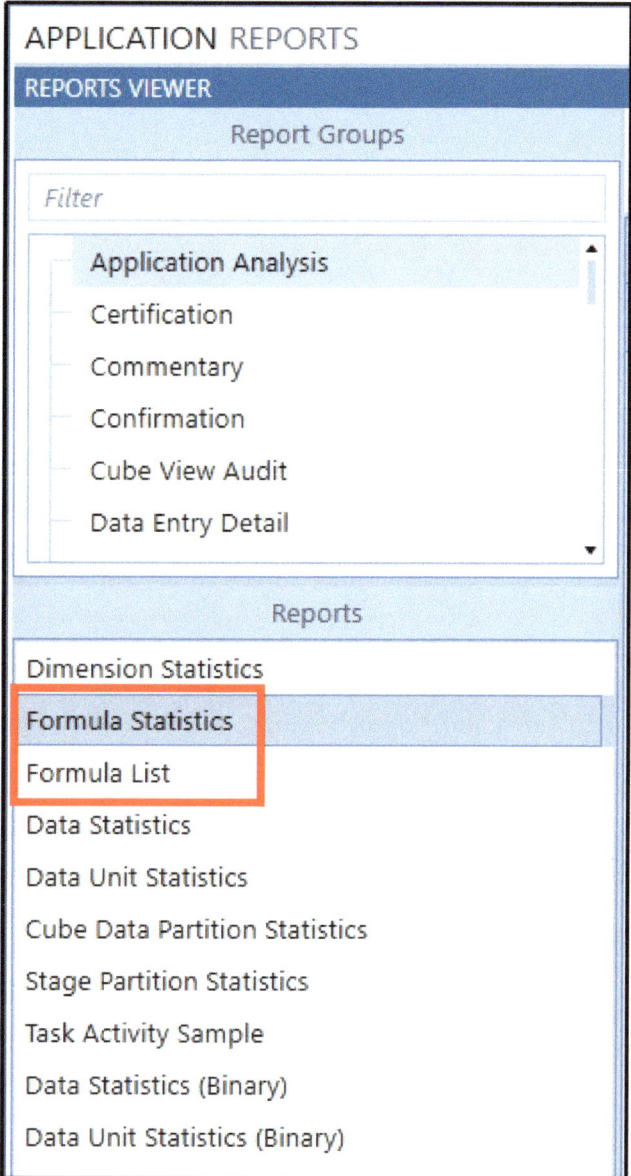

Figure 6.5

Formula Statistics

The Formula Statistics Report will give you a breakdown of each Dimension and how many Members have Member Formulas or Dynamic Calcs assigned to them. Note that this will not include Members that are calculated via Business Rules.

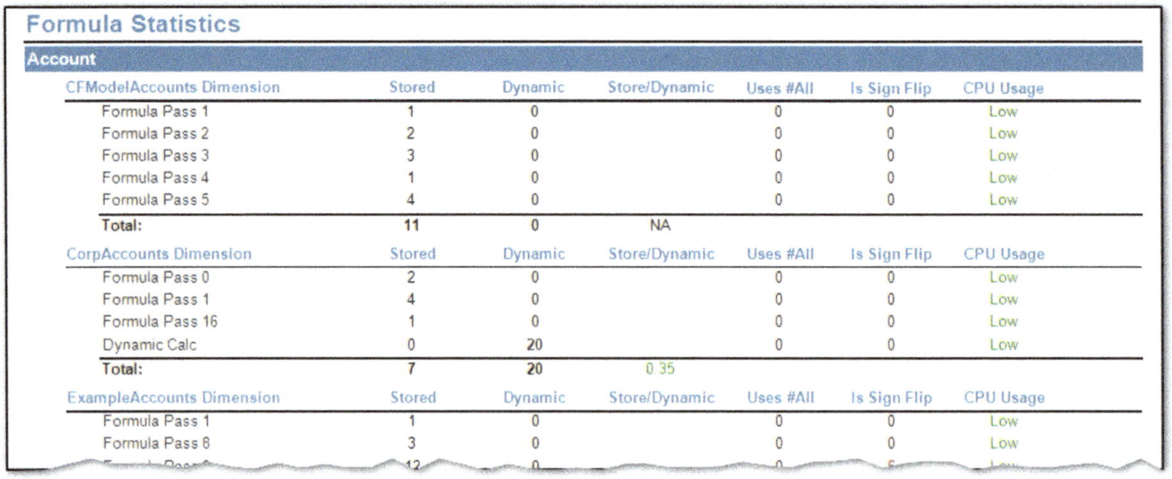

Chapter 6

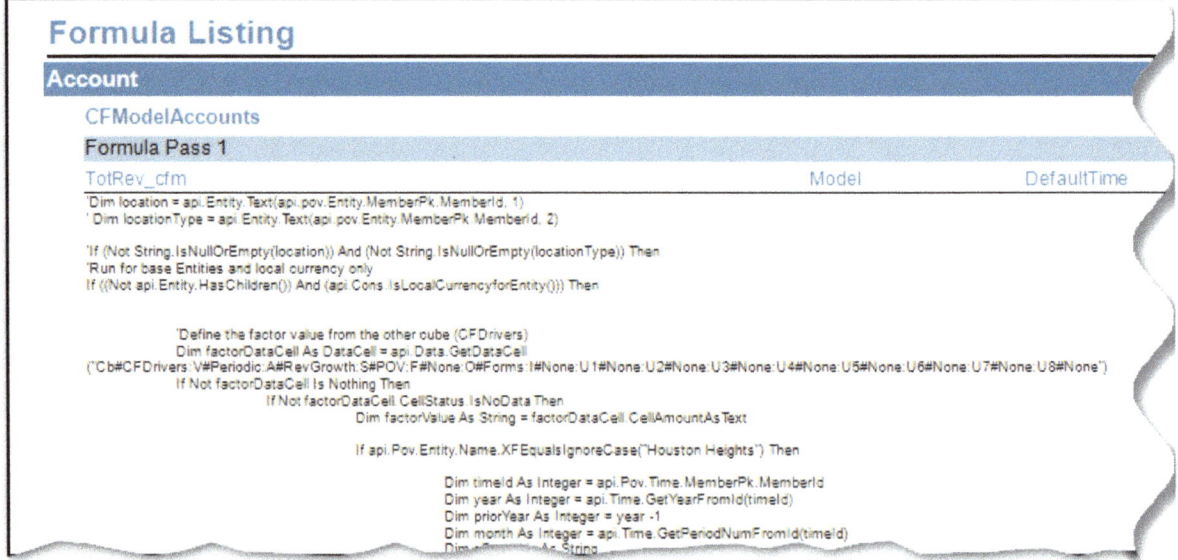

Figure 6.6

Formula List

The Formula List Report shows each Member Formula and its syntax.

Figure 6.7

Calculation Maintenance

At some point, you will (probably very happily) pass the job of maintaining the Calculations built during an implementation to someone else, likely an Administrator. At this point, they will have the daunting job of deciphering and making sense of your code, so they can make any necessary modifications resulting from changes in business processes or underlying data. Ensuring this process goes smoothly requires building Calculations in a maintenance-friendly way, as well as ensuring all your Calculation code is properly commented.

Comments

Comments are text within your code that do not compile or execute. They are strictly there to provide some context and explanation from the code writer. Writing good comments is just as crucial as writing good code.

There are two main components to comments: a header block and inline explanations.

Header

Header comments are at the beginning of each code function or subroutine. They:

1. Identify the Calculation name.

2. Describe the purpose and usage of the Calculation.

3. Document who wrote the code originally (and when), as well as any modifications. Modified dates must include what was changed and who changed it.

4. Note any special maintenance considerations.

```
Namespace OneStream.BusinessRule.Finance.ForecastSales
    Public Class MainClass
        '----------------------------------------------------------------
        'Name:           ForecastSales
        '
        'Purpose:        Calculate a driver based salesforecast based on Price and Volume
        '
        'Usage:          Used in all Forecast scenario types and executed by users in various Fore Cast Workflows
        '
        'Maintenance:    All products added as a base member on U1#Clubs will be included in the filter
        '
        'Created By:     Jon Golembiewski
        'Date Created:   8-21-2021
        '
        'Modifed By:
        'Date Modified:
        '
        '
        '----------------------------------------------------------------
        Public Function Main(ByVal si As SessionInfo, ByVal globals As BRGlobals, ByVal api As FinanceRulesApi, ByVal args A
            Try
                Select Case api.FunctionType
```

Figure 6.8

Inline

It is always better to err on the side of 'over-commenting' versus 'under-commenting.' Try your best to provide a comment for each line or block of 3-5 lines.

Inline comments can be as short as a few words or as long as several sentences. Length is not important; conveying *why* a given block of code does what it does is.

```
'Loop through the cells of the data buffer
For Each sourceCell As DataBufferCell In costDataBuffer.DataBufferCells.Values

    'Retrieve the Inflation Rate from the source Cost Center
    Dim inflationRateDataCell As DataCell = api.Data.GetDataCell("F#None:I#Top:O#Top:A#InflationRate:U1#" & source
    'Check the inflation rate on the Cost Center, if its NoData then retrieve from U1#None
    If inflationRateDataCell.CellStatus.IsNoData Then
        'Get the Inflation Rate on U1#None
        inflationRateDataCell = api.Data.GetDataCell("F#None:I#Top:O#Top:A#InflationRate:U1#None:U2#None:U3#None:
    End If

    'Create a new result cell to eventually add to the resultdata buffer
    'We will inherit the cell properties of the source cell
    Dim resultCell As New DataBufferCell(sourceCell)
```

Figure 6.9

Chapter 6

Regions

Regions are a VB.NET directive that can be used to specify a block of code that can be expanded or collapsed using the outlining feature within the Business Rule Editor. You can place or nest regions within other regions to group similar regions together. This technique is great for organizational purposes within large Business Rules.

Use the `#Region "RegionName"` and `#End Region` syntax to specify a collapsible region within your code.

```
#Region "Region1"

'Some lines of script
'
'
'
'
'
#End Region

#Region "Region2"
'Some lines of script
'
'
'
'
'
#End Region
```

```
24
25              Case Is = FinanceFunctionType.CustomCalculate
26                  If args.CustomCalculateArgs.FunctionName.XFEqu
27
28  [+]                 "Region1"
37
38  [+]                 "Region2"
46
47                  End If
```

Figure 6.10

Maintenance Tips

Maintenance refers to any time a production script needs to be changed or modified due to changes in the application, such as adding Members to Dimensions. The goal should be to minimize any changes to code and narrow maintenance to specific areas of the application, such as the **Dimension Library**.

Time Functions

Time periods or years should *never* be hardcoded into `api.Data.Calculate` formulas.

```
'Calculate next year's sales based on this years sales multiplied by a growth rate
api.Data.Calculate("A#Sales = A#Sales:T#2021M12 * A#GrowthRate:T#2022M1")
```

The above formula is attempting to calculate 2022 Sales based on the last period of the prior year's Sales multiplied by a constant growth rate, which is entered in month 1 of the Forecast year. This formula will work fine for 2022, but once 2023 comes along, the formula is obsolete and maintenance must be performed to update the Calculation for the next year. There is a better way!

Time functions exist that can reference the current Time period being processed.

- `POVPriorYear`
- `POVYear`
- `POVPrior1`, `POVPrior2`, `POVPrior12`, etc.
- `POVNext1`, `POVNext2`, `POVNext12`, etc.
- `POVFirstInYear`

This allows the formula to be dynamic and function correctly in any Time period.

```
'Calculate next years sales base on this years sales multiplied by a growth rate
api.Data.Calculate("A#Sales = A#Sales:T#POVLastInYear * A#GrowthRate:T#POVFirstInYear")
```

The above example may seem painfully obvious but – believe it or not – I have seen the wrong approach taken many times!

> **Note:** The `T#POVLastInYear` and `T#POVFirstInYear` should be used instead of `T#POVPriorYearM12` when possible since these functions will work on Scenarios of quarterly or yearly frequencies as well as monthly.

There are many other Time functions to the ones mentioned. The Member Filter Builder contains a list of available functions.

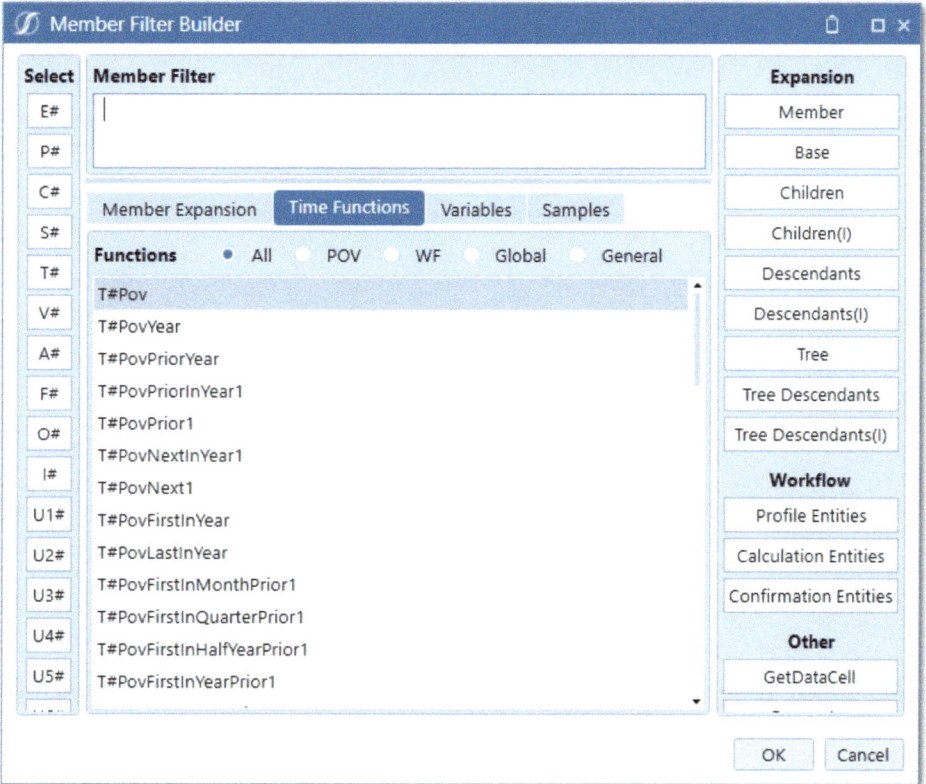

Figure 6.11

Chapter 6

Utilizing Hierarchies

Dimension hierarchies typically exist to support reporting requirements but can also be utilized to support Calculations.

We've seen how Dimension filters can be used to limit the scope of Calculations. If used with Dimension hierarchies, they can also be used to reduce Calculation maintenance. Let's look at an example of a Calculation written by Curly:

```
api.Data.Calculate("A#Sales = RemoveZeros(A#Price * A#Volume)",,,,,"U1#BugZapper, U1#MouseTrap, U1#PestControl")
```

At first glance, this looks like a perfectly good Calculation as it correctly uses a filter to reduce scope. But it is not very maintenance-friendly. If another Cost Center gets added to the Dimension Library, that needs to be included in this Calculation, and the formula will need to be modified by an Admin in the **Business Rule Editor**. Not ideal.

If we look at the hierarchy, we can see why Curly wrote it this way.

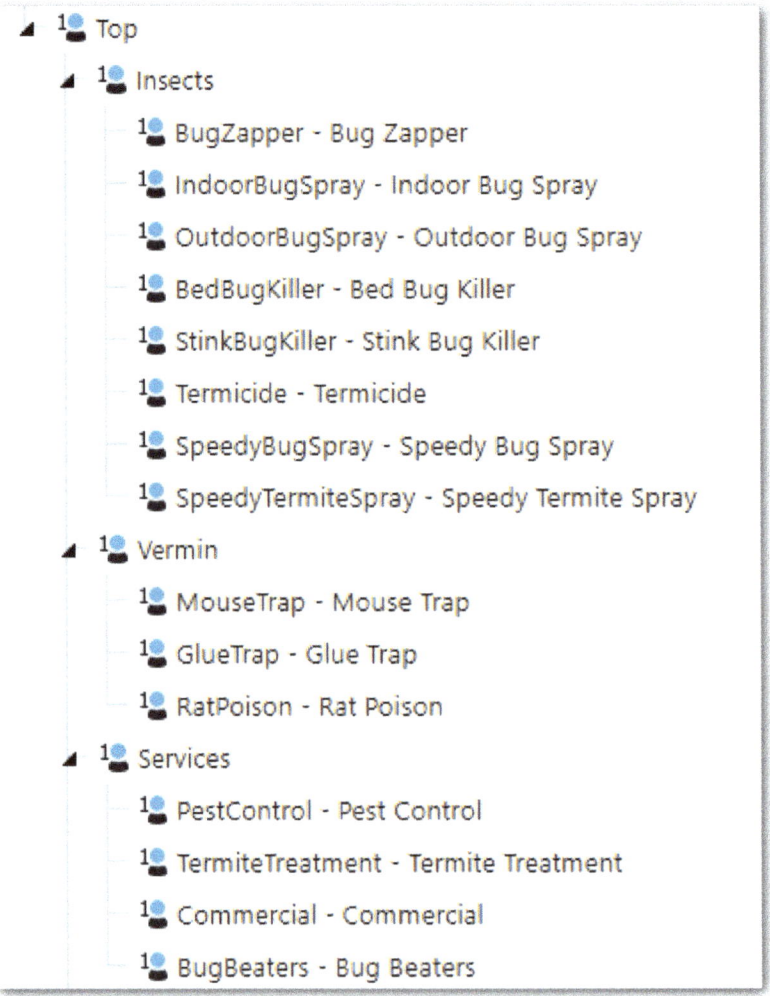

Figure 6.12

We can see that the above hierarchy does not have a common Parent for BugZapper, MouseTrap, and PestControl Products. The very simple solution is to create a new Parent that groups these Members together.

Managing Calculations

Figure 6.13

SalesCalculation is created under another Parent called AlternateHierarchies, which is a sibling of Top, so that it won't cause any double-counting of the included Members.

Our Calculation formula can now be written like this:

```
api.Data.Calculate("A#Sales = RemoveZeros(A#Price * A#Volume)",,,,,"U1#SalesCalculation.Base")
```

A comment should be included in the header of the Calculation that explains that any new Product Member, that should be included in this Calculation, should be added to the U1#SalesCalculation hierarchy.

```
'--------------------------------------------------------------------------------
'Name:              DriverBasedSalesCalc
'Purpose:           Calculate Driver Based Sales for Budget & Forecast Scenarios
'Usage:             Used in all Budget and Forecast Scenario Types and executed by users in various workflows
'                   Runs on all products within the U1#SalesCalculation group
'Maintenance:       All new Products that require this calculation should be added as a child of U1#SalesCalculation
'Created by:        Jon Golembiewski on 1/6/2022
'Edited by:
'--------------------------------------------------------------------------------
```

Creating alternate hierarchies is fairly simple from a technical standpoint and doesn't add any Calculation performance overhead. It is always easier to simply copy a Member beneath a new Parent than it is to change and retest code.

Text Properties

Like alternate hierarchies, text properties can be referenced in Member Filters and used to support Calculations. Let's apply the use of text properties to our previous example:

```
api.Data.Calculate("A#Sales = RemoveZeros(A#Price * A#Volume)",,,,,"U1#BugZapper, U1#MouseTrap, U1#PestControl")
```

Instead of grouping each of the individually referenced Members beneath a newly-created Parent, text properties can be utilized to achieve the same result. Each Member's Text2 property will contain the text SalesCalculation.

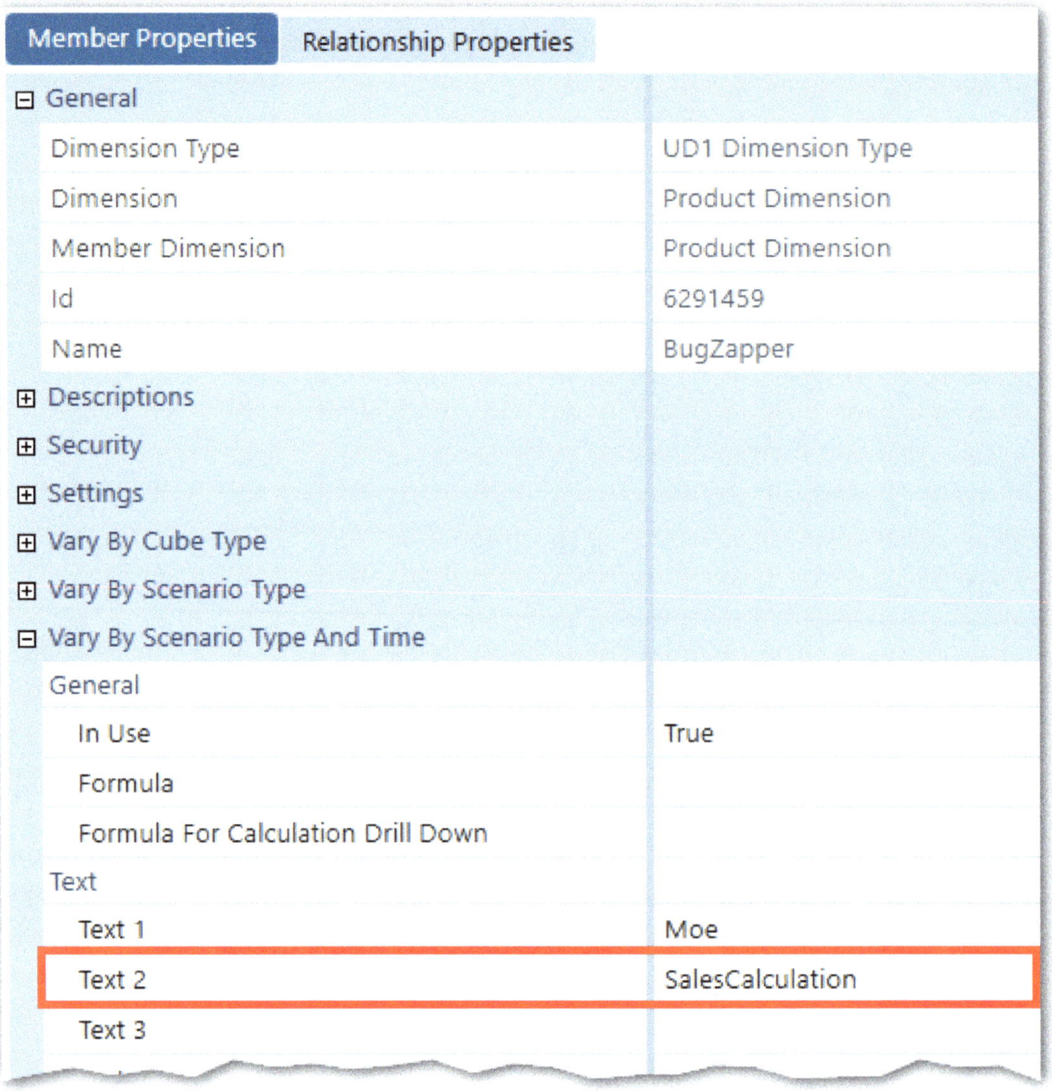

Chapter 6

Figure 6.14

The Dimension filter within our `api.Data.Calculate` function can now use a `Where` clause and reference the `Text2` property.

```
api.Data.Calculate("A#Sales = RemoveZeros(A#Price * A#Volume)",,,,,"U1#Top.Base.Where(Text2 = SalesCalculation")
```

The comment should also be modified to make note of the `Text2` property requirement.

```
'-------------------------------------------------------------------------------------------
'Name:          DriverBasedSalesCalc
'Purpose:       Calculate Driver Based Sales for Budget & Forecast Scenarios
'Usage:         Used in all Budget and Forecast Scenario Types and executed by users in various workflows
'               Runs on all products within the U1#SalesCalculation group
'Maintenance:   All new Products that require this calculation should have a Text2 Property of 'SalesCalculation'
'Created by:    Jon Golembiewski on 1/6/2022
'Edited by:
'-------------------------------------------------------------------------------------------
```

Custom SQL Tables

Using custom SQL tables is another technique that can be employed to reduce maintenance and make your Calculations cleaner and more dynamic. Calculation logic and/or inputs can be stored in a table and then referenced in a Business Rule or Member Formula. Maintenance is then narrowed to changing the table fields to modify Calculation logic or adding rows for new Calculations. Let's take a look at an example of how SQL tables can be used.

Managing Calculations

Use Case

In this example, we have a Forecast Scenario where just about all the data will be calculated. The combination of Account and Cost Center determines the Calculation logic. Due to many Account/Cost Center combinations, this is likely to result in a large number of Calculations leading to a very long Business Rule or a lot of Member Formulas. You can quickly see where this is going – a maintenance nightmare!

Both Dimension hierarchies and text properties can only be defined for a single Member within a Dimension, so those two Methods will not work here. Instead, a SQL Table will be used to store the Account and Cost Center combination along with the Calculation Method and Calculation inputs.

Create the Table

First, a SQL table must be created in the Application Database. This can be done in several ways:

Use the Create Table script property in SQL Table Editor > Component Properties in Dashboards.

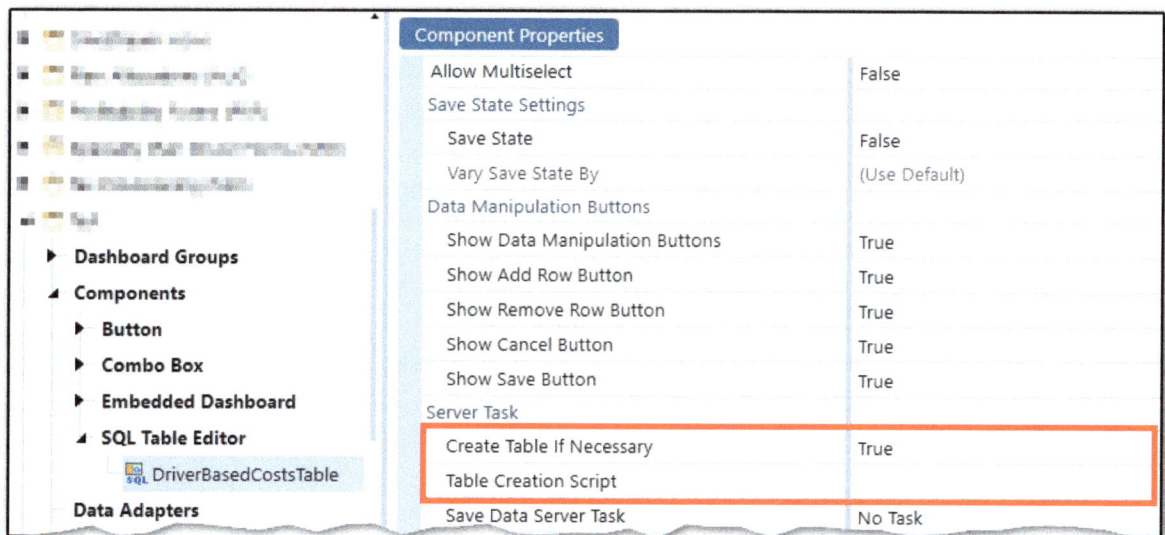

Figure 6.15

Use the **Table Data Manager** Marketplace solution, which provides a User-friendly interface for creating and managing SQL Tables within the Application Database.

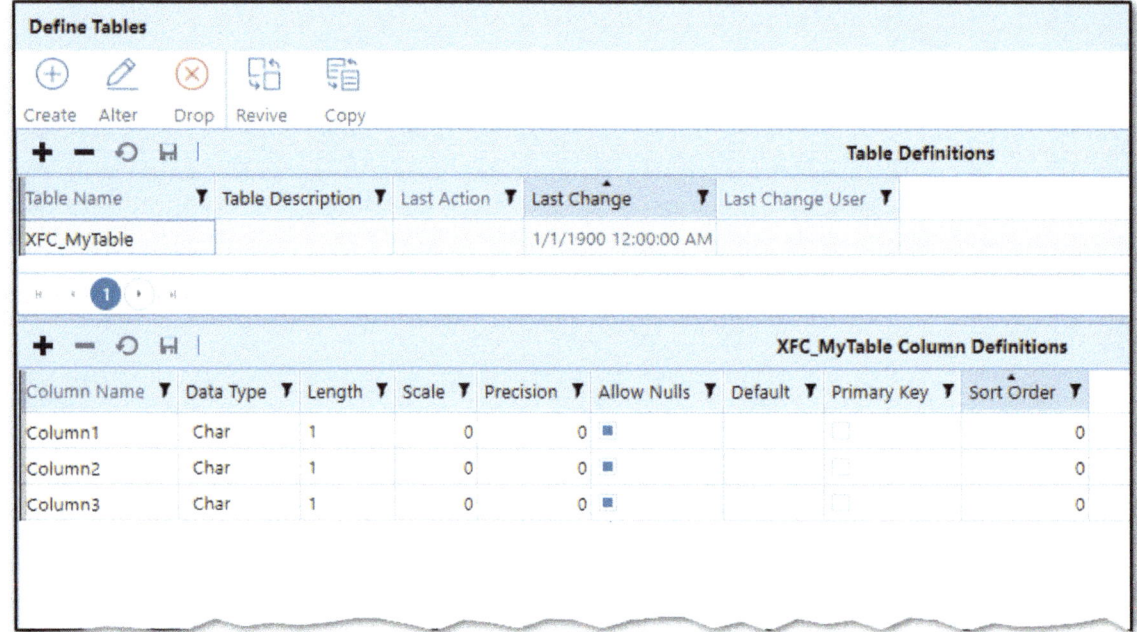

Figure 6.16

Use **SQL Management Studio** on the Application Server (requires server access or assistance from Database Admin).

I typically opt to create tables via Table Data Manager as I am not an expert at writing SQL, and it provides several tools for migration and data extraction for tables created within its framework.

The table – created for our example – will contain the below columns:

- RowID – A unique identifier column used as the Primary Key
- AccountName – Stores the name of the Account
- ProductName – Stores the name of the Product
- CalculationDefinition – Stores the Calculation definition
- CalculationPriceDriverInput – Stores the Price Driver Account name
- CalculationQuantityDriverInput – Stores the Quantity Driver Price name

Populate the Table

Users can interact with SQL tables via Dashboards using a SQL Table Editor Component.

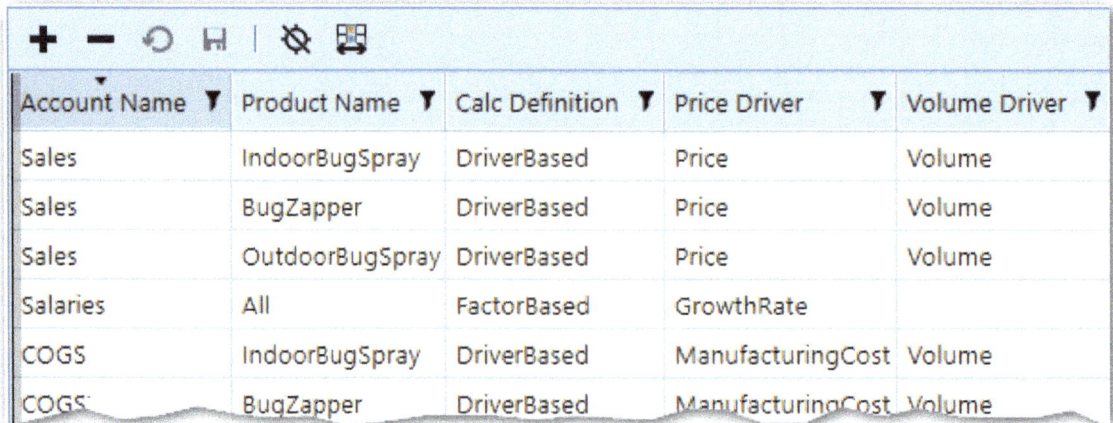

Figure 6.17

Managing Calculations

Exposing this Dashboard to a User via Workflow or OnePlace will allow them to add, delete, or modify rows. The table can also be populated via an Excel file import.

Referencing the Table in a Calculation

To reference the table in a Calculation, we will need to call the table via a SQL query using the `api.Functions.GetCustomBlendDataTable` function and then loop through the rows of the table. For each row iteration, we will run a Calculation using an `api.Data.Calculate` function.

Rule Context

This Calculation will be written in a Business Rule with a **FinanceFunctionType** of Custom Calculate. The Calculation will be executed in the Data Management Step/Sequence.

The Code

```vb
'Build the SQL Statement to get all rows in the table
Dim sql As New Text.StringBuilder
Dim lookupTable = "XFC_CalcDefinitionTable"
sql.AppendLine("SELECT * ")
sql.AppendLine("From " & lookupTable )
'Get the custom SQL table
Dim customSQLTable As DataTable = api.Functions.GetCustomBlendDataTable(BlendCacheLevelTypes.Custom,"Default","Application",sql.ToString)
'Filter the table for only rows that which have a vlaue of 'DriverBased' in the CalculationDefinition column
Dim dataRows As DataRow() = customSQLTable.Select("CalculationDefinition = 'DriverBased'")
    'Check first that there are rows in the table
    If dataRows.Count > 0 Then
        For Each oRow As DataRow In dataRows
            'Get the Account and CostCenter from the table
            Dim accountName = oRow("AccountName")
            Dim productName = oRow("ProductName")
            'Get the Calculation Price and Quantity Drivers
            Dim calcPriceDriverInput = oRow("CalculationPriceDriverInput")
            Dim calcQuantityDriverInput = oRow("CalculationVolumeDriverInput")

            'Clear the Data for the Account and Cost Center
            api.Data.ClearCalculatedData(True,True,True,True,"A#" & accountName & "",,,,"U1#" & productName & "")

            'Build and run the api.Data.Calculate formula using the table variables
            api.Data.Calculate("A#" & accountName & ":U1#" & productName & ":O#Import = " & _
            "A#" & calcPriceDriverInput & ":U1#" & productName & ":O#Top * A#" & calcQuantityDriverInput & ":U1#" & productName & ":O#Top")
        Next
    End If
```

The Breakdown

Get the SQL Table

The first thing our Calculation will do is bring the SQL table into memory using the `api.Functions.GetCustomBlendDataTable` function.

```vb
'Build the SQL Statement to get all rows in the table
Dim sql As New Text.StringBuilder
Dim lookupTable = "XFC_CalcDefinitionTable"
sql.AppendLine("SELECT * ")
sql.AppendLine("From " & lookupTable )
'Get the custom SQL table
Dim customSQLTable As DataTable = api.Functions.GetCustomBlendDataTable(BlendCacheLevelTypes.Custom,"Default","Application",sql.ToString)
```

A SQL statement is built using a **StringBuilder** and passed into the function along with the other required parameters.

Filter the Table using the .Select Method

Once we have the entire table in memory, we can filter it to only include rows with `DriverBased` as the `CalculationDefinition` field.

```vb
'Filter the table for only rows that which have a vlaue of 'DriverBased' in the CalculationDefinition column
Dim dataRows As DataRow() = customSQLTable.Select("CalculationDefinition = 'DriverBased'")
```

Next, we will check to make sure at least one row exists… so we don't waste any processing time if there isn't.

```vb
'Check first that there are rows in the table
If dataRows.Count > 0 Then
```

Chapter 6

Loop through the Table Rows
Once we have the desired table rows, we will loop through each row and bring in each field as a variable.

```
For Each oRow As DataRow In dataRows
    'Get the Account and CostCenter from the table
    Dim accountName = oRow("AccountName")
    Dim productName = oRow("Product")
    'Get the Calculation Price and Quantity Drivers
    Dim calcPriceDriverInput = oRow("CalculationPriceDriverInput")
    Dim calcQuantityDriverInput = oRow("CalculationQuantityDriverInput")
```

Clear the Previously Calculated Data and Execute the Calculation
Now we have everything we need to build the `clear` statement and the formula inside the `api.Data.Calculate` function. The row field variables are passed into the formula string.

```
'Clear the Data for the Account and Cost Center
api.Data.ClearCalculatedData(True,True,True,True,"A#" & accountName & "",,,,"U1#" & productName & "")

'Build and run the api.Data.Calculate formula using the table variables
api.Data.Calculate("A#" & accountName & ":U1#" & productName & ":O#Import = " & _
"A#" & calcPriceDriverInput & ":U1#" & productName & ":O#Top " & "A#" & calcQuantityDriverInput & ":U1#" & productName & ":O#Top")
```

Performance Note

The above example shows the power of using SQL tables to help manage Calculation build and maintenance. It's important to note that the above example could be written more efficiently. Each row will generate an ADC function which calls the Data Unit into memory and then writes back to the database. It is always better for performance to minimize those two actions as much as possible. Instead of using an ADC function within the loop, a Result Data Buffer could be declared outside the loop with result cells added to it in-memory within the loop, and the cells committed to the Cube after the loop with a `SetDataBuffer` function.

Conclusion

Learning how to properly plan, manage, and track Calculations is just as important as learning the skill of writing Calculations. Even the best-written Calculations will fail or fall apart if they aren't written in a maintenance-friendly way. This means including proper commentary and documentation for whoever winds up maintaining them after you're gone. Further, there are several tools and techniques that can reduce and ease maintenance – be sure to deploy them when writing Calculations and you can save yourself (and others) a lot of headaches in the future.

7
Troubleshooting and Performance

Something I've parroted (more than a few times) is the phrase – "First get the Calculation to work, then get it to work faster!"

Both parts of that statement can be equally challenging, and I'm not sure which one I have spent more time on. There is no more helpless a feeling than when a Calculation won't work, and you have tried every solution you can think of to no avail. Your author has spent many hours banging his head against the wall, crying to the heavens for some divine intervention to provide guidance for Calculation issues. Then, there is the completely different – but equally excruciating – pain of trying to troubleshoot a Calculation or Consolidation that produces the correct results, but which the customer complains is taking way too long.

Hopefully, some of my pain and suffering can be of benefit to you. In this chapter, I will divulge some of the best troubleshooting techniques for both getting your Calculations to work – and work fast – as well as explain some common Calculation errors and how to optimize your Calculations for performance. Some of this chapter will be a rehash of the concepts already discussed but should serve as a good refresher.

Troubleshooting

Another phrase that rings true is "Coding is 5% writing the actual code, and 95% testing and troubleshooting." I can probably count on one hand the number of times I've written a Calculation and it executed with the correct results on the first try. Troubleshooting is a skill unto itself and, like anything else, takes practice to master. Understanding the tools available and some common errors will give you a big head start.

Task Activity

Before you can start troubleshooting, you'll need to know whether your Calculation or Consolidation completed successfully and – if it failed – *why*. Task Activity provides this information, and can be accessed either from the top-right menu in the desktop app or from the System tab.

Figure 7.1

…or…

Chapter 7

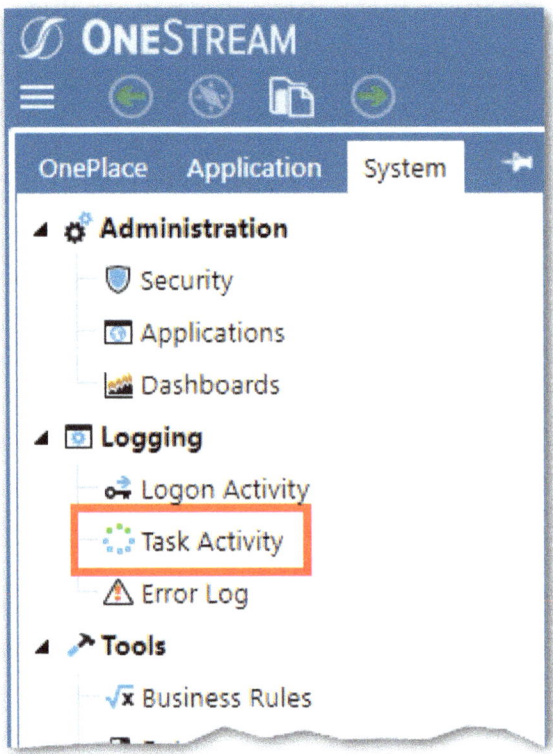

Figure 7.2

The Task Activity table shows the status of all OneStream-related server tasks and can be filtered by Task Type.

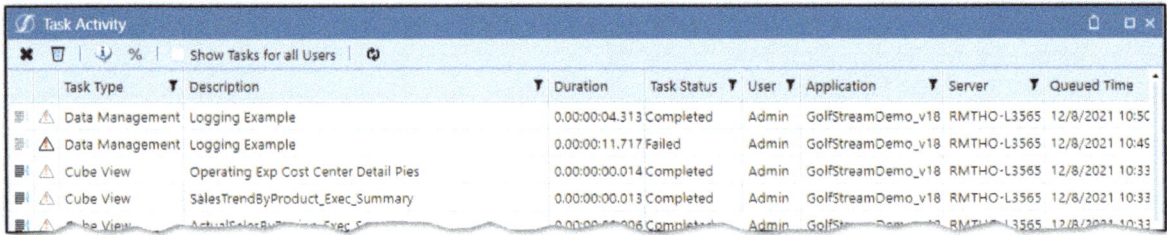

Figure 7.3

For any tasks that have encountered errors, detailed error information is available.

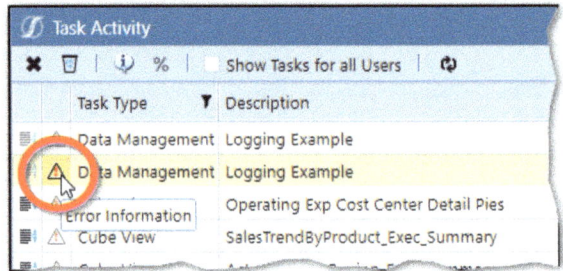

Figure 7.4

Troubleshooting and Performance

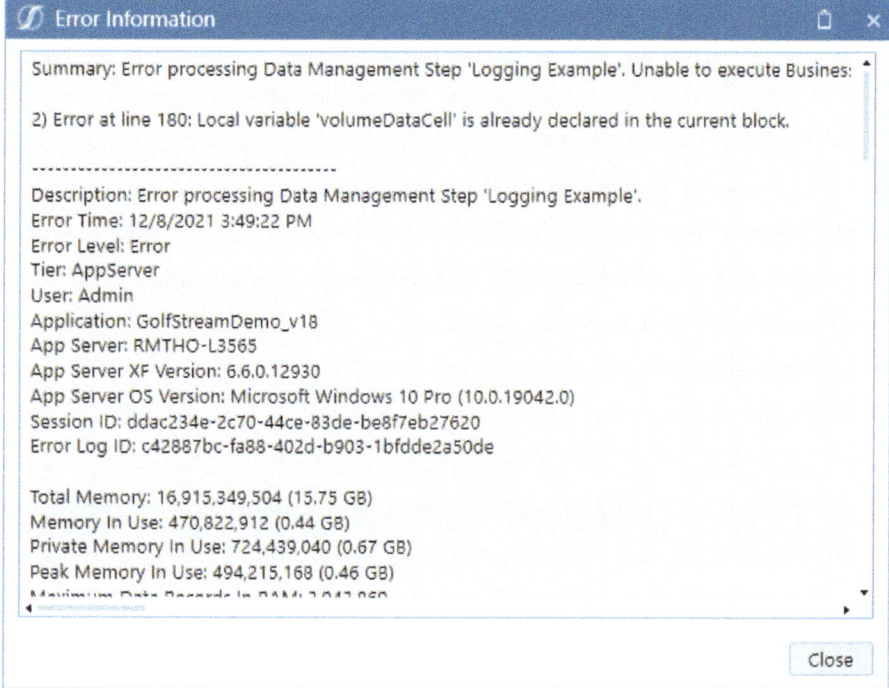

Figure 7.5

Task Activity is a great starting point but should an error be encountered, it won't lead you very far down the road of solving it. Other techniques will need to be deployed – let's continue!

Logging

Logging is perhaps the best tool in the bag for a coder. Coding without logging is like trying to land a plane blind. Logging will allow you to gain insight into what is happening between clicking Execute Calculation and the task completing by letting you log your own messages into the **Error Log**. For example, you may have declared a variable to pull a Member name. If that Member name doesn't exist, then it will likely result in an error, causing the entire Calculation to fail. By logging that variable, you will easily be able to see the root cause of the error.

OneStream has a built-in Error Log, which can be accessed in the System tab.

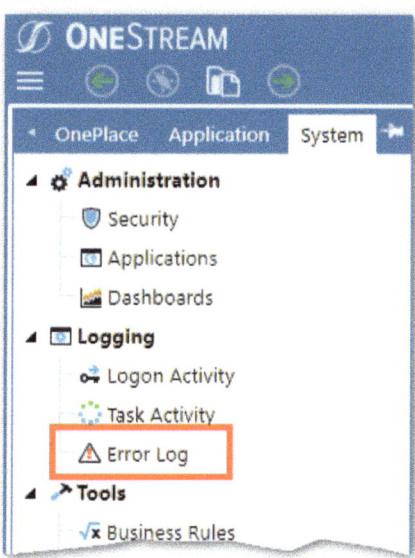

Figure 7.6

Chapter 7

The Error Log contains the following information about the error:

- Description
- Error Time
- Error Level
- User
- Application
- (Server) Tier
- App Server

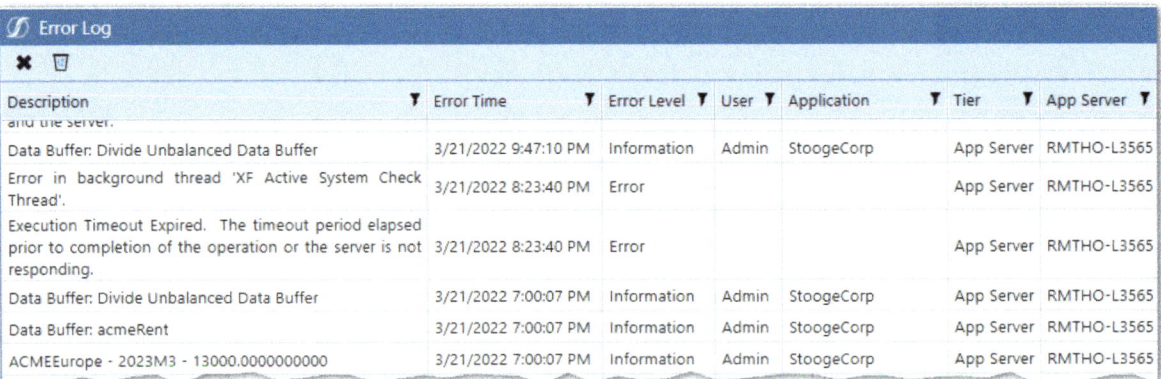

Figure 7.7

The Error Log table is a repository for all errors that occur within OneStream, not just Calculations, so use the filters at the top to find the relevant error.

Writing to the Error Log

Errors that occur during Calculation execution will automatically hit the Error Log. If you want to log your own messages within Calculation Scripts, the Error Log can manually be written to – via API or BRAPI calls.

- `api.LogMessage` – available in Finance Business Rules
- `BRApi.ErrorLog.LogMessage` – available in all rules

> **Note:** Using the API function instead of the BRAPI equivalent generally performs better, so make sure to use the `api.LogMessage` for all Finance Business Rules.

Log a String

The `api.LogMessage` function will allow you to log any string value to the Error Log table.

```
api.LogMessage("String to Log")
```

Upon execution of the Calculation, the string will appear in the Error Log table.

Troubleshooting and Performance

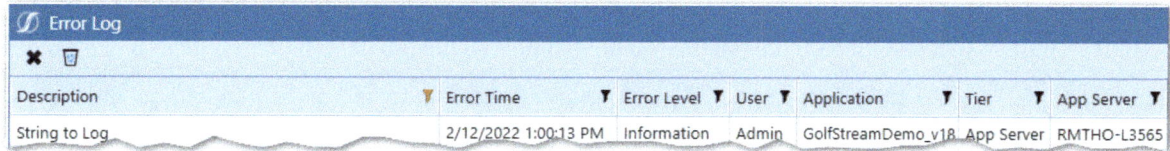

Figure 7.8

By default, Information will show as the Error Level. This can be changed by adding the Error Level argument to the function.

```
api.LogMessage(XFErrorLevel.Error, "String to Log")
```

IntelliSense will show the various options available for the `XFErrorLevel` argument.

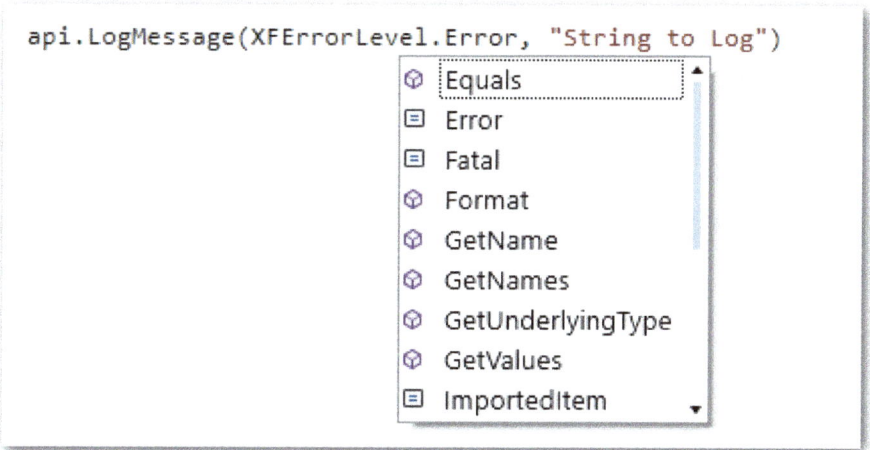

Figure 7.9

Log a Decimal

The `LogMessage` function will only allow the logging of strings, so anything logged using that function must either be a string or be converted to a string. Many objects can be easily converted to a string using the `ToString` or `XFToString` Method. The `XFToString` Method should be used when available as it is culture invariant.

```
Dim myDecimal As Decimal = 123.4
api.LogMessage(myDecimal.XFToString)
```

Logging Lists

Lists will not easily convert to a list, so other techniques can be used:

String.Join

Below is an example of how to log a list of strings using the `String.Join` function with the `vbnewline` keyword:

```
'Create a simple list
Dim myList As New List(Of String)({"A","B","C","D"})
Dim myListAsString As String = String.Join(vbnewline,mylist)

api.LogMessage(mylistAsString.ToString)
```

Chapter 7

The list is logged in the Error Log, with each item appearing on a new line for readability.

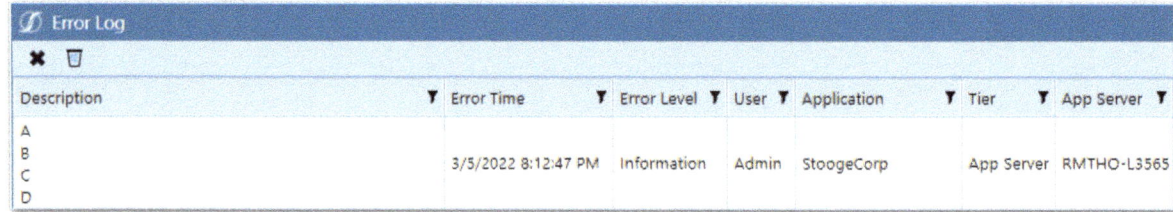

Figure 7.10

Lists of other objects, such as Members, can also be logged using VB.NET Functions.

```vbnet
'Get a list of all product in UD1
Dim productsList As List(Of MemberInfo) = api.Members.GetMembersUsingFilter(api.Dimensions.getDim("Product").DimPk,"UD1#Top.Base")
Dim productListAsString As String = String.Join(vbNewLine, productsList.Select(Function(memInfo) memInfo.Member.Name))
'Log the list to the error log
api.LogMessage(productListAsString)
```

In the above example, the Member name was logged, but other properties of the Member could have been logged instead.

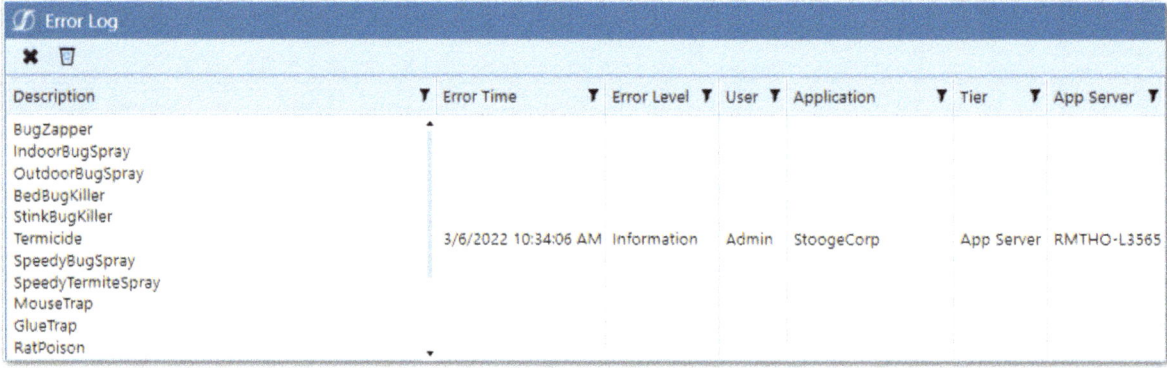

Figure 7.11

For, Each

Lists can also be logged using a `For Each` loop. The above script loops through a list of `MemberInfo` objects and then logs the Member names.

```vbnet
'Get a list of all product in UD1
Dim productsList As List(Of MemberInfo) = api.Members.GetMembersUsingFilter(api.Dimensions.getDim("Product").DimPk,"UD1#Top.Base")
'Create a string builder to add list items to
Dim productListAsString As New Text.StringBuilder
'Loop through the list and add items to the string builder
Dim isFirstItem As Boolean = True
For Each product As MemberInfo In productsList
    If Not isFirstItem Then 'Add a comma to precede all items except the first
        productListAsString.Append("," & product.Member.Name)
    End If
    productListAsString.Append(product.Member.Name)
    isFirstItem = False
Next
'Log the list to the error log
api.LogMessage(productListAsString.ToString)
```

Troubleshooting and Performance

The Member names are displayed in the Error Log, separated by a comma.

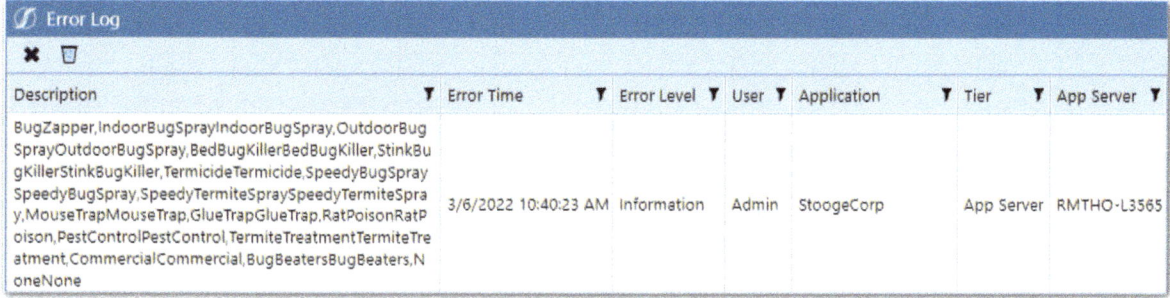

Figure 7.12

> **Note:** Be careful when logging lists with a `For Each` loop when there is a chance of the list containing a high volume of items. This can potentially consume a lot of memory and cause server issues.

Log Data Buffer

For Data Buffers, we can use the `LogDataBuffer` function originally introduced in Chapter 2.

First, declare a Data Buffer using the `api.Data.GetDataBufferUsingFormula` function. Reference the `LogDataBuffer` subfunction by appending `.LogDataBuffer` to the Data Buffer variable.

```
Dim exampleDataBuffer As DataBuffer = api.Data.GetDataBufferUsingFormula("A#Sales")
exampleDataBuffer.LogDataBuffer(api,"Sales Data Buffer", 100)
```

The `LogDataBuffer` function requires you to pass in the API, a string for the name, and an integer for the maximum number of cells. I usually pick 100 for the max number of cells, as anything more is not readable and could overload the server.

The output will appear in the Error Log and show Data Buffer information, as well as all of the data cells within the Buffer.

Chapter 7

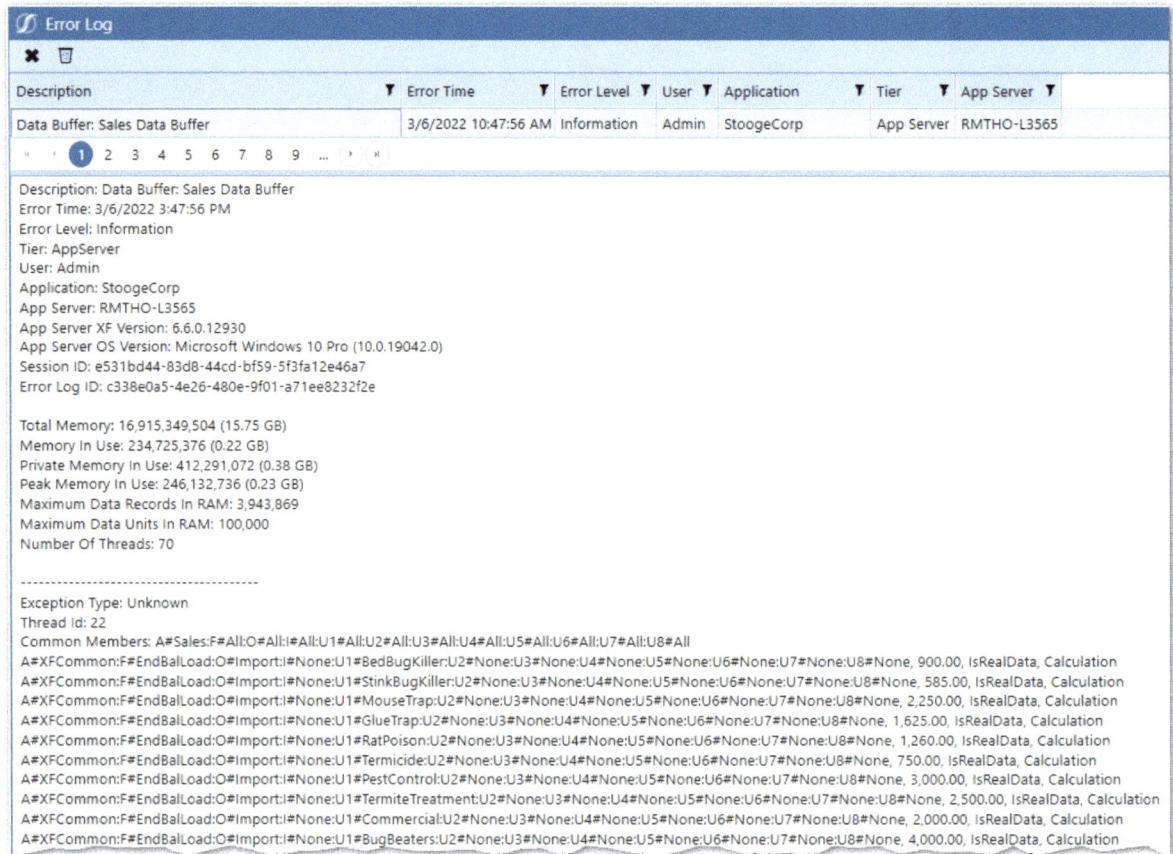

Figure 7.13

If you're getting unexpected (or no) Calculation results, the `LogDataBuffer` function is extremely helpful. You can log each Data Buffer in your `api.Data.Calculate` function and analyze the data cells within to see where Dimensions aren't matching up.

Stopwatch

For longer Calculations, with complex logic, Calculation drill down will only go so far in giving the necessary visibility into what's happening. Using the VB.NET `Stopwatch` function can be very useful in identifying which part of your code is taking the longest to process.

To use the VB.NET `Stopwatch` function, first add the **Diagnostics Library** to your Business Rule header.

```
Imports System
Imports System.Data
Imports System.Data.Common
Imports System.IO
Imports System.Collections.Generic
Imports System.Globalization
Imports System.Linq
Imports Microsoft.VisualBasic
Imports System.Windows.Forms
Imports OneStream.Shared.Common
Imports OneStream.Shared.Wcf
Imports OneStream.Shared.Engine
Imports OneStream.Shared.Database
Imports OneStream.Stage.Engine
Imports OneStream.Stage.Database
Imports OneStream.Finance.Engine
Imports OneStream.Finance.Database
Imports System.Diagnostics
```

Figure 7.14

Create a new `Stopwatch` instance by using the `StartNew` function.

```vb
'Create a new stop watch instance
Dim watch As Stopwatch = Stopwatch.StartNew()
```

After some code logic, log the elapsed time by using the `Elapsed` function.

```vb
'Get the elapsed seconds
Dim elapsedSeconds As Integer = watch.Elapsed.Seconds
'Log the elapsed seconds
api.LogMessage(elapsedSeconds.XFToString)

'Stop the watch
watch.Stop()
```

The below script shows all the functions used together to time a Member List loop.

```vb
'Create a new stop watch instance
Dim watch As Stopwatch = Stopwatch.StartNew()
'Loop through a Member List and do something that takes time
'Get a list of all product in UD1
Dim productsList As List(Of MemberInfo) = api.Members.GetMembersUsingFilter(api.Dimensions.getDim("Product").DimPk,"UD1#Top.Base")
'Create a string builder to add list items to
Dim productListAsString As New Text.StringBuilder
'Loop through the list and pause for 1 second using Thread.Sleep
For Each product As MemberInfo In productsList
    threading.Thread.Sleep(1000)
Next

'Get the elapsed seconds
Dim elapsedSeconds As Integer = watch.Elapsed.Seconds
'Log the elapsed seconds
api.LogMessage(elapsedSeconds.XFToString)

'Stop the watch
watch.Stop()
```

Rubber Duck Debugging

A popular troubleshooting method, known in the coding world as Rubber Duck Debugging, is a simple yet highly effective way of solving a coding issue when all other options have been exhausted.

Rubber Duck Debugging refers to a method of troubleshooting where you articulate your problem to an inanimate object such as a rubber duck. The idea is that by explaining what your code is doing – step by step – you will hit upon the solution in the process. This method is similar to trying to teach a complex subject back to someone in order to gain a deeper understanding. The change in perspective allows you to step back from the problem and analyze it differently.

Figure 7.15

As stupid as it sounds, your author employs this method quite often. There have been many times I have picked up an inanimate object (or telephoned a colleague) and, in the midst of explaining the problem, discovered the answer. When you're out of options, this method is always worth a shot!

Calculation Performance Troubleshooting

Once you get all your Calculations working with expected results, you may find that they are running slower than what is deemed acceptable by the customer. There are several tools available to help troubleshoot performance issues.

Calculation Drill Down

There will likely be dozens, if not hundreds, of Calculations that run during the Data Unit Calculation Sequence. If a Calculation of a Data Unit is running unusually slowly, then finding the culprit can be a daunting task, akin to finding a needle in a haystack.

Luckily, the Calculation drill down tool is available to help pinpoint the exact Calculation(s) causing the issue.

Calculate with Logging

To enable functionality to drill down to Calculation details, Consolidate or Calculate With Logging must be run.

From Data Management:

Figure 7.16

Troubleshooting and Performance

From a Cube View, a Force Consolidate With Logging is run on `ACMEGroup`:

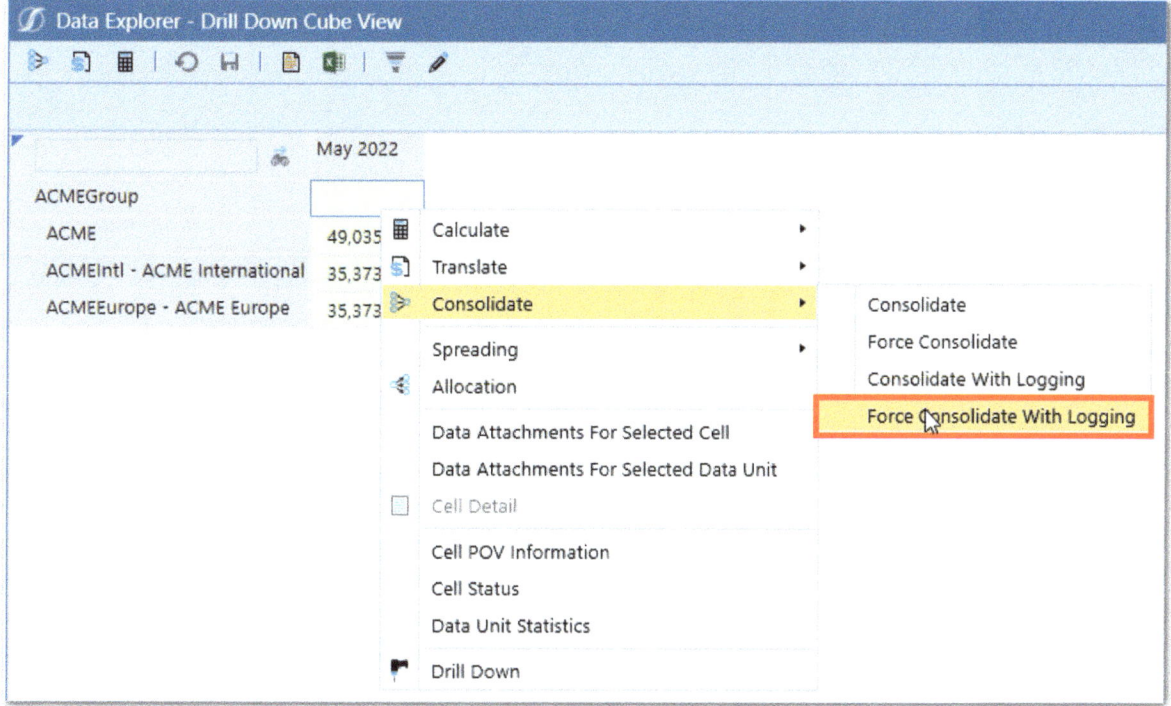

Figure 7.17

Viewing the Result
Once the Calculation with logging finishes, you can view the results by clicking Child Steps in the Task Activity.

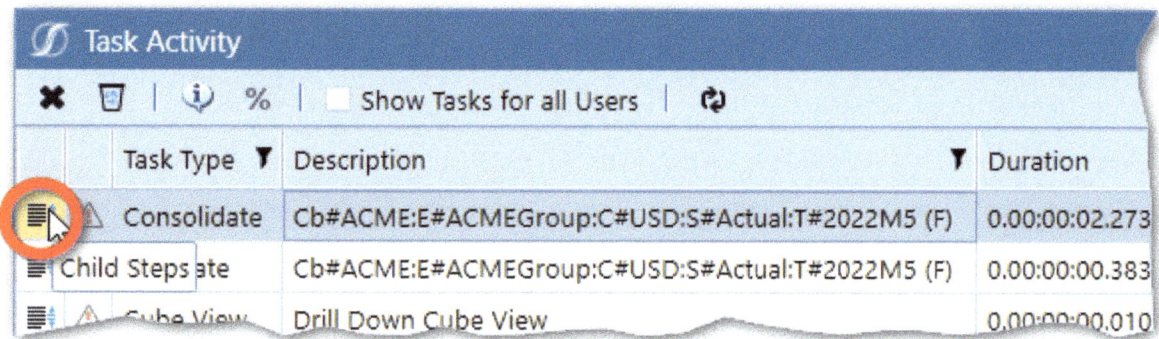

Figure 7.18

Each Child step can be drilled into further, showing details for each step of the DUCS along with the duration. After drilling into `ACMEGroup` in `2022M5`, all the dependent Data Units are shown.

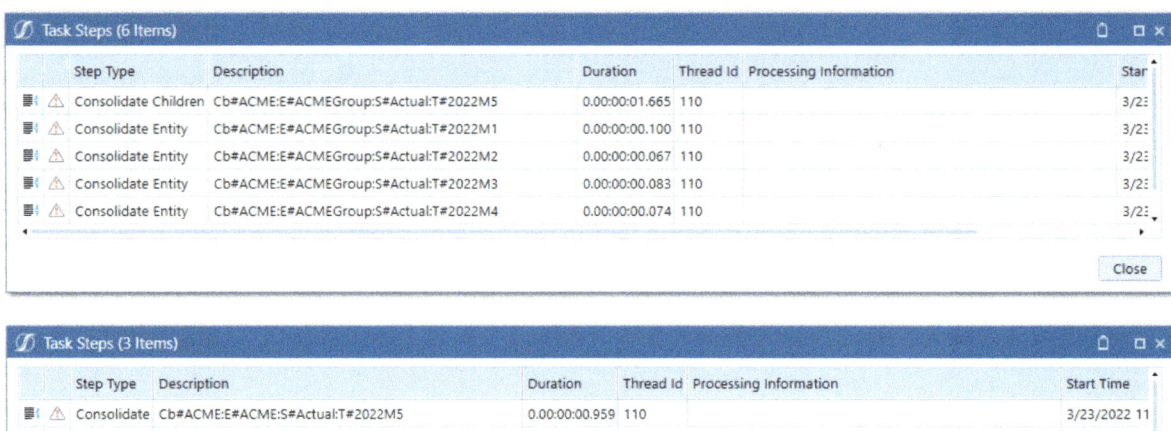

Figure 7.19

Each of the Child steps can be drilled into further to see each Consolidation Member that was processed.

Figure 7.20

Since all our Calculations run on `C#Local`, we will drill into Calculate Local.

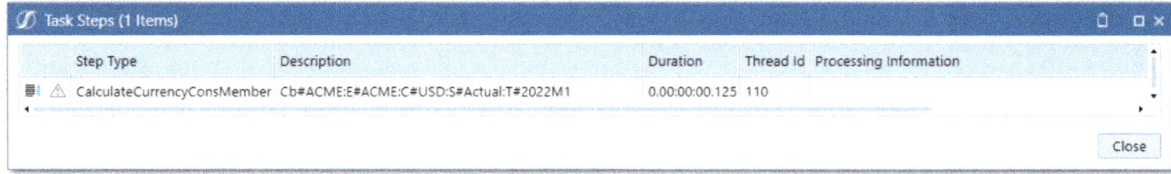

Figure 7.21

Next, we drill into the `CalculateCurrencyConsMember`.

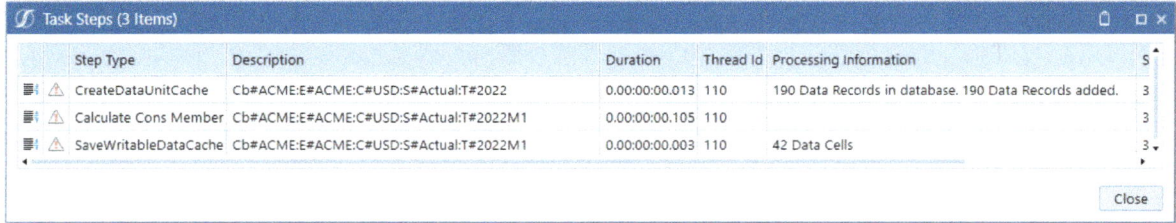

Figure 7.22

Before going further, notice the CreateDataUnitCache step, which will give us some visibility into the number of data records that are brought into cache (memory). This number is exactly what is referred to when talking about **Data Unit Size**.

The CalculateConsMember step will give us a breakdown of each step of the DUCS that was performed on this Data Unit.

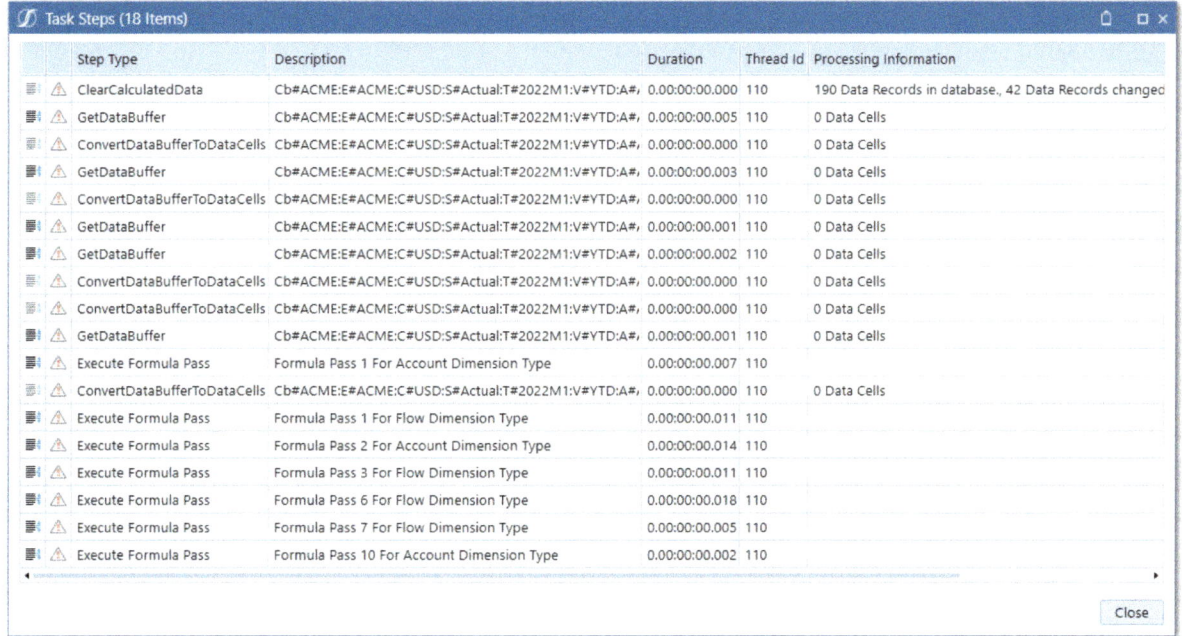

Figure 7.23

Next, individual Formula Passes and Business Rules can be drilled into.

Chapter 7

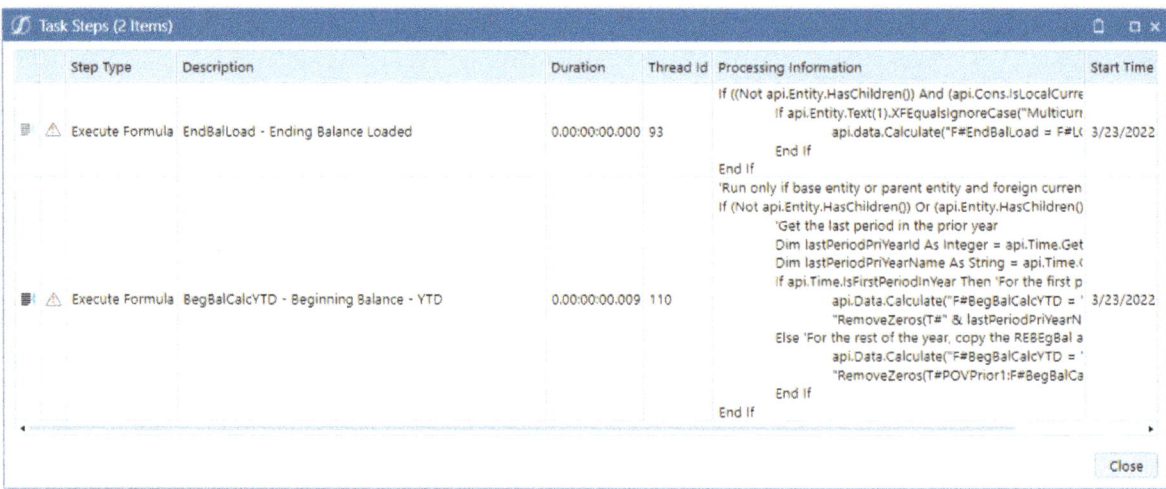

Figure 7.24

Finally, we can drill into the individual formulas.

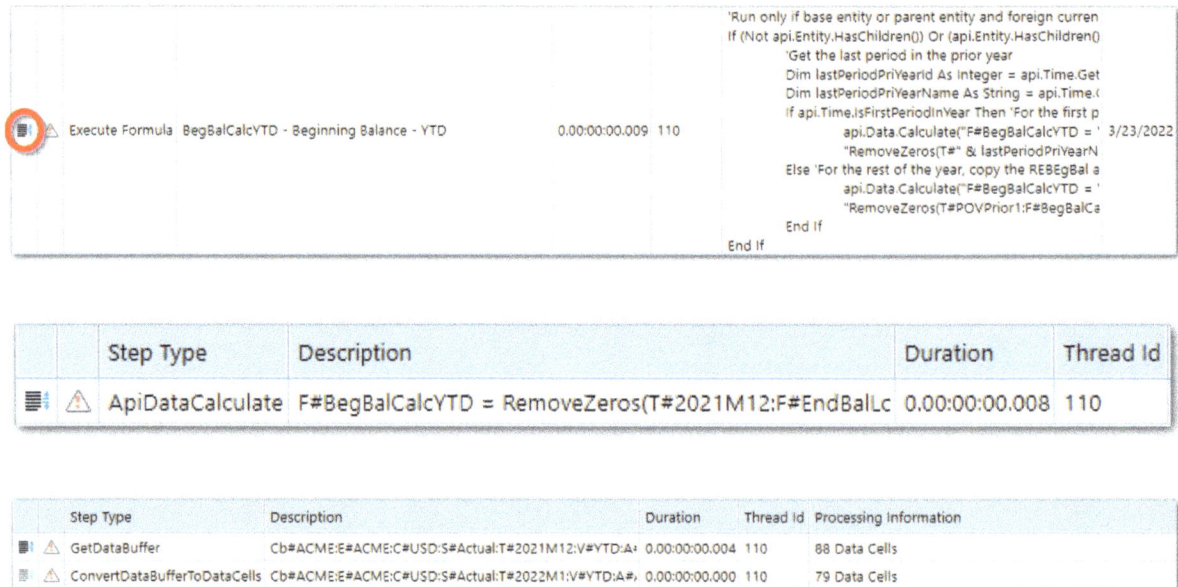

Figure 7.25

We can actually see the detailed breakdown of steps that the `api.Data.Calculate` function takes to derive the calculated data. Pretty cool, right?

This level of visibility into what the Calculation Engine is doing is a crucial tool to have in the bag for troubleshooting Calculations.

> **Note:** Calculation drill down is only available for Calculations that run inside the Data Unit Calculation Sequence. Individual functions within custom Calculations can be analyzed in isolation using Data Management. Also, be aware that running a Calculate or Consolidate With Logging adds significant processing time.

Common Calculation Errors

If your Calculation isn't working, it's likely due to one of two things. Either your Calculation resulted in an error and thus didn't complete, or your Calculation successfully completed but produced incorrect (or no) results. As anybody who has used any software before knows, some error messages are more helpful than others, so knowing the most common errors and how to solve them will save you hours of time.

Calculation Not Producing Results

Probably the most frustrating situation is when your Calculation is seemingly working as designed, running without errors, but the result data is not correct. For these situations, there is usually a data inconsistency that requires you to fix the underlying data (e.g., by remapping or adjusting your Calculation formula).

The best technique to tackle these situations is to use a combination of a Cube View and the `LogDataBuffer` function to obtain visibility into the data. A Cube View can be used to view the source and result intersections side by side, and leverage the drill down functionality. Let's look at an example:

```
api.Data.Calculate("A#Salaries:O#Import = RemoveZeros(A#Headcount:O#Top * A#AverageSalary:O#Top)",True)
```

The above formula is very simple, but it isn't producing the expected results. The first thing to do is set up a Cube View and confirm that there is data in both the Headcount and Average Salary Accounts.

	Headcount	Average Salary	Salaries & Benefits
Sales	2.00	1,500.00	
Marketing	3.00	2,000.00	
HR - Human Resources	2.00	1,800.00	
IT - Information Technology	4.00	1,600.00	
Legal	1.00	2,500.00	
Admin - Administrative	5.00	1,100.00	
Manufacturing	8.00	1,000.00	
Facilities	2.00	1,000.00	
Packaging	1.00	900.00	
PackagingMaterials - Packaging Materials			
ShippingPrep - Shipping Preparation			
ShippingTransportation - Shipping Transportation			
None			

Figure 7.26

We can see that data exists for both of our inputs, yet we still don't see the desired output in the Salaries & Benefits Account. Further investigation is required.

From here, we can drill into the underlying data in two ways:
- Drill down into the Headcount and Average Salary data from the Cube View.
- Log each of the respective Data Buffers in the Calculation.

Chapter 7

Drill Down From the Cube View
We can drill down into any cell by right-clicking and selecting Drill Down to access the Drill Down menu.

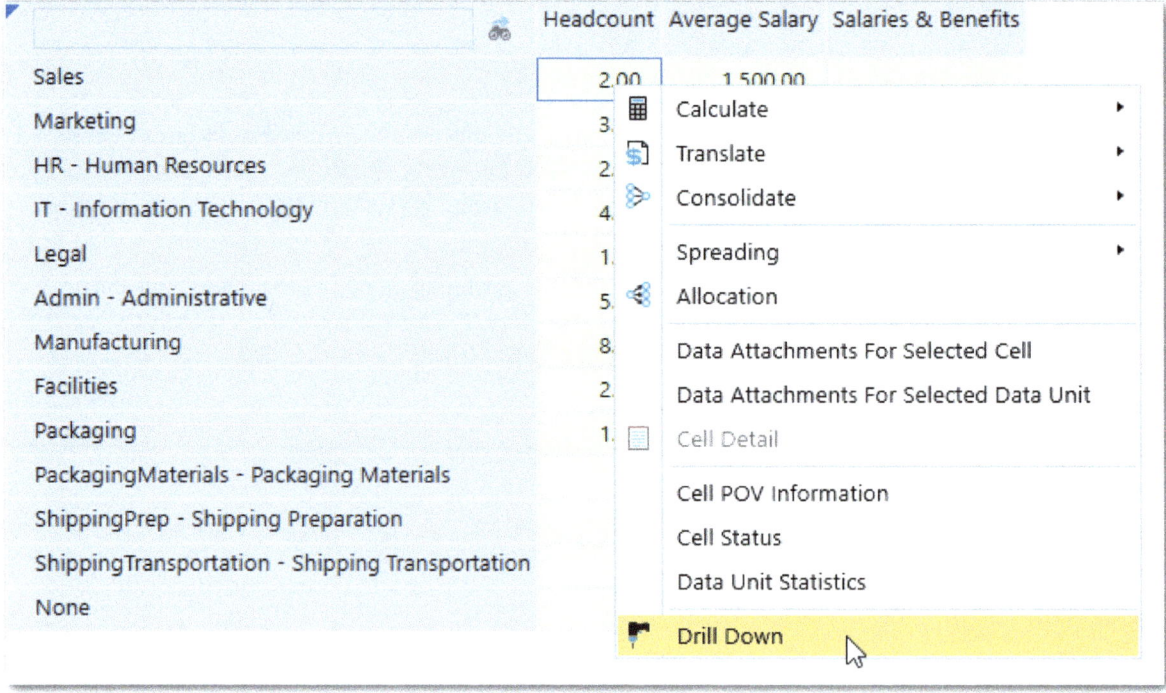

Figure 7.27

From the Drill Down menu, the data cell can be further drilled into. All Aggregated Data Below Cell will show us any Base-level data below the cell.

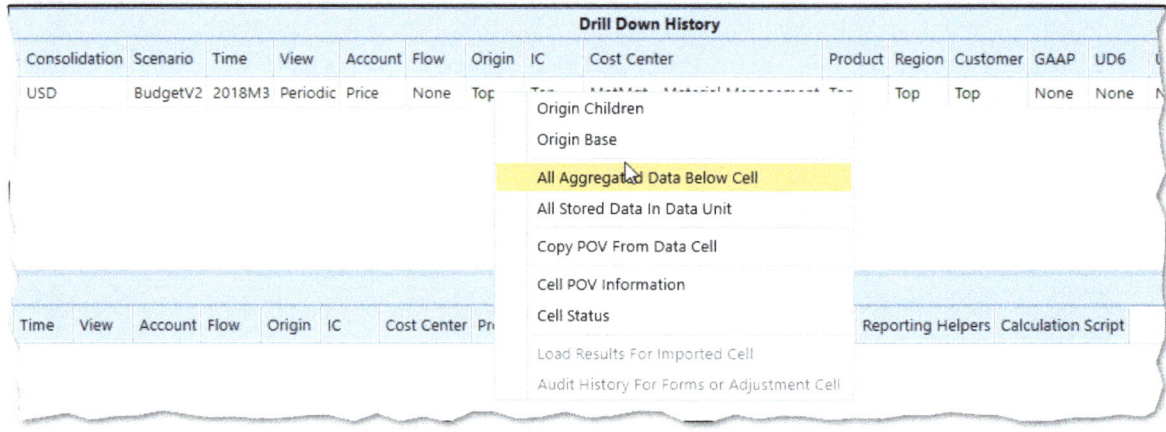

Figure 7.28

We can now see the POV detail for the Base-level data used in the Calculation.

Figure 7.29

Troubleshooting and Performance

We will also do this for the Average Salary data for the same Cost Center.

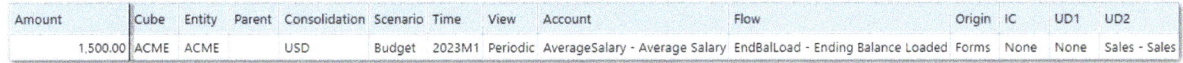

Figure 7.30

After comparing the dimensionality between the two data cells, you can see the data for the two Accounts are at different Flow Dimensions.

Figure 7.31

Log the Data Buffers

As an alternative to the Cube View Drill Method, we can add Data Buffer logging to our Calculation Script, run the Calculation again, and compare the results of each in the Error Log.

```
api.Data.Calculate("A#Salaries:O#Import = RemoveZeros(A#Headcount:O#Top * A#AverageSalary:O#Top)",True)

Dim headcountDataBuffer As DataBuffer = api.Data.GetDataBufferUsingFormula("A#Headcount:O#Top")
Dim averageSalaryDataBuffer As DataBuffer = api.Data.GetDataBufferUsingFormula("A#AverageSalary:O#Top")
headcountDataBuffer.LogDataBuffer(api,"Headcount Data Buffer", 100)
averageSalaryDataBuffer.LogDataBuffer(api,"Average Salary Data Buffer", 100)
```

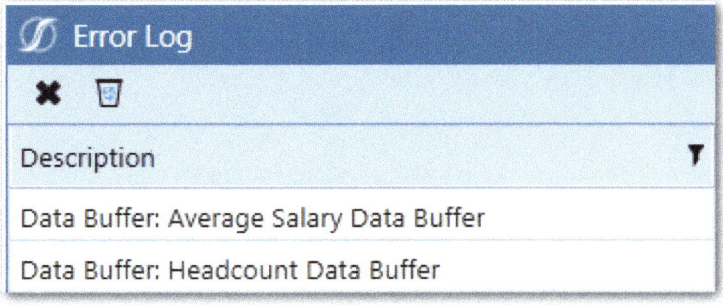

Figure 7.32

Average Salary Data Buffer:

```
Common Members: A#AverageSalary:F#All:O#Top:I#All:U1#All:U2#All:U3#All:U4#All:U5#All:U6#All:U7#All:U8#All
A#XFCommon:F#EndBalLoad:O#XFCommon:I#None:U1#None:U2#HR:U3#None:U4#None:U5#None:U6#None:U7#None:U8#None, 1,800.00, IsRealData, Input
A#XFCommon:F#EndBalLoad:O#XFCommon:I#None:U1#None:U2#Marketing:U3#None:U4#None:U5#None:U6#None:U7#None:U8#None, 2,000.00, IsRealData, Input
A#XFCommon:F#EndBalLoad:O#XFCommon:I#None:U1#None:U2#IT:U3#None:U4#None:U5#None:U6#None:U7#None:U8#None, 1,600.00, IsRealData, Input
A#XFCommon:F#EndBalLoad:O#XFCommon:I#None:U1#None:U2#Legal:U3#None:U4#None:U5#None:U6#None:U7#None:U8#None, 2,500.00, IsRealData, Input
A#XFCommon:F#EndBalLoad:O#XFCommon:I#None:U1#None:U2#Admin:U3#None:U4#None:U5#None:U6#None:U7#None:U8#None, 1,100.00, IsRealData, Input
A#XFCommon:F#EndBalLoad:O#XFCommon:I#None:U1#None:U2#Manufacturing:U3#None:U4#None:U5#None:U6#None:U7#None:U8#None, 1,000.00, IsRealData, Input
A#XFCommon:F#EndBalLoad:O#XFCommon:I#None:U1#None:U2#Sales:U3#None:U4#None:U5#None:U6#None:U7#None:U8#None, 1,500.00, IsRealData, Input
A#XFCommon:F#EndBalLoad:O#XFCommon:I#None:U1#None:U2#Facilities:U3#None:U4#None:U5#None:U6#None:U7#None:U8#None, 1,000.00, IsRealData, Input
A#XFCommon:F#EndBalLoad:O#XFCommon:I#None:U1#None:U2#Packaging:U3#None:U4#None:U5#None:U6#None:U7#None:U8#None, 900.00, IsRealData, Input
```

Figure 7.33

Chapter 7

Headcount Data Buffer:

```
Common Members: A#Headcount:F#All:O#Top:I#All:U1#All:U2#All:U3#All:U4#All:U5#All:U6#All:U7#All:U8#All
A#XFCommon:F#None:O#XFCommon:I#None:U1#None:U2#HR:U3#None:U4#None:U5#None:U6#None:U7#None:U8#None, 2.00, IsRealData, Input
A#XFCommon:F#None:O#XFCommon:I#None:U1#None:U2#Marketing:U3#None:U4#None:U5#None:U6#None:U7#None:U8#None, 3.00, IsRealData, Input
A#XFCommon:F#None:O#XFCommon:I#None:U1#None:U2#IT:U3#None:U4#None:U5#None:U6#None:U7#None:U8#None, 4.00, IsRealData, Input
A#XFCommon:F#None:O#XFCommon:I#None:U1#None:U2#Legal:U3#None:U4#None:U5#None:U6#None:U7#None:U8#None, 1.00, IsRealData, Input
A#XFCommon:F#None:O#XFCommon:I#None:U1#None:U2#Admin:U3#None:U4#None:U5#None:U6#None:U7#None:U8#None, 5.00, IsRealData, Input
A#XFCommon:F#None:O#XFCommon:I#None:U1#None:U2#Manufacturing:U3#None:U4#None:U5#None:U6#None:U7#None:U8#None, 8.00, IsRealData, Input
A#XFCommon:F#None:O#XFCommon:I#None:U1#None:U2#Sales:U3#None:U4#None:U5#None:U6#None:U7#None:U8#None, 2.00, IsRealData, Input
A#XFCommon:F#None:O#XFCommon:I#None:U1#None:U2#Facilities:U3#None:U4#None:U5#None:U6#None:U7#None:U8#None, 2.00, IsRealData, Input
A#XFCommon:F#None:O#XFCommon:I#None:U1#None:U2#Packaging:U3#None:U4#None:U5#None:U6#None:U7#None:U8#None, 1.00, IsRealData, Input
```

Figure 7.34

We can also see the mismatch in the Flow Member by comparing the Headcount and Average Salary Data Buffers above.

Fixing the Issue

Remember, from earlier in the book, that when Data Buffer math occurs, only the data cells with matching dimensionality are processed. In our case, the two Data Buffers do not have any matching cells due to the difference in the Flow Dimension.

Now that we've located the issue, there are a few ways to solve it:

- Fix the underlying data if it was inputted or mapped from a file incorrectly.

- Adjust the Member Scripts in the formula to *include* the Flow Dimension so that the Flow is part of Common Members in the Data Buffer.

If the data is deemed to be correct, then adjusting the Member Script is the only option. The formula can be rewritten as below:

```
api.Data.Calculate("A#Salaries:O#Import:F#EndBalLoad = " & _
"RemoveZeros(A#Headcount:O#Top:F#None * A#AverageSalary:O#Top:F#EndBalLoad)",True)
```

Logging the new Data Buffers will show that the Flow Dimension has moved to the Common Members part of both Data Buffers.

```
Common Members: A#AverageSalary:F#EndBalLoad:O#Top:I#All:U1#All:U2#All:U3#All:U4#All:U5#All:U6#All:U7#All:U8#All
A#XFCommon:F#XFCommon:O#XFCommon:I#None:U1#None:U2#HR:U3#None:U4#None:U5#None:U6#None:U7#None:U8#None, 1,800.00, IsRealData, Input
A#XFCommon:F#XFCommon:O#XFCommon:I#None:U1#None:U2#Marketing:U3#None:U4#None:U5#None:U6#None:U7#None:U8#None, 2,000.00, IsRealData, Input
A#XFCommon:F#XFCommon:O#XFCommon:I#None:U1#None:U2#IT:U3#None:U4#None:U5#None:U6#None:U7#None:U8#None, 1,600.00, IsRealData, Input
A#XFCommon:F#XFCommon:O#XFCommon:I#None:U1#None:U2#Legal:U3#None:U4#None:U5#None:U6#None:U7#None:U8#None, 2,500.00, IsRealData, Input
A#XFCommon:F#XFCommon:O#XFCommon:I#None:U1#None:U2#Admin:U3#None:U4#None:U5#None:U6#None:U7#None:U8#None, 1,100.00, IsRealData, Input
A#XFCommon:F#XFCommon:O#XFCommon:I#None:U1#None:U2#Manufacturing:U3#None:U4#None:U5#None:U6#None:U7#None:U8#None, 1,000.00, IsRealData, Input
A#XFCommon:F#XFCommon:O#XFCommon:I#None:U1#None:U2#Sales:U3#None:U4#None:U5#None:U6#None:U7#None:U8#None, 1,500.00, IsRealData, Input
A#XFCommon:F#XFCommon:O#XFCommon:I#None:U1#None:U2#Facilities:U3#None:U4#None:U5#None:U6#None:U7#None:U8#None, 1,000.00, IsRealData, Input
A#XFCommon:F#XFCommon:O#XFCommon:I#None:U1#None:U2#Packaging:U3#None:U4#None:U5#None:U6#None:U7#None:U8#None, 900.00, IsRealData, Input
```

```
Common Members: A#Headcount:F#None:O#Top:I#All:U1#All:U2#All:U3#All:U4#All:U5#All:U6#All:U7#All:U8#All
A#XFCommon:F#XFCommon:O#XFCommon:I#None:U1#None:U2#HR:U3#None:U4#None:U5#None:U6#None:U7#None:U8#None, 2.00, IsRealData, Input
A#XFCommon:F#XFCommon:O#XFCommon:I#None:U1#None:U2#Marketing:U3#None:U4#None:U5#None:U6#None:U7#None:U8#None, 3.00, IsRealData, Input
A#XFCommon:F#XFCommon:O#XFCommon:I#None:U1#None:U2#IT:U3#None:U4#None:U5#None:U6#None:U7#None:U8#None, 4.00, IsRealData, Input
A#XFCommon:F#XFCommon:O#XFCommon:I#None:U1#None:U2#Legal:U3#None:U4#None:U5#None:U6#None:U7#None:U8#None, 1.00, IsRealData, Input
A#XFCommon:F#XFCommon:O#XFCommon:I#None:U1#None:U2#Admin:U3#None:U4#None:U5#None:U6#None:U7#None:U8#None, 5.00, IsRealData, Input
A#XFCommon:F#XFCommon:O#XFCommon:I#None:U1#None:U2#Manufacturing:U3#None:U4#None:U5#None:U6#None:U7#None:U8#None, 8.00, IsRealData, Input
A#XFCommon:F#XFCommon:O#XFCommon:I#None:U1#None:U2#Sales:U3#None:U4#None:U5#None:U6#None:U7#None:U8#None, 2.00, IsRealData, Input
A#XFCommon:F#XFCommon:O#XFCommon:I#None:U1#None:U2#Facilities:U3#None:U4#None:U5#None:U6#None:U7#None:U8#None, 2.00, IsRealData, Input
A#XFCommon:F#XFCommon:O#XFCommon:I#None:U1#None:U2#Packaging:U3#None:U4#None:U5#None:U6#None:U7#None:U8#None, 1.00, IsRealData, Input
```

Figure 7.35

Data Buffer math now works, and we can see the correct results.

Troubleshooting and Performance

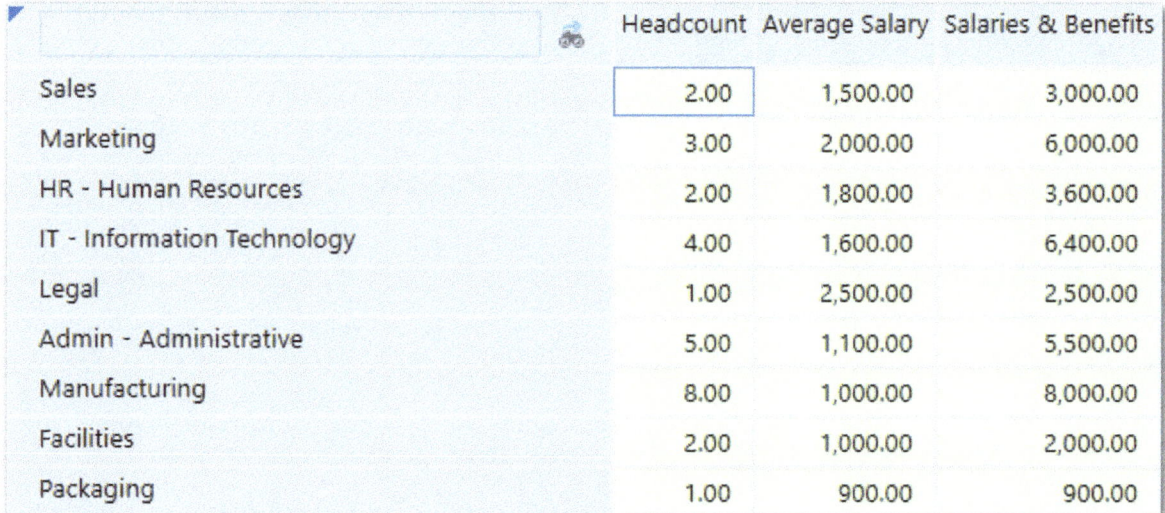

Figure 7.36

Calculation Producing Inconsistent or No Results

A Calculation runs once, and you see the right number. After calculating a second time, the number changes. A third time, it produces the right number again. Around and around you go. Or maybe you check and verify that your data is correct, and yet a Calculation still produces no results. This behavior is usually a symptom of an issue with **Formula Passes**.

If a formula has a dependency on other calculated data, then that data needs to be calculated in a Formula Pass or Business Rule that executes earlier in the Data Unit Calculation Sequence. If two formulas are executing on the same Formula Pass within the same Dimension and have a dependency, inconsistent results will occur since each Formula Pass is multi-threaded. This means that one might execute before the other in one Calculation instance, and vice-versa on another.

A good tip to isolate whether you have a Formula Pass issue – when seeing inconsistent or no results – is to change the formula to run on Formula Pass 16, which is the last pass in the sequence. This will ensure that all other Calculations run before it does. If the Calculation produces correct and consistent results, you have found the issue. From there, you'll need to do some further investigation to isolate which formula is on the wrong pass.

Tracking Calculation dependencies should be done early in the Calculation design phase using the dependency column in the Calculation Matrix introduced in the previous chapter.

Compilation Error

Compilation errors occur when there is a mistake or typo in the syntax in your code. OneStream compiles all Business Rule code at runtime, but you can run a **compile check** within the Business Rule editor to check your code before execution.

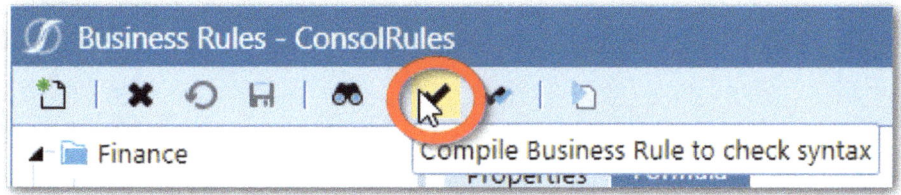

Figure 7.37

If a compilation error occurs, the message will give you some helpful information, such as the line on which the error occurred and the reason for the error.

Chapter 7

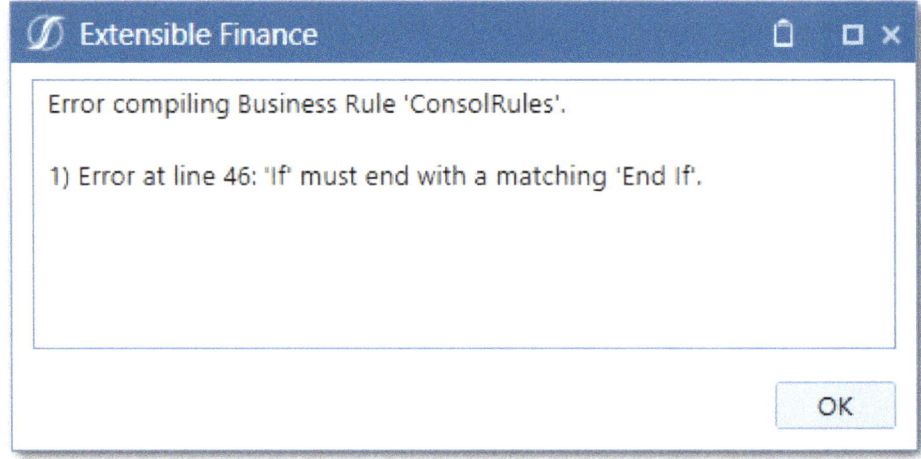

Figure 7.38

To resolve the error, simply fix the syntax and compile again until the Rule compiles successfully.

Invalid Formula Script

Compilation errors won't catch errors within the formula string of functions, such as `api.Data.Calculate` or `api.Data.GetDataBufferUsingFormula`. Those will be thrown as runtime errors.

Invalid Member Name

```
api.Data.Calculate("A#Sales = RemoveZeros(A#Priec * A#Volume)")
```

The above formula string contains a typo – `A#Priec` should be `A#Price`. When the Calculation is executed, it will fail.

Figure 7.39

The error can be viewed by clicking the Error icon or by navigating to Task Activity and viewing it there.

Troubleshooting and Performance

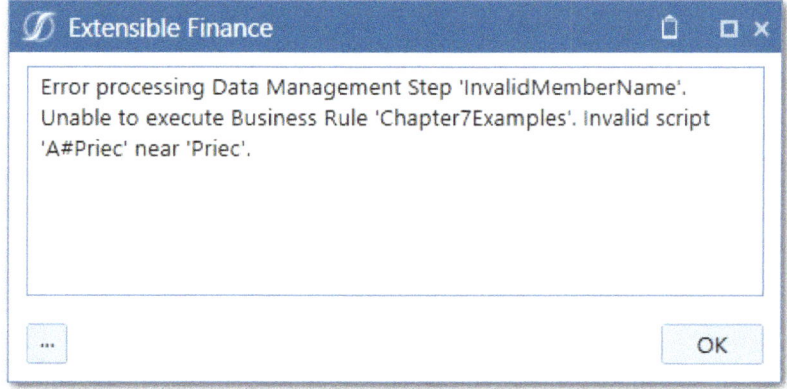

Figure 7.40

The error shows that there was an invalid script due to there being no `Priec` Member in the Account Dimension. To correct this, simply fix the typo.

Unclosed Parentheses

When you have a formula that requires a lot of parentheses, it can be menacing to try to match up all the opening and closing parentheses.

```
api.Data.Calculate("A#COGS = RemoveZeros(MultiplyUnbalanced(A#ManufacturingCost, " & _
"(1 + A#InflationRate:U1#None), U1#None)")
```

An untrained eye may not notice that a parenthesis is missing after `U1#None`. When executing the formula, the below error will be thrown.

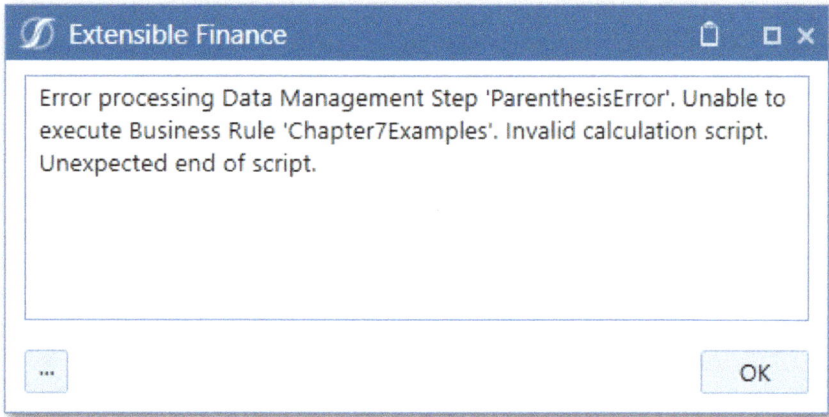

Figure 7.41

Unbalanced Buffer

As discussed in Chapter 3, Data Buffer math can only be performed on Data Buffers that have the same Common Members.

```
api.Data.Calculate("A#COGS = RemoveZeros(A#ManufacturingCost * (1 + A#InflationRate:U1#None)")
```

The above formula will result in an error.

163

Chapter 7

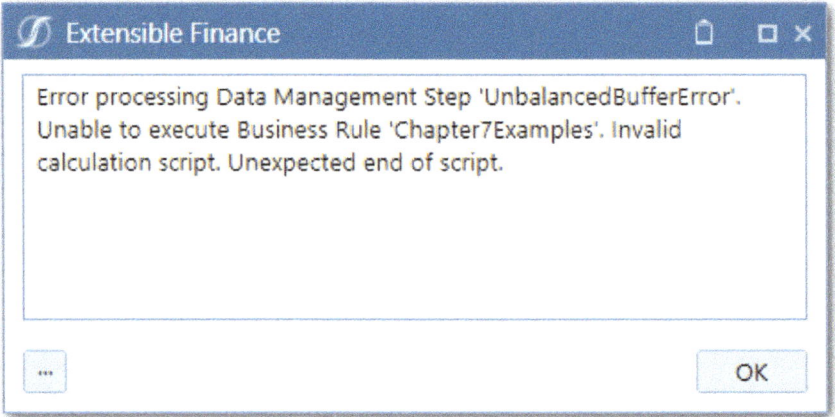

Figure 7.42

The error can be resolved by using the **Unbalanced Functions** explained in Chapter 3.

```
api.Data.Calculate("A#COGS = RemoveZeros(MultiplyUnbalanced(A#ManufacturingCost, " & _
"(1 + A#InflationRate:U1#None), U1#None))")
```

Declaring New Result Cell Outside of Loop

When using the Data Buffer Cell Loop, the new result cell should be declared within the loop.

```
'Loop through the cells of the data buffer
For Each sourceCell As DataBufferCell In costDataBuffer.DataBufferCells.Values

    Dim resultCell As New DataBufferCell(sourceCell)
```

It seems logical to declare the new result cell outside of the loop – to save processing time – but this will result in only the first cell being added to the Result Data Buffer.

Duplicate Members in Filter

When using Dimension filters in the `api.Data.Calculate` function, a filter that contains duplicate Members will result in an error.

```
api.Data.Calculate("A#Sales = RemoveZeros(A#Price * A#Volume)" & _
"",,,,,"U1#Insects.Base, U1#BugZapper")
```

The above formula contains a filter with duplicate Members. `U1#CourseMgt` is a Base Member of `U1#Services`, so would be included twice when OneStream resolves the filter to a Dictionary object.

Figure 7.43

When executing the Calculation, the following error message will be shown:

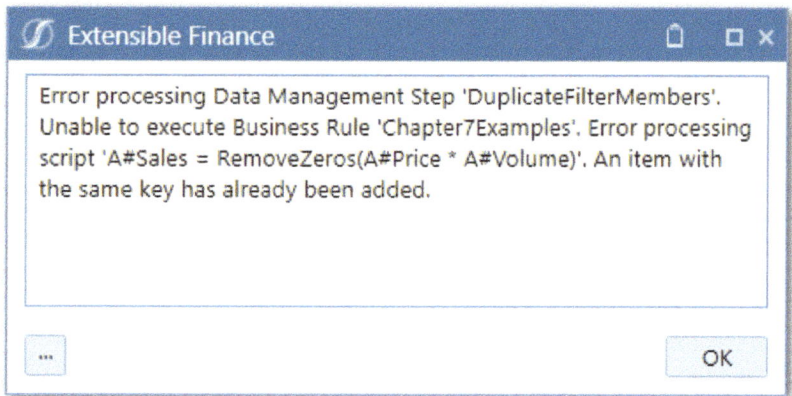

Figure 7.44

OneStream converts the Member Filter into a Dictionary with a unique **Key Value pair** for each Member in the filter. Since Dictionaries cannot contain duplicate items, the error results.

Undefined Members

When using the Data Buffer Cell Loop Method, all Dimensions in the Result Data Buffer must be set. If not explicitly defined, all Data Buffer cells will be set to a default for each Dimension (#None for Account, Flow, and UDs, and #Import for Origin).

```
'Create a result data buffer and destination info to add the cells to later
Dim resultDataBuffer As DataBuffer = New DataBuffer()
Dim destinationInfo As ExpressionDestinationInfo = api.Data.GetExpressionDestinationInfo("")

'Declare starting data buffer to loop through
Dim priceDataBuffer As DataBuffer = api.Data.GetDataBufferUsingFormula("RemoveZeros(A#Price)")

'Loop through the cells of the data buffer
For Each sourceCell As DataBufferCell In priceDataBuffer.DataBufferCells.Values

    'Retrieve the Inflation Rate from the source Cost Center
    Dim volumeDataCell As DataCell = api.Data.GetDataCell("F#EndBalLoad:I#Top:O#Top:A#Volume:U1#" &

    'Create a new result cell to eventually add to the result data buffer
    Dim resultCell As New DataBufferCell()

    'Do the logic to calculate the result amount
    resultcell.CellAmount = sourceCell.CellAmount * volumeDataCell.CellAmount
    resultcell.CellStatus = DataCellStatus.CreateDataCellStatus(False,False)
    'Add the new cell to the Result Data Buffer
    resultdatabuffer.SetCell(si,resultcell)

Next
```

Figure 7.45

In the above script, DestinationInfo is blank and the result cell does not inherit the properties of the source cell, which means no Dimensions are defined for the result cell. When we log the Result Data Buffer, we can see all of the Dimensions are set to defaults.

Common Members: Not Used
A#None:F#None:O#Import:I#None:U1#None:U2#None:U3#None:U4#None:U5#None:U6#None:U7#None:U8#None, 96.00, IsRealData, NotStored

Figure 7.46

While this will not cause an error, it can cause unexpected results as data will be written to None Members, which is likely not the desired result.

This can be resolved by using the DestinationInfo object or by explicitly defining the result cells to set the resulting Data Buffer Dimensions.

Unresolved Members

As we learned in Chapter 4, each Data Buffer Cell can be set to a Member by either inheriting the information from the source cell or by explicitly setting the Data Buffer cell's MemberIds equal to an existing MemberId. If the MemberId is set to XFCommon (inherited from the source cell) or inadvertently set to an invalid Member, an error will occur.

Troubleshooting and Performance

```vb
'Create a result data buffer and destination info to add the cells to later
Dim resultDataBuffer As DataBuffer = New DataBuffer()
Dim destinationInfo As ExpressionDestinationInfo = api.Data.GetExpressionDestinationInfo("O#Import:I#None")

'Declare starting data buffer to loop through
Dim priceDataBuffer As DataBuffer = api.Data.GetDataBufferUsingFormula("RemoveZeros(A#Price)")

'Loop through the cells of the data buffer
For Each sourceCell As DataBufferCell In priceDataBuffer.DataBufferCells.Values

    'Retrieve the Inflation Rate from the source Cost Center
    Dim volumeDataCell As DataCell = api.Data.GetDataCell("F#EndBalLoad:I#Top:O#Top:A#Volume:U1#" & sourceCell

    'Create a new result cell inheriting the properties of the source cell
    Dim resultCell As New DataBufferCell(sourceCell)

    'Do the logic to calculate the result amount
    resultcell.CellAmount = sourceCell.CellAmount * volumeDataCell.CellAmount
    resultcell.CellStatus = DataCellStatus.CreateDataCellStatus(False,False)
    'Add the new cell to the Result Data Buffer
    resultdatabuffer.SetCell(si,resultcell)

Next

resultdatabuffer.LogDataBuffer(api,"Result Data Buffer",100)

api.data.SetDataBuffer(resultDataBuffer,destinationInfo)
```

Figure 7.47

The above example results in an error because common Members were unresolved in the Result Data Buffer.

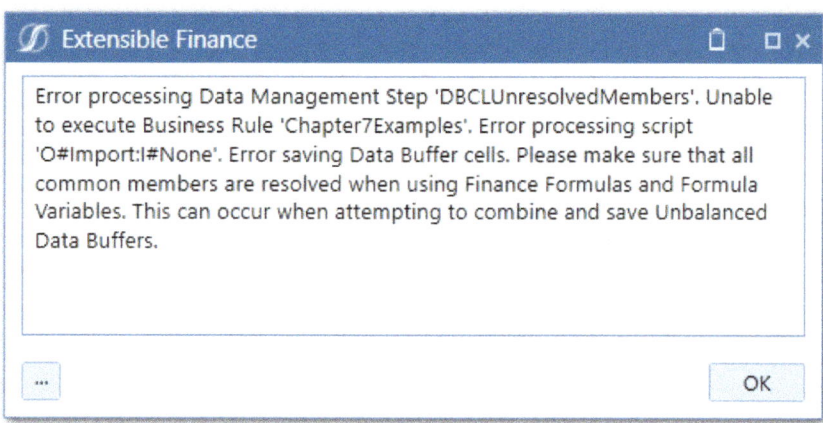

Figure 7.48

When declaring the result cell inside the loop, the properties of the source cell were inherited.

```vb
'Create a new result cell inheriting the properties of the source cell
Dim resultCell As New DataBufferCell(sourceCell)
```

The Source Data Buffer has Account in its Common Members, so that is what is inherited in the result cell. Without explicitly setting the Account to the result cell, or defining it in the DestinationInfo, XFCommon will be used. We can see the logged Result Data Buffer below:

Chapter 7

```
Common Members: Not Used
A#XFCommon:F#EndBalLoad:O#Import:I#None:U1#BugZapper:U2#None:U3#None:U4#None:U5#None:U6#None:U7#None:U8#None, 1,050.00, IsRealData, NotStored
A#XFCommon:F#EndBalLoad:O#Import:I#None:U1#IndoorBugSpray:U2#None:U3#None:U4#None:U5#None:U6#None:U7#None:U8#None, 1,400.00, IsRealData, NotStored
A#XFCommon:F#EndBalLoad:O#Import:I#None:U1#OutdoorBugSpray:U2#None:U3#None:U4#None:U5#None:U6#None:U7#None:U8#None, 1,750.00, IsRealData, NotStored
A#XFCommon:F#EndBalLoad:O#Import:I#None:U1#BedBugKiller:U2#None:U3#None:U4#None:U5#None:U6#None:U7#None:U8#None, 900.00, IsRealData, NotStored
A#XFCommon:F#EndBalLoad:O#Import:I#None:U1#StinkBugKiller:U2#None:U3#None:U4#None:U5#None:U6#None:U7#None:U8#None, 585.00, IsRealData, NotStored
A#XFCommon:F#EndBalLoad:O#Import:I#None:U1#MouseTrap:U2#None:U3#None:U4#None:U5#None:U6#None:U7#None:U8#None, 2,250.00, IsRealData, NotStored
```

Figure 7.49

This means that the common Members are unresolved and the error is thrown. To resolve it, the Account can be defined in the `DestinationInfo` or by explicitly setting the result cell.

```
Dim destinationInfo As ExpressionDestinationInfo = api.Data.GetExpressionDestinationInfo("A#Sales:O#Import:I#None")


'Set the result cell to the destination account
resultcell.DataBufferCellPk.AccountId = api.Members.GetMemberId(DimTypeId.Account, "Sales")
```

This error can also occur if the result cell is set to an invalid Member.

```
'Set the result cell to the destination account
resultcell.DataBufferCellPk.AccountId = api.Members.GetMemberId(DimTypeId.Account, "A#Sales")
```

The above example attempts to set the result cell Account to the Sales Account; however, it is done incorrectly as the `GetMemberId` function accepts the Member name only (without the `A#` Dimension tag). The result is that the Account Dimension is left off the Data Buffer cell.

```
Common Members: Not Used
F#EndBalLoad:O#Import:I#None:U1#BugZapper:U2#None:U3#None:U4#None:U5#None:U6#None:U7#None:U8#None, 1,050.00, IsRealData, NotStored
F#EndBalLoad:O#Import:I#None:U1#IndoorBugSpray:U2#None:U3#None:U4#None:U5#None:U6#None:U7#None:U8#None, 1,400.00, IsRealData, NotStored
F#EndBalLoad:O#Import:I#None:U1#OutdoorBugSpray:U2#None:U3#None:U4#None:U5#None:U6#None:U7#None:U8#None, 1,750.00, IsRealData, NotStored
F#EndBalLoad:O#Import:I#None:U1#BedBugKiller:U2#None:U3#None:U4#None:U5#None:U6#None:U7#None:U8#None, 900.00, IsRealData, NotStored
F#EndBalLoad:O#Import:I#None:U1#StinkBugKiller:U2#None:U3#None:U4#None:U5#None:U6#None:U7#None:U8#None, 585.00, IsRealData, NotStored
F#EndBalLoad:O#Import:I#None:U1#MouseTrap:U2#None:U3#None:U4#None:U5#None:U6#None:U7#None:U8#None, 2,250.00, IsRealData, NotStored
F#EndBalLoad:O#Import:I#None:U1#GlueTrap:U2#None:U3#None:U4#None:U5#None:U6#None:U7#None:U8#None, 1,625.00, IsRealData, NotStored
F#EndBalLoad:O#Import:I#None:U1#RatPoison:U2#None:U3#None:U4#None:U5#None:U6#None:U7#None:U8#None, 1,260.00, IsRealData, NotStored
```

Figure 7.50

Invalid Destination Script

The **Destination Member Script** (the part of the formula to the left of the equal sign) in an `api.Data.Calculate` function should only contain Account-level Dimensions.

```
api.Data.Calculate("E#ACME:A#Sales = RemoveZeros(A#Price * A#Volume)")
```

Adding Data Unit Dimensions to the destination script will result in an error.

Troubleshooting and Performance

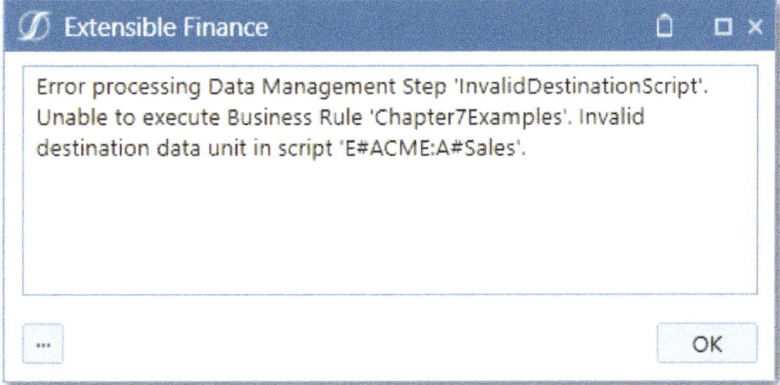

Figure 7.51

The Data Unit information is provided to the Calculation at runtime and is not included in the Data Buffer. Additionally, data can only be written to the current Data Unit being processed.

To filter a Calculation to only process for certain Data Units (Entity in this case), refer to the Data Unit Dimensions in preceding `If` statements.

```
If api.Pov.Entity.Name.XFEqualsIgnoreCase("ACME") Then
    api.Data.Calculate("A#Sales = RemoveZeros(A#Price * A#Volume)")
End If
```

Object Not Set to Instance of an Object

This error is particularly frustrating due to its vagueness.

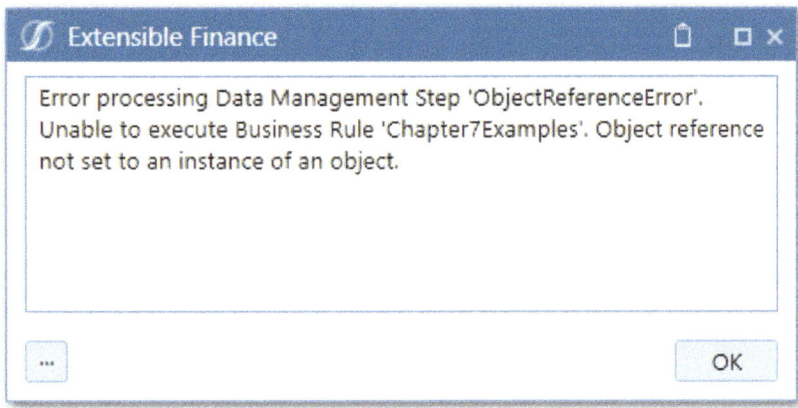

Figure 7.52

This error generally means that an argument in one of your functions did not resolve to a value.

```
Dim UD1DimPk As DimPk  '= api.Dimensions.GetDim("Product").DimPk
Dim memberFilter As String = "U1#Insects.Base"
api.Members.GetMembersUsingFilter(UD1DimPk,memberFilter)
```

The above script passes arguments into the `GetMembersUsingFilter` function. The `DimPk` argument has been declared but not set. When the `GetMembersUsingFilter` gets processed, the 'Object reference not set…' error will be thrown.

Chapter 7

```
Dim UD1DimPk As DimPk = api.Dimensions.GetDim("Product").DimPk
Dim memberFilter As String = "U1#Insects.Base"
api.Members.GetMembersUsingFilter(UD1DimPk,memberFilter)
```

Defining the `UD1DimPk` variable will resolve the error. In this simple example, the culprit for the error is easy to find. If the error is encountered for a rule that is longer and more complex, it can be much more difficult to find the function causing it. Using the logging function, plus some good old trial and error will be your go-to tools.

One last note. Often, a compilation will tip you off – before an error is encountered – with a warning that a variable has *not been* set to a value before it is used. Pay attention to compilation warnings.

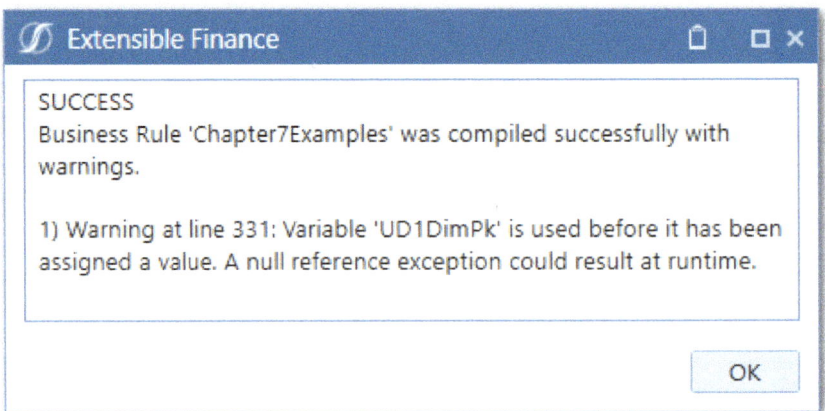

Figure 7.53

Given Key Not Present in Dictionary

When using Custom Calculate functions, parameters can be passed in via **Name Value Pairs**.

```
Dim myParameter As String = args.CustomCalculateArgs.NameValuePairs("MyParameter")
'Execute the calculation
api.Data.Calculate("A#Cost:U1#" & myParameter & " = " & _
"A#Price:U1#" & myParameter & " * A#Volume:U1#" & myParameter & "")
```

If the parameters are not defined in the Data Management Step, in which the Custom Calculate function is called, then an error will occur.

Troubleshooting and Performance

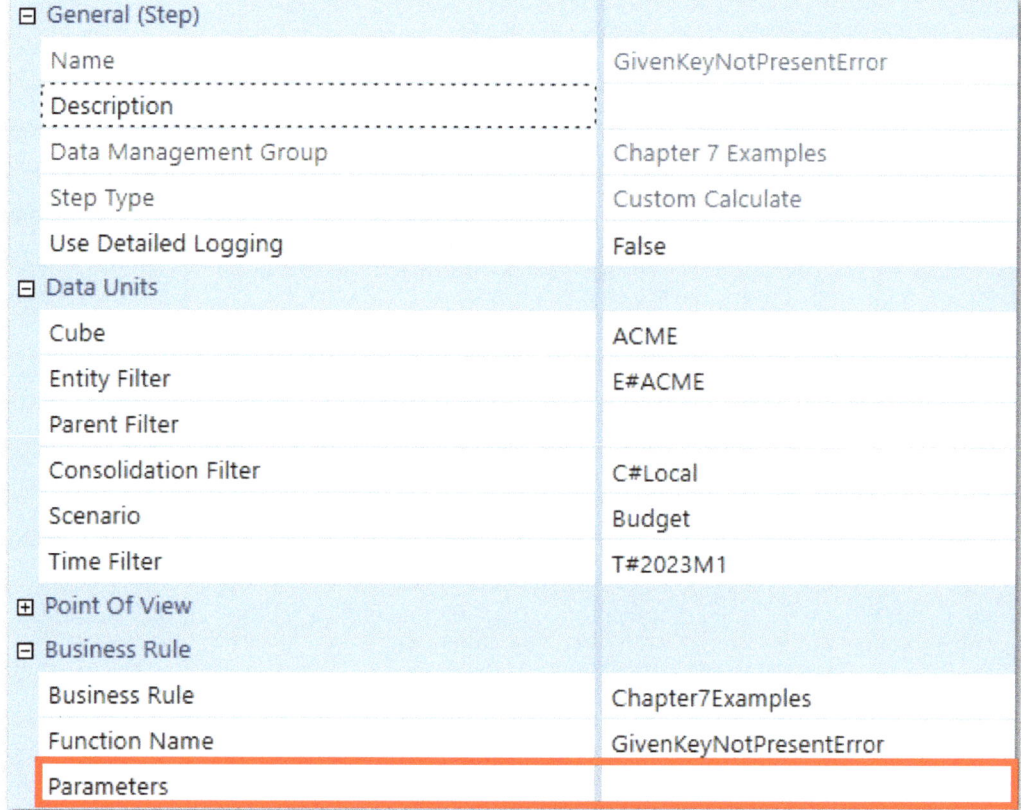

Figure 7.54

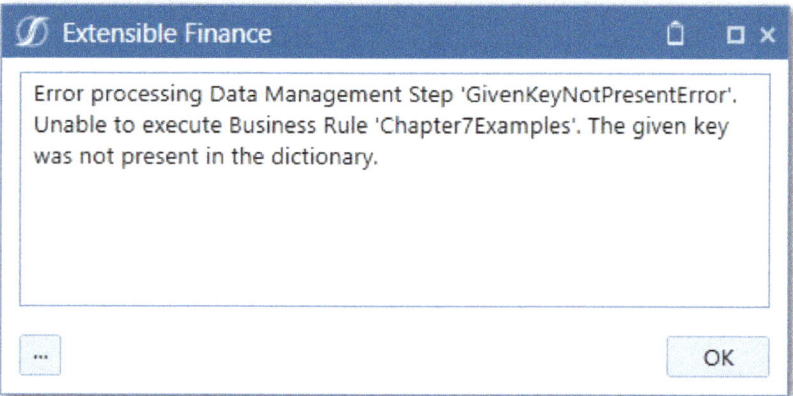

Figure 7.55

There are several things to consider here. First, using `XFGetValue` to retrieve the parameter value will allow us to set a default value if the parameter value cannot be found.

```
Dim myParameter As String = args.CustomCalculateArgs.NameValuePairs.XFGetValue("MyParameter",String.Empty)
```

In this case, we will use a default value of an empty string. As is, the rule will still result in an error because U1 will not be defined in the ADC function. We will add some logic to check the parameter value so that the `api.Data.Calculate` function does not execute if the parameter is blank.

Chapter 7

```
Dim myParameter As String = args.CustomCalculateArgs.NameValuePairs.XFGetValue("MyParameter",String.Empty)
If Not myParameter Is Nothing Then
    'Execute the calculation
    api.Data.Calculate("A#Cost:U1#" & myParameter & " = " & _
    "A#Price:U1#" & myParameter & " * A#Volume:U1#" & myParameter & "")
End If
```

Finally, to fix the root cause of the error, we must define the parameter in the Data Management step.

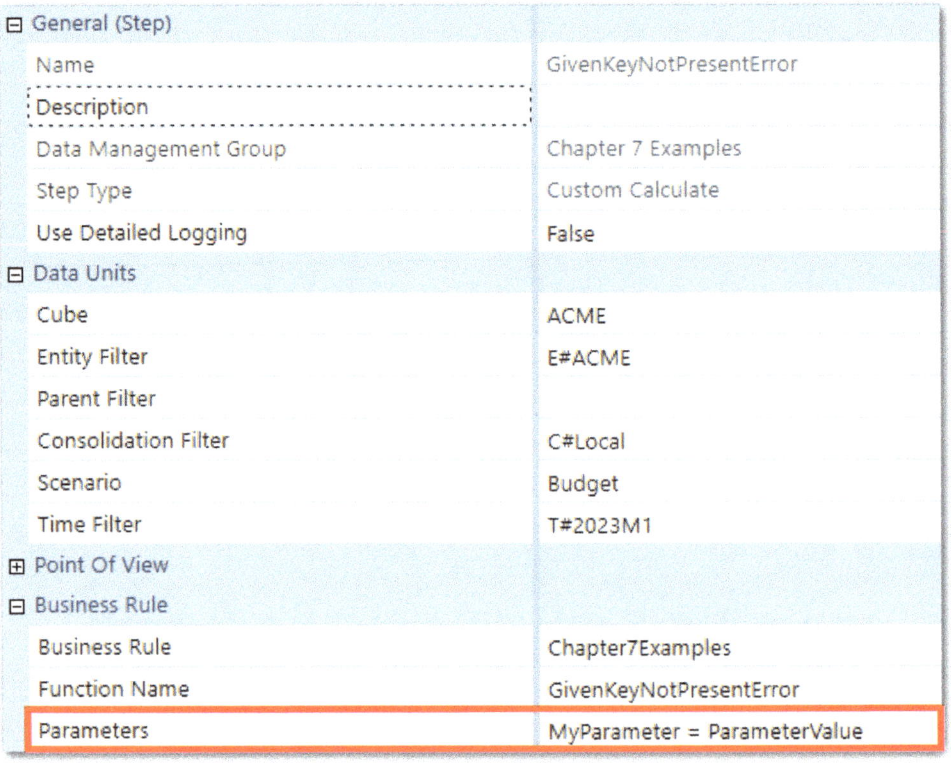

General (Step)	
Name	GivenKeyNotPresentError
Description	
Data Management Group	Chapter 7 Examples
Step Type	Custom Calculate
Use Detailed Logging	False
Data Units	
Cube	ACME
Entity Filter	E#ACME
Parent Filter	
Consolidation Filter	C#Local
Scenario	Budget
Time Filter	T#2023M1
Point Of View	
Business Rule	
Business Rule	Chapter7Examples
Function Name	GivenKeyNotPresentError
Parameters	MyParameter = ParameterValue

Figure 7.56

One last thing is to make sure to add a comment to the rule that notes the parameter definition.

Calculation Performance

Performance boils down to speed, period. While its definition is clear, how it is measured and what it is measured against is not. Typically, it is measured by the time between when the 'Execute Calc' button is clicked to when the results are available to view. Acceptable performance can mean different things to different customers. Even within a single company, it can mean different things to different Users!

It's important to set benchmarks and expectations upfront. Benchmarks can be derived from legacy systems, but it's important to remember that it may not always be an apples-to-apples comparison as more data and functionality is typically present in OneStream. At the end of the day, it is always better to under-promise and over-deliver than the alternative, so set expectations accordingly.

Overview

When it comes to Calculation and Consolidation performance within an application, there are a number of things that can affect performance:

- Hardware and Server Settings

- Cube Design
- Formula Efficiency

A Note on Multi-threading

Before we move further, let's make sure we understand a key feature within the OneStream Calculation Engine. As the OneStream Finance Engine processes Consolidations or Calculations, it multi-threads sibling Data Units. In other words, OneStream tries to process multiple Data Units at the same time when possible.

For example, all Base Entities could theoretically be processed at the same time during a Consolidation. You may have noticed that Consolidations usually reach >90% relatively quickly, and then the last 10% drags. Since the percentage is based on the number of Data Units processed – compared to the total – and multi-threading increases at the lower levels, it makes sense that this dynamic occurs.

The multi-threading concept will be mentioned often in the following settings, so it's important to understand exactly what it refers to.

Hardware and Server Settings

When trying to speed up Calculations or Consolidations, the first idea people have is to increase the hardware specs. If you want your car to go faster, get a bigger engine with more horsepower, right? It's important that hardware is right-sized for the requirements of your application, but increasing hardware is no replacement for well-written Calculations. In fact, hardware increases provide linear performance increases at best, while code optimization often provides an exponential performance increase.

This section will highlight much of what was discussed in Chapter 14 of the OneStream Foundation Handbook. I strongly suggest referencing that book for more details on performance tuning for Calculations, as well as more broadly across the full OneStream product.

Server Structure

Typically, servers are structured so that certain server actions only take place on a *specific* set of servers. For example, data import actions might take place on a dedicated Data Integration Server.

Typical environments will have:

- **General Application Server** – processes User navigation clicks, Cube View execution, Dashboard execution, Report execution. These tasks are mostly single-threaded in nature and are not intensive on the CPU of the server.

- **Stage Application Server** – processes Stage activity in the Stage Engine (Load and Transform, Journals, Forms, Analytic Blend processing). These tasks are multi-threaded in nature and are processor-intensive.

- **Consolidation Application Server** – processes all Consolidation activity in the Finance Engine (Process Cube, Consolidate, Translate, Calculate). These tasks are multi-threaded in nature and are processor-intensive.

- **Data Management Server** – processes all data management sequences in the system. Tasks are multi-threaded in nature and are processor-intensive. The server is, typically, a workhorse for long-running Administrator tasks or dedicated to running Analytic Blend tasks in the system.

For some implementations, there may be dedicated Data Management Servers as well – so that long-running tasks or processes can be directed there if needed.

Server Designation

Certain tasks can be directed at a specific server through Data Management Sequences. This can be a very useful tool to help ease the burden that a few long-running tasks can have on the overall server environment.

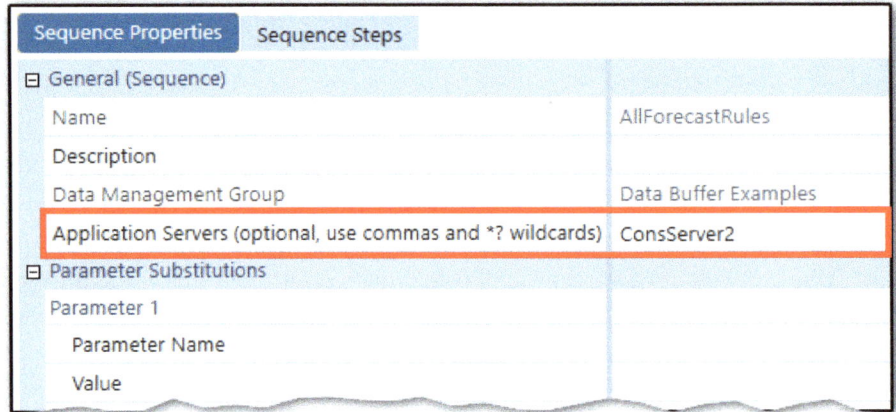

Figure 7.57

CPU Specs

The size and clock speed of the CPUs on the Consolidation Server will have a direct effect on its performance.

- 3.7 GHz chips perform a Consolidation up to two times faster than 2.0 GHz chips.
- Higher clock speeds mean faster execution times.
- Since parallelism is limited on Parent Entities, faster processors allow for Parent Calculations to complete faster.

Multi-threading Settings

There are also multi-threading settings contained in the **Application Server Configuration File** that are available for performance tuning on the Consolidation Engine. These settings can be adjusted to best suit your situation and can be viewed in the Environment section in the System tab and changed in the server configuration files.

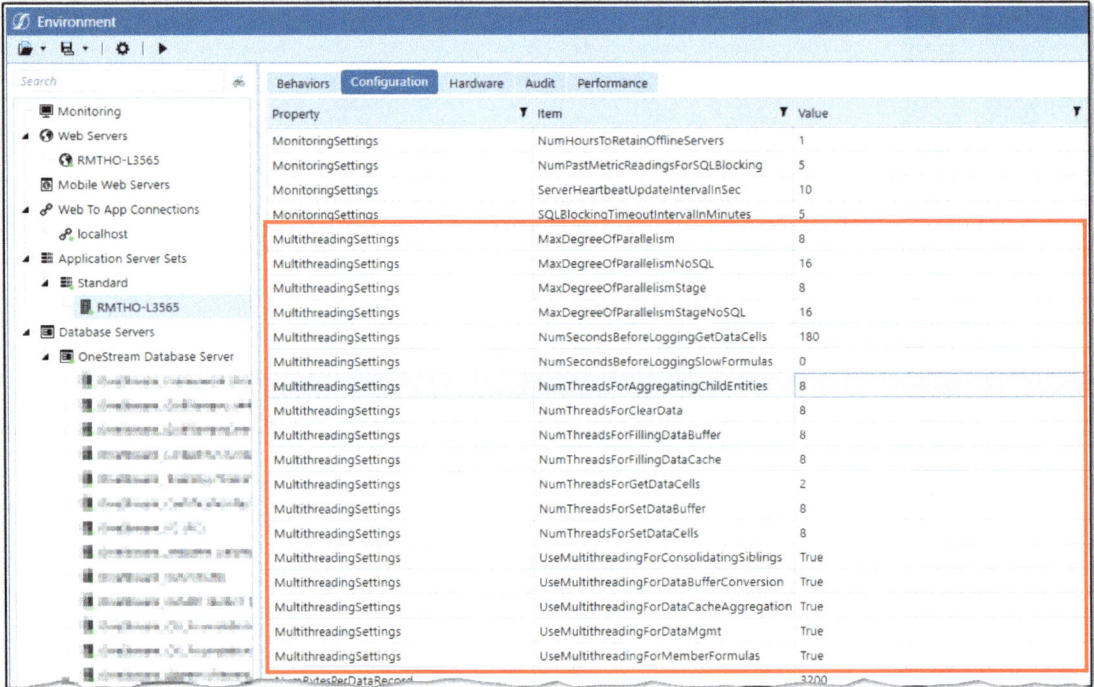

Figure 7.58

Refer to the OneStream Foundation Handbook for more details on how to access and fine-tune these settings.

Cube Design

Cube design plays a major role in Calculation and Consolidation performance. Even perfectly written Calculations will not perform well in a poorly-designed Cube. This section will cover the key design factors that most heavily influence performance.

Data Unit Size and Volume

As we know, Calculations deal primarily with Data Buffers, which are subsets of data records in a Data Unit. By that logic, we can deduce that larger Data Units mean more data records that need to be processed in our Calculations… which will take longer. Makes sense, right?

Reducing Data Unit size as much as possible will directly improve performance. There are a couple of ways Data Unit size can be reduced:

- Utilize Extensibility within Entities and Cubes
- Increase the number of Entities
- No unnecessary storing of data in the Cube
- Reduce data sparsity
- Limit the number of Dimensions as much as possible

Utilize Extensibility

Extensibility can be used to reduce data redundancy and volume at Parent-level Entity Members.

Let's take a situation in which two Base Entities roll up to a Parent. Base Entity 1 is a manufacturing facility and only uses Manufacturing Cost Centers. Base Entity 2 is a Service Provider and only uses Services Cost Centers. Consolidating the detailed Cost Center data from both Entities to their Parent Entity would be completely redundant and provide no additional analytic value. Deploying Extensibility would allow the Cost Center detail to collapse to one 'summary' Member at the Parent Entity. If an analyst wanted to see the Cost Center details, they could simply drill down into each of the Base Entities for insight into those details.

Extensibility is a dense subject that I won't be able to do justice to in the context of this section. There has been a lot written about it in the OneStream Foundation Handbook, and I'm sure more will be written about it in the future, so please refer to other resources for a deeper dive into Extensibility.

Increase The Number of Entities

Spreading the same data set across more Entities can decrease overall Data Unit size and better take advantage of multi-threading.

Let's take an extreme example in which all data is packed into a single Entity which means that there is essentially one very large Data Unit to process. The number of records that would need to be brought into memory for every Calculation would likely overload the processor. In addition, no multi-threading could take place, so all but one processor would be sitting idle. The obvious solution would be to increase the number of Data Units so that the data is 'spread out' evenly over more Entities. This will both better utilize multi-threading, plus reduce the amount of memory that needs to be consumed to retrieve the Data Buffers used in Calculations.

While there are certainly benefits, using the same Entity Dimension across Scenario Types is not always the right move. Data Unit size or process disparities may drive some Scenario Types to use a different Entity Dimension. Look across all available Dimensions and make the optimal choice.

Note that in most Actual reporting situations, there is no flexibility in what the Entity Dimension is – as the Legal Entity needs to drive the Consolidation and Eliminations. For situations where there is more liberty around what the Entity Dimension is (e.g., forecasting or budgeting), then careful consideration should be given, based on Data Unit size. Also, remember that the Entity Dimension can be used for other things than Legal Entities. For example, a project Planning application might benefit by having projects in the Entity Dimension rather than Legal Entities, to allow all projects to be processed in parallel and aggregated when needed. You can reuse the Legal Entity names you might already have in the Entity Dimension for your Consolidation application in a UD Dimension since Member names need to be unique by Dimension Type but can be repeated in different Dimensions.

Optimize Entity Hierarchies

It's best to avoid flat Entity structures with a lot of Children rolling up a Parent as multi-threading will not be optimized. Also, one-to-one Entity to Parent Relationships should be avoided as this creates unnecessary storage points.

Don't Store Unnecessary Data in the Cube

Cubes are not designed to hold large volumes of transactional data. Putting unnecessary or misplaced data in the Cube can lead to Calculation performance issues. Individual employee data, projects, and asset registers are some good examples of the Types of data that typically do not belong in the Cube and are better served within other tools on the OneStream platform.

Consolidation/Calculation Execution Efficiency

The standard Consolidation algorithm (introduced back in Chapter 1) is responsible for aggregating and storing data within the Entity Dimension hierarchies. As this happens, financial intelligence is applied in the form of currency Translations, Intercompany elimination logic, share percentages, and Parent Journal adjustments. Some of this logic is unnecessary for some processes and can be left out by using C#Aggregated, which only runs currency Translation and share percentages, mostly focusing on the straight Aggregation and storage of data.

Use C#Aggregation When Possible

While results will vary, in some situations, using C#Aggregated can be up to 90% faster than a normal Consolidation. Executing an Aggregation can be accomplished by using C#Aggregated in the Consolidation Filter instead of C#Local with a Calculation Type of Consolidate.

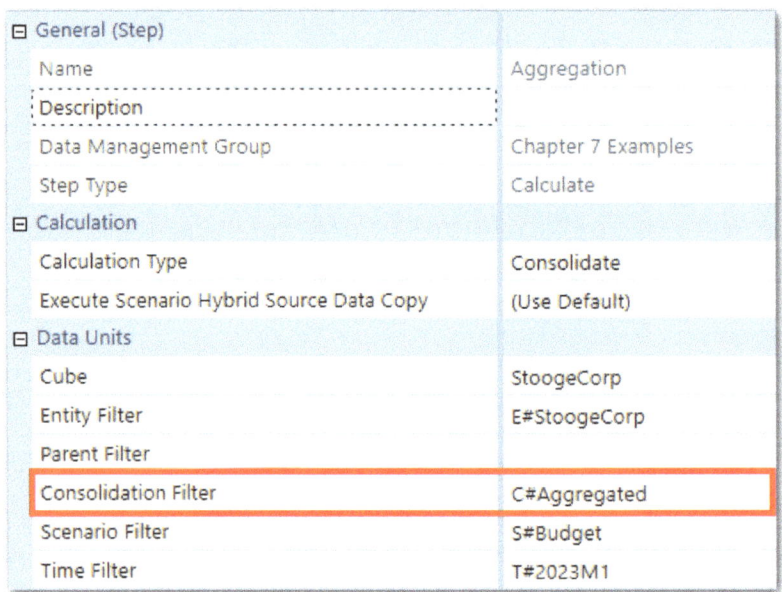

Figure 7.59

After execution, the data from E#ACME will be aggregated to its Parent, StoogeCorp, with the data appearing in C#Aggregated.

Troubleshooting and Performance

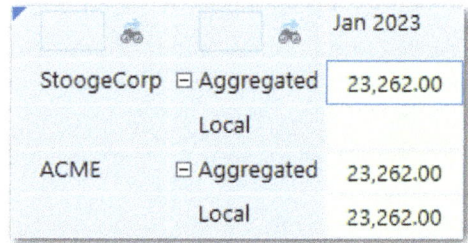

Figure 7.60

You will notice that `C#Local` will not have data at `StoogeCorp` as data will only be stored there when running a Consolidation with `C#Local` specified in the Consolidation Filter.

Using `C#Aggregated` runs currency Translation and calculates percentage ownership. It does not run Intercompany elimination logic, nor account for Parent Journal adjustments, nor does it process other Consolidation Members.

Don't Force Consolidate/Calculate If Unnecessary

While `C#Aggregated` is most often applied to Planning processes where strict accounting and statutory requirements are not necessary, Actual reporting and Consolidation-focused processes will likely use the standard Consolidation algorithm.

Calculations and Consolidations both execute the DUCS for Data Unit(s) specified at runtime. If running a regular Consolidate, **Calculation Status** is considered before OneStream decides whether it needs to process the Data Unit. If using the *Force* Consolidate option, Calculation Status is ignored and *all* Data Units are processed.

Since Calculation Status determines whether data has changed since the last Calculation, Force Calculation is most often unnecessary as it will waste time processing Data Units that have not changed. For example, when Consolidating period 6, using Force Consolidate would start in period 1 and consolidate all Data Units in periods 1-5 before processing all Data Units in period 6. Unless there was a significant metadata change, this would be completely unnecessary as data for those periods would be closed and the data unchanged. Regular Consolidate should be used and only impacted Data Units in period 6 would be processed.

Formula Efficiency

Writing efficient code comes down to a few principles:

- Don't repeat yourself! Avoid redundancy in your code and work with the OneStream Calculation Engine and not against it.
- Use performance-friendly coding techniques.
- Eliminate unnecessary data processing. Ensure Calculations are not creating data for unwanted data intersections or filling the database with unnecessary zeros.

Things to Do

This section will cover various tips and techniques that will help ensure Calculations are written effectively and efficiently. Lock them into habit!

Use Custom Calculate When Possible

When building Cube Calculations, you have the option to use two Finance Function Types – Calculate or Custom Calculate. The Calculate function runs within the Data Unit Calculation Sequence, which is an all-or-nothing exercise. This means that every time a Calculation or Consolidation is run, the entire DUCS is executed – all formulas, all Business Rules. While there are many situations where this is needed, it does come with a lot of overhead and isn't always necessary. Custom Calculate allows a Calculation to run outside of the DUCS, allowing the scope of the Calculation to be narrowed.

Let's take a situation where the Actual and Forecast Scenarios are both using Legal Entity as the Entity Dimension. The Consolidation team – which is responsible for Actuals – is perfectly happy to perform all their Calculations in the DUCS. The FP&A team, which is responsible for the Forecast, has department managers within each Entity who submit and calculate data for their respective departments only.

Having Forecast Calculations run in the DUCS would mean that every time a department manager wants to run Calculations for their department, they would run Calculations for the other departments as well, since the entire Data Unit gets processed. This process would be very inefficient and cause the server to be overloaded with unnecessary Calculations.

By using the Custom Calculate Function Type instead, Calculations can be linked to a User's Workflow with department-specific parameters passed into the rule, ensuring that each manager is only processing their respective departments.

Like the one described above, there are many situations where utilizing the Custom Calculate Finance Function Type can improve overall Calculation performance.

Align Entity Dimensions with Calculations

Entity Dimensions are often shared across Scenario Types and are, in fact, required if you want to leverage Scenario Type Extensibility (sometimes referred to as **Horizontal Extensibility**) within the same Cube. In many situations, this is perfectly suitable if Calculations align to the Entity Dimension for different Scenario Types.

However, in the example described above, where Actuals calculate by Legal Entity and the Planning Scenarios calculate by Department, it may be better to use Department as the Entity for Planning Scenario Types. This would require some additional setup and maintenance as two Department Dimensions would need to be maintained (one in Entity and one in a UD) and data copying rules would need to include logic to pivot the Dimensions.

Correctly aligning the Entity Dimension with Calculations for each Scenario Type can save a lot of headaches plus streamline Calculation build and improve performance.

Use Dynamic Calculations Instead of Stored Calculations (and vice versa)

Dynamic Calculations (covered in Chapter 5) do not run during Consolidations or Calculations and, therefore, do not have any impact on performance there. While Dynamic Calculations do not affect stored Calculation times, they will increase the amount of time it takes to render a Report in which they are referenced. However, in some cases, a Report could take several minutes or even time out if there are complex (or a high volume of) Dynamic Calculations running. In this case, it may make sense to move Dynamic Calculations to stored Calculations and sacrifice some additional Calculation time so that a key Report can run in a timely manner.

It's important to find a balance between stored and Dynamic Calculations and understand that utilizing each affects performance in different ways. Scrutinize each Calculation in the Inventory and determine the best way to write it. After testing, assumptions can be adjusted.

Use RemoveZeros on All Data Buffers

Way back in Chapter 1, we introduced data Cell Status types. NoData and Zeros can exist in the Cube for several reasons and, in many cases, are treated like any other Data Records when it comes to how they are processed in a Data Buffer. In almost all situations, there is no reason to include Zeros or NoData in Data Buffers used in Calculations. OneStream has two functions that can be used to automatically remove NoData or Zero Amount cells from Data Buffers.

- `RemoveNoData` – Removes cells with a Cell Status of NoData.
- `RemoveZeros` – Removes cells with an amount of 0 *and* cells with a Cell Status of NoData.

Troubleshooting and Performance

It should be standard practice to use these functions in all Calculations. Their application in an `api.Data.Calculate` function is shown below:

```
api.Data.Calculate("A#Sales = RemoveZeros(A#Price * A#Volume)")
```

Limit Data Unit Scope

This concept was already introduced in Chapter 3. Use `If` statements – preceding your Calculations – to filter Data Unit Dimensions to which the Calculation should not run. The most common is:

```
If api.Cons.IsLocalCurrencyForEntity() AndAlso Not api.Entity.HasChildren()
```

This will ensure the Calculation only runs for the Local Consolidation Member and Base Entities.

Limit Account-Level Dimension Scope in Data Buffers

This concept was also introduced in Chapter 3. Filters can be used to filter cells from Data Buffers and reduce the number of cells written to the database. Each Calculation should be scrutinized to determine the Members of each Dimension that are relevant.

```
api.Data.Calculate("A#Sales = RemoveZeros(A#Price * A#Volume)",,,,,"U1#Insects.Base")
```

Use Global Variables

OneStream Calculation routines usually involve running the same rule for multiple Data Units, often in parallel. Any variable declared in a rule will be brought into memory again and again for each Data Unit in the sequence. Most of the time, we are happy with this because the variable value may change based on the Data Unit. However, if the variable does not change throughout the duration of the rule sequence, it is a waste of processing time to continually refresh the variable.

Global variables are special variables that are stored in memory for the duration of the runtime of the task session. For example, with a Data Management sequence with multiple steps, the GV will persist through all steps.

They can be called into memory once and then continually referred to through the duration of the rule. Globals are passed into every rule by default.

```
10  Imports OneStream.Shared.Common
11  Imports OneStream.Shared.Wcf
12  Imports OneStream.Shared.Engine
13  Imports OneStream.Shared.Database
14  Imports OneStream.Stage.Engine
15  Imports OneStream.Stage.Database
16  Imports OneStream.Finance.Engine
17  Imports OneStream.Finance.Database
18  Imports System.Diagnostics
19
20  Namespace OneStream.BusinessRule.Finance.Chapter7Examples
21      Public Class MainClass
22          Public Function Main(ByVal si As SessionInfo, ByVal globals As BRGlobals, ByVal api As FinanceRulesApi, ByVal args As FinanceRulesArgs) As Object
23              Try
24                  Select Case api.FunctionType
25
26                      Case Is = FinanceFunctionType.CustomCalculate
```

Figure 7.61

Below are some key functions when interacting with Globals:

- `GetObject` – retrieves an object from the Globals Dictionary
- `SetObject` – sets an object to the Globals Dictionary
- `GetStringValue` – retrieves a string from the Globals Dictionary

Chapter 7

- `SetStringValue` – sets a string to the Globals Dictionary
- `CType` – changes the data Type of an object

Use IntelliSense to see the full menu of functions.

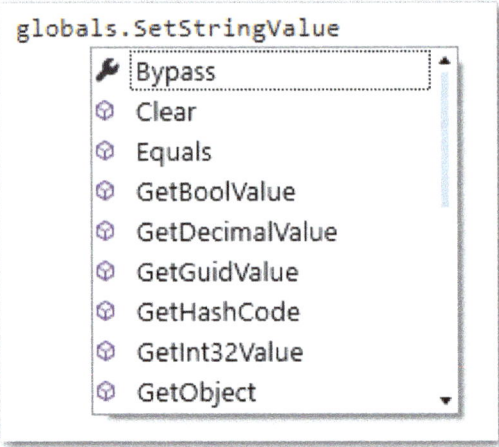

Figure 7.62

Globals are a Dictionary of items and Key Value pairs that can be added using functions like `SetObject` or `SetStringValue`.

```
Dim myString As String = "Hello"
globals.SetStringValue(myString,"MyString)
```

When using Global Variables, it's a good idea to use an `If` statement to first check if a global variable already exists. If not, then the variable can be initialized and added to Globals. If it does exist, then use the `Get` function to retrieve it from memory. The Data Buffer variable can now be used in multiple ADC functions.

```
Dim myStringValue As String = String.Empty 'Start with an empty string
'Check globals first to see if the string has already been set
If globals.GetStringValue("myString") Then 'The variable already exists in globals
    myStringValue = globals.GetStringValue("myString")
Else 'The variable hasn't been set to globals yet
    Dim myString As String = "Hello"
    globals.SetStringValue(myString,"myString") 'Set the string value to globals
End If
```

Global variables will persist through an entire Data Management Sequence, so they can even be worked to reuse variables across multiple Business Rules or functions. They should be especially considered when retrieving objects that are process-intensive, such as:

- Data Tables
- Objects retrieved using BRAPI functions

Formula Variables

We have learned how to declare Data Buffer variables using the `api.Data.GetDataBuffer` and `api.Data.GetDataBufferUsingFormula` functions...

```
Dim volumeDataBuffer As DataBuffer = api.Data.GetDataBufferUsingFormula("A#Volume")
```

Formula variables allow Data Buffer variables to be passed into the formula string of an `api.Data.Calculate` function. Use `api.Data.FormulaVariable.SetDataBufferVariable` and pass in the Data Buffer variable along with a name string.

```
api.Data.FormulaVariables.SetDataBufferVariable("Volume", volumeDataBuffer, True)
```

The last argument is a `True`/`False` value for 'Uses Indexes to Optimize Repeat Filtering', and using `True` will reuse the same Data Buffer using `FilterMembers` and improve performance if the same variable is used multiple times. After naming the Data Buffer, use a dollar sign (`$`) and the name when referencing it in the formula string.

```
api.Data.Calculate("A#Sales = RemoveZeros($Price * $Volume)")
api.Data.Calculate("A#COGS = RemoveZeros(A#ManufacturingCost * $Volume)")
```

The performance benefits come from being able to call the Data Buffer into memory once and then reusing the Data Buffer in multiple `api.Data.Calculate` functions.

Use DimConstants

`DimConstants` are enumerations of standard Dimension Member names in OneStream. When making string comparisons against default Members, always use the `DimConstant` instead of a string comparison of the name.

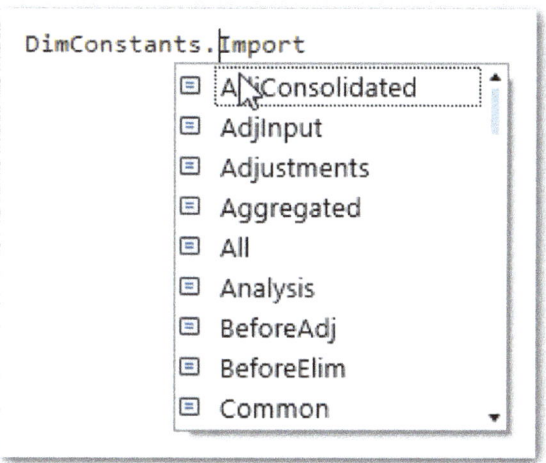

Figure 7.63

String comparisons can be error-prone if there are hidden or unsupported characters from text copied into rules from other sources. Even if they work as expected, they will run less efficiently than using `DimConstants`.

Below is an incorrect string comparison to a default OneStream Member, `"Elimination"`:

```
If api.Pov.Cons.Name.XFEqualsIgnoreCase("Elimination") Then
```

Now, the more efficient, less error-prone version using `DimConstants`:

```
If api.Pov.Cons.MemberId = dimconstants.Elimination Then
```

Using `DimConstants` (and other enumerables) executes faster because only integers need to be compared. These should always be used when possible.

Chapter 7

Things to Avoid

There are a lot of ways to write rules that are inefficient but which seem perfectly logical to do (and which can even produce correct results). If you don't know any better, it can be easy to commit the below crimes and end up with performance problems.

Unnecessary Calculations in the Cube

As mentioned above, transactional data should not go into Cubes as it will bloat Data Units and slow down Calculations and Consolidations. Some people may think they need to put this data in the Cube because it needs complex Calculation logic to run on it, but OneStream offers several other options for the storing and running of Calculations on this type of data.

The **Specialty Planning** suite of MarketPlace solutions offers a robust Calculation Engine that is designed to run on transaction data sets. Data is calculated in relational tables and then summarized and imported into the Cube. **BI Blend** can also perform simple arithmetic on large data sets; so, if Calculations are relatively simple, this tool can be leveraged.

Shifting Calculations for this type of data outside the Cube will greatly improve overall Calculation performance.

Copying Data in the DUCS

Though not technically a Calculation, copying or seeding data between Scenarios or Cubes is often done using a Finance Rule. The most common example is copying Actual data to the Forecast (e.g., for the first six months of a 6+6 Forecast).

A common mistake is to put this formula in the Target Scenario's formula. The thinking is that it executes first in the DUCS, and then all other formulas can follow. Since the Actual data should not change after the initial copy, it is wasteful to continue clearing the data and re-copying each time a Consolidation or Calculation is done.

A better way would be to use a Custom Calculate and set the data to `isDurable = True`. Doing it this way will allow the data copy rule to run once, with the Durable data setting, ensuring the data does not clear on subsequent Calculations or Consolidations. If there is a change in the Actual data, the copy rule can always be run on demand.

Inside vs. Outside Loops

Since loops are repetitive in nature, special care should be taken on what is done inside the loop versus outside.

These types of loops are most often seen within Finance Rules:

- Data Buffer Cell Loops
- Member List Loops
- Data Table Row Loop

In general, it is best to avoid writing to the Cube (or to the database in general) within a loop. Writing to the database is a resource-expensive task. Querying the database should also be minimized as much as possible inside loops. Let's look at a few common examples:

Using Api.Data.Calculate Inside a Loop

This one violates both querying and writing to the database within a loop. To review, the ADC function brings the entire Data Unit into memory, creates a new Result Data Buffer, and then commits that Data Buffer to the Cube. For Data Units with a lot of records, that can be a lot of work! If you are calling an ADC function inside a loop, you could be repeating this potentially hundreds of times.

```
Dim ud1DimPk As DimPk = api.Dimensions.GetDim("Product").DimPk
Dim productList As List(Of MemberInfo) = api.Members.GetMembersUsingFilter(ud1DimPk,"UD1#Top.Base")

For Each product As MemberInfo In productList
    'Check the Product text 2 field
    Dim productText2 As String = api.UD1.Text(product.Member.MemberId,2)
    'only run the logic for Product with DriverBasedCostCalc as text 1
    If productText2.XFEqualsIgnoreCase("SalesCalculation") Then
        api.Data.Calculate("A#Cost:U1#" & product.Member.Name & " = " & _
        "RemoveZeros(A#Price:U1#" & product.Member.Name & " * A#Volume:U1#" & product.Member.Name & ")")
    End If
Next
```

At first glance, the above rule may seem logical. Since stored Calculations process for an entire Data Unit, there is no context of Account-level Dimensions. So, the only way to write logic on UD1 Members is to loop through them. This thinking is incorrect as logic can be applied to Data Buffers via filters or by using the Eval for advanced filtering.

The above example could be written in one ADC function using a UD1 filter instead of a loop and If statement.

```
api.Data.Calculate("A#Cost = A#Price * A#Volume)"" & _
",,,,,"UD1#Top.Base.Where(Text2 = SalesCalculation)")
```

I have found that there are few times where looping through a Member List makes sense. It is almost always better to use an ADC function if possible, or loop through a Data Buffer instead. When looping through a Data Buffer, you have dimensional context for each cell you are looping through, which you can easily transfer to the result cell or for retrieving data cells. When looping through a Member List, you only have context for the Dimension you are looping through, making its use very limited.

Using Api.Data.SetCell or SetDataCell Inside the Loop

If you are moving bricks from one side of your yard to the other, you wouldn't carry one brick at a time, would you? Hopefully not. Instead, you might load them into a wheelbarrow and transport them all at once. This would save both time and energy.

Think of data cells as bricks and a Data Buffer as a wheelbarrow. Instead of writing each data cell individually to the Cube within a loop, you can add them to a Data Buffer in memory and then write them all to the Cube after the loop has completed.

Below is the 'brick-by-brick' method:

Chapter 7

```vb
'Declare starting data buffer to loop through
Dim priceDataBuffer As DataBuffer = api.Data.GetDataBufferUsingFormula("RemoveZeros(A#Price)")

'Clear previously calculated data
api.Data.ClearCalculatedData(True,True,True,True,"A#Sales")

'Loop through the cells of the data buffer
For Each sourceCell As DataBufferCell In priceDataBuffer.DataBufferCells.Values
    'Retrieve the volume data cell using source cell POV
    Dim volumeDataCell As DataCell = api.Data.GetDataCell("F#EndBalLoad:I#Top:O#Top:A#Volume:U1#" & sourceCell.

    'Create a new result cell to eventually add to the resultdata buffer
    'We will inherit the cell properties of the source cell
    Dim resultCell As New DataBufferCell(sourceCell)

    'Set the result cell to the destination account
    resultcell.DataBufferCellPk.AccountId = api.Members.GetMemberId(dimtypeid.Account, "Sales")

    'Do the logic to calculate the result amount
    resultcell.CellAmount = sourceCell.CellAmount * volumeDataCell.CellAmount

    'Set the cell into the cube
    api.Data.SetDataCell(resultcell.DataBufferCellPk.GetMemberScript(api), resultcell.CellAmount,False,True)

Next
```

Figure 7.64

This rule starts with a loop through a Data Buffer and then creates a result cell. After manipulating the result cell, it is written to the Cube inside the loop. While this rule will actually work correctly, it is *much* less efficient than the 'wheelbarrow' method shown below:

```vb
'Create a result data buffer and destination info to add the cells to later
Dim resultDataBuffer As DataBuffer = New DataBuffer()
Dim destinationInfo As ExpressionDestinationInfo = api.Data.GetExpressionDestinationInfo("")

'Declare starting data buffer to loop through
Dim priceDataBuffer As DataBuffer = api.Data.GetDataBufferUsingFormula("RemoveZeros(A#Price)")

'Loop through the cells of the data buffer
For Each sourceCell As DataBufferCell In priceDataBuffer.DataBufferCells.Values
    'Retrieve the volume data cell using source cell POV
    Dim volumeDataCell As DataCell = api.Data.GetDataCell("F#EndBalLoad:I#Top:O#Top:A#Volume:U1#" &

    'Create a new result cell to eventually add to the resultdata buffer
    'We will inherit the cell properties of the source cell
    Dim resultCell As New DataBufferCell(sourceCell)

    'Set the result cell to the destination account
    resultcell.DataBufferCellPk.AccountId = api.Members.GetMemberId(dimtypeid.Account, "Sales")

    'Do the logic to calculate the result amount
    resultcell.CellAmount = sourceCell.CellAmount * volumeDataCell.CellAmount

    'Add the cell to the Result Data Buffer
    resultDataBuffer.SetCell(si, resultCell)
Next

'Save the Data Buffer using the Result Data Buffer and Destination Info
api.Data.SetDataBuffer(resultdatabuffer,destinationinfo)
```

Figure 7.65

Our 'wheelbarrow' is our Result Data Buffer and is created before the loop. As we loop through the Data Buffer cell, result cells (bricks) are added to the result buffer (wheelbarrow) in memory, and

Troubleshooting and Performance

the entire result buffer is written to the Cube after the loop completes. This will perform much faster than the brick-by-brick method.

> **Note:** Always write to the Cube outside of loops!

Api.Data.ClearCalculatedData

When using Custom Calculate Finance Function Types, it is necessary to include Clear Calculated Data scripts at the beginning of each Calculation. This is because the calculated data is not automatically cleared as it is in the DUCS.

Following the same principles, as per the previous examples, always clear the data before starting a loop.

```
'Clear previously calculated data
api.Data.ClearCalculatedData(True,True,True,True,"A#Sales")

'Loop through the cells of the data buffer
For Each sourceCell As DataBufferCell In priceDataBuffer.DataBufferCells.Values
    'Retrieve the volume data cell using source cell POV
```

Figure 7.66

Lookup of Constants

Below is an example where a Member name does not change throughout the entire loop but is looked up in each loop iteration.

```
'Create a result data buffer and destination info to add the cells to later
Dim resultDataBuffer As DataBuffer = New DataBuffer()
Dim destinationInfo As ExpressionDestinationInfo = api.Data.GetExpressionDestinationInfo("")

'Declare starting data buffer to loop through
Dim priceDataBuffer As DataBuffer = api.Data.GetDataBufferUsingFormula("RemoveZeros(A#Price)")

'Loop through the cells of the data buffer
For Each sourceCell As DataBufferCell In priceDataBuffer.DataBufferCells.Values
    'Retrieve the volume data cell using source cell POV
    Dim volumeDataCell As DataCell = api.Data.GetDataCell("F#EndBalLoad:I#Top:O#Top:A#Volume:U1#" &

    'Create a new result cell to eventually add to the resultdata buffer
    'We will inherit the cell properties of the source cell
    Dim resultCell As New DataBufferCell(sourceCell)

    'Set the result cell to the destination account
    resultcell.DataBufferCellPk.AccountId = api.Members.GetMemberId(dimtypeid.Account, "Sales")

    'Do the logic to calculate the result amount
    resultcell.CellAmount = sourceCell.CellAmount * volumeDataCell.CellAmount

    'Add the cell to the Result Data Buffer
    resultDataBuffer.SetCell(si, resultCell)
Next

'Save the Data Buffer using the Result Data Buffer and Destination Info
api.Data.SetDataBuffer(resultdatabuffer,destinationinfo)
```

Figure 7.67

The Sales Account Member ID is being looked up again and again, even though the same value is being returned each time. Pulling this function outside of the loop will save processing time.

```vb
'Create a result data buffer and destination info to add the cells to later
Dim resultDataBuffer As DataBuffer = New DataBuffer()
Dim destinationInfo As ExpressionDestinationInfo = api.Data.GetExpressionDestinationInfo("")

Dim salesAccountId As Integer = api.Members.GetMemberId(dimtypeid.Account, "Sales")

'Declare starting data buffer to loop through
Dim priceDataBuffer As DataBuffer = api.Data.GetDataBufferUsingFormula("RemoveZeros(A#Price)")

'Loop through the cells of the data buffer
For Each sourceCell As DataBufferCell In priceDataBuffer.DataBufferCells.Values
    'Retrieve the volume data cell using source cell POV
    Dim volumeDataCell As DataCell = api.Data.GetDataCell("F#EndBalLoad:I#Top:O#Top:A#Volume:U1#"

    'Create a new result cell to eventually add to the resultdata buffer
    'We will inherit the cell properties of the source cell
    Dim resultCell As New DataBufferCell(sourceCell)

    'Set the result cell to the destination account
    resultcell.DataBufferCellPk.AccountId = salesAccountId

    'Do the logic to calculate the result amount
    resultcell.CellAmount = sourceCell.CellAmount * volumeDataCell.CellAmount

    'Add the cell to the Result Data Buffer
    resultDataBuffer.SetCell(si, resultCell)
Next

'Save the Data Buffer using the Result Data Buffer and Destination Info
api.Data.SetDataBuffer(resultdatabuffer,destinationinfo)
```

Figure 7.68

Alternatively, the Sales Account can be set in the `DestinationInfo` and applied to the Result Data Buffer when writing the Data Buffer to the Cube in the `SetDataBuffer` function.

```vb
'Create a result data buffer and destination info to add the cells to later
Dim resultDataBuffer As DataBuffer = New DataBuffer()
Dim destinationInfo As ExpressionDestinationInfo = api.Data.GetExpressionDestinationInfo("A#Sales")

Dim salesAccountId As Integer = api.Members.GetMemberId(dimtypeid.Account, "Sales")

'Declare starting data buffer to loop through
Dim priceDataBuffer As DataBuffer = api.Data.GetDataBufferUsingFormula("RemoveZeros(A#Price)")

'Loop through the cells of the data buffer
For Each sourceCell As DataBufferCell In priceDataBuffer.DataBufferCells.Values
    'Retrieve the volume data cell using source cell POV
    Dim volumeDataCell As DataCell = api.Data.GetDataCell("F#EndBalLoad:I#Top:O#Top:A#Volume:U1#" &

    'Create a new result cell to eventually add to the resultdata buffer
    'We will inherit the cell properties of the source cell
    Dim resultCell As New DataBufferCell(sourceCell)

    'Set the result cell to the destination account
    resultcell.DataBufferCellPk.AccountId = salesAccountId

    'Add the cell to the Result Data Buffer
    resultDataBuffer.SetCell(si, resultCell)
Next

'Save the Data Buffer using the Result Data Buffer and Destination Info
api.Data.SetDataBuffer(resultdatabuffer,destinationinfo)
```

Figure 7.69

Using Api.Data.ClearCalculatedData in DUCS

Clearing data in Calculations that run in the DUCS is unnecessary (assuming the 'Clear Calculated Data' Scenario property is set to `True`) as clearing previously calculated data is the first step in the sequence.

Stacking Api.Data.Calculate Functions With Similar Logic

Multiple ADC functions with the same logic can be condensed into one that uses filters.

```
api.Data.Calculate("A#Sales:U1#BugZapper = RemoveZeros(A#Price:U1#BugZapper * A#Volume:U1#BugZapper)")
api.Data.Calculate("A#Sales:U1#MouseTrap = RemoveZeros(A#Price:U1#MouseTrap * A#Volume:U1#MouseTrap)")
api.Data.Calculate("A#Sales:U1#PestControl = RemoveZeros(A#Price:U1#PestControl * A#Volume:U1#PestControl)")
```

The above ADC functions all use the same logic. The entire Data Unit is called into memory with each one. Using filters and Member hierarchies, they can be condensed to one, reducing the number of times the Data Unit is called into memory.

```
api.Data.Calculate("A#Sales = RemoveZeros(A#Price * A#Volume)",,,,,"UD1#SalesCalculation.Base")
```

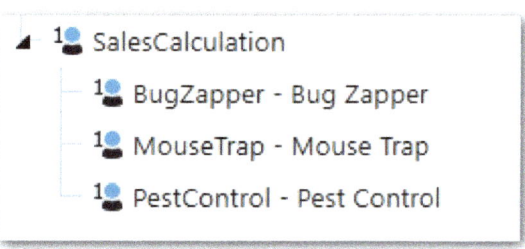

Figure 7.70

Using BRAPI Calls

BRAPI calls are used to call functions in another Engine within the platform, such as the Data Integration Engine. For example, if I am writing a Parser Rule and need to retrieve a Member name, I would need to access the Finance Engine and use the `GetMemberName` function from the Finance BRAPI Library. In many cases, there are available API functions that are equivalent to BRAPI functions.

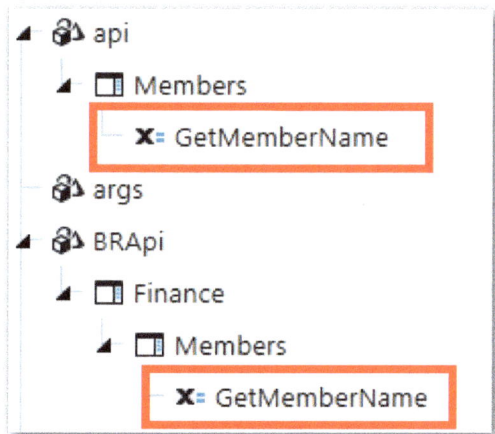

Figure 7.71

Chapter 7

To the unknowing person, it may seem like these functions behave the same... which would be incorrect. While they may produce the same result, the BRAPI function is doing more in the background, which can cause performance issues.

When calling a BRAPI function, a new database connection is opened to connect to that Engine. Using BRAPI calls within a Finance Rule can cause an overload of database connections during multi-threading and ultimately result in degraded performance or a dropped database connection, resulting in an error.

There may be times when it is necessary to call a BRAPI function from a Finance Rule, but it's important to consider the performance implications and limit the number of times it is called. Furthermore, always check for an equivalent function in the API library.

```
'Use this
Dim memberNameApi As String = api.Members.GetMemberName(DimTypeId.Account,memberId)
'Not this
Dim memberNameBrApi As String = BrApi.Finance.Members.GetMemberName(si, DimTypeId.Account,memberId)
```

Hardcoding Time Periods

Time periods can be referenced in `If` statements preceding rules or added to Source Data Buffer Member Scripts to pull data from a specific period within a year.

```
api.Data.Calculate("A#Salaries = RemoveZeros(T#POVPriorYearM12:A#Salaries * (1 + A#InflationRate))")
```

The above formula takes the prior year's ending balance and multiplies it by an inflation rate to derive a forecasted cost. The problem is that this assumes that the Scenario is monthly, which may be true for all Scenarios at the time the rule is written, but which may change over time as additional Scenarios are added. Instead, leverage functions that do not depend on specific Time periods.

```
Dim lastPeriodInYearId As Integer = api.Time.GetLastPeriodInYear()
Dim lastPeriodInYearName As String = api.Members.GetMemberName(dimtypeid.Time, lastPeriodInYearId)
api.Data.Calculate("A#Salaries = RemoveZeros(T#" & lastPeriodInYearName & ":A#Salaries * (1 + A#InflationRate))")
```

Using the `LastPeriodInYear` function will guarantee the formula works for a Scenario with any time frequency.

Another example is referencing Time periods in a preceding `If` statement:

```
Dim curMonth As Integer = TimeDimHelper.GetSubComponentsFromId(api.Pov.Time.MemberId).Month
'Check if the current month is first
If curMonth = 1 Then
    api.Data.Calculate("F#BegBal = T#" & lastPeriodInYearName & ":F#BegBal")
Else
    api.Data.Calculate("F#BegBal = T#POVPrior1:F#BegBal")
End If
```

For Quarterly or Yearly Scenarios, the first month will not be 1, so this will not work. Instead, use the `FirstPeriodInYear` function.

```
If api.Time.IsFirstPeriodInYear Then
    api.Data.Calculate("F#BegBal = T#" & lastPeriodInYearName & ":F#BegBal")
Else
    api.Data.Calculate("F#BegBal = T#POVPrior1:F#BegBal")
End If
```

Forgetting to Comment Out Logging

When using log functions for testing and troubleshooting, make sure they are commented out when the code is moved into production. Your author has, unproudly, crashed a server or two for committing this offense.

System Diagnostics Solution

As a direct response to seeing common patterns of rule-writing mistakes, resulting in poorly performing Applications, a solution was developed to help identify these issues. **System Diagnostics** is available on the OneStream Marketplace and should be installed in every environment.

The solution consists of four main pages:

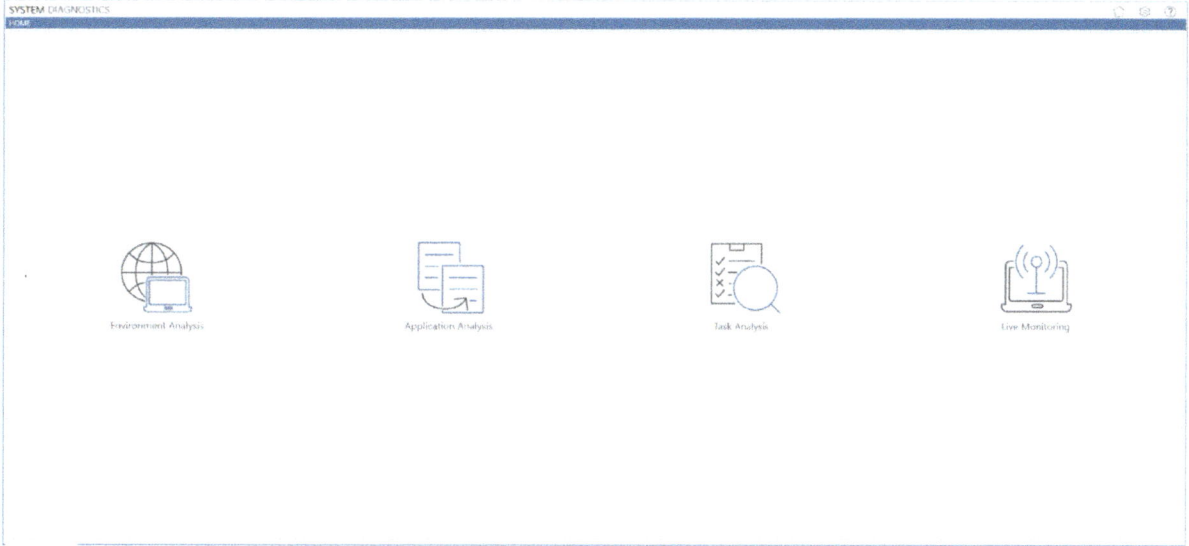

Figure 7.72

The Application Analysis page contains insight relevant to Calculations and Consolidation performance.

Snapshots of the Application can be taken for any year in which there is loaded data.

Chapter 7

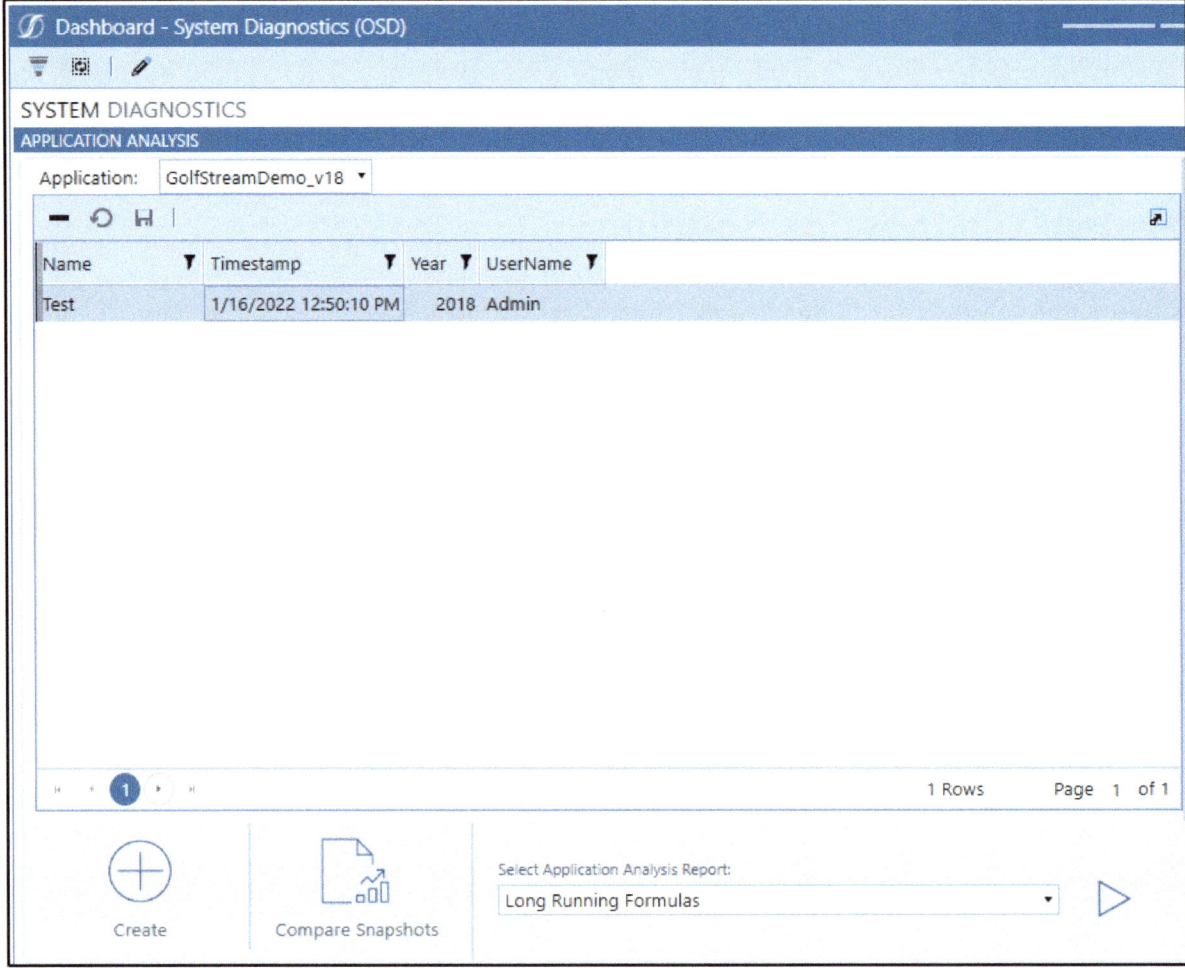

Figure 7.73

After creating a snapshot, various application metrics will be displayed.

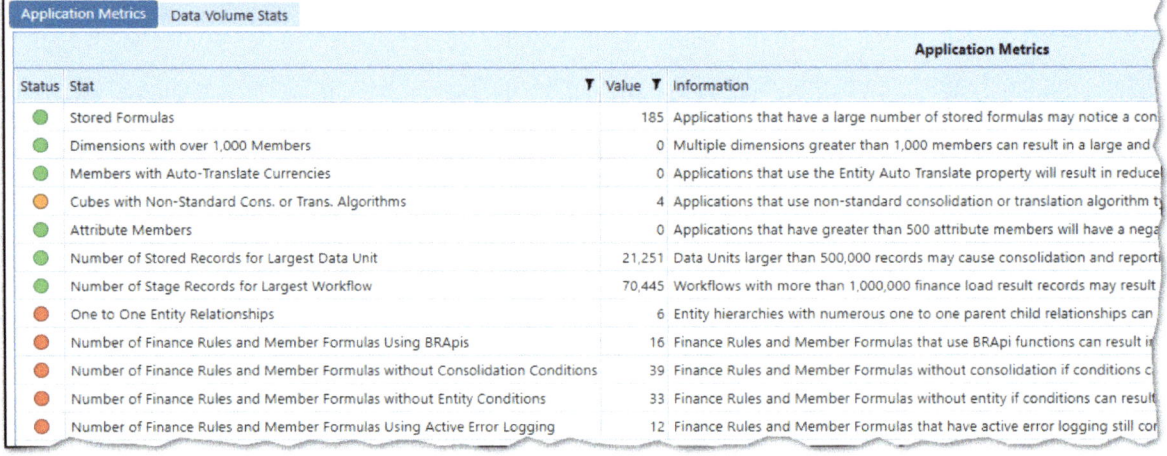

Figure 7.74

These metrics help locate problem areas relating to Cube design, size, and formula efficiency.

Data volume statistics can give further insight into Data Units that have a large number of data records and which may perform slower.

Troubleshooting and Performance

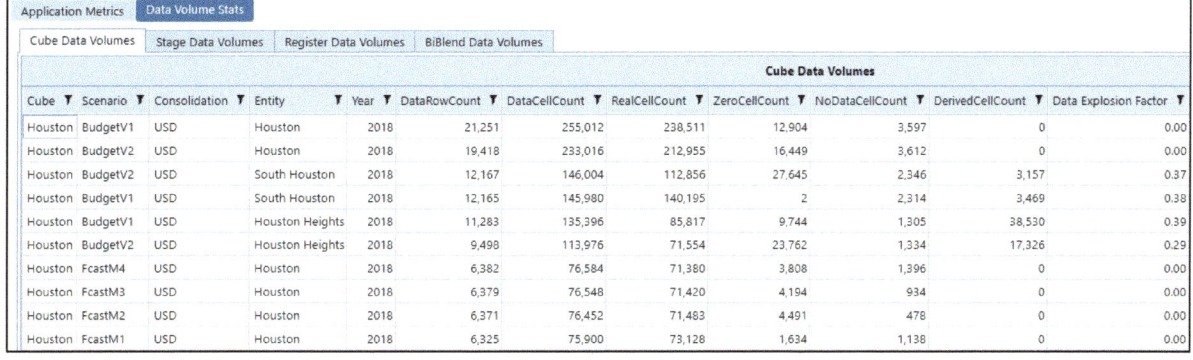

Figure 7.75

The Long Running Formulas Report can identify any Calculation in the DUCS that is taking longer than a specific benchmark. In order for this Report to run correctly, settings to enable long-running formula monitoring and parameters must be set in the server configuration files.

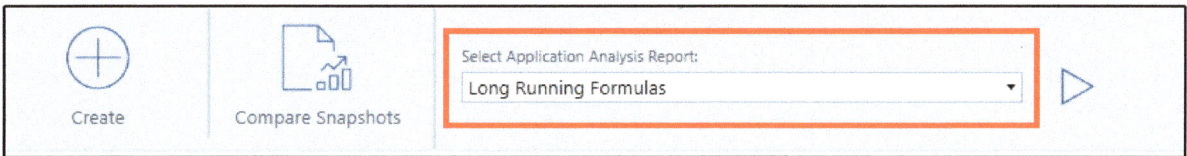

Figure 7.76

System Diagnostics is a great tool that can help Consultants and Administrators monitor applications and help identify root causes of performance issues.

Conclusion

As I said earlier in the chapter, most of a Calculation writer's time is spent testing, troubleshooting, and optimizing performance. Hopefully, the above catalog of tools, techniques, and common errors can save you hours of time!

8
Common Rule Examples

Calculations largely exist to enhance and refine data to provide the clarity required to make better business decisions. This chapter will discuss real-world use cases for Calculations that you are likely to encounter in a typical OneStream implementation. No two situations are the same, so it is highly unlikely any of these Calculations can be used in the exact way presented. They are simply meant to provide some context around the concepts discussed in the previous chapters.

As we tackle each example, I will explain the requirements of the Calculation and give background to the data and metadata requirements. Further, I will break down the code and explain the functions used… and why.

Balance Sheet and Flow Calculations

If you have Balance Sheet data anywhere in your application, you will also need Calculations to provide supporting movement detail. Account balances are loaded from a source system, and details of the Account movements over time are calculated. These Calculations are stored within the Flow Dimension, and work in conjunction with the Account Dimension to provide insight into Balance Sheet Account movements from period to period.

Balance Sheet Calculations

While most Balance Sheet Accounts in an Actual Scenario are imported from a source system, there are a handful of Accounts that are almost always calculated. These Calculations are typically stored in Member Formulas – as they run for a specific Account – and should run in the DUCS so that they are cleared and recalculated to reflect any changes in data they are dependent on. This is primarily due to the cascading nature of the Calculations. If imported Balance Sheet data changes, then all Balance Sheet and Flow formulas will need to be cleared and recalculated.

Current Year Net Income

The Current Year Net Income (`CurYearNetIncome`) Account pulls the YTD Net Income from the Income Statement into the equity section of the Balance Sheet. In most cases, this is accomplished using a simple `api.Data.Calculate` function.

```
'Pull Net Income from the P&L into Retained Earnings. Ran in local and USD due to difference in translation rates
'between the P&L and B/S
If (Not api.Entity.HasChildren()) Or (api.Entity.HasChildren() And api.Cons.IsForeignCurrencyForEntity()) Then
    api.Data.Calculate("A#CurYearNetIncome:V#YTD:O#Import:F#EndBalLoad:I#None:U1#None:U2#None = " & _
    "RemoveZeros(A#NetIncome:V#YTD:O#Top:F#EndBalLoad:I#Top:U1#Top:U2#Top)")
End If
```

> **Note:** Throughout this chapter (and the book more generally), many of the code snippets for rule examples are presented line by line with detailed explanations. Screenshots of the code – as presented in the OneStream Business Rule Editor – are used instead of showing the code as plain text and we know that this can sometimes be difficult to read in the print edition of the book. A full application with all referenced code examples (and more) is available to download at: www.OneStreamPress.com/FRC

Chapter 8

Reduce Data Unit Scope

The preceding `If` statement is used to reduce Data Unit scope. This Calculation runs specifically on Base Entities but does not filter down to Local only as it should calculate on the translated amount as well. This is because the Income Statement translates at a *different rate*, so that needs to be captured. The Calculation also runs for foreign currency Parent Entities with Auto-Translation currencies, if used.

Collapsing Detail

Origin, Flow, Intercompany, UD1, and UD2 Dimensions are included in the formula Member scripts so the detail for those Dimensions is collapsed. This is because the Income Statement data contains more dimensional detail than Balance Sheet Accounts so that detail does not need to be copied.

Key Account Properties

Formula Pass

Since this Calculation will run as part of the DUCS, it will need to be assigned a Formula Pass. FormulaPass2 will be used in case there are any calculated Accounts within the Income Statement which would use FormulaPass1, so that they run prior to this Calculation. If any additional Formula Passes are needed within the Income Statement, a later pass can be used.

Is Consolidated

The default setting for this property is `Conditional (True if no Formula Type (default))` which means that if a Formula Pass is assigned, the Account will not Consolidate. The Is Consolidated property should be changed to True to ensure the calculated results consolidate.

Allow Input

Since this Account will only hold calculated data, the Allow Input property should be changed to False.

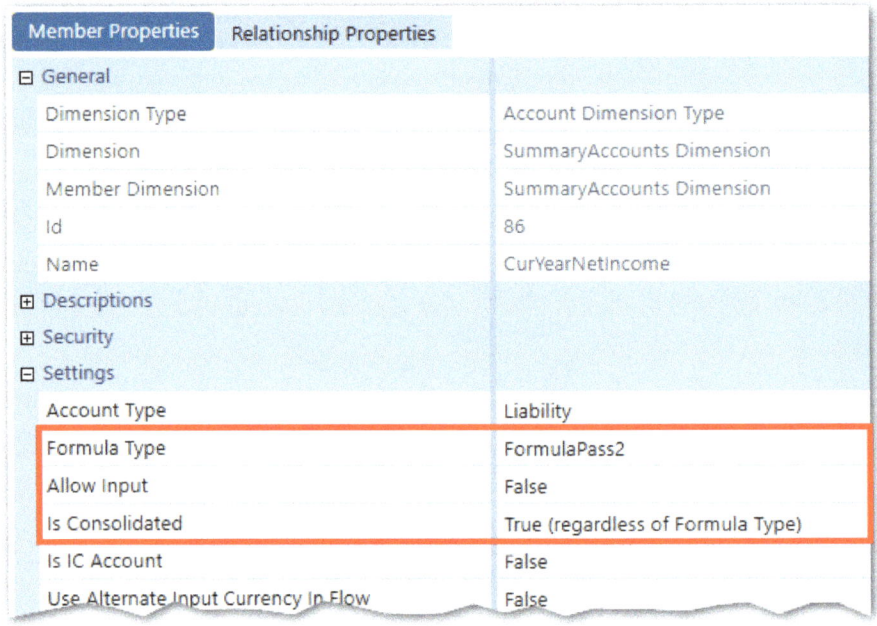

Figure 8.1

Results

After execution of the Calculation, the Current Year Net Income Account within the Balance Sheet matches the YTD Net Income Account within the Income Statement.

Common Rule Examples

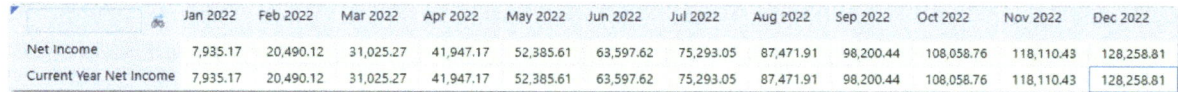

Figure 8.2

Retained Earnings Beginning Balance

The ending retained earnings balance from the prior year will need to be carried forward via a Calculation and stored in a dedicated Account (REBegBal) within the Equity section of the Balance Sheet.

```
'Copy the Retained Earnings account from the prior year to the RE Beg Bal Account
'Ran In local And USD due To difference In translation rates
If (Not api.Entity.HasChildren()) Or (api.Entity.HasChildren() And api.Cons.IsForeignCurrencyForEntity()) Then
    'Get the last period in the prior year
    Dim lastPeriodPriYearId As Integer = api.Time.GetLastPeriodInPriorYear
    Dim lastPeriodPriYearName As String = api.Time.GetNameFromId(lastPeriodPriYearId)
    If api.Time.IsFirstPeriodInYear Then 'For the first period, copy the data from the Prior Year RE Account
        api.Data.Calculate("A#REBegBal:V#YTD:O#Import:F#EndBalLoad:I#None:U1#None:U2#None = " & _
        "RemoveZeros(A#RE:T#" & lastPeriodPriYearName & ":V#YTD:O#Top:F#EndBalLoad:I#Top:U1#Top:U2#Top)")
    Else 'For the rest of the year, copy the REBEgBal account from the prior period
        api.Data.Calculate("A#REBegBal:V#YTD:O#Import:F#EndBalLoad:I#None:U1#None:U2#None = " & _
        "RemoveZeros(A#REBegBal:T#POVPrior1:V#YTD:O#Top:F#EndBalLoad:I#Top:U1#Top:U2#Top)")
    End If
End If
```

Reduce Data Unit Scope

The preceding If statement is used to reduce Data Unit scope. This Calculation runs specifically on Base Entities but does not filter down to Local only as it should copy the already translated amount from the Prior Year and not re-translate at the current rate.

Only Pull from the Prior Year Once

The api.Time.IsFirstPeriodInYear function is used so that the prior year is only referenced once. An api.Data.Calculate will copy forward the Ending Balance from the Retained Earnings Parent Account (RE).

For the rest of the periods, data is simply brought forward from the prior period REBegBal Account, which was calculated in the first ADC function. This will increase performance as retrieving data from prior years takes more processing time since a different data table needs to be referenced.

Collapsing Detail

Details for Origin, Flow, Intercompany, UD1, and UD2 Dimensions are not needed for analytical purposes so those Dimensions are collapsed in the Formula Member scripts.

Key Account Properties

Formula Pass

Since the Calculation only references data from prior periods, FormulaPass1 can be used since there are no dependencies. The Is Consolidated property is set to True to ensure the calculated data consolidates.

Is Consolidated

The default setting for this property is Conditional (True if no Formula Type (default)) which means that if a Formula Pass is assigned, the Account will not Consolidate. The Is Consolidated property should be changed to True to ensure the calculated results consolidate.

Chapter 8

Allow Input

Since this Account will only hold calculated data, the Allow Input property should be changed to False. Data for this Account from the source system (if available) will be bypassed (ignored).

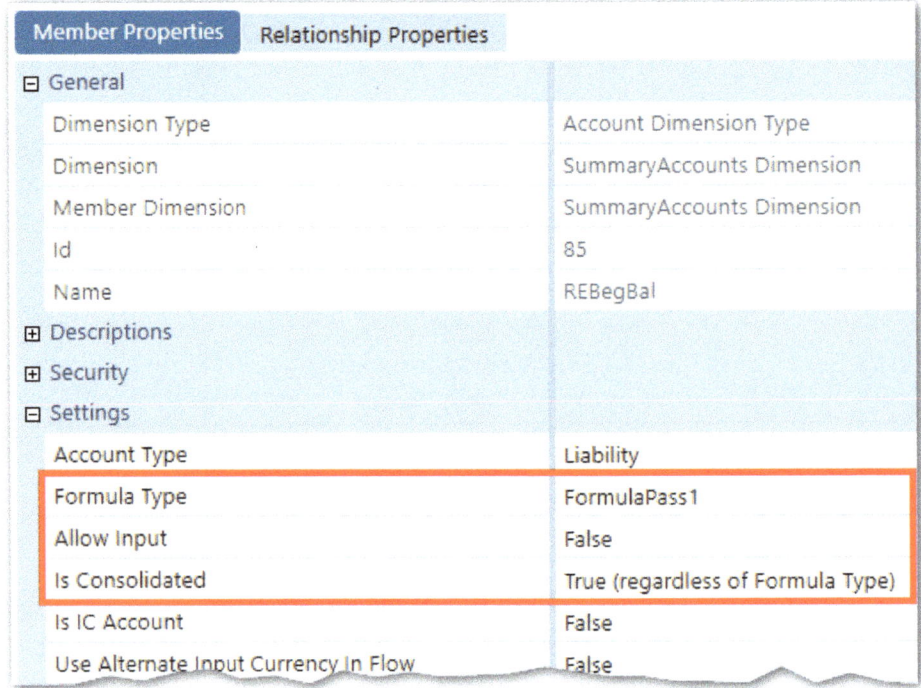

Figure 8.3

Flow Calculations

As stated above, one of the primary functions of the Flow Dimension is to track the details of Balance Sheet Account movements over time. The Flow Dimension tells the story of what happened to an Account balance from period to period and is used to support reporting requirements such as currency impact analysis and Cash Flow.

While there is not one Flow Dimension configuration to fit every situation, we will go through an example of one that is commonly used in practice, and which can be modified to fit customer-specific requirements. The Flow Dimension setup we will use assumes that Ending Balances are loaded to Balance Sheet Accounts from the source system. In some less-common situations, monthly Balance Sheet activity or movements can be loaded. In this case, the Flow Members would be similar, but the Calculations required would be different.

Dimension Member Setup

The Flow Dimension set up will have four main components:

- Beginning Balance
- Activity
- FX
- Ending Balance

These groups will contain a mix of calculated and non-calculated Members and will exist as siblings within the hierarchy.

Common Rule Examples

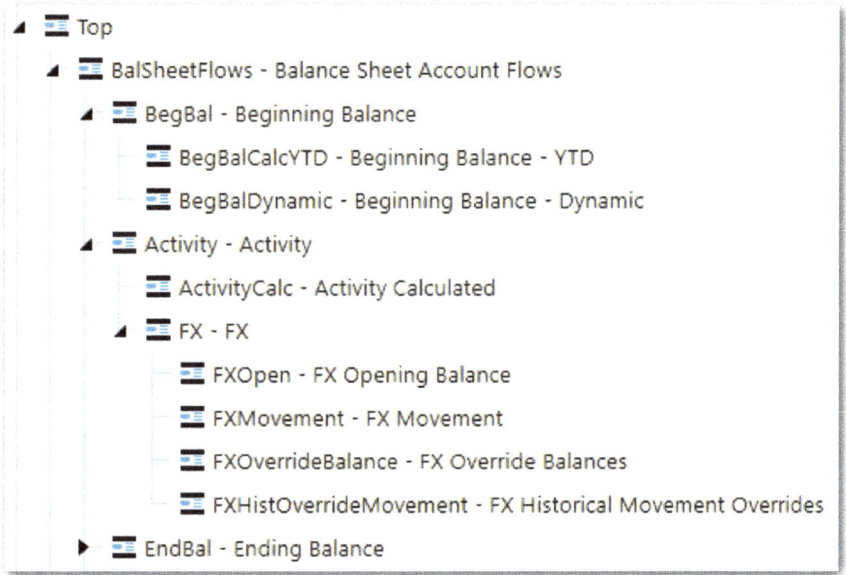

Figure 8.4

The Aggregation Weight property in Relationship Properties will be set to 0 for Beginning Balance and Activity, so that only the loaded Ending Balance aggregates to the Top Member.

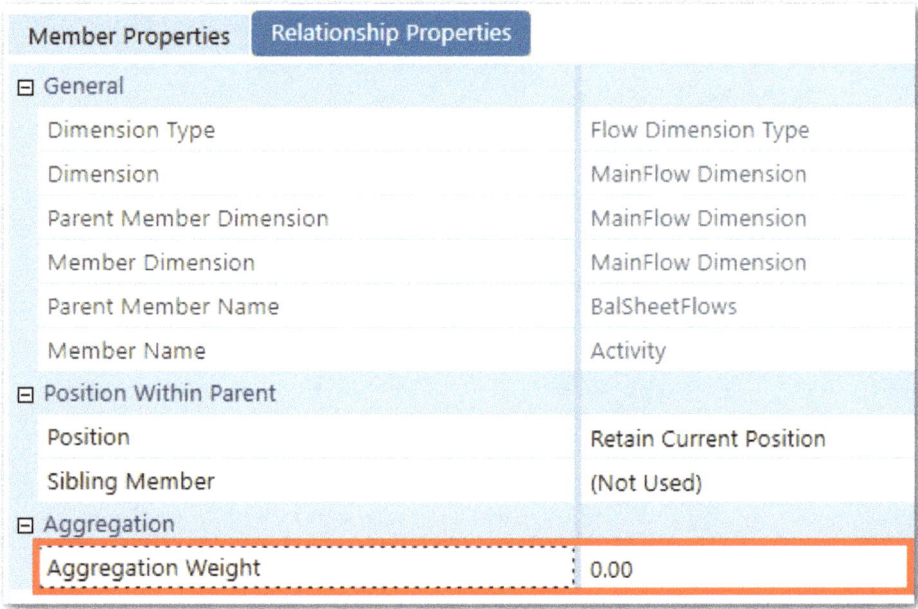

Figure 8.5

Chapter 8

Calculations

Beginning Balance

The Beginning Balance section is made up of two Members.

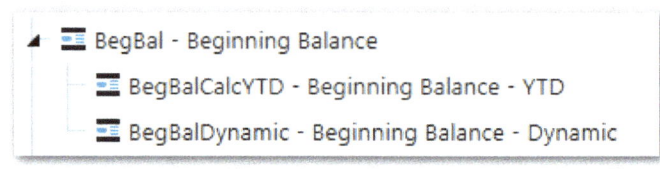

Member Name	Description of Use	Calculated?
BegBalYTD	Calculates the beginning Balance of the Account	Y
BegBalDynamic	Dynamically calculates the correct beginning balance based on the View member	Y (Dynamic)

Figure 8.6

BegBalCalcYTD

```
'Run only if base entity or parent entity and foreign currency
If (Not api.Entity.HasChildren()) Or (api.Entity.HasChildren() And api.Cons.IsForeignCurrencyForEntity()) Then
    'Get the last period in the prior year
    Dim lastPeriodPriYearId As Integer = api.Time.GetLastPeriodInPriorYear
    Dim lastPeriodPriYearName As String = api.Time.GetNameFromId(lastPeriodPriYearId)
    If api.Time.IsFirstPeriodInYear Then 'For the first period, copy the data from the Prior Year RE Account
        api.Data.Calculate("F#BegBalCalcYTD = " & _
        "RemoveZeros(T#" & lastPeriodPriYearName & ":F#EndBalLoad)","A#BalanceSheet.Base")
    Else 'For the rest of the year, copy the REBEgBal account from the prior period
        api.Data.Calculate("F#BegBalCalcYTD = " & _
        "RemoveZeros(T#POVPrior1:F#BegBalCalcYTD)","A#BalanceSheet.Base")
    End If
End If
```

The rule starts with an `If` statement to reduce Data Unit scope to only Base Entities or foreign currency Parent Entities. For this Calculation, we do not want to let the foreign currency Entities translate at the current exchange rates since the beginning balance is translated at the prior year's rate, so the Calculation is not restricted to run only at Local Currency. The Calculation will also run at all Base Entities as well as foreign currency Parent Entities.

After declaring some time-based variables, an `If` statement will check if the current period being processed is the first period in the year and, if so, pull the ending balance from the prior year. For all other periods, the prior period's balance gets pulled into the current period. We perform this check so that we reduce the number of times the prior year's data is referenced – due to it being more computationally expensive. Also, note the use of a filter in the ADC function to restrict the Calculation to Accounts that are only within the Balance Sheet.

BegBalDynamic

As the name suggests, the `BegBalCalcYTD` Flow Member is meant to show Year-To-Date beginning balances. If `BegBalCalcYTD` is referenced in Reports with View Members other than YTD, the YTD balance will be displayed regardless of the view frequency selected.

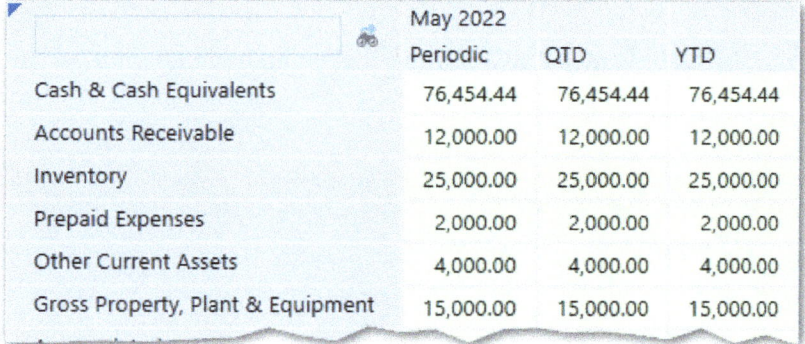

Figure 8.7

The above Report shows the `BegBalCalcYTD` Member for May (period 5) across MTD, QTD, and YTD frequencies. Assuming the balance has changed over the year (it has in this case), each of these values should be different. To solve this, a dynamically-calculated Member is created, which displays the correct balance – based on the View Member in the POV.

```
'Get the view member from the Cube View POV
Dim currView As ViewMember = ViewMember.GetItem(api.Pov.View.MemberPk.MemberId)
'Prior QTR member ID
Dim priorQtr As Integer = api.Time.GetLastPeriodInPriorQuarter(api.Pov.Time.MemberId)
'Prior QTR name
Dim priorQtrName As String = api.Time.GetNameFromId(priorQtr)
'Get prior year period ID
Dim priorYearId As Integer = TimeDimHelper.GetPriorYearPeriodId(api.Pov.Time.MemberId)
'Get the last period in the year - this will work for scenarios with any frequency
Dim lastPeriodInYear As String = TimeDimHelper.GetNameFromId(api.Time.GetLastPeriodInYear(priorYearId))

'Return the correct Beginning Balance based on the View
If currView.Name = "YTD" Then
    Return api.Data.GetDataCell("F#EndBal:T#" & lastPeriodInYear & "")
Else If currView.Name = "Periodic" Then
    Return api.Data.GetDataCell("F#EndBal:T#PovPrior1")
Else If currView.Name = "QTD" Then
    Return api.Data.GetDataCell("F#EndBal:T#" & priorQtrName & "")
Else
    Return Nothing
End If
```

The Formula Type and Account Type properties are set to DynamicCalc

Referencing the dynamically calculated Member now correctly displays the beginning balance, based on the View Member in the column.

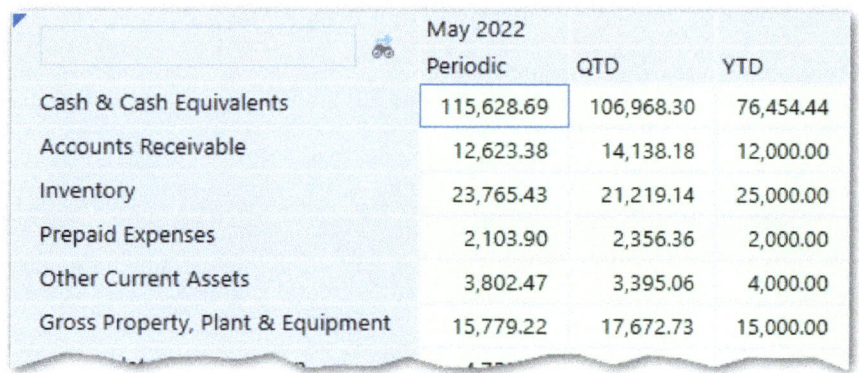

Figure 8.8

Chapter 8

Activity

The `ActivityCalc` Member is meant to show the change in the Account from the beginning balance.

Figure 8.9

ActivityCalc

The `ActivityCalc` Member is meant to show the YTD change in the Account from the beginning balance.

```
'If base Entity and local currency
If (Not api.Entity.HasChildren()) AndAlso api.Cons.IsLocalCurrencyForEntity() Then
    api.Data.Calculate("F#ActivityCalc = " & _
    "RemoveZeros(F#EndBal - F#BegBal)","A#BalanceSheet.Base.Remove(CTA)")
End If
```

An `api.Data.Calculate` function is used to subtract the `BegBal` from the `EndBal` for Balance Sheet Accounts only (excluding the CTA Account, which is covered later). Ensure that the Formula Pass used is later than the Formula Pass on `EndBal` or `BegBal` which are referenced in the formula.

> **Note:** The `ActivityCalc` Member will display correctly across all View Members unlike the `BegBalCalcYTD` Member. This is due to `ActivityCalc` having the Switch Type property set to True which means data in this Member will be switched to behave like a Revenue/Expense Account.
>
> Figure 8.10

FX

The FX section of the Flow Dimension is meant to capture the effects of foreign exchange rates on Account balances over time. Since the Ending Balance of an Account is comprised of the sum of Beginning Balance and Activity, different exchange rates may apply to each. Because of this, the FX effect is broken out into multiple Members.

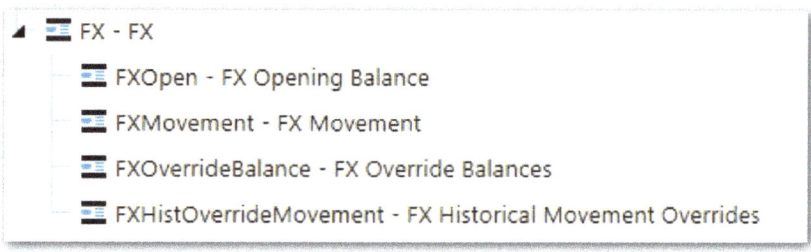

Figure 8.11

FX exposure is important for a company to understand to analyze pure Account movements. Changes in balances on the surface may appear as a positive or negative change in cash, but analyzing the FX proves what the true effect on cash inflows or outflows was. Why is this important? Take Account Receivable, for example. If the balance in Accounts Receivable went down from period to period, it may appear as though the company is collecting cash. If you are able to break down the A/R Account into its pure activity versus FX exposure, you can analyze just how much, if any, the company collected.

With the OneStream Flow Dimension, the Calculation and reporting of FX and CTA are simplified. FX Members are created and attached to each Balance Sheet Account, with rules (described later) to calculate the components of FX. This allows a User to be able to report and analyze every Account by its FX exposure.

Formulas

All the formulas for these Members will have a preceding `If` statement to only calculate at foreign currency Entities.

```
If api.Cons.IsForeignCurrencyForEntity() Then    'If foreign currency
```

FXOpen

The `FXOpen` Member calculates the effect of exchange rate changes on the opening balance. Put another way, the Calculation will determine the difference between the beginning balance which was translated at last year's rate and the beginning balance translated at the current period's rates.

```
'ID of the current time being processed
Dim timeId As Integer = api.Pov.Time.MemberPk.MemberId
'FX Rate Type for Assets/Liabilities
Dim rateTypeClosing As FxRateType = api.FxRates.GetFxRateTypeForAssetLiability()
'Current Closing Rate
Dim closingRate As Decimal =  api.FxRates.GetCalculatedFxRate(rateTypeClosing,timeId)

If api.Cons.IsForeignCurrencyForEntity() Then    'If foreign currency
    api.Data.Calculate("F#FXOpen:V#YTD = RemoveZeros((F#BegBal:C#Local:V#YTD * " & _
    "" & api.Data.DecimalToText(closingRate) & ") - " & _
    "F#BegBal:V#YTD)","A#BalanceSheet.Base.Remove(CTA)")
End If
```

The above Calculation retrieves the current Closing Rate using the `api.FxRates.GetCalculatedFxRates` function. The rate is then multiplied by the Local Currency balance and subtracted from the `BegBal` Flow Member. Remember that the

Chapter 8

`BegBalCalcYTD` Flow Member pulls the *already translated* balance from the prior year since the Calculation scope was not limited to Local currency.

Even though the full balance is translated at the current rate, the `FXOpen` Member will show the effect of rate changes on the beginning balance.

FXMovement

The `FXMovement` Member calculates the FX effect on the Account activity. The formula below captures three components of the FX Movement:

- FX on the current movement: calculates the FX on the current movement (the difference between the current closing rates and current average rates).

- FX on the prior movement: calculates the FX on the prior movement (the difference between the current closing rates and prior average rates).

- FX on the override movement: calculates the FX on movements which have been overridden (difference between average rate and the rate the movement was overridden with).

An `If` Statement makes a distinction between the first period of the year and all others, since periods other than the first will have no prior movements to consider.

```
Dim timeId As Integer = api.Pov.Time.MemberPk.MemberId
Dim rateTypeClosing As FxRateType = api.FxRates.GetFxRateTypeForAssetLiability()
Dim rateTypeAverage As FxRateType = api.FxRates.GetFxRateTypeForRevenueExp()
Dim closingRate As Decimal = api.FxRates.GetCalculatedFxRate(rateTypeClosing,timeId)
Dim averageRate As Decimal = api.FxRates.GetCalculatedFxRate(rateTypeAverage,timeId)

If api.Cons.IsForeignCurrencyForEntity() Then     'If foreign currency
    If api.Time.IsFirstPeriodInYear Then
        api.Data.Calculate("F#FXMovement:V#YTD = " & _
        "RemoveZeros((F#ActivityCalc:C#Local:V#Periodic * " & _
        "(" & api.Data.DecimalToText(closingRate) & " - " & api.Data.DecimalToText(averageRate) & ")) + " & _
        "((F#ActivityCalc:C#Local:V#Periodic * " & api.Data.DecimalToText(averageRate) & ") - " & _
        "F#ActivityCalc:V#Periodic))","A#BalanceSheet.Base.Remove(CTA)")
    Else
        api.Data.Calculate("F#FXMovement:V#YTD = " & _
        "RemoveZeros((F#ActivityCalc:C#Local:V#Periodic * " & _
        "(" & api.Data.DecimalToText(closingRate) & " - " & api.Data.DecimalToText(averageRate) & ")) + " & _
        "((F#ActivityCalc:C#Local:V#YTD:T#PovPrior1 * " & api.Data.DecimalToText(closingRate) & ") - " & _
        "F#ActivityCalc:V#YTD:T#PovPrior1) + " & _
        "((F#ActivityCalc:C#Local:V#Periodic * " & api.Data.DecimalToText(averageRate) & ") - " & _
        "F#ActivityCalc:V#Periodic))","A#BalanceSheet.Base.Remove(CTA)")
    End If
End If
```

FXOverrideBalance and FXHistoricalOverrideMovement

If any Members are translated at rates other than the current rate – for example, historical transactional rate or the Retained Earnings Beginning Balance – the FX effect will be captured in these Members.

CTA – Cumulative Translation Adjustment

CTA, or Cumulative Translation Adjustment, is the Calculation of the cumulative Balance Sheet exposure as a result of the difference in FX rates for each reporting period and is reported in OCI (other comprehensive income). At each reporting period date, Balance Sheet Accounts are either translated at the closing rate, historical exchange rate, or weighted average rate, which results in changes attributable only to the differences in these rates. For example, a functional currency balance could not change from period to period, but the reporting currency balance could, due to the exchange rate used.

CTA reported on the Balance Sheet is the summation of the FX (explained in detail in the prior section) for each individual Balance Sheet Account.

Common Rule Examples

Formula

```
If api.Cons.IsForeignCurrencyForEntity() Then
    api.Data.Calculate("V#YTD:A#CTA:I#None:U1#None:U2#None = " & _
    "RemoveZeros(V#YTD:A#BalanceSheet:I#Top:U1#Top:U2#Top)",,"F#Activity.Base")

    api.Data.Calculate("V#YTD:A#CTA:F#EndBalLoad:I#None:U1#None:U2#None = " & _
    "RemoveZeros(A#CTA:F#BegBal:I#Top:U1#Top:U2#Top + " & _
    "V#YTD:A#CTA:F#Activity:I#Top:U1#Top:U2#Top)")
End If
```

Calculation

The Calculation of CTA uses two ADC functions. The first calculates the CTA for each Base Flow Member of `Activity` (via the filter) by summing the Balance Sheet.

The second ADC function calculates the CTA for the `EndBalLoad` Flow Member by adding the CTA from the `BegBal` and `Activity` Flow Members.

CTA Proof

As part of a company's audit, they are often asked to provide proof of the Calculation of the Translation adjustment in CTA. This is no longer a disconnected, separate process to calculate a proof and make sure it reconciles to the CTA balance. The FX by Account can be totaled and moved to the CTA Account so that the Calculation of CTA is the proof. If the Calculation of FX by Account is not correct, the Balance Sheet won't balance in the translated currency.

The below CTA Proof Report can be set up to show the balance sheet balancing across all Members of the Flow Dimension, as shown in the last row. If any out-of-balance exists, it can be traced to the specific Flow component(s) and Account(s), as shown in the last column.

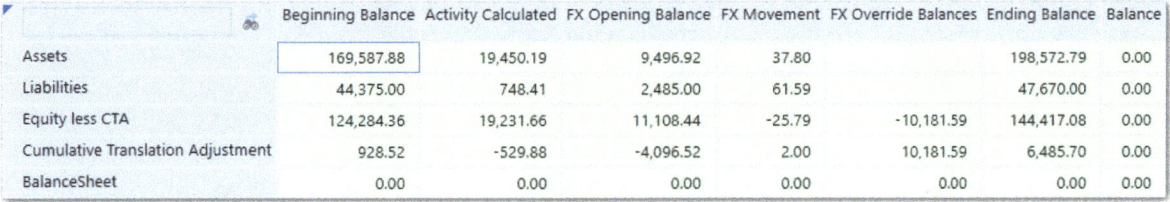

	Beginning Balance	Activity Calculated	FX Opening Balance	FX Movement	FX Override Balances	Ending Balance	Balance
Assets	169,587.88	19,450.19	9,496.92	37.80		198,572.79	0.00
Liabilities	44,375.00	748.41	2,485.00	61.59		47,670.00	0.00
Equity less CTA	124,284.36	19,231.66	11,108.44	-25.79	-10,181.59	144,417.08	0.00
Cumulative Translation Adjustment	928.52	-529.88	-4,096.52	2.00	10,181.59	6,485.70	0.00
BalanceSheet	0.00	0.00	0.00	0.00	0.00	0.00	0.00

Figure 8.12

> **Note:** Much of the knowledge in the Balance Sheet and Flow Calculations section, as well as the next section, was borrowed heavily from Chapter 4 of the OneStream Foundation Handbook, written by Eric Osmanski. Please refer to that book and chapter for additional detail.

Chapter 8

Consolidation Calculations

Consolidation Calculations are Calculations that are meant to follow GAAP principles for how to record the necessary accounting entries related to internal investments. The Entities that have been invested in by the reporting corporation are sometimes owned less than 100% and thus require entries to reflect the partial ownership. This section will explain Calculations for two common ownership situations. Note that these Calculations are specific to GAAP accounting rules and different accounting rules will exist in other countries. These Calculations also require a deep knowledge of accounting principles in addition to technical Calculation knowledge.

Equity Pickup (EPU)

Background and Business Case

The proper Consolidation of Entities is based on accounting guidelines. Under U.S. GAAP, there are two Consolidation models – the **Variable Interest Entity Model** (VIE) and the **Voting Interest Entity Model** (VOE).

The VIE model is applied first and was designed to accommodate situations in which control is demonstrated in ways other than through voting interests. Under the VIE model, an Entity is consolidated when the Parent Entity has significant power over the activities of the VIE and has significant economic exposure to the gains or losses of the VIE. Consolidation under the VIE model also has different measurement, presentation, and disclosure requirements that need to be considered. If the conditions to consolidate under the VIE model do not apply, or if it is an exception to the VIE model, then the voting interest model would then be applied.

Under the voting interest model, full Consolidation is used when a Parent Entity has a controlling financial interest, and the percentage ownership of the subsidiary is greater than or equal to 50%. Under this Method, the financial statements of the subsidiary are consolidated into the Parent. Whether a Parent Entity is required to present consolidated financial statements under IFRS is based on its control of the investee. Control is defined as when a Parent Entity has power over the investee, has rights to returns due to its involvement, and can influence its returns from the investee based on its power. When all three control elements are present, the financial statements of the subsidiary are consolidated into the Parent.

The Parent company records the amount owned as an investment in the subsidiary, and the subsidiary records the same amount in equity. All Intracompany transactions – including the investment and equity – are eliminated during Consolidation so that the values are not overstated. If ownership is less than 100%, the Parent company will record in equity, and on the Income Statement, the noncontrolling interest in the subsidiary – which is equal to the subsidiary's equity at the percentage not owned by the Parent.

Under the voting interest model, the **Equity Method** is typically used when the percentage ownership of the investee is between 20 and 50%, and the investor has significant influence. The balances of the investee/subsidiary are *not* consolidated under the Equity Method; instead, the investor records an investment on the balance sheet equal to its ownership share of the investee's equity balance. For each period, the investor increases (or decreases) its investment by its ownership share of the investee's net income (loss), known as equity pickup. The ownership share of net income (loss) is also recorded on the investor's Income Statement separately.

Equity Pickup (EPU) is the process of revaluing the investments of an investor to reflect the current value of its proportionate share of the investee's equity balance. OneStream allows for the automation of these entries – including **layered ownership models** – by entering ownership percentages, defining the Calculation sequence, and developing a rule to generate the entries. These rules will record the impact of the increase (assuming net income rises for the period on the part of the investee) or decrease (under circumstances where the investee incurs a net loss) in the investor's ownership share of the investee.

There are multiple methods at your disposal to record the equity pickup. The following discussion will cover the most common method.

Example

For our example, the Stooges have decided to take their large pile of cash accrued from killing insects and make some investments in other companies. They set up an Entity named Cheatum Investments and make their first investment in Gypsum Good Antiques, taking a 30% stake. Larry, who has the most accounting skills of the three, now has the responsibility of devising a Calculation to correctly record the investment.

Cube Setup

First, Larry makes a few changes within the Cube settings so that the Consolidation Rules work correctly.

The Calculation settings are modified so that Calculate Share Cons Member If No Data and Calculate Elimination Cons If No Data are set to True. This forces those Members to calculate which is necessary to write to the elimination Member of the Consolidation Member.

A Business Rule is also created (explained later) named ConsolRules and is assigned to the Cube so that it runs during the DUCS.

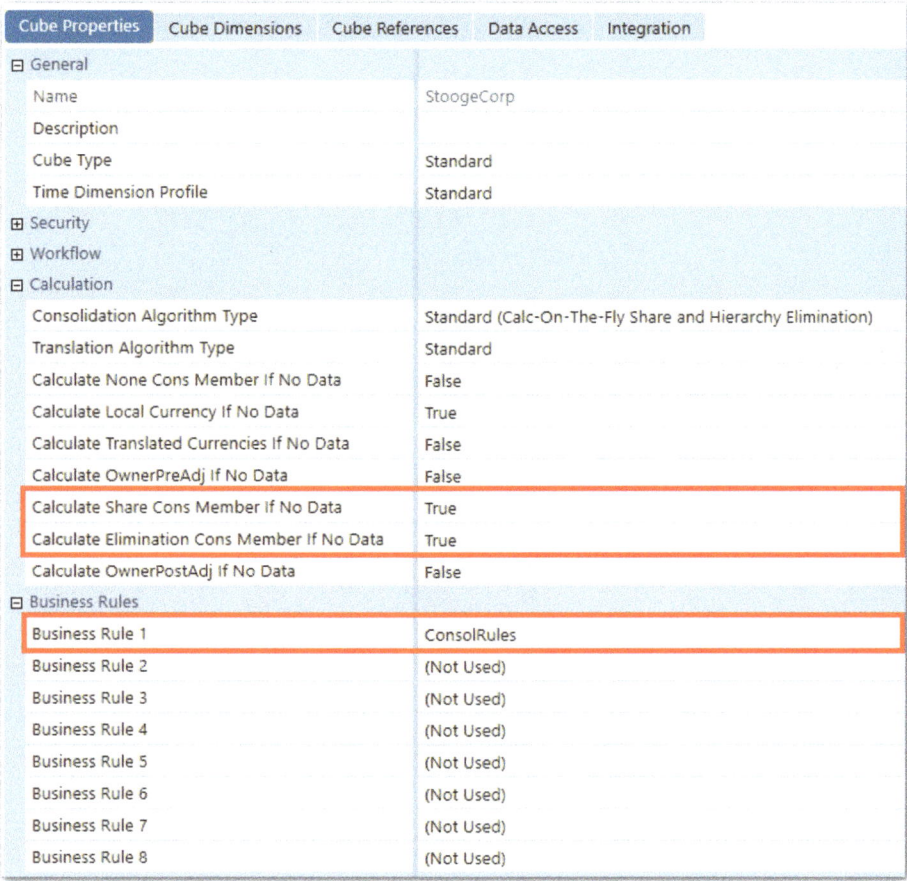

Figure 8.13

Metadata Setup

Entities

Larry creates the new Entities, `Cheatum Investments` and `Gypsum Good Antiques`, within a SubGroup:

Chapter 8

Figure 8.14

`GGAInc` is set up as a sibling of its owner, `CheatumInvestments`. Larry must also configure various properties within the Entities so that the Calculation works correctly.

The 30% ownership of Gypsum (the subsidiary/investee), by Cheatum (the investor), needs to be entered in the Relationship Properties tab of the Entity Dimension.

The attributes within the Relationship Properties tab reflect this percentage ownership. The tab can be found within the Entity Dimensions settings, as follows:

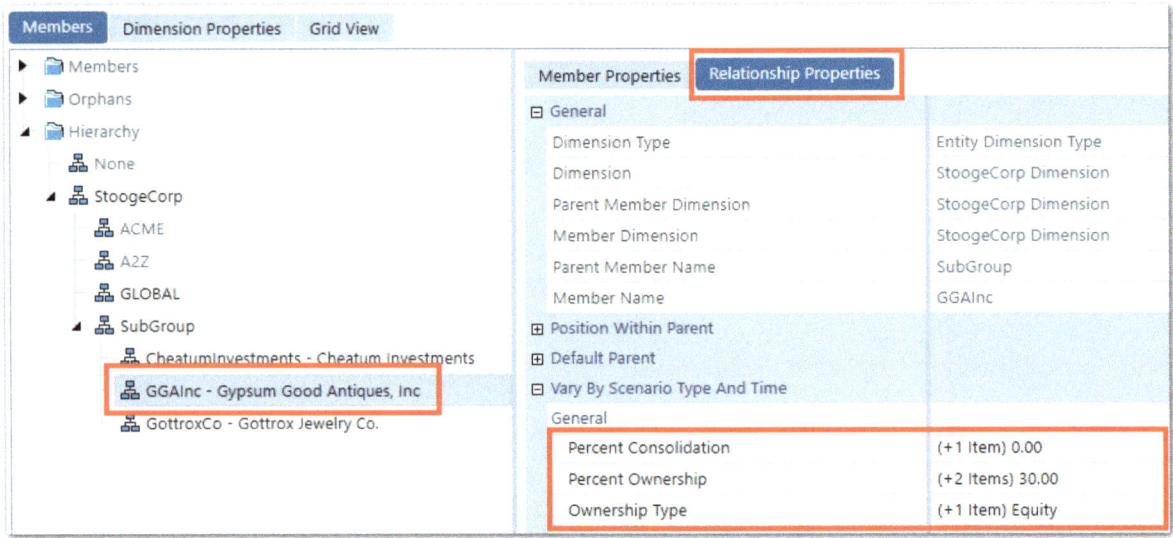

Figure 8.15

The Percent Ownership property is then set within the Varying Member Property panel, as illustrated below:

Common Rule Examples

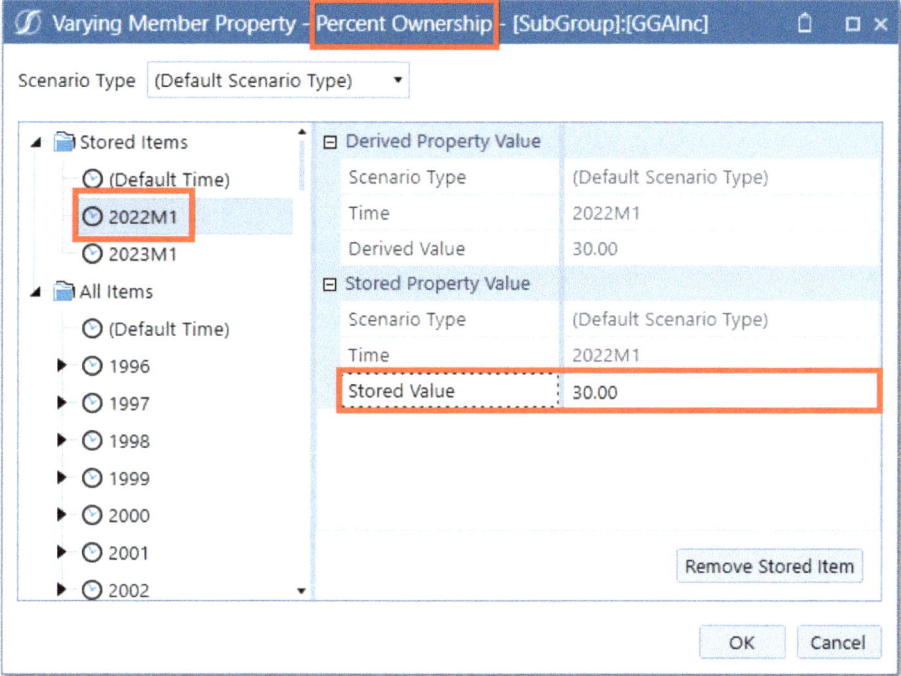

Figure 8.16

Note that the percentages can vary by Scenario Type and Time period. In the example above, the percentage ownership of 30 will be in effect for all periods, starting with 2022M1, until a different percentage is entered in a future period. In this example, the percentage is increased to 40, starting in 2023M1:

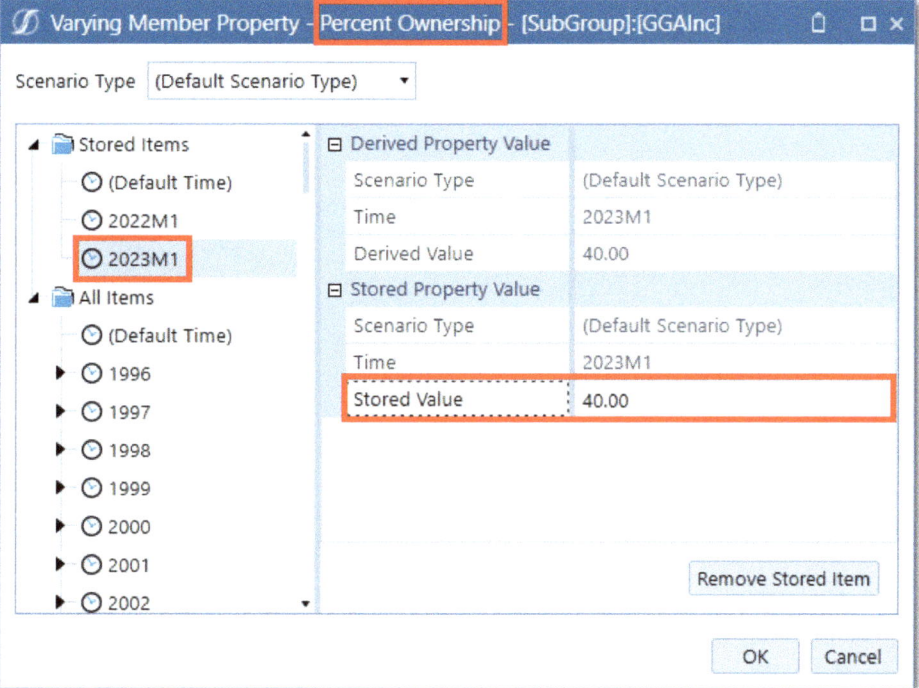

Figure 8.17

In addition to the Percent Ownership of the subsidiary/investee, the Percent Consolidation property also needs to be entered in the relationship properties.

Chapter 8

Like Percent Ownership, the Percent Consolidation can also vary by Scenario Type and Time period. The Percent Consolidation for Entities that are non-consolidating but for which an equity pickup is being recorded – as is the case for GGAInc (Gypsum Good Antiques) – will be zero. Given that the default Percent Consolidation within OneStream is 100, the value of zero (0) needs to be entered for GGAInc, as shown below:

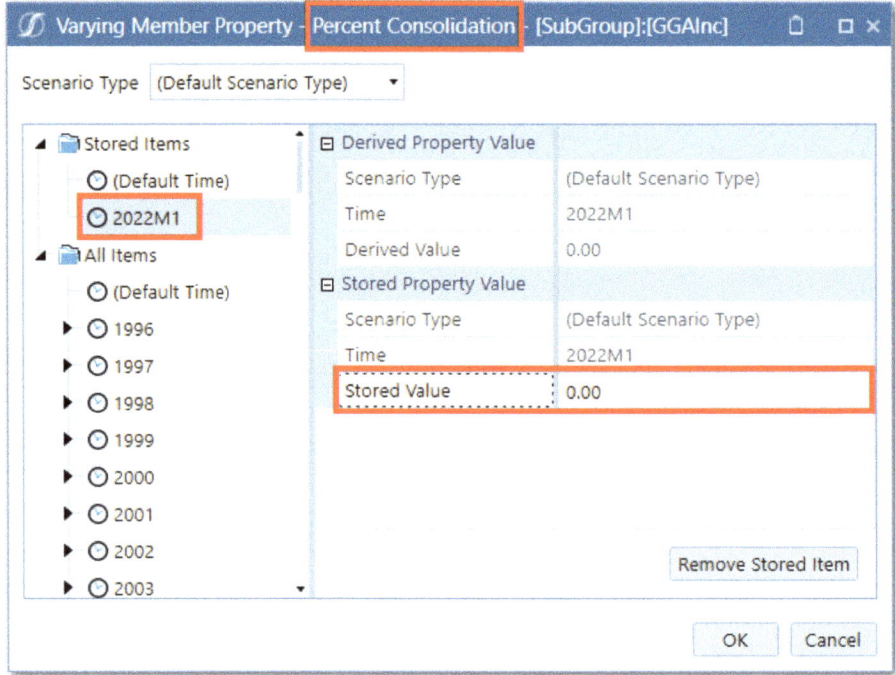

Figure 8.18

Larry also configures the Ownership Type property, which will be utilized by the Calculation which creates the EPU entry. The recommended value for this Type of ownership (e.g., GGAInc to its Parent SubGroup) is Equity, as seen below:

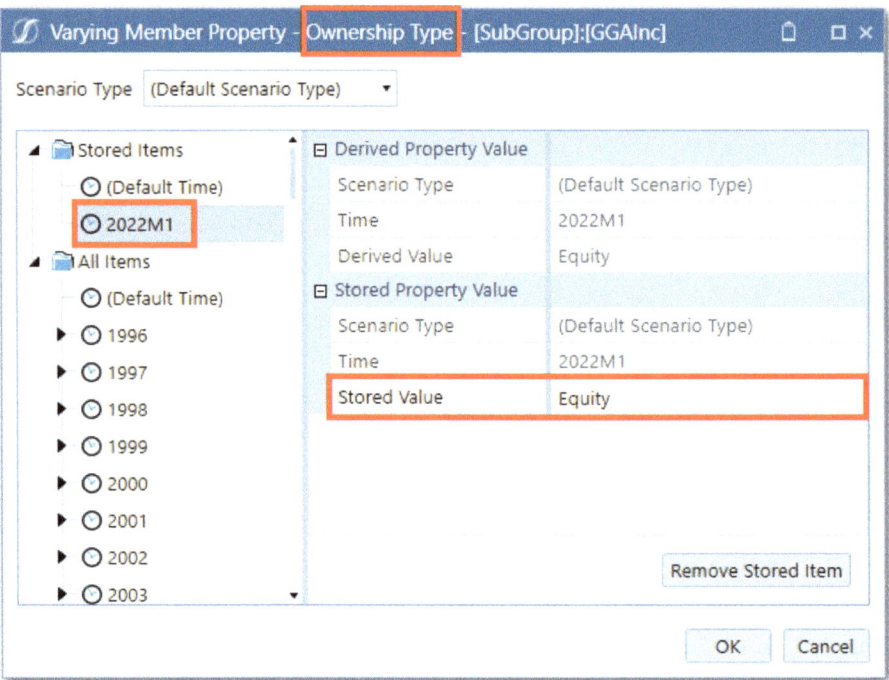

Figure 8.19

Common Rule Examples

Further, Larry also changes the Ownership Type of `CheatumInvestments` to Holding which identifies it as the investor.

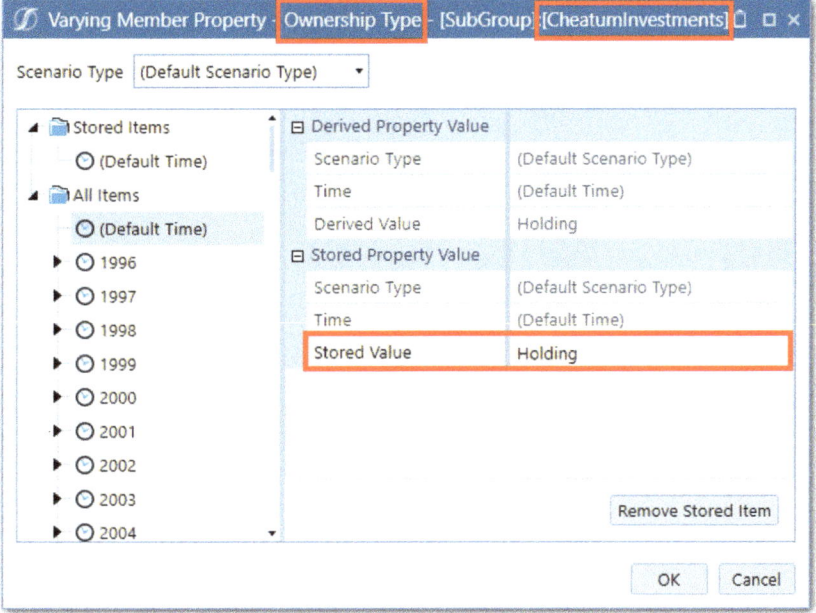

Figure 8.20

Note: The Ownership Type property is strictly a label that can be referenced in Business Rules and does not change the Consolidation behavior by itself.

Larry also sets the Sibling Consolidation Pass setting for `CheatumInvestments` to a value greater than the minimum value for each of the sibling Entities for which the holding company is picking up earnings via the EPU Calculation. This is due to the multi-threading concept introduced in Chapter 2 which means that sibling Entities process at the same time.

As shown in the diagram below, `CheatumInvestments` has been assigned Pass 4.

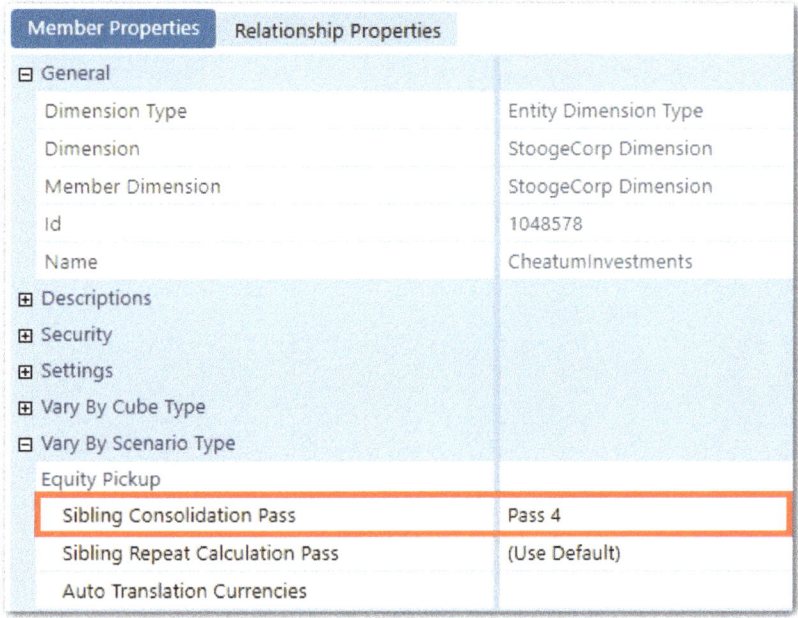

Figure 8.21

Chapter 8

This indicates that Cheatum will execute after all its sibling Entities, whose Sibling Consolidation Pass setting is Pass 1 (or lower than Pass 4), ensuring that the data required for the EPU entry, including a potential currency Translation, processes in the correct order.

> **Note:** The default setting for the Sibling Consolidation Pass is Pass 1.

Accounts

The Investment in Subsidiary Account(s) needs to be identified with a text field attribute that provides an additional filter used to determine how the entry should be recorded. An example of this setup is illustrated below. Account `InvestmentInSubs` (IC Investments in Subsidiary) has been populated with a Text 1 attribute of Investment.

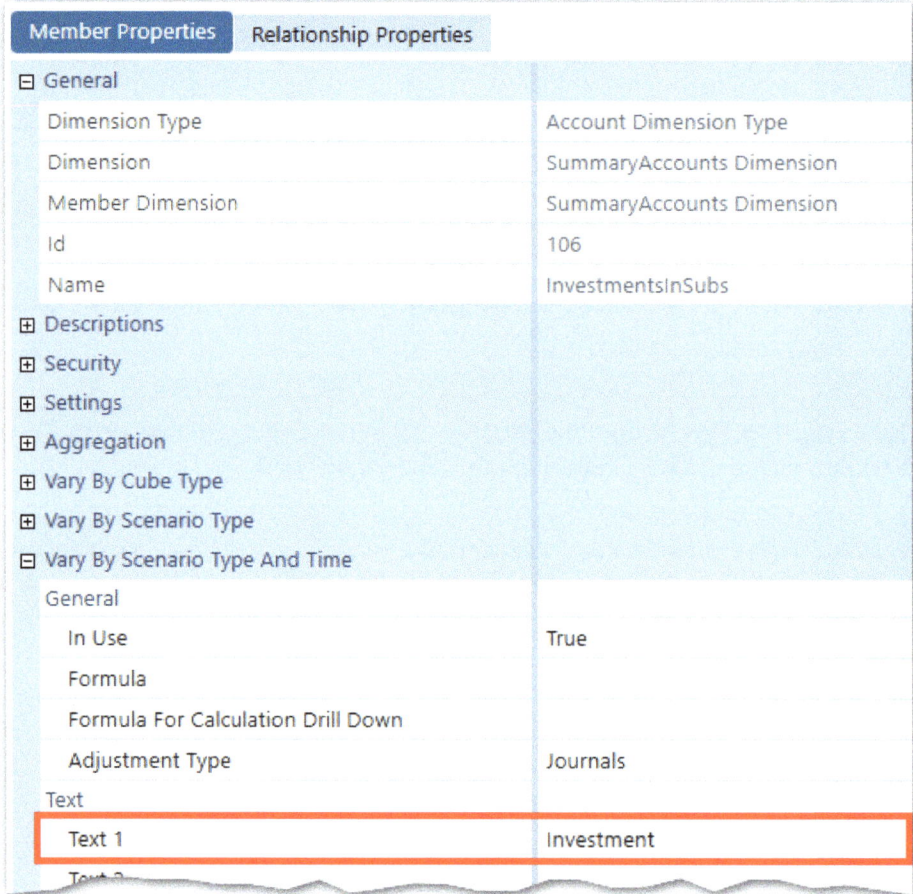

Figure 8.22

That value will then initiate the recording of the EPU entry within the Consolidation Business Rules. As discussed earlier, it is imperative that this Account is enabled for IC detail:

Common Rule Examples

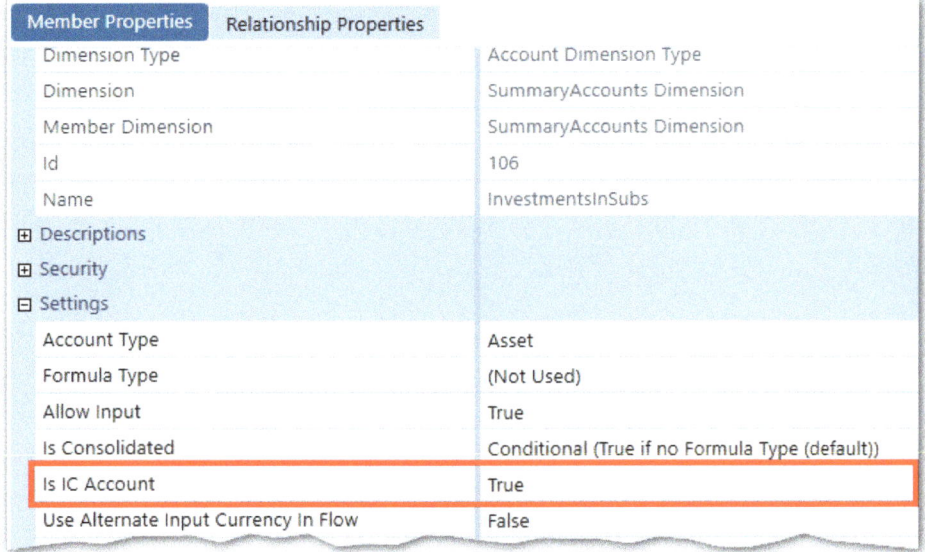

Figure 8.23

This enables the investee to be identified within the data being processed and the proper Net Income amount can be obtained from that legal Entity.

Data Type Dimension

Lastly, Larry decides he wants to track the source of the various Consolidation Rules (and to provide a detailed audit trail Report to his auditors) so he creates a DataType Dimension in UD5. The Members within this Dimension will relate to the entries made by the Consolidation Calculations.

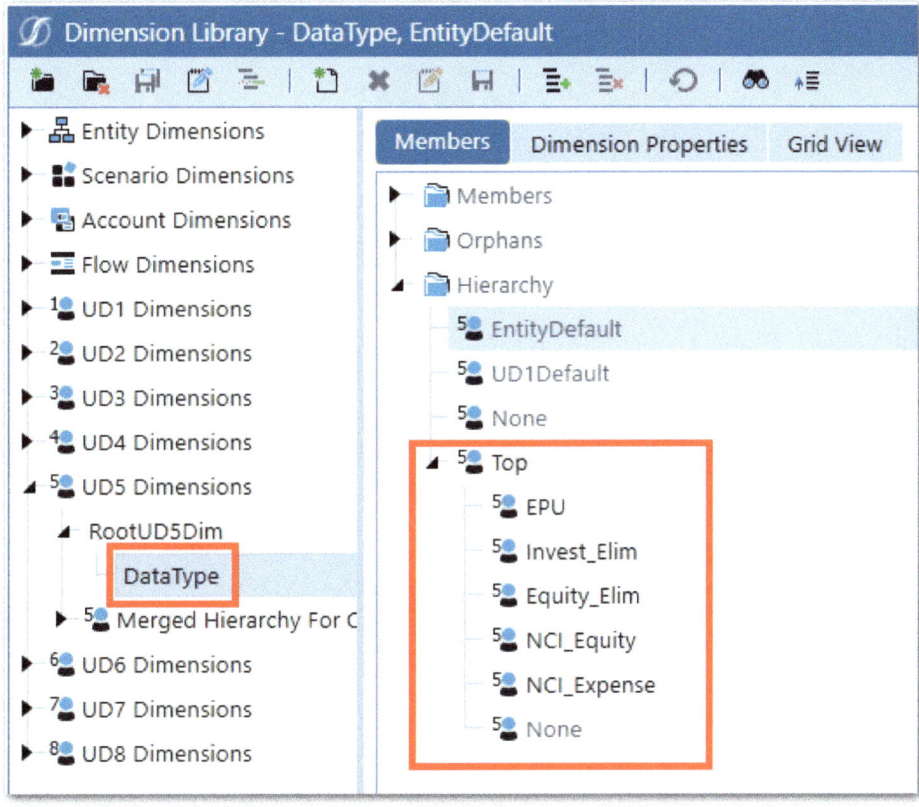

Figure 8.24

Chapter 8

Data Setup

The data that drives a Calculation is in both the Cheatum Investments holding company (the Entity that has recorded the investment in its subsidiary) and Gypsum Good Antiques (the subsidiary).

Larry first records the investment in the `InvestmentInSubs` Account for Cheatum, specifying Gypsum as the Intercompany partner.

Gypsum will then submit their financials each month and their results will appear in the Net Income Account.

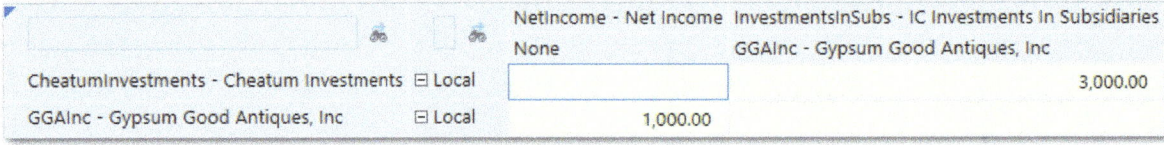

Figure 8.25

Rule Abstract

This rule is recording the entry to adjust the **Investment in Subsidiary** and **Equity in Earnings from Subsidiary Investments** (Profit and Loss Account) to reflect Cheatum's proportionate share of Gypsum's earnings for each period.

The Code Breakdown - Section 1

```
22  #Region "Global_Variables"
23      Const topBalShtAcctName As String = "BalanceSheet"          'Top of Balance Sheet hierarchy Account Name
24      Const invEqElimClearAcctName As String = "InvestmentInSubsPlug"  ' Clearing/Plug Account Name for Investment and Subsid Equity Elims
25      Const nciEquityCpStkName As String = "NCIEquityCommonStock" ' NCI Equity-Cap Stock Account Name
26      Const nciEquityCurYrIncName As String = "NCIEquityCYRetEarn" ' NCI Equity-Curr Yr Earnings Account Name
27      Const netIncAcctName As String = "NetIncome"                ' Net Income Account Name
28      Const eqtyInEarnAcctName As String = "InvSubEarnings"       ' Equity In Earnings (Income from Subs) Account Name
29      Const nciExpAcctName As String = "NonControllingInterest"   ' NCI Expense Account Name
30      Const flowEndBalName As String = "EndBalLoad"               ' Flow Dim Ending Balance Member Name
31      Const flowAddsName As String = "RF_Investments_Additions"   ' Flow Dim Additions/Movements Member Name
32      Const ud5EpuName As String = "EPU"                          ' UD5 (DataType Dim) Equity Pickup Member Name
33      Const ud5InvestElimName As String = "Invest_Elim"           ' UD5 (DataType Dim) Invest in Subs Elim Member Name
34      Const ud5EqtyElimName As String = "Equity_Elim"             ' UD5 (DataType Dim) Equity Elim Member Name
35      Const ud5NciEqtyReclName As String = "NCI_Equity"           ' UD5 (DataType Dim) NCI Equity Reclass Member Name
36      Const ud5NciExpName As String = "NCI_Expense"               ' UD5 (DataType Dim) NCI Expense Member Name
37      Const invSubsAcctText1 As String = "INVESTMENT"             ' Text1 value for Investment in Subsidiary Acctts
38      Const subsidEquityAcctText1 As String = "EQUITY"            ' Text1 value for Subsidiary Equity Accts
39  #End Region 'Global_Variables
40
41  #Region "Main"
42      Public Function Main(ByVal si As SessionInfo, ByVal globals As BRGlobals, ByVal api As FinanceRulesApi, ByVal args As FinanceRulesArgs) As Object
43          Try
44              Select Case api.FunctionType
45                  Case Is = FinanceFunctionType.Calculate
46                      If api.Pov.Cons.Name = "Elimination" Then
47                          Dim invEqElimClearingAcctId As Integer = api.Members.GetMemberId(DimTypeId.Account, invEqElimClearAcctName)
48                          If api.Entity.OwnershipType().ToString.Equals("Holding") Then
49                              Call Book_EPU_InvElim(si, globals, api, invEqElimClearingAcctId)
```

Abstract

The code in this section initializes variables and then determines whether we are processing the appropriate intersection of data to book the EPU entry. A description of the processing taking place within the major blocks is as follows:

Lines 23-38

```
23      Const topBalShtAcctName As String = "BalanceSheet"          'Top of Balance Sheet hierarchy Account Name
24      Const invEqElimClearAcctName As String = "InvestmentInSubsPlug"  ' Clearing/Plug Account Name for Investment and Subsid Equity Elims
25      Const nciEquityCpStkName As String = "NCIEquityCommonStock" ' NCI Equity-Cap Stock Account Name
26      Const nciEquityCurYrIncName As String = "NCIEquityCYRetEarn" ' NCI Equity-Curr Yr Earnings Account Name
27      Const netIncAcctName As String = "NetIncome"                ' Net Income Account Name
28      Const eqtyInEarnAcctName As String = "InvSubEarnings"       ' Equity In Earnings (Income from Subs) Account Name
29      Const nciExpAcctName As String = "NonControllingInterest"   ' NCI Expense Account Name
30      Const flowEndBalName As String = "EndBalLoad"               ' Flow Dim Ending Balance Member Name
31      Const flowAddsName As String = "RF_Investments_Additions"   ' Flow Dim Additions/Movements Member Name
32      Const ud5EpuName As String = "EPU"                          ' UD5 (DataType Dim) Equity Pickup Member Name
33      Const ud5InvestElimName As String = "Invest_Elim"           ' UD5 (DataType Dim) Invest in Subs Elim Member Name
34      Const ud5EqtyElimName As String = "Equity_Elim"             ' UD5 (DataType Dim) Equity Elim Member Name
35      Const ud5NciEqtyReclName As String = "NCI_Equity"           ' UD5 (DataType Dim) NCI Equity Reclass Member Name
36      Const ud5NciExpName As String = "NCI_Expense"               ' UD5 (DataType Dim) NCI Expense Member Name
37      Const invSubsAcctText1 As String = "INVESTMENT"             ' Text1 value for Investment in Subsidiary Acctts
38      Const subsidEquityAcctText1 As String = "EQUITY"            ' Text1 value for Subsidiary Equity Accts
```

Initialize variables, which identify various Member Names that are referenced in other subroutines within the Business Rule.

Lines 45-49

```
45              Case Is = FinanceFunctionType.Calculate
46                  If api.Pov.Cons.Name = "Elimination" Then
47                      Dim invEqElimClearingAcctId As Integer = api.Members.GetMemberId(DimTypeId.Account, invEqElimClearAcctName)
48                      If api.Entity.OwnershipType().ToString.Equals("Holding") Then
49                          Call Book_EPU_InvElim(si, globals, api, invEqElimClearingAcctId)
```

Determine whether we are processing the Elimination Member of the Consolidation Dimension and, if so, determine if the Ownership Type attribute of the current (POV) Entity Relationship has been set to `Holding` for the current period being processed. If those conditions have been met, the subroutine `Book_EPU_InvElim` is called, where the actual EPU entry will be created.

Section 2

```
68              Dim destinationInfo As ExpressionDestinationInfo = api.Data.GetExpressionDestinationInfo("V#Periodic")
69              Dim resultDataBuffer As DataBuffer = New DataBuffer()
70              Dim parentCurrencyName As String = api.Entity.GetLocalCurrency(api.Pov.Parent.MemberId).Name
71              Dim sourceScript As String = "V#YTD:C#" & parentCurrencyName & ":F#EndBalLoad:O#Top:U1#Top:U2#Top:U3#None:U4#None:U5#Top:U6#None:U7#None:U8#None" & _
72                  " + C#OwnerPreAdj:F#Top:O#Top:U1#Top:U2#Top:U3#None:U4#None:U5#Top:U6#None:U7#None:U8#None"
73              Dim filterMembersString As String = "[A#" & topBalShtAcctName & ".Base.Where(Text1 = '" & invSubsAcctText1 & "')]"
74              Dim sourceDataBuffer As DataBuffer = api.Data.GetDataBufferUsingFormula("FilterMembers(" & sourceScript & ", " & _
75                  filterMembersString & ")", DataApiScriptMethodType.Calculate, False, False)
76              If sourceDataBuffer.DataBufferCells.Count > 0 Then
77                  For Each bCell As DataBufferCell In sourceDataBuffer.DataBufferCells.Values
78                      If (Not bCell.CellStatus.IsNoData) And bCell.CellAmount <> 0 Then
79                          Dim subsidEntName As String = bCell.DataBufferCellPk.GetICName(api)
80                          If subsidEntName <> "None" Then
81                              Dim subsidEntId As Integer = api.Members.GetMemberId(DimTypeId.Entity, subsidEntName)
82                              Dim subsidConsMethod As String = api.Entity.OwnershipType(subsidEntId, api.Pov.Parent.MemberId).ToString
83                              Dim subsidPctCon As Decimal = api.Entity.PercentConsolidation(subsidEntId, api.Pov.Parent.MemberId) * .01
84                              Dim subsidPctOwn As Decimal = api.Entity.PercentOwnership(subsidEntId, api.Pov.Parent.MemberId) * .01
85                              'api.LogMessage(api.Pov.Entity.Name & " - " & subsidPctOwn.XFToString)
86                              If subsidConsMethod = "Equity" AndAlso subsidPctCon = 0 AndAlso subsidPctOwn > 0 Then
87                                  Call Post_EPU_Entry(si, globals, api, resultDataBuffer, bCell, subsidEntName, subsidPctOwn)
88                              ElseIf (subsidConsMethod = "NonControllingInterest" OrElse subsidConsMethod = "FullConsolidation") AndAlso _
89                                  (subsidPctOwn > 0 AndAlso subsidPctCon > 0) Then
90                                  Call Post_InvElim(si, globals, api, resultDataBuffer, bCell, invEqElimClearingAcctId)
91                              End If    'If subsidConsMethod = "Equity" AndAlso subsidPctCon = 0 AndAlso subsidPctOwn > 0
92                          End If    'If subsidEntName <> "None"
93                      End If    'If (Not bCell.CellStatus.IsNoData) And bCell.CellAmount <> 0
94                  Next 'bCell
95              End If    'If sourceDataBuffer.DataBufferCells.Count > 0
96              If resultDataBuffer.DataBufferCells.Count > 0 Then
97                  api.Data.SetDataBuffer(resultDataBuffer, destinationInfo)
98              End If    'If resultDataBuffer.DataBufferCells.Count > 0
99          Catch ex As Exception
100             Throw ErrorHandler.LogWrite(si, New XFException(si, ex))
101         End Try
102     End Sub 'Book_EPU_InvElim
```

Abstract

This section obtains the investment in subsidiary data that drives the entry, along with the appropriate ownership percentages. It then calls a subroutine that contains the rules that create the balanced entry. A description of the processing taking place within the major blocks is as follows:

Lines 68-69

```
68              Dim destinationInfo As ExpressionDestinationInfo = api.Data.GetExpressionDestinationInfo("V#Periodic")
69              Dim resultDataBuffer As DataBuffer = New DataBuffer()
```

Declare a Result Data Buffer and Destination Info object which will be used throughout the rule.

Lines 70-75

```
70              Dim parentCurrencyName As String = api.Entity.GetLocalCurrency(api.Pov.Parent.MemberId).Name
71              Dim sourceScript As String = "V#YTD:C#" & parentCurrencyName & ":F#EndBalLoad:O#Top:U1#Top:U2#Top:U3#None:U4#None:U5#Top:U6#None:U7#None:U8#None" & _
72                  " + C#OwnerPreAdj:F#Top:O#Top:U1#Top:U2#Top:U3#None:U4#None:U5#Top:U6#None:U7#None:U8#None"
73              Dim filterMembersString As String = "[A#" & topBalShtAcctName & ".Base.Where(Text1 = '" & invSubsAcctText1 & "')]"
74              Dim sourceDataBuffer As DataBuffer = api.Data.GetDataBufferUsingFormula("FilterMembers(" & sourceScript & ", " & _
75                  filterMembersString & ")", DataApiScriptMethodType.Calculate, False, False)
```

Define the filter for the data required and declare the Data Buffer that is then looped through in the rows below.

Chapter 8

Lines 77-93

```
77                  For Each bCell As DataBufferCell In sourceDataBuffer.DataBufferCells.Values
78                      If (Not bCell.CellStatus.IsNoData) And bCell.CellAmount <> 0 Then
79                          Dim subsidEntName As String = bCell.DataBufferCellPk.GetICName(api)
80                          If subsidEntName <> "None" Then
81                              Dim subsidEntId As Integer = api.Members.GetMemberId(DimTypeId.Entity, subsidEntName)
82                              Dim subsidConsMethod As String = api.Entity.OwnershipType(subsidEntId, api.Pov.Parent.MemberId).ToString
83                              Dim subsidPctCon As Decimal = api.Entity.PercentConsolidation(subsidEntId, api.Pov.Parent.MemberId) * .01
84                              Dim subsidPctOwn As Decimal = api.Entity.PercentOwnership(subsidEntId, api.Pov.Parent.MemberId) * .01
85                              'api.LogMessage(api.Pov.Entity.Name & " - " & subsidPctOwn.XFToString)
86                              If subsidConsMethod = "Equity" AndAlso subsidPctCon = 0 AndAlso subsidPctOwn > 0 Then
87                                  Call Post_EPU_Entry(si, globals, api, resultDataBuffer, bCell, subsidEntName, subsidPctOwn)
88                              ElseIf (subsidConsMethod = "NonControllingInterest" OrElse subsidConsMethod = "FullConsolidation") AndAlso _
89                                  (subsidPctOwn > 0 AndAlso subsidPctCon > 0) Then
90                                  Call Post_InvElim(si, globals, api, resultDataBuffer, bCell, invEqElimClearingAcctId)
91                              End If    'If subsidConsMethod = "Equity" AndAlso subsidPctCon = 0 AndAlso subsidPctOwn > 0
92                          End If    'If subsidEntName <> "None"
93                      End If    'If (Not bCell.CellStatus.IsNoData) And bCell.CellAmount <> 0
```

Loop through the Data Buffer that includes the Investment in Subsidiary data and process each record. Determine if the subsidiary (IC Member) has been assigned a Consolidation Method of `Equity` for the Parent being consolidated if the percent Consolidation is zero and if the percent ownership is greater than zero. If all of these conditions have been met, call the subroutine to record the balanced entry for the EPU (note that lines 88–90 relate to the elimination of Investment in Subsidiary when there is majority ownership, discussed separately in the Noncontrolling Interest section).

Lines 95-98

```
95              End If    'If sourceDataBuffer.DataBufferCells.Count > 0
96              If resultDataBuffer.DataBufferCells.Count > 0 Then
97                  api.Data.SetDataBuffer(resultDataBuffer, destinationInfo)
98              End If    'If resultDataBuffer.DataBufferCells.Count > 0
```

Write the data (the EPU entry line items) included in the Results Buffer to the database.

Section 3

```
104     Private Sub Post_EPU_Entry(ByVal si As SessionInfo, ByVal globals As BRGlobals, ByVal api As FinanceRulesApi, ByRef resultDataBuffer As DataBuffer, _
105             ByVal bCell As DataBufferCell, ByVal subsidEntName As String, ByVal subsidPctOwn As Decimal)
106         Dim sourcePov As String = ":F#Top:O#Top:I#Top:U1#Top:U2#Top:U3#None:U4#None:U5#Top:U6#None:U7#None:U8#None"
107         Dim parentCurrencyName As String = api.Entity.GetLocalCurrency(api.Pov.Parent.MemberId).Name
108         Dim netIncSubsidAmt As Decimal = api.Data.GetDataCell("V#Periodic:C#" & parentCurrencyName & ":E#" & subsidEntName & ":A#" & netIncAcctName & sourcePov).CellAmount
109         netIncSubsidAmt = netIncSubsidAmt & api.Data.GetDataCell("V#Periodic:C#OwnerPreAdj:E#" & subsidEntName & ":A#" & netIncAcctName & sourcePov).CellAmount
110         '-----------------------------------------------------------
111         ' DR (assuming positive Net Inc) the Investment in Subsidiary account:
112         '-----------------------------------------------------------
113         Dim resultCell1 As New DataBufferCell(bCell)
114         resultCell1.DataBufferCellPk.FlowId = api.Members.GetMemberId(DimTypeId.Flow, flowEndBalName)
115         resultCell1.DataBufferCellPk.OriginId = DimConstants.Elimination
116         resultCell1.DataBufferCellPk.UD1Id = DimConstants.None
117         resultCell1.DataBufferCellPk.UD2Id = DimConstants.None
118         resultCell1.DataBufferCellPk.UD3Id = DimConstants.None
119         resultCell1.DataBufferCellPk.UD4Id = DimConstants.None
120         resultCell1.DataBufferCellPk.UD5Id = api.Members.GetMemberId(DimTypeId.UD5, ud5EpuName)
121         resultCell1.DataBufferCellPk.UD6Id = DimConstants.None
122         resultCell1.DataBufferCellPk.UD7Id = DimConstants.None
123         resultCell1.DataBufferCellPk.UD8Id = DimConstants.None
124         resultCell1.CellAmount = netIncSubsidAmt * subsidPctOwn
125         resultDataBuffer.SetCell(api.SI, resultCell1, True)
126         '-----------------------------------------------------------
127         ' CR the Equity in Earnings account:
128         '-----------------------------------------------------------
129         Dim resultCell2 As New DataBufferCell(resultCell1)
130         resultCell2.DataBufferCellPk.AccountId = api.Members.GetMemberId(DimTypeId.Account, eqtyInEarnAcctName)
131         resultCell2.DataBufferCellPk.FlowId = api.Members.GetMemberId(DimTypeId.Flow, flowEndBalName)
132         resultDataBuffer.SetCell(api.SI, resultCell2, True)
133     End Sub 'Post_EPU_Entry
```

Abstract

This section (encapsulated within the `Post_EPU_Entry` subroutine) computes and records the line items within the EPU entry. It emulates posting a manual Journal entry for EPU. The first portion of the code obtains the net income from the subsidiary for which we are recognizing our portion of income in the consolidating earnings and creates the debit and credit line-item entries. A description of the processing taking place within the major blocks is as follows:

Lines 106-109

```
106        Dim sourcePov As String = ":F#Top:O#Top:I#Top:U1#Top:U2#Top:U3#None:U4#None:U5#Top:U6#None:U7#None:U8#None"
107        Dim parentCurrencyName As String = api.Entity.GetLocalCurrency(api.Pov.Parent.MemberId).Name
108        Dim netIncSubsidAmt As Decimal = api.Data.GetDataCell("V#Periodic:C#" & parentCurrencyName & ":E#" & subsidEntName & ":A#" & netIncAcctName & sourcePov).CellAmount
109        netIncSubsidAmt = netIncSubsidAmt & api.Data.GetDataCell("V#Periodic:C#OwnerPreAdj:E#" & subsidEntName & ":A#" & netIncAcctName & sourcePov).CellAmount
```

Obtain the net income from the subsidiary that we have an investment in and for which we are recording our proportionate share of their earnings for this period.

Lines 113-125

```
113        Dim resultCell1 As New DataBufferCell(bCell)
114        resultCell1.DataBufferCellPk.FlowId = api.Members.GetMemberId(DimTypeId.Flow, flowEndBalName)
115        resultCell1.DataBufferCellPk.OriginId = DimConstants.Elimination
116        resultCell1.DataBufferCellPk.UD1Id = DimConstants.None
117        resultCell1.DataBufferCellPk.UD2Id = DimConstants.None
118        resultCell1.DataBufferCellPk.UD3Id = DimConstants.None
119        resultCell1.DataBufferCellPk.UD4Id = DimConstants.None
120        resultCell1.DataBufferCellPk.UD5Id = api.Members.GetMemberId(DimTypeId.UD5, ud5EpuName)
121        resultCell1.DataBufferCellPk.UD6Id = DimConstants.None
122        resultCell1.DataBufferCellPk.UD7Id = DimConstants.None
123        resultCell1.DataBufferCellPk.UD8Id = DimConstants.None
124        resultCell1.CellAmount = netIncSubsidAmt * subsidPctOwn
125        resultDataBuffer.SetCell(api.SI, resultCell1, True)
```

Record the impact to the Investment in Subsidiary Account. If the subsidiary's earnings are positive for the period, this will represent a debit to the Investment Account. The net income is multiplied by the holding company's percentage ownership in the subsidiary.

Lines 129-132

```
129        Dim resultCell2 As New DataBufferCell(resultCell1)
130        resultCell2.DataBufferCellPk.AccountId = api.Members.GetMemberId(DimTypeId.Account, eqtyInEarnAcctName)
131        resultCell2.DataBufferCellPk.FlowId = api.Members.GetMemberId(DimTypeId.Flow, flowEndBalName)
132        resultDataBuffer.SetCell(api.SI, resultCell2, True)
```

Record the impact to the Equity in Earnings Account within the Income Statement. If the subsidiary's earnings are positive for the period, this will represent a credit to the Earnings Account. The net income is multiplied by the holding company's percentage ownership in the subsidiary.

Results

Following a Consolidation of the SubGroup, the EPU Calculation books the entry to both the `InvestInSubs` and `InvSubsEarnings` Accounts, accounting for the 30% ownership percentage of the $300 Net Income.

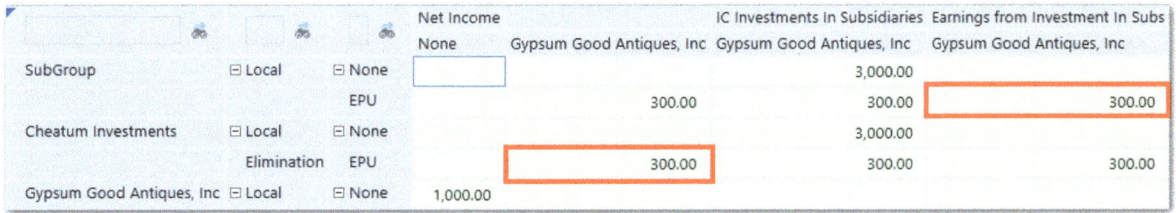

Figure 8.26

Noncontrolling Interest (NCI)

Generally speaking, under US GAAP accounting, companies with >50 percent (majority) ownership of another company, but below 100 percent, are required to consolidate 100 percent of the subsidiary's financials into their own financial statements. However, as stated above, a reporting Entity must consolidate any legal Entity in which it has a controlling financial interest.

Chapter 8

The appropriate accounting treatment applied for investments with majority ownership is the **Consolidation Method**.

To reflect the fact that the acquirer owns less than 100 percent of the consolidated assets and liabilities, a new equity line item titled **Noncontrolling Interests** is created and will reflect the amount of equity possessed by the minority shareholders external to the legal Entity being reported.

As for the income statement, the subsidiary's income statement will also be consolidated into the combined income statement. As such, the consolidated net income reflects the share of net income that belongs to the Parent common shareholders, while also displaying the consolidated net income that does not belong to the Parent. A separate line item that represents the portion of net income that belongs to the minority shareholders will be netted (subtracted, assuming positive income) from the net income (loss) attributable to the shareholders of the reporting Entity. It is typically labeled as "Earnings attributable to noncontrolling interests" or something very similar. The Calculation must be performed on a monthly basis, given that the minority ownership percentage can change throughout time.

Example

For the Stooges' next venture, they purchase a 70% controlling stake in the Gottrox Jewelry Company, again with Cheatum Investments as the holding company.

Metadata

Entities

Larry first creates the new Entity within the SubGroup Parent, again as a sibling of the investor company, Cheatum Investments.

Figure 8.27

CheatumInvestments is the holding company that has recorded an Investment in Subsidiary for GottroxCo which is 70% owned by the SubGroup consolidated structure and thus will be consolidated into the SubGroup Legal Entity accordingly, with the appropriate accounting entries recorded to reflect the ownership interests of the minority stockholders.

Larry enters the Percent Ownership of Gottrox in the Relationship Properties.

Common Rule Examples

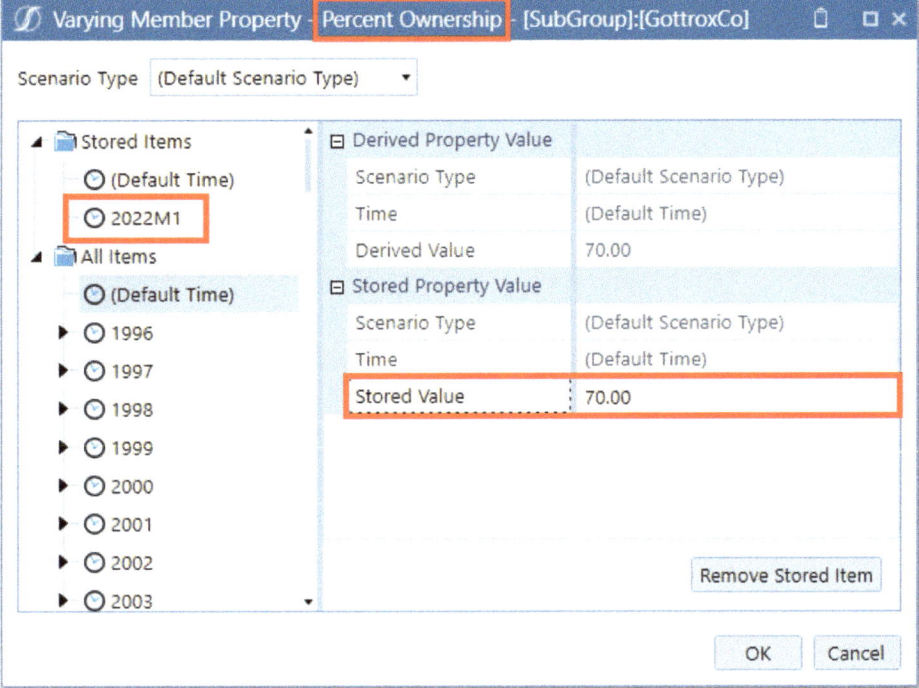

Figure 8.28

As mentioned earlier, the percentages can vary by Scenario Type and Time period. In the example above, the percentage ownership of 70 will be in effect for all periods, starting with 2022M1, until a different percentage is entered in a future Time period.

In addition to the Percent Ownership of Gottrox, Larry also considers the Percent Consolidation. Given that the default Consolidation percentage within OneStream is 100, the amount does not necessarily have to be modified in the relationship settings, but it should be verified. The Percent Consolidation for Gottrox and Cheatum will be set to (absorb the default value of) 100, as shown below:

Figure 8.29

Chapter 8

The final setting that is pertinent for the relationship properties is Ownership Type. The Business Rules that create the NCI entry will refer to this setting. The recommended value for this Type of ownership (e.g., `GottroxCo` to its Parent `SubGroup`) is Non-Controlling Interest, as seen below.

Figure 8.30

This label may seem contradictory to the ownership structure, as the Parent company indeed possesses a *controlling* interest in the subsidiary, but in this case, we have chosen this label to reference the fact that we will be automating the entries to record the *noncontrolling* interest aspect of our ownership in a special section of equity on the Balance Sheet entitled "Noncontrolling interests" and a line item on the Income Statement entitled "Net income attributable to noncontrolling interest."

The other option is to leave this setting at the default value of Full Consolidation and initiate the rule that records the NCI through examination of the percentage ownership (testing for a value less than 100 percent) in combination with the percentage Consolidation (i.e., 100% for NCI). Both options are valid.

Accounts

The next step is for Larry to identify the Equity Accounts for which the balance will be eliminated during the Consolidation process. These Accounts need to be identified with a text field attribute which will initiate the elimination of the balance and the reclassification of the minority ownership percentage (calculated as 1 minus the percentage ownership) portion of the balance into the Noncontrolling Interest subsection (within the Equity section) of the balance sheet. An example of this setup is illustrated below. Account `Stock` (`Common Stock`) has been populated with a Text 1 attribute of Equity.

Common Rule Examples

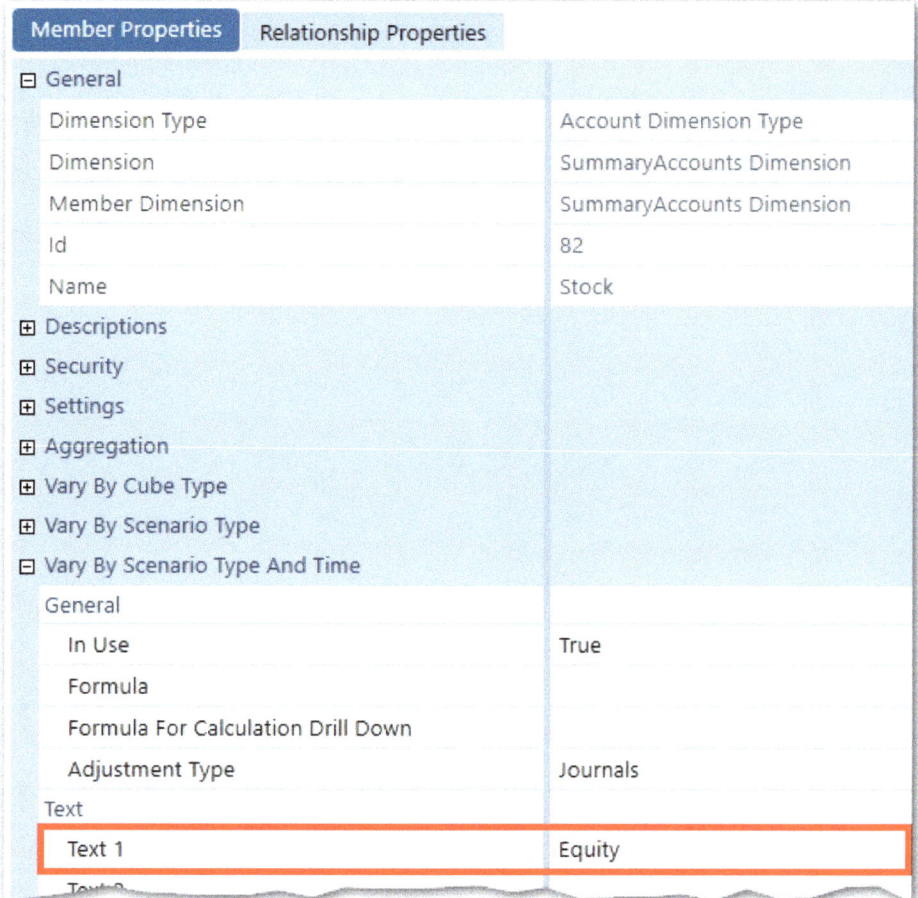

Figure 8.31

That value will then initiate the recording of the NCI entry within the Consolidation Business Rules, as explained below.

In addition to the Equity Accounts being eliminated and partially reclassified to the NCI section, Larry identifies other Accounts utilized in the Business Rule that creates the NCI adjustment, as follows:

1. The NCI Equity Account(s) that is the recipient of the reclassed equity (minority ownership portion). This Account can be stored in a parameter, a text field (for each of the core Equity Accounts that are being eliminated), or in a variable within the Consolidation Rules, amongst other options. Example Accounts appear below:

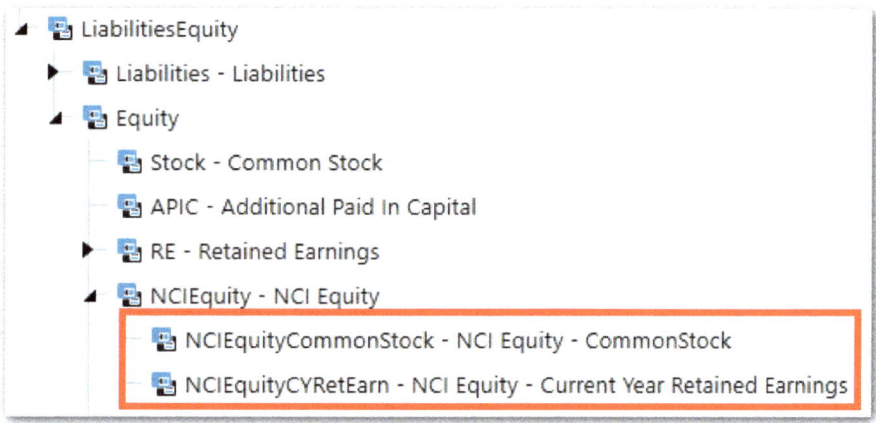

Figure 8.32

2. The `InvestmentsInSubsPlug` Account is utilized as a 'Clearing Account' in the elimination of the Gottrox (subsidiary) equity (and corresponding investment in subsidiary that exists within Cheatum (holding company)). Like the NCI Equity Account(s), this Account can be stored in a parameter, a text field, or in a variable within the Consolidation Rules, amongst other options. An example Account appears below:

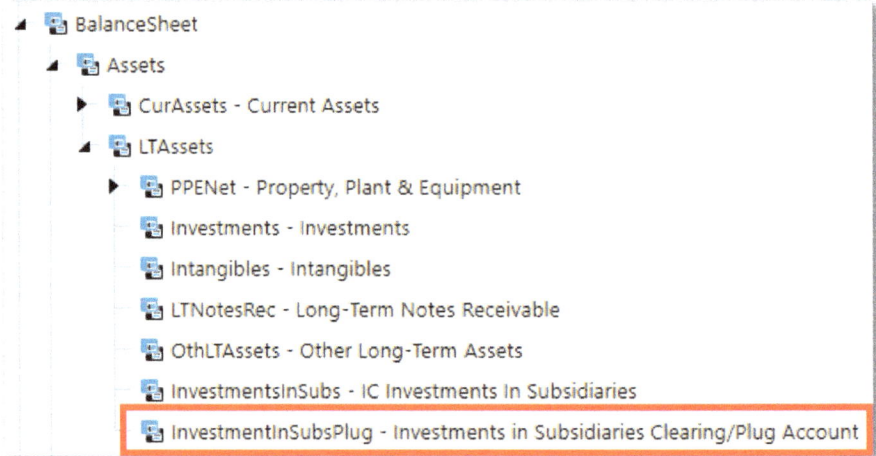

Figure 8.33

3. The NCI Expense Account is utilized to post the adjustment of net income to recognize the portion attributable to the minority stakeholders. Like the above Accounts, this Account can be stored in a parameter, a text field, or in a variable within the Consolidation Rules, amongst other options. An example Account appears below:

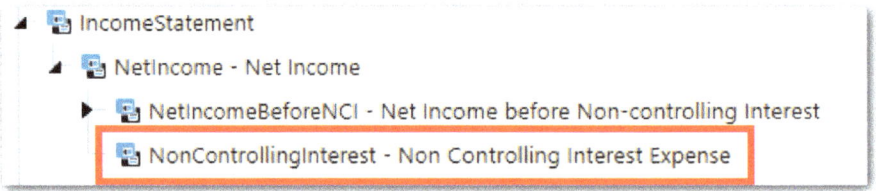

Figure 8.34

Data Description

The data that drives this Calculation is located in the subsidiary that is owned less than 100% (but most likely greater than 50%). The data will exist in the Stockholders Equity section:

In addition to the Equity Accounts, we also utilize the data in the Net Income (Parent-level) Account within the Income Statement section of the Chart of Accounts:

Common Rule Examples

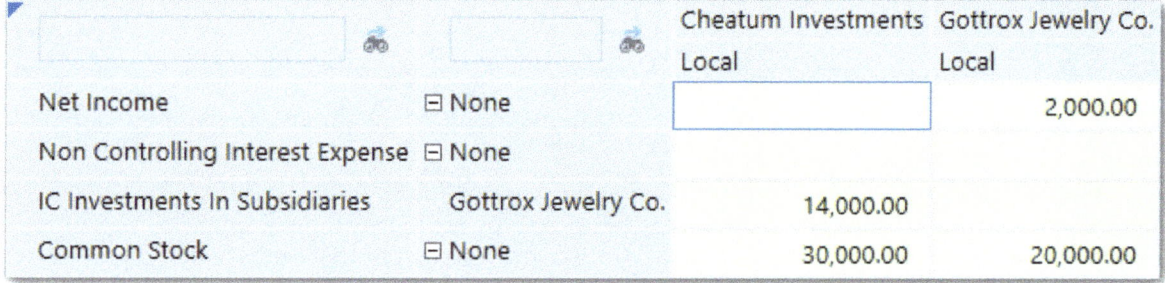

Figure 8.35

Rule Abstract

This rule records the entry to eliminate subsidiary equity and reclassify/identify the minority stockholder's portion of equity on the Balance Sheet and earnings (loss) within the Income Statement for each period.

Code Breakdown

Section 1

```
22  #Region "Global_Variables"
23      Const topBalShtAcctName As String = "BalanceSheet"           'Top of Balance Sheet hierarchy Account Name
24      Const invEqElimClearAcctName As String = "InvestmentInSubsPlug" ' Clearing/Plug Account Name for Investment and Subsid Equity Elims
25      Const nciEquityCpStkName As String = "NCIEquityCommonStock"  ' NCI Equity-Cap Stock Account Name
26      Const nciEquityCurYrIncName As String = "NCIEquityCYRetEarn" ' NCI Equity-Curr Yr Earnings Account Name
27      Const netIncAcctName As String = "NetIncome"                 ' Net Income Account Name
28      Const eqtyInEarnAcctName As String = "InvSubEarnings"        ' Equity In Earnings (Income from Subs) Account Name
29      Const nciExpAcctName As String = "NonControllingInterest"    ' NCI Expense Account Name
30      Const flowEndBalName As String = "EndBalLoad"                ' Flow Dim Ending Balance Member Name
31      Const flowAddsName As String = "RF_Investments_Additions"    ' Flow Dim Additions/Movements Member Name
32      Const ud5EpuName As String = "EPU"                           ' UD5 (DataType Dim) Equity Pickup Member Name
33      Const ud5InvestElimName As String = "Invest_Elim"            ' UD5 (DataType Dim) Invest in Subs Elim Member Name
34      Const ud5EqtyElimName As String = "Equity_Elim"              ' UD5 (DataType Dim) Equity Elim Member Name
35      Const ud5NciEqtyReclName As String = "NCI_Equity"            ' UD5 (DataType Dim) NCI Equity Reclass Member Name
36      Const ud5NciExpName As String = "NCI_Expense"                ' UD5 (DataType Dim) NCI Expense Member Name
37      Const invSubsAcctText1 As String = "INVESTMENT"              ' Text1 value for Investment in Subsidiary Acctts
38      Const subsidEquityAcctText1 As String = "EQUITY"             ' Text1 value for Subsidiary Equity Accts
39  #End Region 'Global_Variables
40
41  #Region "Main"
42      Public Function Main(ByVal si As SessionInfo, ByVal globals As BRGlobals, ByVal api As FinanceRulesApi, ByVal args As FinanceRulesArgs) As Object
43          Try
44              Select Case api.FunctionType
45                  Case Is = FinanceFunctionType.Calculate
46                      If api.Pov.Cons.Name = "Elimination" Then
47                          Dim invEqElimClearingAcctId As Integer = api.Members.GetMemberId(DimTypeId.Account, invEqElimClearAcctName)
48                          If api.Entity.OwnershipType().ToString.Equals("Holding") Then
49                              Call Book_EPU_InvElim(si, globals, api, invEqElimClearingAcctId)
50                          ElseIf api.Entity.OwnershipType().ToString.Equals("NonControllingInterest") Then
51                              Call Book_NCI(si, globals, api, invEqElimClearingAcctId)
```

Abstract

The code in this section initializes variables and then determines whether we are processing the appropriate intersection of data to book the EPU entry. A description of the processing taking place within the major blocks is as follows:

Lines 23-39

```
23      Const topBalShtAcctName As String = "BalanceSheet"           'Top of Balance Sheet hierarchy Account Name
24      Const invEqElimClearAcctName As String = "InvestmentInSubsPlug" ' Clearing/Plug Account Name for Investment and Subsid Equity Elims
25      Const nciEquityCpStkName As String = "NCIEquityCommonStock"  ' NCI Equity-Cap Stock Account Name
26      Const nciEquityCurYrIncName As String = "NCIEquityCYRetEarn" ' NCI Equity-Curr Yr Earnings Account Name
27      Const netIncAcctName As String = "NetIncome"                 ' Net Income Account Name
28      Const eqtyInEarnAcctName As String = "InvSubEarnings"        ' Equity In Earnings (Income from Subs) Account Name
29      Const nciExpAcctName As String = "NonControllingInterest"    ' NCI Expense Account Name
30      Const flowEndBalName As String = "EndBalLoad"                ' Flow Dim Ending Balance Member Name
31      Const flowAddsName As String = "RF_Investments_Additions"    ' Flow Dim Additions/Movements Member Name
32      Const ud5EpuName As String = "EPU"                           ' UD5 (DataType Dim) Equity Pickup Member Name
33      Const ud5InvestElimName As String = "Invest_Elim"            ' UD5 (DataType Dim) Invest in Subs Elim Member Name
34      Const ud5EqtyElimName As String = "Equity_Elim"              ' UD5 (DataType Dim) Equity Elim Member Name
35      Const ud5NciEqtyReclName As String = "NCI_Equity"            ' UD5 (DataType Dim) NCI Equity Reclass Member Name
36      Const ud5NciExpName As String = "NCI_Expense"                ' UD5 (DataType Dim) NCI Expense Member Name
37      Const invSubsAcctText1 As String = "INVESTMENT"              ' Text1 value for Investment in Subsidiary Acctts
38      Const subsidEquityAcctText1 As String = "EQUITY"             ' Text1 value for Subsidiary Equity Accts
```

Initialize variables that are referenced in other subroutines within the Business Rule.

Chapter 8

Lines 46-51

```
46              If api.Pov.Cons.Name = "Elimination" Then
47                  Dim invEqElimClearingAcctId As Integer = api.Members.GetMemberId(DimTypeId.Account, invEqElimClearAcctName)
48                  If api.Entity.OwnershipType().ToString.Equals("Holding") Then
49                      Call Book_EPU_InvElim(si, globals, api, invEqElimClearingAcctId)
50                  ElseIf api.Entity.OwnershipType().ToString.Equals("NonControllingInterest") Then
51                      Call Book_NCI(si, globals, api, invEqElimClearingAcctId)
```

These lines determine whether we are processing the Elimination Member of the Consolidation Dimension and, if so, will determine if the Ownership Type attribute of the current (POV) Entity Relationship has been set to `NonControllingInterest` for the current period being processed. If those conditions have been met, the subroutine `Book_NCI` is called, where the actual NCI entry will be created. Note that rows 47-48 pertain to the Equity Pickup entry, discussed previously.

Section 2

```
171  Private Sub Book_NCI(ByVal si As SessionInfo, ByVal globals As BRGlobals, ByVal api As FinanceRulesApi, ByVal invEqElimClearingAcctId As Integer)
172      Dim pctCon As Decimal = api.Entity.PercentConsolidation() * .01
173      Dim pctOwn As Decimal = api.Entity.PercentOwnership() * .01
174      Dim pctNci As Decimal = 1 - pctOwn
175      Dim originElimMbrId As Integer = DimConstants.Elimination
176      Dim destinationInfo As ExpressionDestinationInfo = api.Data.GetExpressionDestinationInfo("V#Periodic")
177      Dim resultDataBuffer As DataBuffer = New DataBuffer()
178      Dim parentCurrencyName As String = api.Entity.GetLocalCurrency(api.Pov.Parent.MemberId).Name
179      Dim sourceScript As String = "V#YTD:C#" & parentCurrencyName & ":F#Top:O#Top:I#Top:U1#Top:U2#Top:U3#None:U4#None:U5#Top:U6#None:U7#None:U8#None" & _
180          " + C#OwnerPreAdj:F#Top:O#Top:I#Top:U1#Top:U2#Top:U3#None:U4#None:U5#Top:U6#None:U7#None:U8#None"
181      Dim filterMembersString As String = "[A#" & topBalShtAcctName & ".Base.Where(Text1 = '" & subsidEquityAcctText1 & "')]"
182      Dim sourceDataBuffer As DataBuffer = api.Data.GetDataBufferUsingFormula("FilterMembers(" & sourceScript & ", " & _
183          filterMembersString & ")", DataApiScriptMethodType.Calculate, False, False)
184      If sourceDataBuffer.DataBufferCells.Count > 0 Then
185          Dim nciEqtyAcctId As Integer = api.Members.GetMemberId(DimTypeId.Account, nciEquityCpStkName)
186          Dim ud5EquityElimMbrId As Integer = api.Members.GetMemberId(DimTypeId.UD5, ud5EqtyElimName)
187          For Each bCell As DataBufferCell In sourceDataBuffer.DataBufferCells.Values
188              If (Not bCell.CellStatus.IsNoData) And bCell.CellAmount <> 0 Then
189                  Call Post_NCI_EqElim(si, globals, api, resultDataBuffer, bCell, invEqElimClearingAcctId)
190                  If pctNci > 0 Then
191                      Call Post_NCI_ReclEqty(si, globals, api, resultDataBuffer, bCell, invEqElimClearingAcctId, pctNci)
192                  End If    'If pctNci > 0
193              End If    'If (Not bCell.CellStatus.IsNoData) And bCell.CellAmount <> 0
194          Next  'bCell
195      End If    'If sourceDataBuffer..DataBufferCells.Count > 0
196      If resultDataBuffer.DataBufferCells.Count > 0 Then
197          api.Data.SetDataBuffer(resultDataBuffer, destinationInfo)
198      End If    'If resultDataBuffer.DataBufferCells.Count > 0
199      If pctNci > 0 Then
200          Call Post_NCI_Exp(si, globals, api, pctNci)
201      End If    'If pctNci > 0
202  End Sub  'Book_NCI
```

Abstract

This section obtains the investment in subsidiary data that drives the entry, along with the appropriate ownership percentages and then calls a subroutine that contains the rules that create the balanced entry. A description of the processing taking place within the major blocks is as follows:

Lines 172-174

```
172      Dim pctCon As Decimal = api.Entity.PercentConsolidation() * .01
173      Dim pctOwn As Decimal = api.Entity.PercentOwnership() * .01
174      Dim pctNci As Decimal = 1 - pctOwn
```

Obtain the Entity relationship percentages (Consolidation, ownership) and initialize variables.

Lines 175-183

```
175      Dim originElimMbrId As Integer = DimConstants.Elimination
176      Dim destinationInfo As ExpressionDestinationInfo = api.Data.GetExpressionDestinationInfo("V#Periodic")
177      Dim resultDataBuffer As DataBuffer = New DataBuffer()
178      Dim parentCurrencyName As String = api.Entity.GetLocalCurrency(api.Pov.Parent.MemberId).Name
179      Dim sourceScript As String = "V#YTD:C#" & parentCurrencyName & ":F#Top:O#Top:I#Top:U1#Top:U2#Top:U3#None:U4#None:U5#Top:U6#None:U7#None:U8#None" & _
180          " + C#OwnerPreAdj:F#Top:O#Top:I#Top:U1#Top:U2#Top:U3#None:U4#None:U5#Top:U6#None:U7#None:U8#None"
181      Dim filterMembersString As String = "[A#" & topBalShtAcctName & ".Base.Where(Text1 = '" & subsidEquityAcctText1 & "')]"
182      Dim sourceDataBuffer As DataBuffer = api.Data.GetDataBufferUsingFormula("FilterMembers(" & sourceScript & ", " & _
183          filterMembersString & ")", DataApiScriptMethodType.Calculate, False, False)
```

Specify criteria pertinent to defining the Source and Result Data Buffers. A source script is defined and passed into the `GetDataBuffer` function. An empty Result Data Buffer and `DestinationInfo` objects are declared and will be used later.

Lines 184-194

```
184            If sourceDataBuffer.DataBufferCells.Count > 0 Then
185                Dim nciEqtyAcctId As Integer = api.Members.GetMemberId(DimTypeId.Account, nciEquityCpStkName)
186                Dim ud5EquityElimMbrId As Integer = api.Members.GetMemberId(DimTypeId.UD5, ud5EqtyElimName)
187                For Each bCell As DataBufferCell In sourceDataBuffer.DataBufferCells.Values
188                    If (Not bCell.CellStatus.IsNoData) And bCell.CellAmount <> 0 Then
189                        Call Post_NCI_EqElim(si, globals, api, resultDataBuffer, bCell, invEqElimClearingAcctId)
190                        If pctNci > 0 Then
191                            Call Post_NCI_ReclEqty(si, globals, api, resultDataBuffer, bCell, invEqElimClearingAcctId, pctNci)
192                        End If    'If pctNci > 0
193                    End If    'If (Not bCell.CellStatus.IsNoData) And bCell.CellAmount <> 0
194                Next 'bCell
```

Loop through the Data Buffer that includes the subsidiary equity data and process each record. Call the subroutine (Post_NCI_EqElim) that will post the elimination of the subsidiary equity (row 189) and the subroutine (Post_NCI_ReclEqty) to post the reclassification of equity into the NCI Equity section of the balance sheet (row 191).

Lines 196-198

```
196            If resultDataBuffer.DataBufferCells.Count > 0 Then
197                api.Data.SetDataBuffer(resultDataBuffer, destinationInfo)
198            End If    'If resultDataBuffer.DataBufferCells.Count > 0
```

Write the data for the equity elimination and NCI Equity reclass entry line items included in the results buffer to the database.

Lines 199-201

```
199            If pctNci > 0 Then
200                Call Post_NCI_Exp(si, globals, api, pctNci)
201            End If    'If pctNci > 0
```

Check if the percent ownership is greater than 100 and if so, call the subroutine (Post_NCI_Exp) that will post the entry for NCI Expense on the Income Statement, and the offset to the Retained Earnings section of the Balance Sheet.

Section 3

```
206    Private Sub Post_NCI_EqElim(ByVal si As SessionInfo, ByVal globals As BRGlobals, ByVal api As FinanceRulesApi, ByRef resultDataBuffer As DataBuffer, _
207                ByVal bCell As DataBufferCell, ByVal invEqElimClearingAcctId As Integer)
208        '-----------------------------------------------------------------
209        '    Record the Equity Elimination
210        '-----------------------------------------------------------------
211        '-----------------------------------------------------------------
212        ' DR (clear) the equity account balance:
213        '-----------------------------------------------------------------
214        Dim resultCell1 As New DataBufferCell(bCell)
215        resultCell1.DataBufferCellPk.FlowId = api.Members.GetMemberId(DimTypeId.Flow, flowEndBalName)
216        resultCell1.DataBufferCellPk.OriginId = DimConstants.Elimination
217        resultCell1.DataBufferCellPk.ICId = DimConstants.None
218        resultCell1.DataBufferCellPk.UD1Id = DimConstants.None
219        resultCell1.DataBufferCellPk.UD2Id = DimConstants.None
220        resultCell1.DataBufferCellPk.UD3Id = DimConstants.None
221        resultCell1.DataBufferCellPk.UD4Id = DimConstants.None
222        resultCell1.DataBufferCellPk.UD5Id = api.Members.GetMemberId(DimTypeId.UD5, ud5EqtyElimName)
223        resultCell1.DataBufferCellPk.UD6Id = DimConstants.None
224        resultCell1.DataBufferCellPk.UD7Id = DimConstants.None
225        resultCell1.DataBufferCellPk.UD8Id = DimConstants.None
226        resultCell1.CellAmount = bCell.CellAmount * -1
227        resultDataBuffer.SetCell(api.SI, resultCell1, True)
228        '-----------------------------------------------------------------
229        ' CR the investment/equity clearing account:
230        '-----------------------------------------------------------------
231        Dim resultCell2 As New DataBufferCell(resultCell1)
232        resultCell2.DataBufferCellPk.AccountId = invEqElimClearingAcctId
233        resultDataBuffer.SetCell(api.SI, resultCell2, True)
234    End Sub 'Post_NCI_Entry_EqElim
```

Chapter 8

Abstract

This section will post the elimination of the equity for the subsidiary that is owned by the holding company being consolidated.

Lines 214-227

```vb
214         Dim resultCell1 As New DataBufferCell(bCell)
215         resultCell1.DataBufferCellPk.FlowId = api.Members.GetMemberId(DimTypeId.Flow, flowEndBalName)
216         resultCell1.DataBufferCellPk.OriginId = DimConstants.Elimination
217         resultCell1.DataBufferCellPk.ICId = DimConstants.None
218         resultCell1.DataBufferCellPk.UD1Id = DimConstants.None
219         resultCell1.DataBufferCellPk.UD2Id = DimConstants.None
220         resultCell1.DataBufferCellPk.UD3Id = DimConstants.None
221         resultCell1.DataBufferCellPk.UD4Id = DimConstants.None
222         resultCell1.DataBufferCellPk.UD5Id = api.Members.GetMemberId(DimTypeId.UD5, ud5EqtyElimName)
223         resultCell1.DataBufferCellPk.UD6Id = DimConstants.None
224         resultCell1.DataBufferCellPk.UD7Id = DimConstants.None
225         resultCell1.DataBufferCellPk.UD8Id = DimConstants.None
226         resultCell1.CellAmount = bCell.CellAmount * -1
227         resultDataBuffer.SetCell(api.SI, resultCell1, True)
```

Post the elimination of the subsidiary equity balance. This entry will be a debit, assuming a positive balance in the source Equity Account.

Lines 231-233

```vb
231         Dim resultCell2 As New DataBufferCell(resultCell1)
232         resultCell2.DataBufferCellPk.AccountId = invEqElimClearingAcctId
233         resultDataBuffer.SetCell(api.SI, resultCell2, True)
```

Post the offset to the investment in the subs/subsidiary Equity Clearing Account. This entry will be a credit, assuming a positive balance in the source Equity Account.

Section 4

```vb
238     Private Sub Post_NCI_ReclEqty(ByVal si As SessionInfo, ByVal globals As BRGlobals, ByVal api As FinanceRulesApi, ByRef resultDataBuffer As DataBuffer, _
239         ByVal bCell As DataBufferCell, ByVal invEqElimClearingAcctId As Integer, ByVal pctNci As Decimal)
240         '-----------------------------------------------------------------
241         '    Record the NCI (Equity) Entry
242         '-----------------------------------------------------------------
243         '-----------------------------------------------------------------
244         ' DR the investment/equity clearing account:
245         '-----------------------------------------------------------------
246         Dim resultCell1 As New DataBufferCell(bCell)
247         resultCell1.DataBufferCellPk.AccountId = invEqElimClearingAcctId
248         resultCell1.DataBufferCellPk.FlowId = api.Members.GetMemberId(DimTypeId.Flow, flowEndBalName)
249         resultCell1.DataBufferCellPk.ICId = DimConstants.None
250         resultCell1.DataBufferCellPk.OriginId = DimConstants.Elimination
251         resultCell1.DataBufferCellPk.UD1Id = DimConstants.None
252         resultCell1.DataBufferCellPk.UD2Id = DimConstants.None
253         resultCell1.DataBufferCellPk.UD3Id = DimConstants.None
254         resultCell1.DataBufferCellPk.UD4Id = DimConstants.None
255         resultCell1.DataBufferCellPk.UD5Id = api.Members.GetMemberId(DimTypeId.UD5, ud5NciEqtyReclName)
256         resultCell1.DataBufferCellPk.UD6Id = DimConstants.None
257         resultCell1.DataBufferCellPk.UD7Id = DimConstants.None
258         resultCell1.DataBufferCellPk.UD8Id = DimConstants.None
259         resultCell1.CellAmount = bCell.CellAmount * pctNci
260         resultDataBuffer.SetCell(api.SI, resultCell1, True)
261         '-----------------------------------------------------------------
262         ' CR the non-controlling interest equity account balance:
263         '-----------------------------------------------------------------
264         Dim resultCell2 As New DataBufferCell(resultCell1)
265         resultCell2.DataBufferCellPk.AccountId = api.Members.GetMemberId(DimTypeId.Account, nciEquityCpStkName)
266         resultDataBuffer.SetCell(api.SI, resultCell2, True)
267     End Sub 'Post_NCI_Entry_ReclEqty
```

Abstract

This section will post the reclassification of the minority ownership portion of subsidiary equity from the primary equity section to the Noncontrolling Interest equity section.

Lines 246-260

```vb
246         Dim resultCell1 As New DataBufferCell(bCell)
247         resultCell1.DataBufferCellPk.AccountId = invEqElimClearingAcctId
248         resultCell1.DataBufferCellPk.FlowId = api.Members.GetMemberId(DimTypeId.Flow, flowEndBalName)
249         resultCell1.DataBufferCellPk.ICId = DimConstants.None
250         resultCell1.DataBufferCellPk.OriginId = DimConstants.Elimination
251         resultCell1.DataBufferCellPk.UD1Id = DimConstants.None
252         resultCell1.DataBufferCellPk.UD2Id = DimConstants.None
253         resultCell1.DataBufferCellPk.UD3Id = DimConstants.None
254         resultCell1.DataBufferCellPk.UD4Id = DimConstants.None
255         resultCell1.DataBufferCellPk.UD5Id = api.Members.GetMemberId(DimTypeId.UD5, ud5NciEqtyReclName)
256         resultCell1.DataBufferCellPk.UD6Id = DimConstants.None
257         resultCell1.DataBufferCellPk.UD7Id = DimConstants.None
258         resultCell1.DataBufferCellPk.UD8Id = DimConstants.None
259         resultCell1.CellAmount = bCell.CellAmount * pctNci
260         resultDataBuffer.SetCell(api.SI, resultCell1, True)
```

Post the offset (see next row for details) to the investment in the subs/subsidiary Equity Clearing Account. This entry will be a debit, assuming a positive balance in the source Equity Account.

Lines 264-266

```vb
264         Dim resultCell2 As New DataBufferCell(resultcell1)
265         resultCell2.DataBufferCellPk.AccountId = api.Members.GetMemberId(DimTypeId.Account, nciEquityCpStkName)
266         resultDataBuffer.SetCell(api.SI, resultCell2, True)
```

Post the minority ownership portion of the equity balance to the Noncontrolling Interest Equity Account. The amount is calculated as the balance within the Equity Account multiplied by the minority ownership percentage. This entry will be a credit, assuming a positive balance in the source Equity Account.

Section 5

```vb
269   Private Sub Post_NCI_Exp(ByVal si As SessionInfo, ByVal globals As BRGlobals, ByVal api As FinanceRulesApi, pctNci As Decimal)
270         Dim parentCurrencyName As String = api.Entity.GetLocalCurrency(api.Pov.Parent.MemberId).Name
271         Dim sourcePov As String = ":F#Top:O#Top:I#Top:U1#Top:U2#Top:U3#None:U4#None:U5#Top:U6#None:U7#None:U8#None"
272         Dim netIncParentCurr As Decimal  = api.Data.GetDataCell("V#Periodic:C#" & parentCurrencyName & ":A#" & netIncAcctName & sourcePov).CellAmount
273         netIncParentCurr = netIncParentCurr + api.Data.GetDataCell("V#Periodic:C#OwnerPreAdj:A#" & netIncAcctName & sourcePov).CellAmount
274         If netIncParentCurr <> 0 AndAlso pctNci <> 0 Then
275             Dim destPov1 As String = ":O#Elimination:I#None:U1#None:U2#None:U3#None:U4#None:U5#" & ud5NciExpName & ":U6#None:U7#None:U8#None"
276             Dim priorPdYtdNciExp As Decimal = 0
277             If Not api.Time.IsFirstPeriodInYear() Then
278                 priorPdYtdNciExp = api.Data.GetDataCell("V#YTD:T#PovPrior1:A#" & nciExpAcctName & ":F#" & flowEndBalName & destPov1).CellAmount
279             End If   'If Not api.Time.IsFirstPeriodInYear()
280             Dim currPdNciExp As Decimal = netIncParentCurr * pctNci
281             '-----------------------------------------------------------------
282             ' DR (assuming positive Net Inc) the NCI Expense account:
283             '-----------------------------------------------------------------
284             api.Data.Calculate("V#Periodic:A#" & nciExpAcctName & ":F#" & flowEndBalName & destPov1 & " = " & currPdNciExp)
285             '-----------------------------------------------------------------
286             ' CR the NCI Equity account:
287             '-----------------------------------------------------------------
288             api.Data.Calculate("A#" & nciEquityCurYrIncName & ":F#" & flowAddsName & destPov1 & " = " & currPdNciExp + priorPdYtdNciExp)
289         End If    'If netIncParentCurr <> 0 AndAlso pctNci <> 0
290   End Sub  'Post_NCI_Entry_NciExp
```

Abstract

This section will post the entry to the NCI Expense Account and the corresponding amount to the NCI Equity Account in order to accurately report the net income attributable to minority ownership shareholders and reclassify the current year income in the standard Retained Earnings section of the Balance Sheet to the NCI Equity section.

Lines 270-273

```vb
270         Dim parentCurrencyName As String = api.Entity.GetLocalCurrency(api.Pov.Parent.MemberId).Name
271         Dim sourcePov As String = ":F#Top:O#Top:I#Top:U1#Top:U2#Top:U3#None:U4#None:U5#Top:U6#None:U7#None:U8#None"
272         Dim netIncParentCurr As Decimal = api.Data.GetDataCell("V#Periodic:C#" & parentCurrencyName & ":A#" & netIncAcctName & sourcePov).CellAmount
273         netIncParentCurr = netIncParentCurr + api.Data.GetDataCell("V#Periodic:C#OwnerPreAdj:A#" & netIncAcctName & sourcePov).CellAmount
```

Obtain the periodic Net Income for the subsidiary.

Chapter 8

Lines 274-279

```
274        If netIncParentCurr <> 0 AndAlso pctNci <> 0 Then
275            Dim destPov1 As String = ":O#Elimination:I#None:U1#None:U2#None:U3#None:U4#None:U5#" & ud5NciExpName & ":U6#None:U7#None:U8#None"
276            Dim priorPdYtdNciExp As Decimal = 0
277            If Not api.Time.IsFirstPeriodInYear() Then
278                priorPdYtdNciExp = api.Data.GetDataCell("V#YTD:T#PovPrior1:A#" & nciExpAcctName & ":F#" & flowEndBalName & destPov1).CellAmount
279            End If    'If Not api.Time.IsFirstPeriodInYear()
```

For all periods beyond M1, obtain the prior period YTD NCI Expense amount using an `api.Data.GetDataCell` function.

Line 280

```
280            Dim currPdNciExp As Decimal = netIncParentCurr * pctNci
```

Calculate the current period NCI expense by multiplying the Net Income by the percent ownership.

Line 284

```
284            api.Data.Calculate("V#Periodic:A#" & nciExpAcctName & ":F#" & flowEndBalName & destPov1 & " = " & currPdNciExp)
```

Post the minority ownership portion of the current period Net Income to the NCI Expense Account. The amount is determined by multiplying the periodic Net Income by the minority ownership percentage. It will be a debit, assuming positive earnings for the period.

Line 288

```
288            api.Data.Calculate("A#" & nciEquityCurYrIncName & ":F#" & flowEndBalName & destPov1 & " = " & currPdNciExp + priorPdYtdNciExp)
```

Adjust the NCI Equity Account (for current year earnings) to include the minority ownership portion of current period Net Income. For the first period in the year, the amount is determined by multiplying the periodic Net Income by the minority ownership percentage. For all other periods, it will include the current period amount (mentioned above) plus the prior period YTD amount. It will be a credit, assuming positive earnings for the period.

Results

After executing the rule, the portion of Net Income not owned by Cheatum (600) is eliminated and consolidated to the Non-Controlling Expense Account at the `SubGroup` Entity. The same 600 is also eliminated from the Current Year Retained Earning Account to reflect the reduction in Net Income. The Investment In Subsidiary and Common Stock Account balances are also fully eliminated.

		SubGroup Local	Elimination	Cheatum Investments Local	Elimination	Gottrox Jewelry Co. Local	Elimination
Net Income	None	1,400.00				2,000.00	-600.00
	Gottrox Jewelry Co.						
Non Controlling Interest Expense	None	600.00					600.00
IC Investments In Subsidiaries	Gottrox Jewelry Co.	0.00		14,000.00	-14,000.00		
Investments in Subsidiaries Clearing/Plug Account	None	-14,000.00					-14,000.00
	Gottrox Jewelry Co.	14,000.00			14,000.00		
Common Stock	None	30,000.00		30,000.00		20,000.00	-20,000.00
NCI Equity - CommonStock	None	6,000.00					6,000.00
NCI Equity - Current Year Retained Earnings	None	600.00					600.00

Figure 8.36

Variations

Variations in requirements and specific situations may require tweaking the method of calculating EPU and NCI presented above. For example, ownership percentage of the subsidiary may need to be calculated based on voting rights, or shares held, which can change from period to period. In this case, ownership percentage can be determined within a separate Calculation and stored in a specific Account. As stated in the beginning of this chapter, these examples are not meant to suit every situation and should be used as a frame of reference for writing complex Consolidation Calculations.

Seeding Rules

Seeding rules refer to rules that copy data from one Scenario to another. These types of rules are very common in almost every application due to OneStream's unique ability to support data for multiple business processes. For example, Year-To-Go Forecast Scenarios typically require historical Actual data to arrive at a full-year view, or Budgets may use Actual data as a starting point in which a growth rate is applied.

OneStream has several ways to copy data from Scenario to Scenario:

- Data Management Copy Steps
- Hybrid Source Data Scenarios
- Finance Business Rules

Of the above Methods, Finance Business Rules offer the most flexibility. Since this book focuses on Finance Business Rules, I will go through examples that utilize this approach. Other Methods may fit best for a particular situation, however, and should be taken into consideration.

What Rule Type to Use?

By their very nature, seeding rules are often one-time exercises that are performed to copy data from a Scenario or Time period which is closed. Because of this, **Custom Calculate** is the logical choice as the method of executing seeding rules; it allows the rules to run once or on an ad-hoc basis and does not have to be cleared and re-calculated each time the DUCS is executed.

If data from the source Scenario changes frequently, it may make sense to execute the rule in a **Scenario Formula** that will run as part of the DUCS. It's important to understand the implications of running this rule in the DUCS as the data will be cleared and recopied each time a Calculation or Consolidation takes place.

The right rule type to use is largely situational but – in most cases – Custom Calculate is the most efficient as it can be executed on demand. In our Forecast seeding examples explained below, Actual data should not change after it is copied. In this case, Custom Calculate makes the most sense.

IsDurable and ClearCalculatedData

Using Custom Calculate rules would mean that the isDurableData property should be set to True for all Calculations and a preceding `ClearCalculatedData` script would need to be included as well.

Simple Copy Data Example

Let's start with a very simple example of a seeding rule:

```
If args.CustomCalculateArgs.FunctionName.XFEqualsIgnoreCase("SimpleSeeding") Then

    'Only run for Base Entities and Local currency
    If (Not api.Entity.HasChildren()) And api.Cons.IsLocalCurrencyForEntity()
        'Clear previously calculated Data
        api.Data.ClearCalculatedData(True,True,True,True)
        'Copy budget scenario to the Fcst_M1 scenario
        api.Data.Calculate("S#Fcst_M1 = RemoveZeros(S#Budget)",True)
    End If
```

The above script copies all data from the Budget Scenario to the Fcst_M1 Scenario. Note that we are able to use Scenario in the Destination Script. This means that *all* data from Budget will be copied to `Fcst_M1`. Integrating logic to only copy certain Entities, Accounts, or Time can make your seeding rules much more dynamic, so you'll likely need the full arsenal of Business Rule writing skills you've learned so far in this book to tackle more complex requirements.

Next, let's look at a situation with a bit more complexity.

Forecast Seeding Example

In this example, we will seed data for a Forecast Scenario. This Scenario, named `Fcst_M4`, will contain three months of Actual data and nine months of Forecast to arrive at a full-year projection.

Scenario:	Forecast_M4											
Plan Period:	1	2	3	4	5	6	7	8	9	10	11	12
Data:	Actual	Actual	Actual	Forecast	Forecast	Forecast	Forecast	Forecast	Forecast	Forecast	Forecast	Forecast

Figure 8.37

To get this rule to work correctly, we will need to perform some logic on the current Time being processed, so that the copy only occurs on months 1-3.

```
'Seeding rule that is NOT dynamic.
'Only run for Base Entities and Local currency
If (Not api.Entity.HasChildren()) And api.Cons.IsLocalCurrencyForEntity()
    'Get the month number from the current time period being processed
    Dim curMonthNumber As Integer = TimeDimHelper.GetSubComponentsFromId(api.Pov.Time.MemberId).Month
    If curMonthNumber.Equals(1) Or
        curMonthNumber.Equals(2) Or
        curMonthNumber.Equals(3) Then
        'Clear previously calculated Data
        api.Data.ClearCalculatedData(True,True,True,True)

        api.Data.Calculate("S#Fcst_M4 = RemoveZeros(S#Actual)",True)
    End If
End If
```

The above rule would work, but it isn't very maintenance-friendly because it would only work for the `Fcst_M4` Scenario. Other Forecast Scenarios would need to have separate rules with identical logic, except for the number of months referenced in the `If` statement. Any changes to the seeding logic would require each rule to be changed. Let's try to write this to be a bit more dynamic, so that we can cover all Forecast Scenarios with one rule. There are a couple of techniques to consider.

Using the Scenario Name

In our example, each Scenario name contains a suffix that denotes the month in which the Forecast is prepared. We can parse out this suffix, using the `InStr` and `Mid` VB.NET functions from the Scenario name, and determine which month to copy in Actuals. Now the same rule can be used for all Forecast Scenarios.

```
'Seeding rule that is based on the month suffix in the scenario name
'Since Forecast_M1 will not contain any Actuals, do not run
If Not api.Pov.Scenario.Name.XFEqualsIgnoreCase("Forecast_M1")
    'Only run for Base Entities and Local currency
    If (Not api.Entity.HasChildren()) And api.Cons.IsLocalCurrencyForEntity()
        'Get the month number from the current time period being processed
        Dim curMonthNumber As Integer = TimeDimHelper.GetSubComponentsFromId(api.Pov.Time.MemberId).Month
        'Get the current scenario name
        Dim curScenarioName As String = api.Pov.Scenario.Name
        'Get the forecast month from the suffix in the scenario name
        Dim curFcstMonth As Integer = Mid(curScenarioName,InStr(curScenarioName,"M")+1,2)
        'Only perform the seeding if the current month is less than the forecast month
        If curMonthNumber < curFcstMonth Then
            'Clear previously calculated Data
            api.Data.ClearCalculatedData(True,True,True,True)

            api.Data.Calculate("S#" & curScenarioName & " = RemoveZeros(S#Actual)",True)
        End If
    End If
End If
```

Using No Input Periods

Scenario Members have a property called **Number Of No Input Periods Per Workflow Unit** that restricts inputs to entire Time periods for a Scenario. This setting is often used in Forecast Scenarios to restrict inputs on already-closed Actual months. This setting can also be referenced in seeding rules to determine which months Actual data should be copied to.

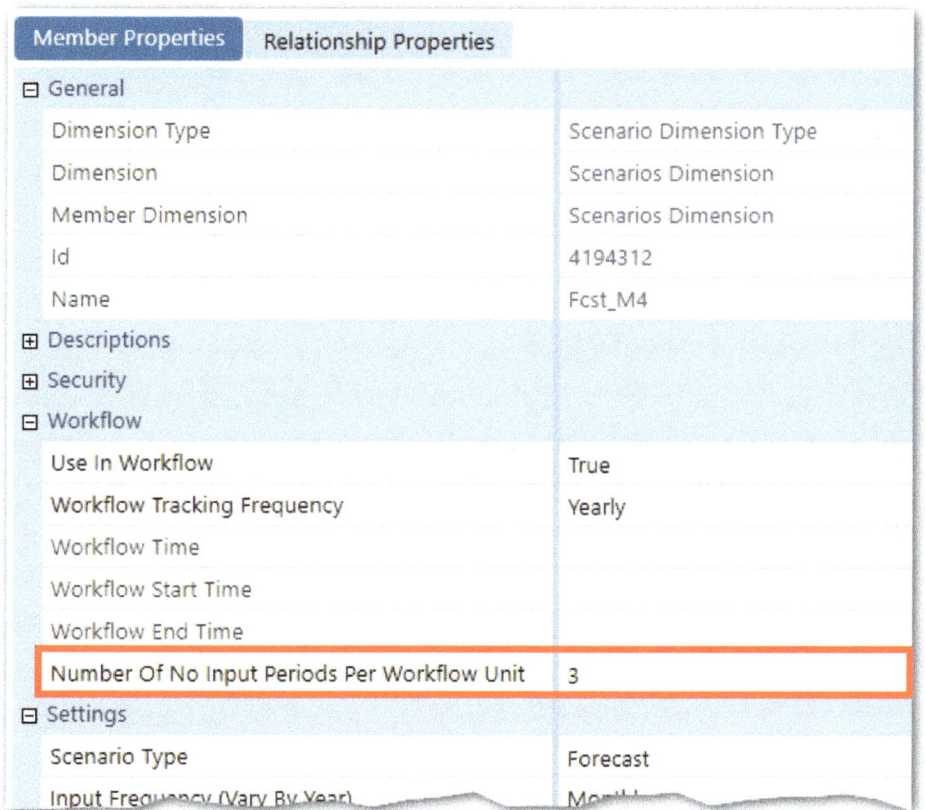

Figure 8.38

The `api.Scenario.GetWorkflowNumNoInputTimePeriods` is used to access the Scenario property, and used in the seeding logic.

Chapter 8

```
'Seeding rule that is based on the numer of No Input Periods in the Scenario Properties
'Since Forecast_M1 will not contain any Actuals, do not run
If Not api.Pov.Scenario.Name.XFEqualsIgnoreCase("Forecast_M1")
    'Only run for Base Entities and Local currency
    If (Not api.Entity.HasChildren()) And api.Cons.IsLocalCurrencyForEntity()
        'Get the month number from the current time period being processed
        Dim curMonthNumber As Integer = TimeDimHelper.GetSubComponentsFromId(api.Pov.Time.MemberId).Month
        'Get the current scenario name
        Dim curScenarioName As String = api.Pov.Scenario.Name
        'Get the forecast month from the No Input Periods Setting
        Dim curFcstMonth As Integer = api.Scenario.GetWorkflowNumNoInputTimePeriods()
        'Only perform the seeding if the current month is less than the forecast month
        If curMonthNumber < curFcstMonth Then
            'Clear previously calculated Data
            api.Data.ClearCalculatedData(True,True,True,True)

            api.Data.Calculate("S#" & curScenarioName & " = RemoveZeros(S#Actual)",True)
        End If
    End If
End If
```

Convert Extended Members

It is possible that dimensionality between the Scenarios that you are seeding may be different due to the use of Extensibility. If seeding from a Scenario with extended dimensionality, the extended Members must be converted to the dimensionality of the target Scenario. The `ConvertDataBufferExtendedMembers` function introduced in Chapter 3 can be used to do this automatically.

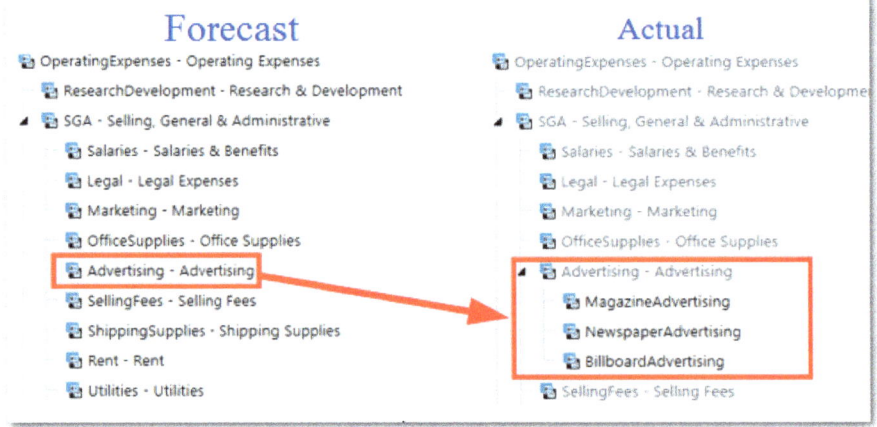

Figure 8.39

We will add this function to our seeding rule to convert the Actual Data Buffer to the dimensionality of the Forecast Scenario. A Data Buffer variable will be used to reference the converted Data Buffer in our `api.Data.Calculate` formula.

```
'Get the Actual Data Buffer and convert it
Dim actualDataBuffer As DataBuffer = api.Data.GetDataBufferUsingFormula("RemoveZeros(S#Actual)")
Dim convertedActualDataBuffer As DataBuffer
convertedActualDataBuffer = api.Data.ConvertDataBufferExtendedMembers(api.Pov.Cube.Name,"Actual",actualDataBuffer)
'Store the converted actual data buffer in a data buffer variable
api.Data.FormulaVariables.SetDataBufferVariable("ConvertedActuals",convertedActualDataBuffer,True)
'Only perform the seeding if the current month is less than the forecast month
If curMonthNumber < curFcstMonth Then
    'Clear previously calculated Data
    api.Data.ClearCalculatedData(True,True,True,True)
    api.Data.Calculate("S#" & curScenarioName & " = $ConvertedActuals",True)
End If
```

Figure 8.40

Allocation Calculations

Often, data needs to be allocated across Dimensions in order to align detail for comparative reporting across Scenarios, add analytic detail, or appropriately assign central costs. Calculations can be a convenient way to create allocations and several techniques we've learned along the way can be applied.

Using Unbalanced Functions

Back in Chapter 3, we introduced unbalanced functions that can be used in an `api.Data.Calculate` formula to perform math on Data Buffers with different dimensionality. These functions can be used for allocations by allocating a single data point over a Dimension using other data to form the allocation percentages. Let's look at an example where Forecast data is allocated over Accounts based on the distribution of Actuals.

In this example, our favorite stooge, Curly, is forecasting total SG&A Expenses for ACME Exterminators. Due to time constraints and available information, he can only Forecast total SG&A Expenses and cannot provide data at the detailed SGA Accounts where Actuals are reported. The CFO, Moe, pokes Curly in the eyes and demands to see the forecasted SG&A expenses at the same level as Actuals. To satisfy Moe, Curly has the idea of allocating the total SG&A expenses based on the detailed costs in Actuals. Luckily, Curly has read this book and remembers the unbalanced functions introduced in Chapter 3 and decides to apply them here.

The Setup

First, Curly sets up a supplemental Account to store the *pre-allocated* operating costs for the Forecast.

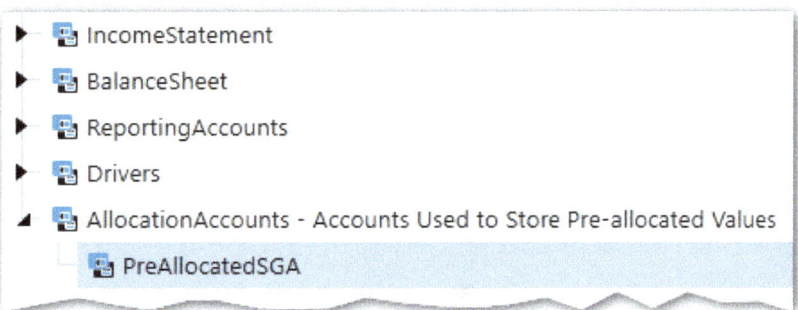

Figure 8.41

Next, he creates a Cube View to input the pre-allocated SG&A expense with the detailed Actuals displayed, which will be used for the allocation.

Chapter 8

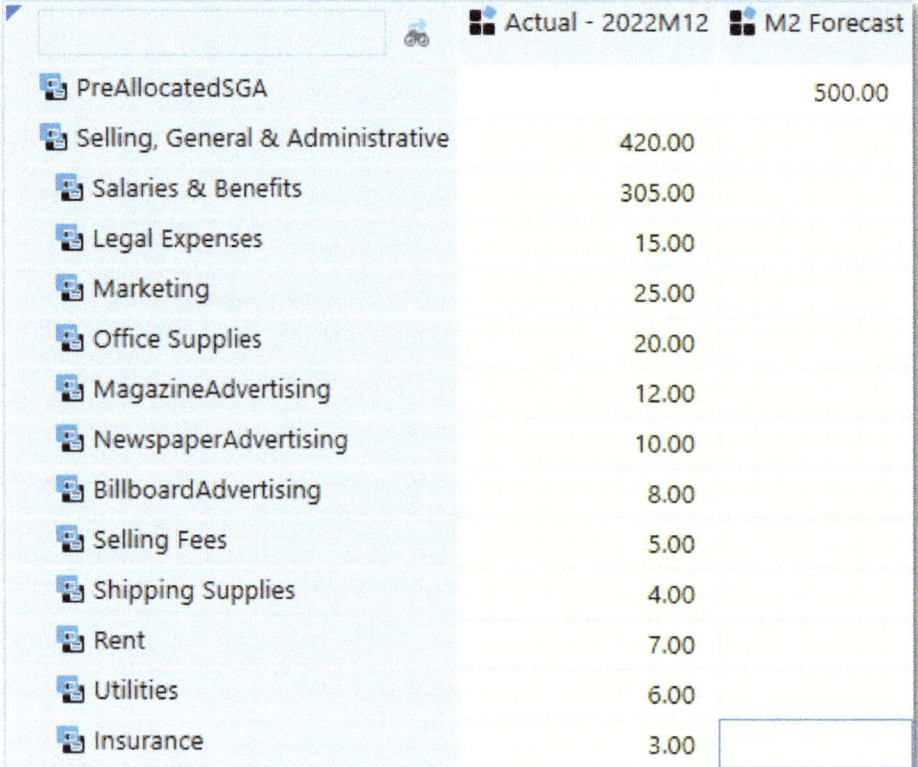

Figure 8.42

The goal is to allocate the 500 input to the `PreAllocatedSGA` Account across the detailed Accounts, based on the Actual data, using a Calculation.

The Calculation

Curly uses the unbalanced functions within an `api.Data.Calculate` function to achieve the above goal.

```
If ((Not api.Entity.HasChildren()) And (api.Cons.IsLocalCurrencyforEntity())) Then
    api.Data.ClearCalculatedData(True,True,True,True,"A#SGA.base")

    api.Data.Calculate("O#Import:I#None:F#EndBalLoad = " & _
    "RemoveZeros(MultiplyUnbalanced(DivideUnbalanced(T#POVPriorYearM12:S#Actual:O#Top:I#Top:F#EndBalLoad, " & _
    "T#POVPriorYearM12:S#Actual:A#SGA:O#Top:I#Top:F#EndBalLoad:U1#Top:U2#Top, A#SGA:U1#Top:U2#Top), " & _
    "A#PreAllocatedSGA:O#Top:I#Top:F#EndBalLoad:U1#None:U2#None, A#PreAllocatedSGA:U1#None:U2#None))","A#SGA.Base")

End If
```

Two nested unbalanced functions are used. Let's work inside out and analyze each one.

First, the `DivideUnbalanced` function takes the Actual data from the last period of the prior year for all SGA Accounts (via the filter) and divides by the total SGA.

```
Dim divideUnbalancedBuffer As DataBuffer
divideUnbalancedBuffer = api.Data.GetDataBufferUsingFormula("FilterMembers(DivideUnbalanced(" & _
"T#POVPriorYearM12:S#Actual:O#Top:I#Top:F#EndBalLoad, " & _
"T#POVPriorYearM12:S#Actual:A#SGA:O#Top:I#Top:F#EndBalLoad:U1#Top:U2#Top, A#SGA:U1#Top:U2#Top),A#SGA.Base)")
```

We can log the result of the `DivideUnbalanced` in a Data Buffer to see the results.

Common Rule Examples

![Figure 8.43 - Common Members data buffer listing with XFCommon allocations]

Figure 8.43

We now have a Data Buffer of our allocation percentages. Notice that the data cells within the Buffer contain details for U2 as well, which the pre-allocated data will inherit in the next step.

Next, we can multiply this Data Buffer by the `PreAllocatedSGA` Account using `MultiplyUnbalanced`. Each allocation percentage cell will get multiplied by the `PreAllocatedOpEx` data cell.

This results in detailed SG&A data adding up to our original 500 in Total Operating expenses. Moe is happy, which means no more eye pokes for Curly today!

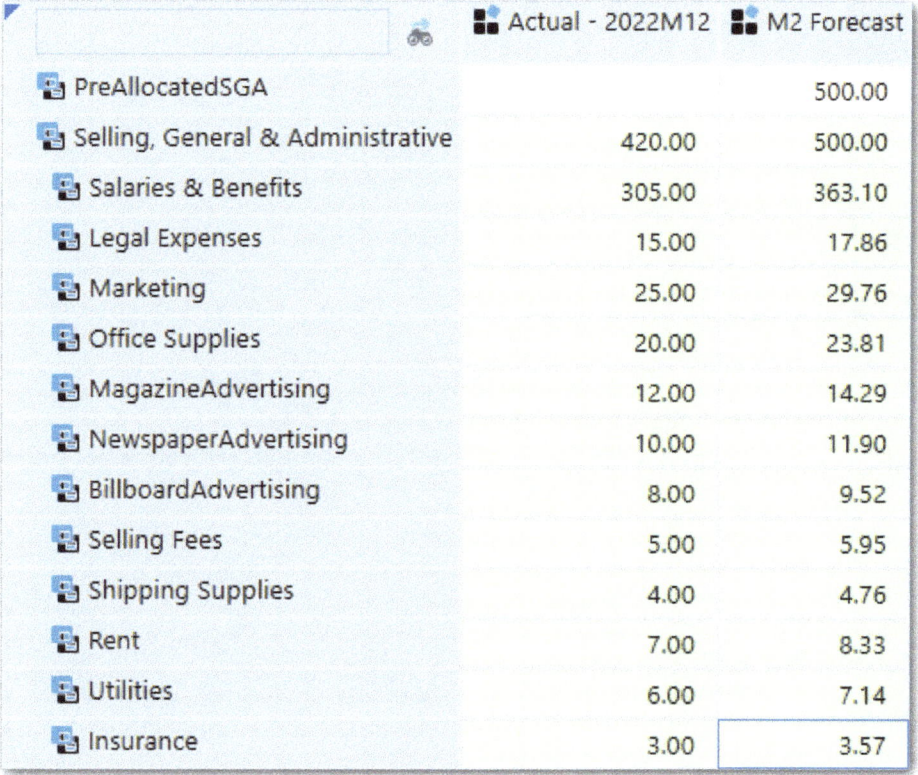

Figure 8.44

Using a Data Buffer Cell Loop

Allocations can also be done using a Data Buffer Cell Loop. Let's solve the same problem as above using the DBCL Method.

Calculation Abstract

Instead of leveraging the unbalanced functions in an ADC function, this Calculation will loop through a Data Buffer of all Actual SGA Expense data cells from the prior year, and use those cells as the basis of the allocation. Before starting the loop, Total SG&A expenses from Actuals and the

Chapter 8

`PreAllocatedOpEx` Account from `Fcst_M2` are retrieved. Actual total SG&A expenses will be used as the allocation denominator and multiplied by the `PreAllocatedOpEx` Account input by Curly.

Calculation Script and Breakdown

```
318  If ((Not api.Entity.HasChildren()) And (api.Cons.IsLocalCurrencyforEntity())) Then
319      'Clear the cells from previous calcs
320      api.Data.ClearCalculatedData(True,True,True,True,"A#SGA.base")
321      'Get the data buffer for the allocation detail cells
322      Dim sourceDataBuffer As DataBuffer
323      sourceDataBuffer = api.Data.GetDataBufferUsingFormula("Filtermembers(RemoveZeros(V#YTD:T#POVPriorYearM12:S#Actual" & _
324                                                          ":O#Top:I#Top:F#EndBalLoad), A#SGA.base)")
325      If Not sourceDataBuffer Is Nothing Then
326          'Create a data buffer that will fill with the source cells during the loop below
327          Dim resultDataBuffer As DataBuffer = New DataBuffer()
328          Dim destinationInfo As ExpressionDestinationInfo = api.Data.GetExpressionDestinationInfo("O#Import:I#None:F#EndBalLoad")
329
330          'Get the Total OpEx Account in the Actual Scenario which will be the denominator of the allocation
331          Dim totSGAValue As Decimal = api.Data.GetDataCell("V#YTD:T#POVPriorYearM12:S#Actual:O#Top:I#Top:A#SGA:F#EndBalLoad" & _
332                                                          ":U1#Top:U2#Top:U3#None:U4#None:U5#None:U6#None:U7#None:U8#None").CellAmount
333          'Get the Pre Allocated OpEx Account from the target scenario which is the amount to allocate
334          Dim preAllocatedSGAValue As Decimal = api.Data.GetDataCell("A#PreAllocatedSGA:I#Top:F#EndBalLoad:O#Top:U1#None:" & _
335                                                          "U2#None:U3#None:U4#None:U5#None:U6#None:U7#None:U8#None").CellAmount
336
337          'Loop through the cells in the data buffer
338          For Each sourceCell As DataBufferCell In sourceDataBuffer.DataBufferCells.Values
339              'Get the source cell amount
340              Dim sourceCellAmount As Decimal = sourceCell.CellAmount
341              'Create a new result cell with same dimensionality as the source cell
342              Dim resultCell As New DataBufferCell(sourceCell)
343
344              If totSGAValue <> 0 Then
345                  resultcell.CellAmount = (sourceCellAmount / totSGAValue) * preAllocatedSGAValue
346              End If
347              'Save the result cell into the result data buffer
348              resultDataBuffer.SetCell(api.SI,resultCell,True)
349          Next
350          'write the resulting new data set to the database.
351          api.Data.SetDataBuffer(resultDataBuffer,destinationInfo,,,,,,,,,,,,,,True)
352
353      End If
354  End If
```

Lines 318-320

```
318  If ((Not api.Entity.HasChildren()) And (api.Cons.IsLocalCurrencyforEntity())) Then
319      'Clear the cells from previous calcs
320      api.Data.ClearCalculatedData(True,True,True,True,"A#SGA.base")
```

The Calculation starts with an `If` statement, which restricts the scope of the Calculation to only run-on Base Entities and the Local Consolidation Member. A `ClearCalculatedData` function is also needed if this script is run as a Custom Calculate. If running this in a Member Formula, or as a Business Rule assigned to the Cube, this can be omitted.

Lines 321-325

```
321      'Get the data buffer for the allocation detail cells
322      Dim sourceDataBuffer As DataBuffer
323      sourceDataBuffer = api.Data.GetDataBufferUsingFormula("Filtermembers(RemoveZeros(V#YTD:T#POVPriorYearM12:S#Actual" & _
324                                                          ":O#Top:I#Top:F#EndBalLoad), A#SGA.base)")
325      If Not sourceDataBuffer Is Nothing Then
```

Next, a Data Buffer object is declared using the `GetDataBufferUsingFormula` for the prior year Actual SGA data. All UD Dimensions are left off the script so that details for those Dimensions (if they exist) will be included. The cells from this Data Buffer will be used as the basis for the allocation. An `If` statement checks to make sure the Data Buffer isn't empty before continuing.

Lines 326-328

```
326          'Create a data buffer that will fill with the source cells during the loop below
327          Dim resultDataBuffer As DataBuffer = New DataBuffer()
328          Dim destinationInfo As ExpressionDestinationInfo = api.Data.GetExpressionDestinationInfo("O#Import:I#None:F#EndBalLoad")
```

A Result Data Buffer is created, which will be used to add cells to – before eventually writing it to the Cube. A `DestinationInfo` object is created and set to the default Members for Origin,

Intercompany, and Flow Dimensions. This will be used to set the data cells in the Result Data Buffer when it is written to the Cube at the end of the rule.

Lines 330-335

```
330        'Get the Total OpEx Account in the Actual Scenario which will be the denominator of the allocation
331        Dim totSGAValue As Decimal = api.Data.GetDataCell("V#YTD:T#POVPriorYearM12:S#Actual:O#Top:I#Top:A#SGA:F#EndBalLoad" & _
332                                         ":U1#Top:U2#Top:U3#None:U4#None:U5#None:U6#None:U7#None:U8#None").CellAmount
333        'Get the Pre Allocated OpEx Account from the target scenario which is the amount to allocate
334        Dim preAllocatedSGAValue As Decimal = api.Data.GetDataCell("A#PreAllocatedSGA:I#Top:F#EndBalLoad:O#Top:U1#None:" & _
335                                         "U2#None:U3#None:U4#None:U5#None:U6#None:U7#None:U8#None").CellAmount
```

Data cell values – which will remain static throughout the Calculation – are retrieved before starting the `For`, `Each` loop. The prior year Total SG&A Expense for Actuals will be used as the denominator value for the allocation. Allocation percentages will be applied to the retrieved `PreAllocated` SGA value input by Curly in the `Fcst_M2` Scenario.

Lines 337-342

```
337        'Loop through the cells in the data buffer
338        For Each sourceCell As DataBufferCell In sourceDataBuffer.DataBufferCells.Values
339            'Get the source cell amount
340            Dim sourceCellAmount As Decimal = sourceCell.CellAmount
341            'Create a new result cell with same dimensionality as the source cell
342            Dim resultCell As New DataBufferCell(sourceCell)
```

These lines begin the `For`, `Each` Loop through the Source Data Buffer Cells. A new Result Data Buffer Cell is created, which inherits all the properties of the Source Cell. The Source Cell Amount is also retrieved, which will be used later.

Lines 344-348

```
344        If totSGAValue <> 0 Then
345            resultcell.CellAmount = (sourceCellAmount / totSGAValue) * preAllocatedSGAValue
346        End If
347        'Save the result cell into the result data buffer
348        resultDataBuffer.SetCell(api.SI,resultCell,True)
```

The allocation logic is performed by taking the Actual SGA Expense Detail Account (source cell Amount divided by the prior year Actual SGA), which creates the allocation percentage that is multiplied by the `PreAllocated` SGA value. An `If` statement is used to check whether the Total SGA is zero which would cause a Divide by Zero error. The result is set equal to the Result Cell and added to the Result Data Buffer.

Lines 349-351

```
349        Next
350        'write the resulting new data set to the database.
351        api.Data.SetDataBuffer(resultDataBuffer,destinationInfo,,,,,,,,,,,,,True)
```

After all the source cells have been processed, the loop ends, and the Result Data Buffer is written to the Cube using the `SetDataBuffer` function.

Allocations Across Entities

The previous examples have demonstrated how to allocate data across Account-level Dimensions within a single Entity. Allocating data from an Entity across other Entities will require some additional considerations. Calculated data in an Entity needed by other Entities for an allocation will not be available due to the multi-threading behaviour of the DUCS. It is also not possible to write data to Entities outside the current one being processed. Have we finally found a Calculation situation that we can't solve?

Chapter 8

The solution to this conundrum involves using a **BRAPI** function to execute a Custom Calculate function for other Entities while another Entity is being processed.

Example

To illustrate this example, we will continue with the previous SG&A allocation example. This allocation was run for the ACME Entity only and Moe instructs Curly that the allocated rent expense is incurred centrally and needs to be allocated to other Entities based on square footage.

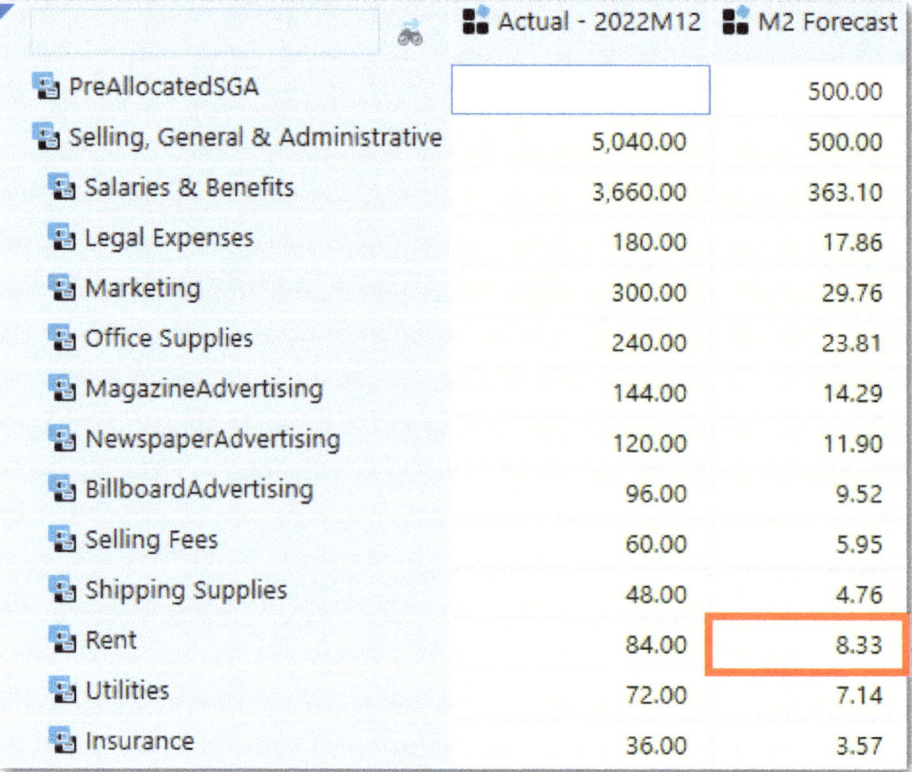

Figure 8.45

The Setup

Curly first sets up a driver Account for `Square Footage` for each Entity to input to.

Figure 8.46

Common Rule Examples

A Form is then created with square footage amounts entered into the `Square Footage` Account by Entity.

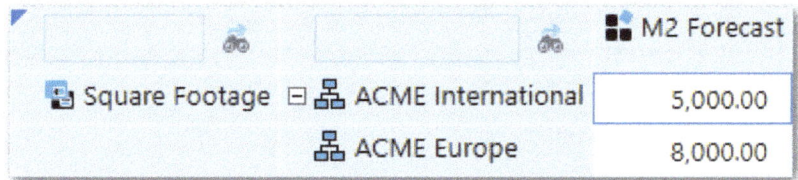

Figure 8.47

He then creates the rent cost allocation rule in a Custom Calculate function and modifies the SGA allocation rule to execute the Custom Calculate in ACME International and ACME Europe after the SGA Allocation for ACME.

Calculation Breakdown

SGA Allocation

The SGA Allocation Calculation that runs for ACME is modified to add a new script to execute the rent allocation Custom Calculate function (starting on line 285).

```
277  If ((Not api.Entity.HasChildren()) And (api.Cons.IsLocalCurrencyforEntity())) Then
278      api.Data.ClearCalculatedData(True,True,True,True,"A#SGA.base")
279
280      api.Data.Calculate("O#Import:I#None:F#EndBalLoad = " & _
281      "RemoveZeros(MultiplyUnbalanced(DivideUnbalanced(T#POVPriorYearM12:S#Actual:O#Top:I#Top:F#EndBalLoad, " & _
282      "T#POVPriorYearM12:S#Actual:A#SGA:O#Top:I#Top:F#EndBalLoad:U1#Top:U2#Top, A#SGA:U1#Top:U2#Top), " & _
283      "A#PreAllocatedSGA:O#Top:I#Top:F#EndBalLoad:U1#None:U2#None, A#PreAllocatedSGA:U1#None:U2#None))","A#SGA.Base")
284
285      'Create a list of entities to execute the custom calculate on
286      Dim entityList As List(Of Member) = api.Members.GetBaseMembers(api.Pov.EntityDim.DimPk,api.Members.GetMemberId(dimtypeid.Entity,"ACMEGroup"))
287      'Get the other data unit dimensions from the POV
288      Dim povCube As String = api.Pov.Cube.Name
289      Dim povScenario As String = api.Pov.Scenario.Name
290      Dim povTime As String = api.Pov.Time.Name
291      'Loop through the entities in the list and execute the custom calculate
292      For Each entity As Member In entityList
293          If Not entity.Name.Equals("ACME") Then 'Do not run for ACME since Rent expense is being distributed FROM this entity
294              'Create a dictionary of required parameters for the custom calculate function
295              Dim brParamDict As New Dictionary(Of String, String) From {{"Cube", povCube},
296                                                                         {"Entity", entity.Name},
297                                                                         {"Consolidation", "Local"},
298                                                                         {"Scenario", povScenario},
299                                                                         {"Time", povTime},
300                                                                         {"View", "YTD"}}
301              'Trigger custom calculate
302              BRApi.Finance.Calculate.ExecuteCustomCalculateBusinessRule(si, "Chapter8Examples", "RentAllocation", brParamDict, CustomCalculateTimeType.CurrentPeriod)
303          End If
304      Next entity
305
306      api.Data.ClearCalculatedData(True,True,True,True,"A#Rent")
307
```

Lines 277-284

```
277  If ((Not api.Entity.HasChildren()) And (api.Cons.IsLocalCurrencyforEntity())) Then
278      api.Data.ClearCalculatedData(True,True,True,True,"A#SGA.base")
279
280      api.Data.Calculate("O#Import:I#None:F#EndBalLoad = " & _
281      "RemoveZeros(MultiplyUnbalanced(DivideUnbalanced(T#POVPriorYearM12:S#Actual:O#Top:I#Top:F#EndBalLoad, " & _
282      "T#POVPriorYearM12:S#Actual:A#SGA:O#Top:I#Top:F#EndBalLoad:U1#Top:U2#Top, A#SGA:U1#Top:U2#Top), " & _
283      "A#PreAllocatedSGA:O#Top:I#Top:F#EndBalLoad:U1#None:U2#None, A#PreAllocatedSGA:U1#None:U2#None))","A#SGA.Base")
```

This part of the Calculation was described above and allocated the `PreAllocatedSGA` costs to the detailed SGA Accounts based on the distribution of Actuals.

Lines 285-290

```
285      'Create a list of entities to execute the custom calculate on
286      Dim entityList As List(Of Member) = api.Members.GetBaseMembers(api.Pov.EntityDim.DimPk,api.Members.GetMemberId(dimtypeid.Entity,"ACMEGroup"))
287      'Get the other data unit dimensions from the POV
288      Dim povCube As String = api.Pov.Cube.Name
289      Dim povScenario As String = api.Pov.Scenario.Name
290      Dim povTime As String = api.Pov.Time.Name
```

The `BRApi.Finance.Calculate.ExecuteCustomCalculateBusinessRule` requires the Dictionary of Name Value pairs which will determine the Data Units for which the rule runs for.

Chapter 8

This is required since the Custom Calculate function is running outside of a Data Management step where the Data Unit would normally be defined.

```
Sub BRApiFinanceCalculate.ExecuteCustomCalculateBusinessRule(si As SessionInfo, brName As String, functionName As String, nameValuePairs As Dictionary(Of String, String), timeType As CustomCalculateTimeType)
```

Figure 8.48

These lines will declare the variables that will define the Data Unit Dimensions. These variables will later be added to the Dictionary which is passed into the `ExecuteCustomCalculateBusinessRule` function. The Entity List is created from the Base Members of the `ACMEGroup` Member which will represent the list of Entities that the rent costs will be allocated to.

Lines 291-293

```
291    'Loop through the entities in the list and execute the custom calculate
292    For Each entity As Member In entityList
293        If Not entity.Name.Equals("ACME") Then 'Do not run for ACME since Rent expense is being distributed FROM this entity
```

The Entity list created in line 293 is looped through. An `If` Statement explicitly skips ACME as this Entity will be in the list but should not have costs allocated to it (since we are allocating costs *from it*).

Lines 294-300

```
294        'Create a dictionary of required parameters for the custom calculate function
295        Dim brParamDict As New Dictionary(Of String, String) From {{"Cube", povCube},
296                                                                   {"Entity", entity.Name},
297                                                                   {"Consolidation", "Local"},
298                                                                   {"Scenario", povScenario},
299                                                                   {"Time", povTime},
300                                                                   {"View", "YTD"}}
```

Inside the Entity List loop, a new Dictionary object is created and the Data Unit parameters are added. The Entity is added from the current loop iterations and the rest of the Data Unit Dimensions are defined from the POV.

Lines 301-302

```
301    'Trigger custom calculate
302    BRApi.Finance.Calculate.ExecuteCustomCalculateBusinessRule(si, "Chapter8Examples", "RentAllocation", brParamDict, CustomCalculateTimeType.CurrentPeriod)
```

The `BRApi.Finance.Calculate.ExecuteCustomCalculateBusinessRule` is called with the Business Rule name, function, and Name Value pairs Dictionary passed in. The last parameter is the `CustomCalculateTimeType` which is an enumerable.

Common Rule Examples

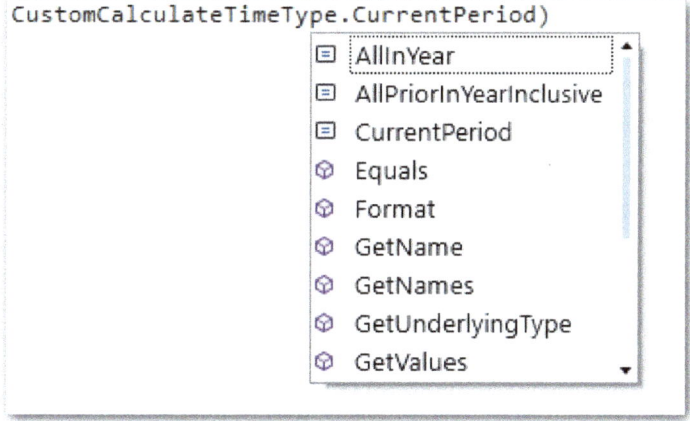

Figure 8.49

`CurrentPeriod` is selected as we only want to execute the function for the current period being processed.

Line 306

```
306    api.Data.ClearCalculatedData(True,True,True,True,"A#Rent")
```

The rent expense for ACME is cleared using the `ClearCalculatedData` function after the data is allocated to the other Entities.

Rent Allocation

```
If ((Not api.Entity.HasChildren()) And (api.Cons.IsLocalCurrencyforEntity())) Then
    api.Data.ClearCalculatedData(True,True,True,True,"A#Rent")
    Dim totalSquareFootage As Decimal = api.Functions.GetEntityAggregationDataCell("E#ACMEGroup:O#Top:I#Top:F#EndBalLoad:A#SquareFootage:" & _
        "U1#None:U2#None:U3#None:U4#None:U5#None:U6#None:U7#None:U8#None").CellAmount

    api.Data.Calculate("A#Rent:I#None:O#Import = RemoveZeros(MultiplyUnbalanced(C#Local:E#ACME:A#Rent:O#Top:I#Top, " & _
        "Divide(A#Squarefootage:O#Top:I#Top:U1#None:U2#None, " & totalSquareFootage & "),U1#None:U2#None))",True)
End If
```

The rent allocation Custom Calculate Function executes an ADC function which takes the total square footage (via the `api.Functions.GetEntityAggregationDataCell` function), and divides by the square footage of each Entity. The result is then multiplied against the total rent from the original allocation in the central Entity (ACME). A `MultiplyUnbalanced` function is used due to differing dimensionality between `Rent` (calculated with Cost Center detail) and `Square Footage` (input at U2#None).

Results

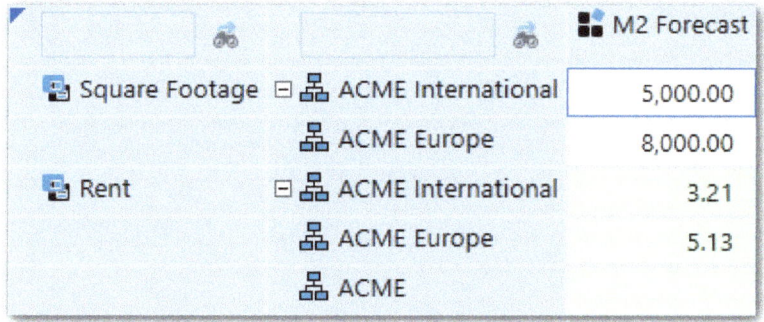

Figure 8.50

Budget and Forecast Calculations

By their very nature, Forecast and Budget Scenarios often rely heavily on Calculations performed in the OneStream Finance Engine. Below are examples of the types of Calculations that are often encountered.

- Driver-Based Calculations – using drivers such as Price and Quantity to derive a Forecast or Budget.

- Factor-Based Calculations – using Actual data as a baseline and applying a growth or inflation rate to derive a Forecast or Budget.

- Seeding Calculations – copying of data (such as Actuals) into a Forecast or Budget to derive a total calendar year of data.

- Allocations – due to timing constraints and availability of data, Forecast or Budget data may lack the same detail as Actuals. Actual data can be used as a basis to allocate data to the detail required for like-for-like comparative reporting.

Throughout this chapter and previous chapters of this book, numerous examples of the above Calculations have been explained and outlined so they won't be repeated here. I am confident in stating that the full arsenal of Calculation skills and techniques learned in this book will certainly be required when building a sophisticated Budget or Forecast solution.

Variance Analysis Calculations

Sometimes referred to as **Waterfall Analysis**, companies use variance analysis to gain insight into Income Statement Account fluctuations from period to period, or Scenario to Scenario. For example, a company may want to analyze why sales decreased 20% from last year; a price decrease or lower sales volume may have contributed to the decline.

Simple variance analysis can be done within Dynamic Calculations if possible. More complex variance analysis may need to consider other data points and can be done in a stored Member Formula or Custom Calculate. The Flow Dimension is a logical place to store these Calculations.

Let's go through a few examples.

Simple Variance

The simplest version of a variance Calculation would be the current period subtracted from the prior period to show the year over year change. A dynamically calculated Flow Member named `SimpleVariance_PY` is created.

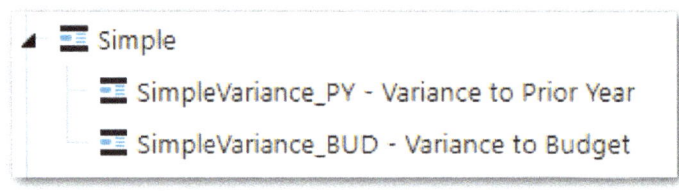

Figure 8.51

Common Rule Examples

Formula Type is set to DynamicCalc:

Figure 8.52

A simple formula within a `GetDataCell` function subtracts the current period (inherited from the Report) from the same period in the prior year, using the `POVPrior12` function.

```
Return api.Data.GetDataCell("BWDiff(F#EndBalLoad, F#EndBalLoad:T#POVPrior12)")
```

The `BWDiff` function is used so that Account Type is taken into consideration. This will treat a decline in revenue Account as negative variance and a decline in expenses as positive.

The `SimpleVariance_PY` Member can be referenced in a Cube View.

Chapter 8

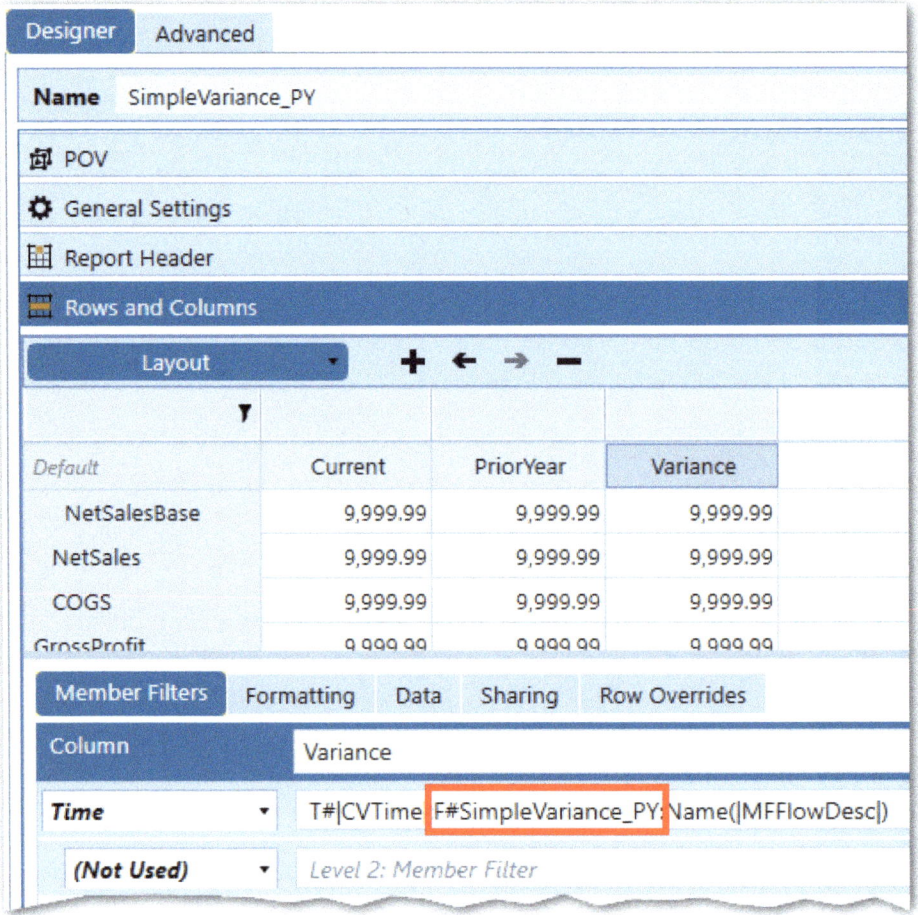

Figure 8.53

A similar Calculation can be written on the `SimpleVariance_BUD` Member to show the variance from Actual to Budget.

```
Return api.Data.GetDataCell("BWDiff(F#EndBalLoad, F#EndBalLoad:S#Budget)")
```

Detailed Variance Calculation

While useful – if only for the purpose of performing quick math in a Report – our simple Calculation doesn't tell much of a story to explain what occurred to cause the variance. An increase in the Cost of Goods Sold Account from a prior period could be due to several factors, such as a higher sales volume or an increase in raw material prices. If this data is available, it can be used in a Calculation to provide a more detailed explanation of the variance. Below are some common variance types:

- Volume – based on the quantity driver associated with a specific Account.
- Price – based on the price driver associated with a specific Account.
- FX – based on the change in exchange rates.
- Mix – acts as a plug between the total variance and the total of the other variances' Members.

Examples of how the above variance types might be calculated will be explained in detail below. Note that these examples are highly dependent on the availability of necessary data. This data can exist in another Cube, Scenario, or an internal or external data table and should have at least some Dimension commonality with the source data.

Dimension Member Setup

Flow Members will be setup to hold the calculated data of each variance type. A suffix of _PM will be used to distinguish that the Members are related to the variance to the Prior Month. Other suffixes can be used too for other variances, such as the variance to Prior Year (_PY) or Budget (_BUD).

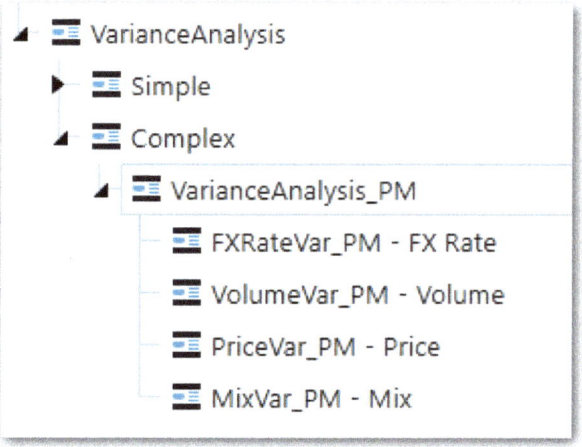

Figure 8.54

FX Rate Variance Calculation

Required Data

To properly calculate the FX Rate effect, data must be available in the transactional currency from the source system. For example, raw materials could be sourced from multiple countries and costs incurred in the local currency. Transactional Currency Flow Members can be set up to store the transactional currency.

Chapter 8

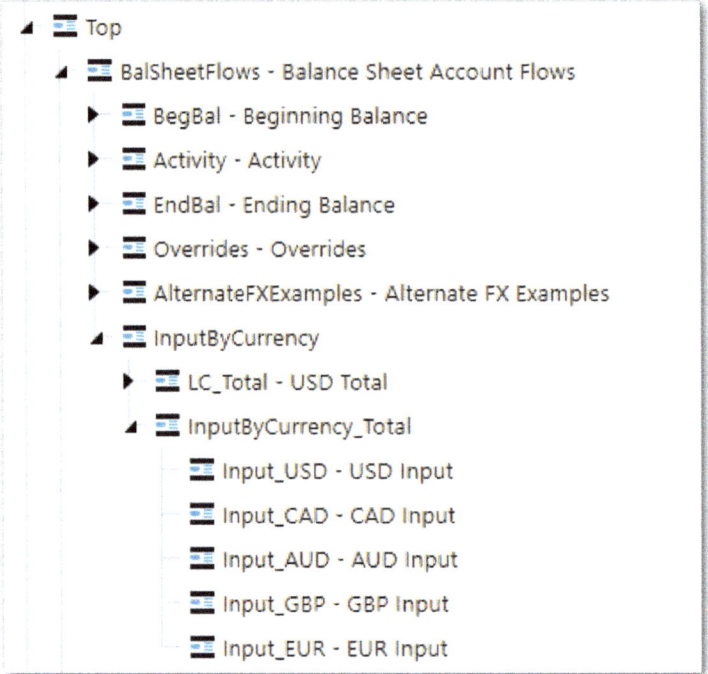

Figure 8.55

FX Rates will also need to be loaded for each transactional currency.

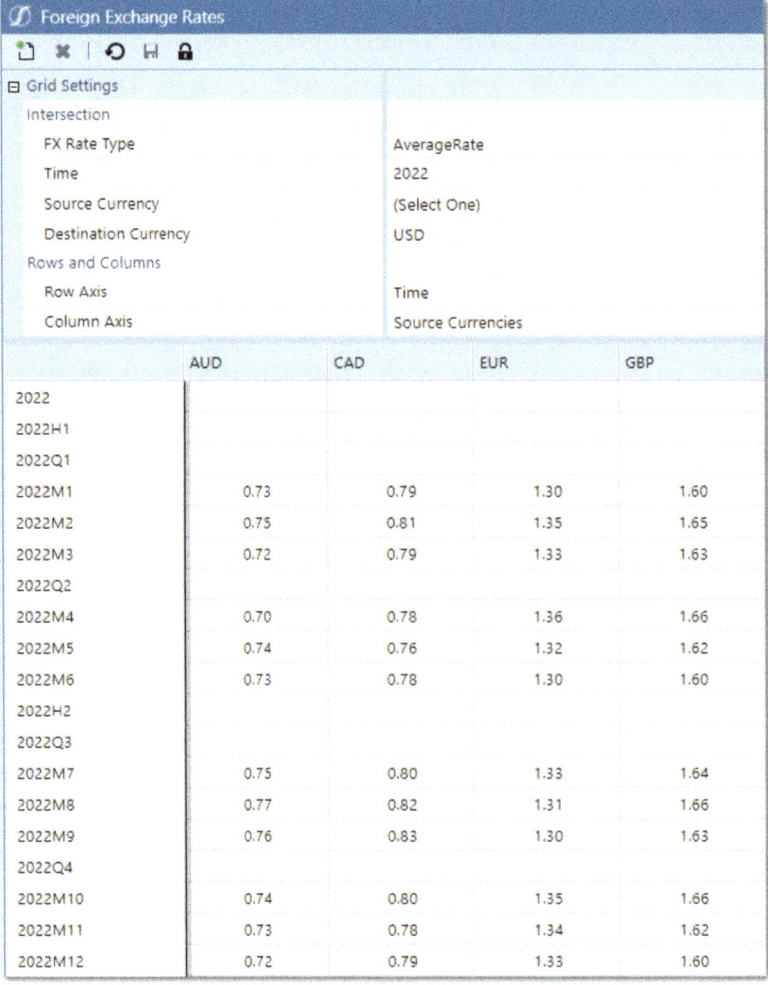

Figure 8.56

The transactional data stored in the above Flow Members will be translated to the Entity's currency during the DUCS and stored in other Flow Members within `LC_Total`.

Figure 8.57

The translated currencies are then aggregated to `LC_Total` and copied into the `EndBalLoad` Member via an `api.Data.Calculate` function.

```
If ((Not api.Entity.HasChildren()) And (api.Cons.IsLocalCurrencyforEntity())) Then
    If api.Entity.Text(1).XFEqualsIgnoreCase("MultiCurrency") Then
        api.data.Calculate("F#EndBalLoad = F#LC_Total")
    End If
End If
```

While the data is ultimately translated and totaled to the reporting currency, the transactional details are still present and can be accessed within the variance Calculation.

Calculation Abstract

Our FX Variance Calculation will use the transactional currency details to determine the effect that FX rates had on sales.

The Calculation will subtract the prior year's transactional currency amount (translated at the current FX rate) by the prior year's transactional currency amount translated at the prior year's FX rate. Written as a formula, it looks like this:

(Prior Period's Transactional Currency Amount * Current Rate) – (Prior Period's Transactional Currency Amount * Prior Rate)

Calculation Script and Breakdown

The Calculation needs to consider the transaction currency amounts stored in the Flow Dimensions and parse the currency from the Flow name so that the rates can be retrieved. This type of analysis cannot be done with an ADC function, so we will deploy the Data Buffer Cell Loop technique.

Chapter 8

```
152    'Run only for local currency and base entities
153    If (api.Cons.IsLocalCurrencyForEntity() And Not api.Entity.HasChildren()) Then
154        'Clear the cells from previous calcs
155        api.Data.ClearCalculatedData(True,True,True,True,,"F#FXRateVar_PM")
156        'Get the data buffer for the comprative period
157        Dim sourceDataBuffer As DataBuffer
158        sourceDataBuffer = api.Data.GetDataBufferUsingFormula("Filtermembers(RemoveZeros(V#Periodic:T#POVPrior1), " & _
159        "A#IncomeStatement.base, F#InputByCurrency_Total.Base)")
160        If Not sourceDataBuffer Is Nothing Then
161            'Create a data buffer that will fill with the source cells during the loop below
162            Dim resultDataBuffer As DataBuffer = New DataBuffer()
163            Dim destinationInfo As ExpressionDestinationInfo = api.Data.GetExpressionDestinationInfo("FXRateVar_PM")
164            'Get some variables from the Data Unit POV that are needed later
165            Dim timeID As Integer = api.pov.Time.MemberId
166            Dim priTimeID As Integer = TimeDimHelper.GetPriorPeriod(timeId)
167            Dim cubeID As Integer = api.pov.Cube.CubeId
168            'Get some variables needed to retrieve the FX Rates
169            Dim destCurrencyID As Integer = Currency.USD.Id 'This assumes USD is the application reporting currency
170            Dim RateTypeRev As FxRateType = api.FxRates.GetFxRateTypeForRevenueExp()
171            'Loop through the cells in the data buffer
172            For Each sourceCell As DataBufferCell In sourceDataBuffer.DataBufferCells.Values
173                'Declare a resultcell which will be used
174                Dim resultCell As New DataBufferCell(sourceCell)
175                'Get the source cell amount
176                Dim sourceCellAmount As Decimal = sourceCell.CellAmount
177                'Get the Flow Name from the source cell being processed
178                Dim flowName As String = sourceCell.DataBufferCellPk.GetFlowName(api)
179                'Parse the currency member out of the source cell flow member
180                Dim sourceCurrencyName As String = Right(flowname,3)
181                Dim sourceCurrencyID As Integer = api.Cons.GetCurrency(sourceCurrencyName).Id
182                'Get the current and prior year's FX Rates
183                Dim curAverageRate As Decimal = api.FxRates.GetCalculatedFxRate(RateTypeRev, cubeId, TimeId, sourceCurrencyID,destCurrencyID)
184                Dim priAverageRate As Decimal = api.FxRates.GetCalculatedFxRate(RateTypeRev, cubeId, priTimeID, sourceCurrencyID,destCurrencyID)
185                'Perform the calculation logic using the source cell amount and the
186                If Not curAverageRate = 0.0 And Not priAverageRate = 0.0 Then
187                    resultcell.CellAmount = (sourceCellAmount * curAverageRate) - (sourceCellAmount * priAverageRate)
188                End If
189                'Save the result cell into the result data buffer
190                resultDataBuffer.SetCell(api.SI,resultCell,True)
191            Next
192            'write the resulting new data set to the database.
193            api.Data.SetDataBuffer(resultDataBuffer,destinationInfo,,,,,,,,,,,,,True)
194        End If
195    End If
```

Lines 152-155

```
152    'Run only for local currency and base entities
153    If (api.Cons.IsLocalCurrencyForEntity() And Not api.Entity.HasChildren()) Then
154        'Clear the cells from previous calcs
155        api.Data.ClearCalculatedData(True,True,True,True,,"F#FXRateVar_PM")
```

The Calculation starts with an `If` statement, which restricts the scope of the Calculation to only execute at Base Entities and the Local Consolidation Member. A `ClearCalculated` data statement is also needed if this script is run as a Custom Calculate. If running this in a Member Formula, or as a Business Rule assigned to the Cube, this can be omitted.

Lines 156-160

```
156    'Get the data buffer for the comprative period
157    Dim sourceDataBuffer As DataBuffer
158    sourceDataBuffer = api.Data.GetDataBufferUsingFormula("Filtermembers(RemoveZeros(V#Periodic:T#POVPrior1), " & _
159    "A#IncomeStatement.base, F#InputByCurrency_Total.Base)")
160    If Not sourceDataBuffer Is Nothing Then
```

Next, a Data Buffer object is declared using the `GetDataBufferUsingFormula` for the prior year's data. Prior year's data is used as the source buffer as opposed to the current year's data because there is no FX Rate effect to calculate if the prior period is 0 (or NoData). A filter is applied to the Data Buffer Cells so that the Calculation only runs for `IncomeStatement` Accounts and transactional currency Flow Members.

Before continuing, an `If` statement checks that the Data Buffer is not empty so that it does not waste processing effort if it is.

Common Rule Examples

Lines 161-163

```
161         'Create a data buffer that will fill with the source cells during the loop below
162         Dim resultDataBuffer As DataBuffer = New DataBuffer()
163         Dim destinationInfo As ExpressionDestinationInfo = api.Data.GetExpressionDestinationInfo("FXRateVar_PM")
```

A Result Data Buffer and destination info object are created, which will be used to add cells to, before eventually writing to the Cube.

Lines 164-170

```
164         'Get some variables from the Data Unit POV that are needed later
165         Dim timeID As Integer = api.pov.Time.MemberId
166         Dim priTimeID As Integer = TimeDimHelper.GetPriorPeriod(timeId)
167         Dim cubeID As Integer = api.pov.Cube.CubeId
168         'Get some variables needed to retrieve the FX Rates
169         Dim destCurrencyID As Integer = Currency.USD.Id 'This assumes USD is the application reporting currency
170         Dim RateTypeRev As FxRateType = api.FxRates.GetFxRateTypeForRevenueExp()
```

These lines declare variables related to the result data cells, POV Members, and FX Rates. Each of these will be used later in the Calculation.

Lines 171-176

```
171         'Loop through the cells in the data buffer
172         For Each sourceCell As DataBufferCell In sourceDataBuffer.DataBufferCells.Values
173             'Declare a resultcell which will be used
174             Dim resultCell As New DataBufferCell(sourceCell)
175             'Get the source cell amount
176             Dim sourceCellAmount As Decimal = sourceCell.CellAmount
```

These lines begin the `For`, `Each` loop through the Source Data Buffer Cells. A new Result Data Buffer Cell is created, which inherits all the properties of the Source Cell. The properties of the Result Data Cell will be manipulated and then eventually added to the Result Data Buffer. The Source Cell Amount is also retrieved, which will be used later.

Lines 177-184

```
177         'Get the Flow Name from the source cell being processed
178         Dim flowName As String = sourceCell.DataBufferCellPk.GetFlowName(api)
179         'Parse the currency member out of the source cell flow member
180         Dim sourceCurrencyName As String = Right(flowname,3)
181         Dim sourceCurrencyID As Integer = api.Cons.GetCurrency(sourceCurrencyName).Id
182         'Get the current and prior year's FX Rates
183         Dim curAverageRate As Decimal = api.FxRates.GetCalculatedFxRate(RateTypeRev, cubeId, TimeId, sourceCurrencyID,destCurrencyID)
184         Dim priAverageRate As Decimal = api.FxRates.GetCalculatedFxRate(RateTypeRev, cubeId, priTimeID, sourceCurrencyID,destCurrencyID)
```

These lines are related to retrieving both the current and prior year's FX Rates. The API function, `GetCalculatedFxRate` will be used, which requires several parameters. `RateType`, `CubeID`, `TimeID`, and `DestinationCurrency` have all been retrieved above the loop. Source currency is parsed from the source cell Flow Member. The Source Data Buffer specifically includes only Base Flow Members from the `InputByCurrency_Total`.

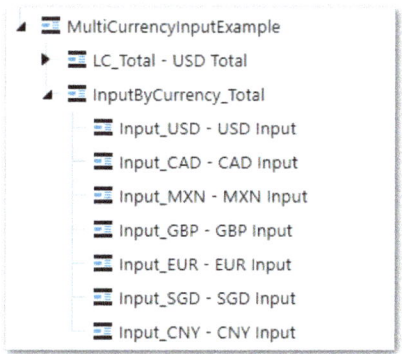

Figure 8.58

Chapter 8

The naming convention of these Members ensures that the currency is always the last three characters in the name. These characters are parsed out and passed into the `GetCalculatedFXRate` function.

Lines 185-188

```
185             'Perform the calculation logic using the source cell amount and the
186             If Not curAverageRate = 0.0 And Not priAverageRate = 0.0 Then
187                 resultcell.CellAmount = (sourceCellAmount * curAverageRate) - (sourceCellAmount * priAverageRate)
188             End If
```

These lines perform the Calculation logic using the retrieved FX Rates and the prior year's Amount (via the Source Cell). The result of the formula is then set equal to the Result Cell's Cell Amount. The Calculation is prevented from running with an `If` statement to check if the FX Rates are 0.

Lines 189-193

```
189             'Save the result cell into the result data buffer
190             resultDataBuffer.SetCell(api.SI,resultCell,True)
191         Next
192         'Write the resulting new data set to the database.
193         api.Data.SetDataBuffer(resultDataBuffer,destinationInfo,,,,,,,,,,,,,True)
```

The Result Cell is added to the Result Data Buffer. After all the Source Cells have been processed, the loop ends, and the Result Data Buffer is written to the Cube using the `SetDataBuffer` function. The `DestinationInfo` object is used to set the Flow Member of all Result Data Buffer Cells to the `FXRateVar_PY` Member.

Price and Volume Variance Calculation

Required Data

To properly calculate the Price and Volume Rate effects, Price and Volume driver data will need to be available for both the Time periods and/or Scenarios that you are comparing. In a driver-based Forecast or Budget, this data will likely already be available. Prices and Volume can also be loaded for Actuals from production systems to support the Calculation. For the sake of this example, we assume that Price and Volume data are available for all periods of Actuals.

Association of Driver to Account

For the Calculation to work, each Account must have a Price and Volume driver associated with it. Again, if the Forecast or Budget is derived using drivers already, this information is available in the Calculation logic which isn't very convenient when needing to reference it in another Calculation.

Text properties on the Account can be used to associate each Account with a driver. For our example, the Text 3 property will store the Price driver and Text 4 will store the Volume driver. Below is an example for both the Sales and COGS Accounts.

Sales:

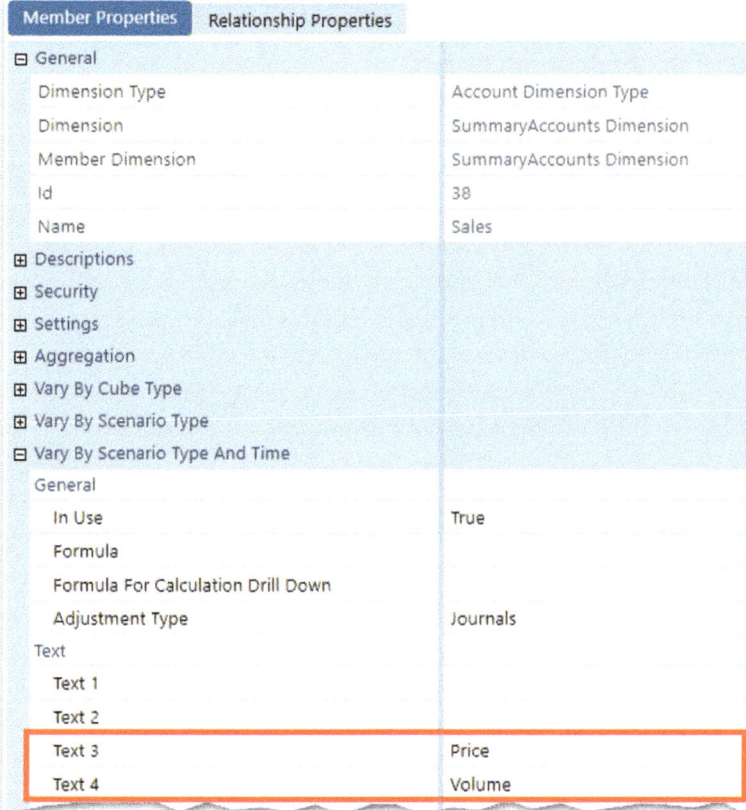

Figure 8.59

COGS:

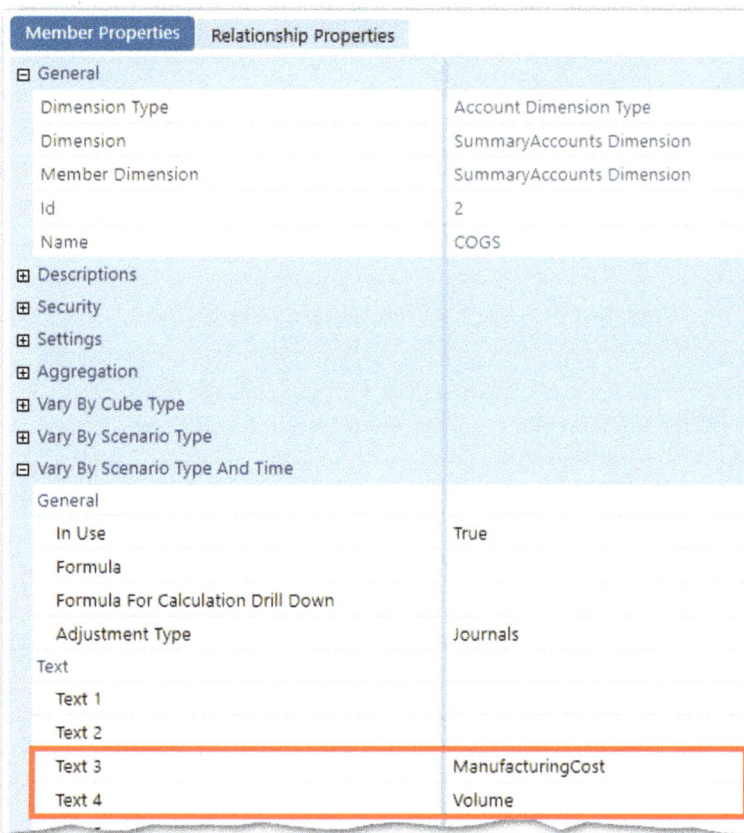

Figure 8.60

Calculation Abstract

Our Price and Volume variance Calculation will use the driver values (determined from the Account Text properties) from the current and comparative periods to measure the impact the changes in the driver values had on the variance.

Price Variance

The formula for the Price variance is:

(Current Volume * (Current Price – Comparative Price)) – FX Rate Variance

Since prices are in USD, the FX Rate Variance (calculated earlier) is backed out.

Volume Variance

The formula for the Volume variance is:

(Comparative Price * Current Volume) – (Comparative Price * Comparative Volume)

Calculation Script and Breakdown

The Calculation will loop through a Data Buffer of all Income Statement Accounts, retrieve the driver data, and perform the Calculation logic.

```vb
200  If (api.Cons.IsLocalCurrencyForEntity() And Not api.Entity.HasChildren()) Then
201      'Clear the cells from previous calcs
202      api.Data.ClearCalculatedData(True,True,True,True,,"F#VolumeVar_PM,F#PriceVar_PM")
203      'Get the data buffer that includes income statement data for both current period and comparative period
204      Dim sourceDataBuffer As DataBuffer
205      sourceDataBuffer = api.Data.GetDataBufferUsingFormula("Filtermembers(RemoveZeros(V#Periodic:T#POVPrior1:O#Top:I#Top:F#EndBalLoad + " & _
206                          "V#Periodic:O#Top:I#Top:F#EndBalLoad), A#IncomeStatement.base)")
207      If Not sourceDataBuffer Is Nothing
208          'Create a result data buffer that will fill with the source cells during the loop below
209          Dim resultDataBuffer As DataBuffer = New DataBuffer()
210          Dim destinationInfo As ExpressionDestinationInfo = api.Data.GetExpressionDestinationInfo("O#Import:I#None")
211          'Get the Member IDs for the target Flow members
212          Dim destFlowIDVolume As Integer = api.Members.GetMemberId(DimType.Flow.Id,"VolumeVar_PM")
213          Dim destFlowIDPrice As Integer = api.Members.GetMemberId(DimType.Flow.Id,"PriceVar_PM")
214          'loop through the cells in the databuffer
215          For Each sourceCell As DataBufferCell In sourceDataBuffer.DataBufferCells.Values
216              'Create new result cells for Price and Volume variances
217              Dim resultCellPrice As New DataBufferCell(sourceCell)
218              Dim resultCellVolume As New DataBufferCell(sourceCell)
219              'Retrieve the source cell member names to be used later
220              Dim sourceAccountName As String = sourceCell.DataBufferCellPk.GetAccountName(api)
221              'Build a member script for all source cell UD Members
222              Dim sourceUDMemberScript As String
223              sourceUDMemberScript = "U1#" & sourceCell.DataBufferCellPk.GetUD1Name(api) & ":" & _
224                  "U2#" & sourceCell.DataBufferCellPk.GetUD2Name(api) & ":" & _
225                  "U3#None:U4#None:U5#None:U6#None:U7#None:U8#None"
226              'Get the FX Rate Variance Amount for this account
227              Dim fxRateVarValue As Decimal = api.Data.GetDataCell("A#" & sourceAccountName & ":F#FXRateVar_PM:I#Top:O#Top:" & sourceUDMemberScript & "").CellAmount
228              'Get the cost values for both the current period and comparative period
229              Dim costValueComp As Decimal = 0.00
230              Dim costValueCurr As Decimal = 0.00
231              costValueComp = api.Data.GetDataCell("V#Periodic:T#POVPrior1:A#" & sourceAccountName & ":F#EndBalLoad:I#Top:O#Top:" & sourceUDMemberScript & "").CellAmount
232              costValueCurr = api.Data.GetDataCell("V#Periodic:A#" & sourceAccountName & ":F#EndBalLoad:I#Top:O#Top:" & sourceUDMemberScript & "").CellAmount

233              'Get the Driver values from the Text fields
234              Dim priceDriverName As String = api.account.Text(sourcecell.DataBufferCellPk.AccountId,3)
235              Dim volumeDriverName As String = api.account.Text(sourcecell.DataBufferCellPk.AccountId,4)
236              'Get the Price & Valume Driver values for both the current period and comparative period
237              Dim priceDriverValueComp As Decimal = 0.00
238              Dim priceDriverValueCurr As Decimal = 0.00
239              Dim volumeDriverValueCurr As Decimal = 0.00
240              Dim volumeDriverValueComp As Decimal = 0.00
241              priceDriverValueComp = api.Data.GetDataCell("V#Periodic:T#POVPrior1:A#" & priceDriverName & ":F#EndBalLoad:I#Top:O#Top:" & sourceUDMemberScript & "").CellAmount
242              priceDriverValueCurr = api.Data.GetDataCell("V#Periodic:A#" & priceDriverName & ":F#EndBalLoad:I#Top:O#Top:" & sourceUDMemberScript & "").CellAmount
243              volumeDriverValueCurr = api.Data.GetDataCell("V#Periodic:A#" & volumeDriverName & ":F#EndBalLoad:I#Top:O#Top:" & sourceUDMemberScript & "").CellAmount
244              volumeDriverValueComp = api.Data.GetDataCell("V#Periodic:T#POVPrior1:A#" & volumeDriverName & ":F#EndBalLoad:I#Top:O#Top:" & sourceUDMemberScript & "").CellAmount
245              'Calculate Price variance
246              resultCellPrice.CellAmount = ((volumeDriverValueCurr * (priceDriverValueCurr - priceDriverValueComp)) - fxRateVarValue)
247              'Calculate Volume variance
248              resultCellVolume.CellAmount = (priceDriverValueComp * volumeDriverValueCurr) - (priceDriverValueComp * volumeDriverValueComp)
249              'Set the result cell Flow Member
250              resultCellVolume.DataBufferCellPk.FlowId = destFlowIDVolume
251              resultCellPrice.DataBufferCellPk.FlowId = destFlowIDPrice
252              'Save the result cell into the result data buffer
253              resultDataBuffer.SetCell(api.SI,resultCellPrice,True)
254              resultDataBuffer.SetCell(api.SI,resultCellVolume,True)
255          Next
256          'Write the resulting new data set to the database.
257          api.Data.SetDataBuffer(resultDataBuffer,destinationInfo,,,,,,,,,,,,True)
258      End If
259  End If
```

Figure 8.61

Lines 200-202

```
200    If (api.Cons.IsLocalCurrencyForEntity() And Not api.Entity.HasChildren()) Then
201        'Clear the cells from previous calcs
202        api.Data.ClearCalculatedData(True,True,True,True,,"F#VolumeVar_PM,F#PriceVar_PM")
```

The Calculation starts with an `If` statement, which restricts the scope of the Calculation to only execute at Base Entities and the Local Consolidation Member. A `ClearCalculatedData` statement is also needed if the script is run as a Custom Calculate. If running the script in a Member Formula, or as a Business Rule assigned the Cube, this can be omitted.

Lines 203-207

```
203        'Get the data buffer that includes income statement data for both current period and comparative period
204        Dim sourceDataBuffer As DataBuffer
205        sourceDataBuffer = api.Data.GetDataBufferUsingFormula("Filtermembers(RemoveZeros(V#Periodic:T#POVPrior1:O#Top:I#Top:F#EndBalLoad + " & _
206                                                              "V#Periodic:O#Top:I#Top:F#EndBalLoad), A#IncomeStatement.base)")
207        If Not sourceDataBuffer Is Nothing
```

Next, a Data Buffer object is declared using the `GetDataBufferUsingFormula`. A math formula is used to add the prior period to the current year. This ensures that data is retrieved even if there is no data for one of the periods since we would still want to calculate a variance even if one of the periods had no data. A filter is applied to the Data Buffer Cells so that the Calculation only runs for `IncomeStatement` Accounts and transactional currency Flow Members.

Before continuing, an `If` statement checks that the Data Buffer is not empty so that it does not waste processing effort if it is.

Lines 208-213

```
208            'Create a result data buffer that will fill with the source cells during the loop below
209            Dim resultDataBuffer As DataBuffer = New DataBuffer()
210            Dim destinationInfo As ExpressionDestinationInfo = api.Data.GetExpressionDestinationInfo("O#Import:I#None")
211            'Get the Member IDs for the target Flow members
212            Dim destFlowIDVolume As Integer = api.Members.GetMemberId(DimType.Flow.Id,"VolumeVar_PM")
213            Dim destFlowIDPrice As Integer = api.Members.GetMemberId(DimType.Flow.Id,"PriceVar_PM")
```

A Result Data Buffer is created that will be used to add cells to, before eventually writing to the Cube. A `DestinationInfo` object is created with a Member script that defines the target Origin and Intercompany Members. Target Flow Members for both the Price and Volume variance Members are also retrieved before starting the loop. Flow is purposely left off the `DestinationInfo` script because we will be adding two result cells to the Result Data Buffer. Since `DestinationInfo` changes *all* cells in the Result Data Buffer, we will set the target Flow Members on the individual result cells using the Members declared above.

Lines 214-220

```
214            'loop through the cells in the databuffer
215            For Each sourceCell As DataBufferCell In sourceDataBuffer.DataBufferCells.Values
216                'Create new result cells for Price and Volume variances
217                Dim resultCellPrice As New DataBufferCell(sourceCell)
218                Dim resultCellVolume As New DataBufferCell(sourceCell)
219                'Retrieve the source cell member names to be used later
220                Dim sourceAccountName As String = sourceCell.DataBufferCellPk.GetAccountName(api)
```

These lines begin the `For`, `Each` loop through the Source Data Buffer Cells. Two new Result Data Buffer Cells are created for both the Volume and Price variance Calculation results. Both of these Result Cells inherit the properties of the source cell. The properties of the result data cells will be manipulated and then eventually added to the Result Data Buffer. The Account Name from the source cell is also retrieved to be used later.

Lines 221-225

```
221             'Build a member script for all source cell UD Members
222             Dim sourceUDMemberScript As String
223             sourceUDMemberScript = "U1#" & sourceCell.DataBufferCellPk.GetUD1Name(api) & ":" & _
224                 "U2#" & sourceCell.DataBufferCellPk.GetUD2Name(api) & ":" & _
225                 "U3#None:U4#None:U5#None:U6#None:U7#None:U8#None"
```

A Member script string is built using information from the source cell for UD1 and UD2. None is used for the other UDs since they are not used in our Cube. This Member script will be used when defining the full POV in the `GetDataCell` function, which will be used in the next lines to retrieve data cells needed for the Calculation.

Lines 226-232

```
226             'Get the FX Rate Variance Amount for this account
227             Dim fxRateVarValue As Decimal = api.Data.GetDataCell("A#" & sourceAccountName & ":F#FXRateVar_PM:I#Top:O#Top:" & sourceUDMemberScript & "").CellAmount
228             'Get the cost values for both the current period and comparative period
229             Dim costValueComp As Decimal = 0.00
230             Dim costValueCurr As Decimal = 0.00
231             costValueComp = api.Data.GetDataCell("V#Periodic:T#POVPrior1:A#" & sourceAccountName & ":F#EndBalLoad:I#Top:O#Top:" & sourceUDMemberScript & "").CellAmount
232             costValueCurr = api.Data.GetDataCell("V#Periodic:A#" & sourceAccountName & ":F#EndBalLoad:I#Top:O#Top:" & sourceUDMemberScript & "").CellAmount
```

These lines retrieve various data cell amounts for the which will be used in the variance Calculation logic. The data cell amounts for the FX Rate Variance (described earlier) and the cell amounts of the Income Statement Account for both the current and prior period are retrieved.

Lines 233-244

```
233             'Get the Driver values from the text fields
234             Dim priceDriverName As String = api.account.Text(sourcecell.DataBufferCellPk.AccountId,3)
235             Dim volumeDriverName As String = api.account.Text(sourcecell.DataBufferCellPk.AccountId,4)
236             'Get the Price & Value Driver values for both the current period and comparative period
237             Dim priceDriverValueComp As Decimal = 0.00
238             Dim priceDriverValueCurr As Decimal = 0.00
239             Dim volumeDriverValueCurr As Decimal = 0.00
240             Dim volumeDriverValueComp As Decimal = 0.00
241             priceDriverValueComp = api.Data.GetDataCell("V#Periodic:T#POVPrior1:A#" & priceDriverName & ":F#EndBalLoad:I#Top:O#Top:" & sourceUDMemberScript & "").CellAmount
242             priceDriverValueCurr = api.Data.GetDataCell("V#Periodic:A#" & priceDriverName & ":F#EndBalLoad:I#Top:O#Top:" & sourceUDMemberScript & "").CellAmount
243             volumeDriverValueCurr = api.Data.GetDataCell("V#Periodic:A#" & volumeDriverName & ":F#EndBalLoad:I#Top:O#Top:" & sourceUDMemberScript & "").CellAmount
244             volumeDriverValueComp = api.Data.GetDataCell("V#Periodic:T#POVPrior1:A#" & volumeDriverName & ":F#EndBalLoad:I#Top:O#Top:" & sourceUDMemberScript & "").CellAmount
```

These lines retrieve the driver data cell Amounts from the Driver Accounts defined in the Text 3 and Text 4 properties of the Account. The Text properties are retrieved using the `api.Account.Text` function with the Account from the source cell passed in. Using the values stored in the Text Properties, the Price and Volume cell amounts are retrieved for both the current and prior periods.

Lines 245-248

```
245             'Calculate Price variance
246             resultCellPrice.CellAmount = ((volumeDriverValueCurr * (priceDriverValueCurr - priceDriverValueComp)) - fxRateVarValue)
247             'Calculate Volume variance
248             resultCellVolume.CellAmount = (priceDriverValueComp * volumeDriverValueCurr) - (priceDriverValueComp * volumeDriverValueComp)
```

The Calculation logic is performed using the inputs retrieved in prior steps and the Result Cell's Cell Amounts are set.

Lines 249-257

```
249             'Set the result cell Flow Member
250             resultCellVolume.DataBufferCellPk.FlowId = destFlowIDVolume
251             resultCellPrice.DataBufferCellPk.FlowId = destFlowIDPrice
252             'Save the result cell into the result data buffer
253             resultDataBuffer.SetCell(api.SI,resultCellPrice,True)
254             resultDataBuffer.SetCell(api.SI,resultCellVolume,True)
255         Next
256         'Write the resulting new data set to the database.
257         api.Data.SetDataBuffer(resultDataBuffer,destinationInfo,,,,,,,,,,,,,,,True)
```

The `FlowIDs` of the Result Data Cells are set to the `PriceVar_PY` and `VolumeVar_PY` Members which were retrieved before the loop. All other Dimensions and properties of the Result Cell will be set using the `DestinationInfo` object or mirror the Source Cell. Next, the Result Cell is added to the Result Data Buffer. After all the Source Cells have been processed, the loop ends, and the Result Data Buffer is written to the Cube using the `SetDataBuffer` function.

Mix Calculation

The Mix Calculation will plug any difference between the total variance and the calculated FX, Price, and Volume variance effects. Differences will exist due to data inaccuracies, accruals or the timing of payments and sales. The Mix Calculation is a simple `api.Data.Calculate` function that subtracts the total variance from the FX, Price, and Volume variance Members.

```
If (api.Cons.IsLocalCurrencyForEntity() And Not api.Entity.HasChildren()) Then
    'Clear the cells from previous calcs
    api.Data.ClearCalculatedData(True,True,True,True,,"F#MixVar_PM")

    api.Data.Calculate("V#Periodic:F#MixVar_PM:I#None:O#Import = (V#Periodic:T#POVPrior1:F#EndBalLoad:I#Top:O#Top + " & _
    "V#Periodic:F#FXRateVar_PM:I#Top:O#Top + V#Periodic:F#PriceVar_PM:I#Top:O#Top + V#Periodic:F#VolumeVar_PM:I#Top:O#Top) - " & _
    "V#Periodic:F#EndBalLoad:I#Top:O#Top","A#IncomeStatement.Base",,,,,,,,,,,,,,,True)

End If
```

Results

After running all three Calculations, the results can be viewed in a Cube View which shows a 'walk' from the prior period to the current period sales amount.

	Prior Month	FX Rate	Price	Volume	Mix	Dec 2022
Sales	18,869.75	-117.32	367.06	-185.00	0.00	18,934.50
Cost of Goods Sold	7,102.57	-41.03	138.17	-69.63	0.00	7,130.08
Price	904.63					916.98
Volume	1,560.60					1,545.30

Figure 8.62

Conclusion

I hope this chapter has helped cement your understanding of the power and vast functionalities contained within the OneStream Finance Engine. The examples outlined in this chapter are far from an exhaustive list of everything you may encounter on a project. Rather, they are meant to provide real-world context of how the concepts and techniques covered in this book can enhance data to solve real-world business problems. Hopefully, at a minimum, these can be used as a starting point which can be adapted to fit specific situations.

Your journey of accumulating OneStream knowledge will not stop after reading this book just as mine hasn't stopped from writing it. There will always be new use cases, product enhancements, and other challenges that will have me using new functions or applying existing knowledge in a different way. I look forward to continuing to learn alongside you! Thanks for reading!

Index

#All - 57

Account-Level Dimensions - 48

Accounts - 210, 218

Action, Button Properties - 27

ActivityCalc - 200

Aggregated Member - 33

Aggregation - 123

Aggregation, In-Memory - 11

Allocation Calculations - 231

Allocation, Entities - 235

Alternate Hierarchies - 124

Api.Data.Calculate - 51, 52, 53, 82, 87, 142

Api.Data.Calculate, Loop - 182

Api.Data.Calculate, Stacking - 187

Api.Data.Calculate, Syntax - 51

Api.Data.ClearCalculatedData - 75, 185, 187

Api.Data.GetDataCell - 106, 107

Api.Data.SetCell, Loop - 183

Api.Members.GetMemberId - 90

Api.Pov Functions - 75

Api.Pov.Account - 64

Application Blending - 118

Application Reports - 130

Application Server Configuration File - 174

Arrays - 44

Auto-Translation Currencies - 194

Balance Sheet Calculations - 193

Balanced Data Buffers - 56

Base-Level Member - 39, 68

BegBalCalcYTD - 198

BegBalDynamic - 198

Beginning Balance - 198

BetterWorse - 113

BetterWorsePercent - 113

BI Blend - 182

BI Blend Engine - 6

Blank Cells - 42

Blending, Drill-Back - 118

Blending, Model - 118

Blending, Relational - 117

BRAPI - 9, 187

Budget Calculations - 240

Business Rule - 102

Business Rule Editor - 7, 9, 12, 136

Business Rule Library - 6

Business Rule, Cube - 22

Business Rule, Dynamic Calculations - 102

Business Rule, Engine Interaction - 6

Business Rule, Finance - 12

Business Rule, Finance, Location - 12

Business Rule, FX Rates, Translation - 20

Business Rule, Member Formulas - 17

Business Rule, Other Business Rules - 17

Button - 77

Button Properties, Action - 27

Button, Dashboard - 27

C#Aggregated - 33, 176

CacheLevel - 120

CacheName - 120

Calculate - 24

Calculate Finance Function Type - 128

Calculate, Logging - 152

Calculate, NoData - 20

Calculated Data, Clear - 75, 142, 185, 227

Calculation - 21, 198

Calculation Abstract - 245, 250

Calculation Drill Down - 15, 152

Calculation Errors, Common - 157

Index

Calculation Location - 128
Calculation Maintenance - 132
Calculation Management - 127
Calculation Matrix - 127, 129
Calculation Needed, CN - 29
Calculation Performance - 172
Calculation Performance, Troubleshooting - 152
Calculation Report - 130
Calculation Run - 21
Calculation Status - 29, 177
Calculation Testing - 129, 130
Calculation Type - 24, 128
Calculation, Allocation - 231
Calculation, Balance Sheet - 193
Calculation, Budget - 240
Calculation, Consolidation - 204
Calculation, Dynamic - 99
Calculation, Efficiency - 176
Calculation, Entity Dimension - 178
Calculation, Equity Pickup - 30
Calculation, Execution - 128
Calculation, Flow - 193, 196
Calculation, Force - 29
Calculation, Forecast - 240
Calculation, FX Rate Variance - 243, 248
Calculation, No Results - 157, 161
Calculation, Reporting - 99
Calculation, Storage Type - 73
Calculation, Stored - 124
Calculation, Variance - 242
Calculation, Variance Analysis - 240
Calculation, Waterfall - 240
Cell - See Data Cell
Classes - 8
CN, Calculation Needed - 29
Code - 8
Collapsing Detail - 69, 70, 194, 195
Collection Classes - 8
Combo Box - 77

Comment Out, Logging - 189
Comments - 133
Common Members - 48, 54
Compilation Error - 161
Compile Check - 161
Conditional Statements - 63
Consolidation Algorithm - 11, 19
Consolidation Calculations - 204
Consolidation Dimension - 21
Consolidation, Custom - 19
Consolidation, Efficiency - 176
Consolidation, Force - 29
Consolidation, Standard - 19
Consolidation, Stored Share, Org-By-Period Elimination - 19
Constants - 60
Constants, Lookup - 185
Copy Data - 227
CPU Specs - 174
Cube - 37
Cube Design - 175
Cube Properties - 18
Cube Setup - 205
Cube View - 26, 103
Cube View, Drill Down - 158
Cube, Building Blocks - 37
Cube, Business Rules - 22
Cube, Data - 39
Cube, Unnecessary Calculations - 182
Cube, Unnecessary Data - 176
Cumulative Translation Adjustment - 202, 203
Currencies, Auto-Translation - 194
Currency, Translated - 64
Current Year, Net Income - 193
Custom Calculate - 21, 24, 30, 75, 177, 227
Custom Calculate, Data Unit Calculation Sequence - 34
Custom Calculate, Trigger - 30
Custom SQL Tables - 138
Custom, Consolidation - 19

Index

Custom, Translation - 20

Dashboard Button - 27
Dashboard, Linking - 76
Data Buffer - 44, 92
Data Buffer Cell Loop - 87, 94, 233
Data Buffer Cell Loop, Eval - 95
Data Buffer Cell Loop, Flexibility - 94
Data Buffer Cell Loop, Guidelines - 98
Data Buffer Cell Loop, Performance - 94
Data Buffer Cell POV - 48
Data Buffer Error, Unbalanced - 96
Data Buffer Math - 53
Data Buffer, Anatomy - 47
Data Buffer, Balanced - 56
Data Buffer, Extensibility - 62
Data Buffer, Fixes - 160
Data Buffer, Log - 46, 149, 159
Data Buffer, Members - 48
Data Buffer, NoData - 49
Data Buffer, Object - 45
Data Buffer, RemoveZeros - 178
Data Buffer, Result - 88
Data Buffer, Scope, Account-Level Dimension - 179
Data Buffer, Visualize - 45
Data Buffer, Zeros - 49
Data Cell - 37
Data Cell Amount - 48, 94
Data Cell POV - 104
Data Cell Primary Key - 37, 55
Data Cell Properties - 107
Data Cell Status - 40, 48, 94
Data Cell Status, Setting - 93
Data Cell, Blank - 42
Data Clearing - 32
Data Description - 220
Data Explosion - 56, 57
Data Integrity - 30
Data Management - 24

Data Management Engine - 6
Data Management Step - 78
Data Quality Engine - 6
Data Script, Clear - 32
Data Storage - 11
Data Type - 8
Data Type Dimension - 211
Data Unit - 11, 25, 29, 43, 55
Data Unit Calculation Sequence - 13, 16, 21, 152, 193
Data Unit Calculation Sequence, All Or Nothing - 30
Data Unit Calculation Sequence, Custom Calculate - 34
Data Unit Calculation Sequence, Data, Copying - 182
Data Unit Calculation Sequence, Trigger - 23
Data Unit Dimension, Destination Script - 55
Data Unit Dimension, Source Scripts - 56
Data Unit Member - 64
Data Unit Scope - 63, 179, 194, 195
Data Unit, Dependent - 29
Data Unit, Sibling - 29
Data Unit, Size - 155, 175
Data Unit, Volume - 175
Data, Calculated, Clear - 185
Data, Copying - 227
Data, Copying, Data Unit Calculation Sequence - 182
Data, Cube - 39
Data, Derived - 42
Data, Durable - 32, 73
Data, Dynamic - 34
Data, Numeric Cube - 39
Data, Numerical - 106
Data, Stored - 34
Data, Textual - 108
Data, Unnecessary, Cube - 176
DataCellEx - 109
DataCellPk - 89
DataCellPk, Source Cell IDs - 90

Index

Debugging, Rubber Duck - 151

Decimal, Log - 147

Dependencies - 128

Dependent Data Units - 29

Derived Data - 42

Derived Values - 43

Design and Requirements - 127

Destination Member Script - 168

Destination Script, Data Unit Dimensions - 55

Destination Script, Invalid - 168

DestinationInfo - 88

Diagnostics Library - 150

Dictionary - 89

DimConstants - 90, 181

Dimension - 10

Dimension Filter - 65, 136

Dimension Library - 16, 134

Dimension Member, Setup - 196, 243

Dimension, Account-Level - 48

Dimension, Consolidation - 21

Dimension, Data Type - 211

Dimension, Entity, Calculation - 178

Dimension, Open - 69

Dimension, Origin - 69

Dimension, Transforming - 94

Dimension, Unbalanced - 59

Dimension, View - 40

Divide by Zero - 235

Divide by Zero, Error - 235

Double Unbalanced - 95

Drill Down, Cube View - 158

Drill-Back Blending - 118

Duplicate Member, Filter - 164

Duplicates - 68

Durable Calculation - 74

Durable Data - 32, 73

DurableCalculatedData - 32

Dynamic Calculation - 99, 102, 178

Dynamic Calculation Script Location - 99

Dynamic Calculation, Business Rules - 102

Dynamic Calculation, GetStageBlendText - 119

Dynamic Calculation, Referencing - 117

Dynamic Calculation, Syntax - 99

Dynamic Calculation, UD8 Dimension - 114

Dynamic Data - 34

Elimination Consolidation Member - 19

Elimination, Org-By-Period, Stored Share, Consolidation - 19

Engine Interaction, Business Rules - 6

Entity - 216

Entity Dimensions, Calculations - 178

Entity, Allocations - 235

Entity, Increase - 175

Equity Method - 204

Equity Pickup - 30, 204

Error Log - 46, 145, 146

Error-Handling - 112

Eval - 80

Eval, Data Buffer Cell Loop - 95

Eval, Filtering - 79

Eval2 - 82

EventArgs - 80

Excel - 44, 104

Extended Member, Conversion - 230

Extensibility - 175

Extensibility, Data Buffers - 62

Extensibility, Horizontal - 178

FieldList - 120

FieldToReturn - 121

Filter - 179

Filter, Dimension - 65, 136

Filtering with Eval - 79

Finance Business Rule - 12

Finance Engine - 5

Finance Engine Functions - 11

Finance Engine Processes - 10

Index

Finance Function Type - 13, 34, 128, 141

Flow Calculation - 193, 196

For, Each - 89, 148

Force Calculate - 29, 177

Force Consolidate - 29, 177

Forecast Calculation - 240

Forecast Seeding - 228

Foreign Exchange - see FX

Formula - 128, 201, 203

Formula Efficiency - 177

Formula List - 132

Formula Pass - 16, 161, 194, 195

Formula Script, Invalid - 162

Formula Statistics - 131

Formula Variables - 61, 180

Full Consolidation - 218

Functions - 112

FX - 201

FX Rate Variance Calculation - 243, 248

FX Rate, Translation, Business Rules - 20

FXHistoricalOverrideMovement - 202

FXMovement - 202

FXOpen - 201

FXOverrideBalance - 202

GAAP Principles - 204

GetDataBufferUsingFormula - 89

GetDataCell - 89

GetStageBlendText, Dynamic Calculation - 119

Given Key, Dictionary - 170

Global Variables - 179

Globals - 180

Growth Rate - 60

Hardware Settings - 173

Header Comments - 133

Hierarchies - 69, 136

Hierarchies, Alternate - 124

Hierarchy Relationships - 29

Horizontal Extensibility - 178

Inline Comments - 133

Input, Allow - 194, 196

Inside Loops - 182

IntelliSense - 10, 147

Invalid Destination Script - 168

Invalid Formula Script - 162

Invalid Member Name - 162

IsConsolidated - 194, 195

IsDurable - 32, 227

Key Account Properties - 194, 195

Key Value Pair - 165

Layered Ownership Models - 204

Limit Account-Level Dimension Scope in Data Buffers - 179

Location, Finance Business Rules - 12

Location, Member Formulas - 14

Log Data Buffer - 149, 159

Log, Decimal - 147

Log, String - 146

Logging - 145

Logging Lists - 147

Logging the Data Buffer - 46

Logging, Comment Out - 189

Lookup, Constants - 185

Loop - 92, 98

Loop, Definition - 98

Loop, Result Cell - 164

Loop, SQL Table Rows - 142

Loops, Inside, Outside - 182

Maintenance Tips - 134

Mapping Table - 94

Member Filter - 53

Member Filter Builder - 65, 113

Member Filter, Applying - 66

Member Filter, Member Duplication - 68

Index

Member Formula - 12, 14, 23, 100
Member Formula Editor - 14
Member Formula, Business Rules - 17
Member Formula, Location - 14
Member List Parameter - 77
Member Name, Invalid - 162
Member Script - 37, 107
Member Script, Destination - 168
Member Script, Source Cell DataBufferCellPk - 91
Member, Aggregated - 33
Member, Base Level - 39
Member, Common - 48, 54
Member, Data Buffers - 48
Member, Data Unit - 64
Member, Duplicate, Filter - 164
Member, Elimination Consolidation - 19
Member, Extended, Conversion - 230
Member, Parent Entity - 39
Member, Share Consolidation - 19
Member, Undefined - 165
Member, Unresolved - 166
Metadata - 216
Metadata Setup - 205
Methods - 8
Microsoft .NET Framework - 8
Model Blending - 118
Multi-threading - 29, 173
Multi-threading, Settings - 174

Name Value Pairs - 77, 112, 170
No Duplicates - 68
No Input Periods - 229
NoData - 42
NoData Calculate Settings - 20
NoData, Data Buffers - 49
NoData, Remove - 71
Noncontrolling Interest - 215
Numerator, Unbalanced Dimensions - 59
Numeric Cube Data - 39

Numerical Data - 106

O#Forms - 69
O#Import - 69
Object, Not Set, Object Instance - 169
OneStream API Library - 9
OnEvalDataBuffer - 81
Org-By-Period Elimination, Consolidation - 19
Org-By-Period Elimination, Consolidation, Stored Share - 19
Origin Dimension - 69
Outside Loops - 182
Ownership Type - 208, 218

Parallel Processing - 29
Parent Entity Member - 39
Performance - 91, 142, 143
Period, No Input - 229
POV Members - 105
Presentation Engine - 6
Prior Year - 195

Real Data - 41
Referencing, Dynamic Calculations - 117
Regions - 134
Relational Blending - 117
RemoveZeros - 93
RemoveZeros, Data Buffers - 178
Report - 124
Report, Application - 130
Result Cell - 89
Result Cell Amount, Setting - 92
Result Cell, Loop - 164
Result Cell, Result Data Buffer - 92
Result Cells, Multiple - 95
Result Data Buffer - 88
Result Data Buffer, Result Cell - 92
ResultCellPk, Setting - 91
Retained Earnings Beginning Balance - 195
Return Statement - 105

Index

Return Text Properties - 109
Rubber Duck Debugging - 151
Rule Abstract - 212, 221
Rule Context - 141

Scenario Formula - 227
Scenario Name - 228
Scenario Type - 64
Scope Information - 128
Scope, Account-Level Dimension, Data Buffers - 179
Scope, Data Unit - 179, 194, 195
Script - 8
Script, Dynamic Calculation - 99
Seeding Rules - 227
Sequences, Data Management - 24
Server Designation - 173
Server Settings - 173
Server Structure - 173
SetDataCell, Loop - 183
SetDimension Extension - 93
Share Consolidation Member - 19
Sibling Consolidation Pass - 209
Sibling Data Units - 29
Sibling Passes - 30
Source Cell DataBufferCellPk, Member Script - 91
Source Cell ID, DataCellPk - 90
Source Cell Member Name - 90
Source Data Cell - 89
Source Script, Data Unit Dimensions - 56
Specialty Planning - 182
SQL Management Studio - 140
SQL Table Rows, Loop - 142
SQL Table, .Select - 141
SQL Table, Calculation Reference - 141
SQL Table, Memory - 141
SQL Table, Populating - 140
SQL Tables, Custom - 138
Stage Engine - 5

Standard, Consolidation - 19
Standard, Translation - 20
Stopwatch - 150
Storage Type - 43, 48
Stored Calculations - 124, 178
Stored Data - 34
Stored Share, Consolidation - 19
Stored Share, Org-By-Period Elimination, Consolidation - 19
String, Log - 146
String.Join - 147
StringBuilder - 141
Substitution Variables - 108
Syntax - 58, 61
Syntax, Dynamic Calculations - 99
System Diagnostics Solution - 189

Table Data Manager - 139
Table, Creation - 139
Task Activity - 143
Testing - 129
Text Properties - 137
Textual Data - 108
Time Functions - 108, 134
Time Periods, Hardcoding - 188
Translated Currency - 64
Translation - 19
Translation, Business Rules, FX Rates - 20
Translation, Custom - 20
Translation, Standard - 20
Troubleshooting - 143

UD8 Dimension, Dynamic Calculations - 114, 115
UD8#None - 116
Unbalanced Data Buffer - 56, 163
Unbalanced Data Buffer Error - 96
Unbalanced Function - 58, 59, 164, 231
Unbalanced, Double - 59, 95
Unclosed Parentheses - 163

Index

Undefined Members - 165
Unnecessary Calculations, Cube - 182
Unnecessary Data, Cube - 176
Unresolved Members - 166

Values, Derived - 43
Variable Interest Entity Model - 204
Variance - 113, 240
Variance Analysis Calculations - 240
Variance Calculation - 242
VariancePercent - 113
Variations - 226
VB.NET Basics - 8
View Dimension - 40
Voting Interest Entity - 204

Waterfall Calculations - 240
WfProfileName - 120
Workflow Engine - 6
Workflow Name - 28
Workflow Process Step - 28
Write Once - 98

Zeros - 42
Zeros, Data Buffers - 49
Zeros, Remove - 71

OneStream Foundation Handbook

The Definitive Reference to Design, Configure and Support Your OneStream Platform.

OneStream is a modern, unified platform that is revolutionizing Corporate Performance Management. This proven alternative to fragmented legacy applications is designed to simplify processes for the most sophisticated, global enterprises. Hundreds of the world's leading companies are turning to OneStream to help with reporting and understanding financial data.

In this practical guide, The Architect Factory team at OneStream Software explains each part of an implementation, and the design of solutions. Readers will learn the core guiding principles for implementing OneStream from the company's top team of experts. Beyond offering a training guide, the focus of this book is on the 'why' of design and building an application.

- Manage your Implementation with the OneStream methodology
- Understand Design and Build concepts
- Build solutions for the Consolidation of financial data, and develop Planning models
- Create Data Integration solutions that will feed your models
- Develop Workflows to guide and manage your End-Users
- Advance your solutions with Rules and Security
- Take advantage of detailed Data Reporting using tools such as Analytic Blend, Advanced Excel reporting, and Dashboarding
- Tune Performance, and optimize your application

OneStream Planning: The Why, How and When

OneStream is a world-class Intelligent Finance Platform that handles the complex planning, consolidation, reporting and other requirements of mid-sized to large enterprises. Whether in retail, financial services, manufacturing or other industries, the OneStream platform provides the means to integrate multiple data sources and utilize a wide range of tools and methodologies to improve business processes and performance. Through OneStream, organizations benefit from unified, real-time, enterprise-wide planning and forecasting.

Aimed at OneStream Planning practitioners, administrators, implementors, and power users alike, as well as Financial close and consolidations practitioners, *OneStream Planning: The Why, How and When* is the first standalone book in the performance management space to cover the power and potential of Planning in OneStream. Drawing from real-world deployments, the book is rooted in easily understood business use cases, and explains approaches (with code) through a comprehensive exploration of the solution. All this is offered within a framework of top functional and technical practice as informed by the authors' decades-long consulting and application development experiences.

- Which should I do – Import or Direct Load, Consolidate or Aggregate?
- How do Data Buffers really work; what is Eval and why should I care? Which approach is fastest and does it really matter?
- Why Multiyear Scenarios should never be Yearly
- Can Thing Planning run in the Spreadsheet? (It can.)
- Combining REST API and Analytic Blend
- Slice Security down to the very tiniest slice
- Pivot Grid or Large Pivot Grid, that is the question
- A book filled with clear use cases
- Exhaustively tested and verified solutions, and extensive source code
- Undocumented features and functionality covered, along with functional and technical good practices

Lightning Source UK Ltd.
Milton Keynes UK
UKHW051143060223
416527UK00008B/201